Learning to Look

A Handbook on Classroom Observation and Teaching Models

Jane A. Stallings

Stanford Research Institute

Wadsworth Publishing Company, Inc.

Belmont, California

Education Editor: Roger Peterson
Production Editor: Catherine Aydelott
Designer: Nancy Benedict
Cartoon Illustrator: Shelley Dieterichs
Technical Illustrator: Carlton Brown

Printed in the United States of America

1 2 3 4 5 6 7 8 9 10——81 80 79 78 77

Library of Congress Cataloging in Publication Data

Stallings, Jane.
   Learning to look.

   Includes bibliographies.
   1. Observation (Educational method).   I. Title.
LB1027.S686   371.3   77-7242
ISBN 0-534-00522-5

WADSWORTH SERIES IN CURRICULUM AND INSTRUCTION

Series Editor: Jack R. Fraenkel, San Francisco State University

Published:

Educational Research: A Guide to the Process, Experimental Edition
    Norman E. Wallen, San Francisco State University

Facing Value Decisions: Rationale-Building for Teachers
    James P. Shaver and William Strong, Utah State University

*Learning to Look: A Handbook on Classroom Observation and Teaching
    Models*
    Jane A. Stallings, Stanford Research Institute

To my teachers, Robert Hess, Eleanor Maccoby, Pauline Sears, Robert Scarf, Fannie Shaftel, and Richard Show, who over many years generously shared their wisdom and insight.

Also to my children, Lisa, Larkin, Joshua, and Shaun, who have shared their lives with me, and from whom I have learned that each person is unique and learns best when allowed to proceed in his or her own way.

Contents

Learning to Look

SERIES FOREWORD

Children's classroom behavior reveals a great deal about their intellectual and emotional development. Unfortunately, much of what children say and do is forgotten or misinterpreted by their teachers and other observers. In today's busy classrooms it is often difficult, if not impossible, for a teacher to remember, or remember accurately, at the end of a crowded and tiring day just exactly what Al, or Maria, or Felix actually said or did.

Nevertheless, teachers need accurate information about what their students say and do in the course of their daily work if they are to help students learn as much and as efficiently as possible. Careful, systematic observation of classroom behavior is one way to get such information. By analyzing the observations, teachers can change the way they teach so as to reinforce or bring about desired behavior. As Dr. Stallings says in her opening chapter, we can learn things about children from observing in the classroom that we cannot learn in any other way. Just *how* to observe is what this book is about.

Dr. Stallings describes clearly and concisely how to observe, systematically record, and analyze students' doings and sayings. She gives examples of observation instruments and tips on choosing a particular instrument, depending on what one wishes to find out. A unique feature of the book is Dr. Stallings' detailed description of one particular observation system. The many exercises allow readers to use the system and thus gain experience in what careful and systematic observation actually involves.

All people involved in education—teachers, teachers in training, supervisors of teachers, college and university professors, and school administrators—will find LEARNING TO LOOK quite useful. It is a valuable and needed contribution to the literature of education.

Jack R. Fraenkel
Series Editor

FOREWORD

This book is the first of its kind. We have had books on classroom observation and other books on models or types of teaching, but no previous work has integrated theory, research, and practice—and certainly not with the richness of detail, illustrative material, and practice exercises to be found here. The result of this integration should be highly rewarding to budding and experienced teachers alike. It should also be helpful to teacher educators, school administrators, and others interested in education.

Dr. Stallings obviously is fully at home with her subject. Her experience as a teacher and researcher is abundantly evident in the book's many realistic anecdotes, practical hints for observers, valid characterizations of teachers and classrooms, and appropriate explorations of the literature on education. Dr. Stallings' years as a classroom teacher combine with her leadership in several major research projects to make what she offers unusually pertinent, vivid, specific, and well balanced. Readers should come away from this book with observational skills that will deepen their understanding of their own and others' teaching, and with an intimate knowledge of what various models of teaching mean for teacher and pupil behavior.

I expect this book to contribute significantly to the improvement of teaching at all age and grade levels. In the long run, all those whose lives are touched by teachers should fare better for what this book provides.

N. L. Gage
Stanford University

PREFACE

Children in classrooms are constantly under their teachers' eye. On the basis of these observations, teachers choose materials and strategies, and make educational decisions about each child. But teachers are bombarded by a bewildering variety of events: Kirsten has lost her lunch money, Bill is blowing up a balloon, Lindsay is laughing at him, José is reversing all of his *p*'s, *g*'s, *b*'s, and *d*'s, Sue needs help with spelling a word, Teresa is helping her, and the rest of the class is trying to finish a writing assignment. *All at the same time.*

By the time the last bell rings, many of these priceless observations are lost. As the sound of the bell dies away, teachers often wonder what happened that they didn't see or hear. In short, teachers have an observation problem.

This book is meant to help you, the reader, with this problem. It is to be used by students preparing to be classroom teachers, by teachers already in the classroom, and by school administrators and supervisors trying to help classroom teachers improve their teaching.

The book has three main objectives. The central one is to help you make systematic observations. You are introduced to a variety of observation systems and shown how to record information about events in the classroom and use the information to guide the students' learning. I have chosen one observation system in particular for you to learn to use. I describe actual situations and present observation experiences with this system in mind. You will need to get involved, try the exercises, and learn some observation codes.

A second objective is to introduce several educational theories that have been developed into models of education. Teachers and potential teachers need to be aware of several different theories of education in order to have a broad base for their teaching decisions.

This book describes five models: the *exploratory* and *group process*
models follow open education theory; the *developmental cognitive*
model enhances cognitive growth; and the *programmed* and *fundamental
school* models focus primarily on developing basic skills. The suggested
readings at the ends of the chapters will guide you to more information
on models that interest you.

I chose these five models because they represent a wide range of
theories: from carefully structured teacher-directed models to open-
classroom models where children initiate their own learning. Of course,
they do not represent all of the existing educational models. Not included, for example, are the Montessori and Slingerland methods.

Third, this book helps you predict how children might grow and
develop within each of the models. These predictions are based upon
findings reported in a large national observation study where teaching practices were found to be strongly related to what happened to
the children.*

The book's organization follows these objectives: the first
chapter discusses the value of classroom observations and describes
several observation systems. Chapter 2 tries to teach you how to
observe systematically using the observation instrument developed at
Stanford Research Institute in Menlo Park, California. Chapter 3
discusses educational points of view. Chapters 4 through 8 describe
the five educational models in theory, practice, and expected results.
At the end of each of these chapters is a completed observation form
showing how the model looks to an observer. Chapter 9 compares the
five models and discusses their strengths and weaknesses.

Jane A. Stallings

ACKNOWLEDGMENTS

The observation system described in this book was researched
and developed at Stanford Research Institute (SRI) in Menlo Park,
California. I want to thank several people there for encouraging
me to write the book: Harvey Dixon, Vice President; Marc Henderson,
Executive Director of the Urban and Social Systems Division; Richard
Marciano, Director of the Education Research Department; and Philip
Sorensen, Senior Analyst. All of them took an interest in my work
and gave me both moral and substantive support. Thanks also to my
friend and colleague at SRI, Mary Wilcox, who read each chapter
with such insight. As a former teacher, she reviewed the manuscript
from the classroom perspective, and had many good suggestions. I'm
also grateful to the extraordinary Classroom Process staff: Dorothy
Booth, Georgia Gillis, Phillip Giesen, and Peggy Needels. We worked
closely together during the past six years, developing the observation system and training materials presented here. Marion Arnot,
Rebecca Cieniewicz, and Brigitte Visor persevered through my scribbles
and misspellings to transform my manuscript into a readable document.

I also thank the reviewers of the manuscript, who offered constructive criticism. Their suggestions contributed significantly to

---

*The total report of this research may be found in Jane A.
Stallings and David Kaskowitz, *Follow Through Classroom Observation
1972-1973*, Menlo Park, Calif.: Stanford Research Institute, 1974.

the book's quality and usability. They are: Arthur Coladarci, Stanford University; Frank Cross, Oregon State University; Jack Fraenkel, San Francisco State University; Norman Furst, Temple University; Robert George, Indiana State University; Thomas L. Good, University of Missouri at Columbia; John Goodlad, University of California, Los Angeles; Shirley Hill, California State University, Fullerton; Lillian Katz, University of Illinois; Autumn Stanley, Wadsworth; E. Paul Torrance, University of Georgia; and Ernest Taub, State University of New York at Stony Brook.

Since the book was written largely for student teachers, I am especially grateful to Daphne Terrell of California State University, Fullerton, and Donna Parker of Oregon State University. These two student teachers reviewed the book and used the observation system in their classrooms. Their observations were practical and pertinent.

Thanks to Dick Greenberg, Roger Peterson, and Catherine Aydelott of Wadsworth. Dick saw the possibility of weaving a book on observation into a book on teaching models. He thought a former teacher could write a useful book for other teachers, and encouraged me to write the book. I hope we have fulfilled his vision. Roger managed the development of the book, consistently finding good reviewers and coaching me through to the finish. And always with consideration and skill, Catherine guided the book and me through the sometimes painful production process.

Last, I want to thank the children—the subjects of the vignettes and case studies. They stimulated my first research questions, and with patience helped me learn to look.

Chapter 1

Introduction: Are You Sure That's What Happened?

"Ms. Strong, Martha won't let anyone else swing!" shouts Kate.

"She pushed me off when I was going really high!" retorts Martha.

"You wouldn't get off!" replies Kate.

"My knee hurts." Martha lunges at Kate to push her down. The teacher puts a restraining arm around each six-year-old girl.

"What happened, girls?" asks Ms. Strong.

"She takes the swing all the time . . . all the time!" chimes in Grace.

"But I just got on!" argues Martha. "Jeannie was swinging and she gave it to me."

"No, sir! She tried to give it to me but you grabbed it. You just had a turn," argues Kate.

What really happened? The teacher must listen patiently to each child and try to fit the pieces together. Later in the day, Martha is again involved in an altercation:

"Ms. Strong, Martha won't let anyone in the store," complains Sue.

"She just took my camera away," adds Grace.

Martha approaches, crying, "Bill pushed me out of the store."

Walking toward the store, the teacher asks, "What's happening here?"

"Martha won't let anyone in the store," responds Bill.

"But they keep taking the cameras and messing them up!" shrieks Martha.

"Did you make the cameras, Martha?" asks the teacher.

"Most of them," she responds. "Jill made two of them."

"Did you want to sell them in the store?"

"Yes, but everyone was just grabbing them and then painting them all up. They are supposed to bring them back at the end of the day."

"I paid you 54¢ for the camera, and I can paint it if I want to," retorts Grace.

"No, it takes too much time to make cameras for you to just mess them up. You are supposed to bring them back. I'll just have to keep making more and more cameras every day." Martha begins to cry.

WHY OBSERVE?

This scene from the play store is Martha's second stormy encounter with other children today. This kind of conflict has become almost a daily event for her. Ms. Strong would like to know more about Martha's behavior. How do the conflicts start? Are they always started by Martha, as it seems? How can one know what is really happening?

Some teachers might ask Martha to explain her behavior. Others might send Martha to the principal's office and hope that her difficulties would be revealed in that discussion. The chances that Martha can explain her behavior to the teacher or to an administrator are slight. But if a systematic observer could watch Martha in the context of her classroom over several days, patterns of behavior might show up and provide the teacher with clues to understanding her. Further, the observed patterns may suggest steps for the teacher to take. Martha might need more positive support for acceptable behavior, or for example, Ms. Strong herself might be setting up some of the situations by having unrealistic expectations of Martha and allowing her more freedom than she can handle. We can learn things about children from observing them in the classroom that we cannot learn any other way. Also, observations of children can help teachers plan better educational programs.

Systematic observation is done objectively according to predefined rules and established operational definitions. It can help classroom teachers, student teachers, and school administrators learn more about the social, emotional, and cognitive development of children. If a child is observed to be shy and introverted, the teacher might organize groups so that the child can work among children who are friendly and not aggressive. If a child is observed enjoying tinkering with machines and examining objects to see how they work, the teacher might plan to have more exploratory materials in the classroom environment. Systematic observations can also make educators more aware of their own behavior and lead to changes in undesirable behavior. Observation is a tool for learning about human behavior—your own or anyone else's. Many eminent learning theorists have developed their theories through careful observations of children. Jean Piaget, one of today's most respected developmental psychologists, developed his learning theory from his observations of his own children, and Alfred Binet's test of intelligence evolved from his observations of normal and retarded children.

For students in the process of becoming teachers, it is important to observe in many classrooms in order to compare and contrast teaching styles. Much can be learned from observing a master teacher handle difficult problems like fights between children. Recording the observation will provide students with a concrete reference instead of just a fading impression of how the teacher handled the fight. Also, students can compare the teacher's behavior with that recommended in a textbook and based on a particular learning theory, such as behavior modification, and decide whose techniques they prefer. For example, a student teacher is observing in Ms. Taylor's fifth-grade classroom. Jim, one of the children, is shooting pumpkin seeds across the room with a rubber band slingshot. Ms. Taylor intervenes, saying firmly, "Give that stuff to me and stay in your seat at recess." This is how Ms. Taylor handles the problem. However, most behavior modification theories, including the one described in the student teacher's textbook, recommend that a teacher ignore undesired behavior and draw attention to desired behavior by praising children in the classroom who are doing what is expected. So, the student teacher has a choice and can better decide which technique he or she prefers. But whatever the students decide, their knowledge and repertoire of teaching techniques will increase from observing others teach.

It is also helpful for education students to observe children in natural settings to see if child behaviors described in textbooks can be identified in the classroom. For example, a student teacher could observe a third-grade classroom where most of the children are likely to be eight years old. Piagetian developmental theory[1] describes children from ages seven to eleven as being in the *concrete* operational stage—that is, the stage at which they are able to think while manipulating objects and to understand and transfer meaning to symbols that represent these objects as in the reading process. These children begin to solve problems in their heads and have less need to manipulate objects physically in order to draw meaning from them. The observer, then, could see how many of the children in the classroom behave in the ways Piaget describes for children in this concrete operational stage. For instance, do most of the children use counting sticks or blocks or weights and measures to solve problems in mathematics? Or do they solve the problems without such aids? If textbook theory is compared with behavior in a classroom, student teachers are more likely to develop an understanding of child growth and development.

School administrators, who must evaluate teachers' performances each year, can use systematic observations in making judgments about the teachers' proficiency. An administrator, for example, can use the observation to identify and study relationships between teaching practices and children's achievement test scores. The administrator can also use the observation as a training device by discussing it with the teacher. Such discussions of the observations are likely to be more helpful in changing classroom teaching techniques than are general, unsupported statements about the teacher's behavior.

Teachers have little time to reflect on or analyze their own behavior; often their perceptions of their behavior and its effect on children differ widely from those of an outside observer, who can see them more objectively. John Goodlad pointed out in his study of elementary teachers that

> . . . there seemed to be a considerable discrepancy between teachers' perceptions of their own innovative behavior and the perceptions of observers. The teachers sincerely thought they were individualizing instruction, encouraging inductive learning, involving children in group processes . . . .[2]

Goodlad's observers concluded, however, that teachers were seldom doing these things. Teachers may be unaware that they often dominate discussions, allow too little response time, or ask simple, direct questions—for example, they ask yes-or-no questions when discussion questions would be more appropriate. An administrator using systematic observation can give teachers objective reviews and help them become better informed and more aware of such problems.

---

[1] See Chapter 6 for a detailed discussion of Piaget's theory.
[2] John I. Goodlad and M. Frances Klein, *Looking Behind the Classroom Door*, 2nd ed. (Worthington, Ohio: Charles A. Jones Publishing, 1974), p. 98.

METHODS OF OBSERVATION

There are many methods for recording observations of children and teachers. One is to record everything that happens in the classroom in narrative description. Another is to record important points through a shorthand system in which a single word, symbol, or letter can stand for an entire event, object, or person. Many checklists, time sample systems, interactive systems, and rating scales, which use a shorthand system, have been developed.

Despite the variety of observation systems, they all have several elements in common:

1. A focus of observation. Whom do you look at or listen to— teacher? child?—what activities, materials, environmental factors do you record?

2. A content focus. What do you want to learn about—motor development, social-emotional development, cognitive development, physical environment, activities?

3. A coding unit. How long do you observe before recording and over how long a period do you observe—three seconds, five minutes, five hours?

4. A means to record data. How do you record data—on audio-tape, videotape, with paper and pencil?

5. A setting. Where do you record—in the classroom, playroom, playground?

6. A purpose. Why are you observing—to study a child, evaluate a program, train other people, conduct a research project?

Narrative Description

During nine years of classroom teaching, I often wished for some reliable account of what was happening to a child who has having problems in living and learning, because it was hard to understand what that one child was experiencing when thirty-five other children also needed attention. Whom did the child in question approach and talk to? Who approached that child? What was the nature of their interaction? How did I, the teacher, respond to the child? What activities did the child become most involved with? What activities did he or she reject? How long did the child stay involved in an activity? How mobile was the child? How often was the child happy or angry, engrossed or lethargic? Answers to these kinds of questions are valuable in planning each child's educational program.

Systematic written descriptions of children can provide these answers. The descriptions can be made by either the classroom teacher or an outside observer. I developed the following description of a student named Frank over a seven-month period. I made written descriptions of Frank, taking twenty minutes for each, at least twice a week. A morning assistant teacher was in charge while I recorded the observations. I also recorded shorter events involving Frank whenever they occurred. I carried a small pad in my pocket to jot down the date, time, and interaction or event. These entries were usually only a few sentences, but the information was important in developing a more complete picture of Frank's life in school and in preparing an educational program for him.

The first day of school Frank came into the second-grade room with his mother. She said, "I have to hurry to work. Be a good boy." He stood shyly just inside the door. His mother had said on his application, "It takes time for Franklin to thaw. He is awfully shy at first." What was he feeling, I wondered, as he looked about the room. How would it feel to be the only black child in a new class—far removed from your neighborhood and everything familiar. Entering a new group is a difficult process for adults or children. There are so many new signals to learn. I tried to imagine myself in a reversed situation, and I felt great admiration for Frank and his mother in making this venture.

Frank had enrolled in our second-grade class. The group into which he came was fortunate and unusual in its possession of physical, mental, and sociological qualifications well above the average. The median for the total battery of California Achievement Tests was in the 97th percentile. The children came primarily from stable, professional homes. Fifteen of them had been in the first-grade class with me. Now in the second grade, we had added four new girls and Frank. Frank's mother had said he was very bright, but he was not performing well in school. He was about four months below grade level in reading. Records from his previous school confirmed this.

On this first day of school Frank sat quietly during the opening meeting, listening while other children shared their summer experiences. He did not venture into this group conversation. At reading time we encouraged the children to choose one of the many books that we had placed around the room. When I read with Frank, I found that his sight vocabulary was relatively good, but that his phonetic and structural analysis skills needed building.

Each morning school started with a group meeting where the children made suggestions of things they wished to study, or discussed some group problem. We found that Frank began to talk in a soft, disturbing patter during these times. He did not join the discussions, but it became increasingly difficult for him to listen and for the others to hear.

The group decided they would like to take turns being chairperson of the morning meetings. On October 26 Susan was the chairperson and she called on Dale.

Dale: Let's study shore birds. My dad took me out to the tidelands on Sunday with his binoculars.

John: Yeah, let's go on a bird hike!

Frank: Bird hike? Bird hike! What's a bird hike? I am tired of doing this.

Frank was apparently voicing his frustration and his question at experiences out of his range. He was, however, finally voicing them. The next record of Frank was made on October 30. It was his turn to be group chairperson. He declined his turn and passed it on to Dale. We wondered if Frank would feel comfortable enough to take his turn the next time around.

During this same time, we found children complaining about Frank's interference with their dramatic play. Each recess and noon the children organized plays. They had costumes, sets, and a stage in the back of the room. Our school was fortunate in having a drama coach who inspired children of all ages to create and perform dramatic adventures. They met with him in dramatics class once a week. Frank never took part, but heckled from the sidelines. The imaginary world in which these children found such delight was not available to him. His life seemed very real and very earnest.

Isabel, the morning assistant teacher, and I decided to read to Frank every chance we had. He seemed not to have heard many of the fantasy stories that children in his group had heard while growing up. We thought he might lack the imagery or imagination that develops through hearing stories. It is not easy to pretend to be a prince, and ogre, an eagle, a dragon, or a unicorn if you've never seen or heard of one. If he lacked this reading experience, then we would try to make up for it in part. Our school librarian agreed to assist in this effort. She asked his assistance in selecting the storybook to be read to the group. He selected a baseball story. At his request, she read additional stories to him for half an hour after school while he waited for his mother. I tried to select stories that would be of interest to him—no fairies or princesses for a while, but pirates and spaceships, and during group story times I kept him close to me. His problem seemed to be sitting still long enough so that he could hear enough words from the story to develop mind pictures. Sometimes I would say, "Everyone close your eyes while I read. See what kind of a picture comes into your mind." It was a new experience for him and he began to enjoy it.

He had a difficult time in creative writing and wrote primarily in his handwriting practice book. Then, one morning during late November, we found Frank copying from his library book, *Big Mac*. He said, "I am going to take this book home and copy more words from it. Then tomorrow I am going to keep on copying it." Isabel said, "That's just fine, Frank. Would you sometime like to write your own story?" Frank said, "I don't know any story, but what I am going to do is put more words into this story." (He indicated the first page of *Big Mac*.) "I am going to put some of my words in it." This was the beginning, a tiny opening to self-expression.

In dramatics class, he only heckled at first. Finally, in the third month, he took a small part as a pirate. Another opening. As he took part in the more formal structure of directed dramatics, he felt easier playing parts within the informal dramatic play of the classroom. And as his reservoir of stories grew, the land of Let's Pretend became more available to him. At the same time, his interaction with the other children improved.

Was Frank's new school environment providing him with opportunities and challenges that might bring his achievement level nearer to his ability? At the end of January we gave him the Stanford Achievement Test as one way of checking. At the end of his first-grade year, Frank had tested four months behind his grade level. Now, in January of his second year, he tested only slightly below grade level in word and paragraph meaning. In social science, spelling, word study skills, and language, he was at grade level. In arithmetic concepts he measured in the 82nd percentile. Clearly he was progressing.

One day in February a class discussion was taking place about what to do when people talk so much that the group can't discuss a problem. Frank was relaxed, and responded.

Julie: I think they should go to the backroom and sit on the couch for fifteen minutes.

Frank: We should send them to Spahr (the dramatics teacher), then they could talk all day.

Here Frank revealed just how tuned in he was to the situation and how he considered it all a little foolish. His humor, as he allowed us to hear more of it, was sophisticated for his age.

Just before Easter vacation, Frank returned from the library with his first book of fairy tales. He had finished *We Read More and More*, and was flying through Stearn's (1966) final book, *Now We Read Everything*. That day, as I crossed the schoolyard to get our coffee from the staff room, Frank called out from the top of the tallest tree, "Look, Jane, I'm an eagle! The highest eagle of them all." And I thought, "You are right, Frank. You are an eagle, or a pirate, or a prince."

Our cool and factual Frank had become a child among children. He is achieving well and shows imagination and creativity.[3]

If it is not possible for classroom teachers to record observations themselves, it may be possible to recruit a friend or hire an observer to do so. Once, in desperation, when I could not understand the behavior of Billy, a particularly disturbing second-grade child, I hired a college student to come in and write a running account of everything he did for two days. From this, I received sixty handwritten pages of narrative.

The information was most valuable. I learned that on the first day, Billy had gotten up and wandered about the room fifty-seven times. Since the school day was five hours long, this was about ten times an hour. He had fallen off his chair fourteen times. He had picked his nose seventeen times and rubbed his eyes twenty-three times. He had received thirteen smiles from me and twenty-seven reprimands—mostly to stop falling off his chair and pay attention. He initiated conversations with other children forty-four times, but the interaction was only one or two sentences long. He spoke to everyone who passed his seat and tried to trip three people, succeeding twice. He was rejected fifteen times by other children who were involved in some activity and was physically pushed away from a group of three who were working on a mural. During recess, he put a blanket over his desk, took his reading workbook, and disappeared underneath. He stayed there for five minutes. The second day's observations were similar, and the picture that emerged was one of a hyperactive, highly distractible child.

Supported by these specific descriptions, I requested conferences with his parents, his doctor, a reading specialist, and the school psychologist. The written account of his behavior enabled me to present factual information with a minimum of inference. As a result of these meetings, an educational program was planned that helped Billy progress in his learning.

A reading specialist was assigned to work with him three times a week outside the classroom. Inside the classroom, I carried out the reading program the specialist prescribed. Billy's pediatrician

---

[3]Adapted from Jane Stallings, "Frank," *Elementary School Guidance and Counseling*, vol. 2, no. 4, pp. 295-298. Copyright 1968 American Personnel and Guidance Association. Reprinted with permission.

prescribed a diet that eliminated artificially colored foods and artificial flavorings in the hope that the change in diet would reduce his hyperactivity. His parents were advised by the school psychologist to be patient with Billy and exert as much calming influence as possible at home. They were encouraged to have realistic expectations regarding his progress toward more controlled behavior.

Billy also needed help, it was decided, in screening out distractible influences within the school environment. Since we had a large room, we decided to build three learning booths. These booths were made by placing three 4' × 5' fiberboard sheets in deep grooves cut into three 4' long 2" × 4" runners. These dividers were then bracketed into the wall, starting at the corner of the room, with just enough space between them for a child's desk. The entrances to the booths were curtained with fireproof cloth. Introducing the booths, as special places where children could learn better, allowed Billy to use them without appearing to have been singled out or sentenced to isolation. In fact the learning booths became so popular with the children that there had to be a sign-up sheet. This did present a slight problem in that I had to see that Billy received as much isolated learning time as he needed.

The narrative type of observation is useful for in-depth case studies such as Billy's. Jean Piaget used narrative to describe his continuous observations of his own children. Recorded daily for several years, these observations provided him with in-depth case studies upon which he based his theory of learning. Other researchers, including Roger Barker and Pauline Sears and Vivian Sherman, have organized and directed narrative observations that are excellent examples of in-depth studies of individual children.[4]

In anthropological studies, a method called ethnographic observing is used to record narratively everything about a family or a tribe. W. J. Tikunoff, D. Berliner, and R. Rist adapted this technique to be used in large-scale studies of teaching processes.[5] Key words, phrases, and ideas are counted and summarized for use in statistical analysis.

Narrative observations, valuable as they can be, do have some limitations, however. First, new observers may find it difficult to select what to record, and, if they do a running account of the entire day, the quality and quantity of the written material is likely to drop off as the day progresses and fatigue sets in. Also, it is sometimes hard to analyze what has been recorded. Among other things, it takes a long time to read through thirty pages and count, for example, how many times Billy left his seat or talked to another person. Finally, although this is a good method for compiling information on just one child, it is difficult to use when observing groups of children or when describing a total classroom environment. For these latter, there are more efficient methods.

---

[4]Roger G. Barker, ed., *The Stream of Behavior* (New York: Appleton-Century-Crofts, 1963); Pauline S. Sears and Vivian S. Sherman, *In Pursuit of Self-Esteem* (Belmont, Calif.: Wadsworth, 1964).

[5]William J. Tikunoff, David C. Berliner, and Ray C. Rist, *An Ethnographic Study of the Forty Classrooms of the Beginning Teacher Evaluation Study Known Sample*, Technical Report No. 75-10-5 (San Francisco, Calif.: Far West Laboratory for Educational Research and Development, 1975).

Pupil Groupings

Fixed and regular for activities	Mostly fixed	Emerge about half the time; fixed half the time	More often emerge spontaneously	Usually emerge spontaneously
1	2	3	4	5

Pupil Differentiation

Almost always work at same activity	Most work at same activity most of the time	Most work at same activity half of the time	Work at different activities more often than not	Usually work at different activities
1	2	3	4	5

Pupil Reinforcement

From other pupils:	Never	Rarely	Occasionally	Frequently	Almost constantly
	1	2	3	4	5

From adults:	Almost constantly	Frequently	Occasionally	Rarely	Never
	5	4	3	2	1

From materials:	Never	Rarely	Occasionally	Frequently	Almost constantly
	1	2	3	4	5

Overall Emotional-Attitudinal Climate

Highly positive	Positive most of the time	Neither positive nor negative	Negative occasionally	Highly negative
5	4	3	2	1
Children appear extremely happy and/or satisfied	Most children appear happy and/or satisfied much of the time	About half appear happy and/or satisfied much of the time	Occasionally pupils appear happy and/or satisfied	Children appear extremely unhappy and/or dissatisfied
5	4	3	2	1

Source: Robert S. Soar, *Follow Through Classroom Process Measurement and Pupil Growth (1970-71)*. Final Report. (Gainesville, Fla.: Institute for Development of Human Resources, University of Florida, 1975.) ERIC Accession No. ED 106 297.

Social Competence Scale

Student _____ Teacher _____

	Always	Very Often	Often	Sometimes	Seldom	Hardly Ever	Never
1. Child can communicate emotional needs to teacher.	1	2	3	4	5	6	7
2. Child seeks adult attention by crying.	1	2	3	4	5	6	7
3. Child needs adult aid for each step of activity.	1	2	3	4	5	6	7
4. Child is responsible in carrying out requests and directions.	1	2	3	4	5	6	7
5. Child seeks physical contact with teacher.	1	2	3	4	5	6	7
6. Child adds freely (verbally or nonverbally) to teacher's suggestions.	1	2	3	4	5	6	7
7. Child expresses open defiance against authority.	1	2	3	4	5	6	7
8. Child shies away and withdraws when approached by other children.	1	2	3	4	5	6	7
9. Child responds with immediate compliance to teacher's direction.	1	2	3	4	5	6	7
10. Child can be independent of adult in having ideas about or planning activities.	1	2	3	4	5	6	7
11. Child frowns, shrugs shoulders, pouts, or stamps foot when suggestion is made by teacher.	1	2	3	4	5	6	7
12. Child can be independent of adult in overcoming difficulties with other children or activities.	1	2	3	4	5	6	7
13. Child needs excessive praise and encouragement from teacher in order to participate in activities.	1	2	3	4	5	6	7
14. Other children seem unwilling to play with this child.	1	2	3	4	5	6	7
15. Child is unwilling to carry out reasonable suggestions from teacher even when having difficulty.	1	2	3	4	5	6	7

Source: Martin Kohn and Bernice Rosman, "A Social Competence Scale and Symptom Checklist for the Preschool Child: Factor Dimensions, Their Cross-Instrument Generality, and Longitudinal Persistence" *Developmental Psychology* 6 (1972), pp. 430-444. Also from M. Kohn, B. Parnes, and B. Rosman, *A Social Competence Scale*, rev. ed. (New York: The William Alanson White Institute, 1976). (There are a total of seventy-two items on the Social Competence Scale.)

SELECTING AN OBSERVATION SYSTEM

Before choosing an observation instrument, you must answer the question: What do I want to learn about children, myself, or other adults participating in the classroom? If you are operating an open classroom, you may want to know, for example, what materials are being used, which learning centers are used most often, to what degree children are working independently, or how often children receive individual attention. Once you know the questions you want to answer, you can select or develop an observation instrument that will collect the data you need.

E. Gil Boyer, Anita Boyer, and Gail Karafin in *Measures of Maturation* review seventy-three observation systems available for use with young children.[8] In this book, they provide a good description of each system and report findings from studies in which each has been used. Their review is summarized here on page 20. In *Mirrors of Behavior*, Anita Simon and E. Gil Boyer review over one hundred observation systems available for use with a wider range of students and for use in a wider range of situations.[9] Richard Brandt, Carol A. Cartwright and G. Phillip Cartwright, and Gary Borich and Susan Madden also have reviews of the observation systems.[10] In addition, most authors of observation systems will be happy to respond to your requests for information or questions about how to use them.

If, after studying available observation systems, you do not find one that will answer your questions, you may need to modify an existing system or develop your own. Chapter 2, which describes the development of an observation system used in the study of the Follow Through Planned Variation Project, may give you ideas on how to do this.

Chapter 2 may also help you develop observation skills. Such skills are essential to good teaching, for no matter how many students a teacher has, he or she rarely thinks in terms of "the class." A teacher thinks of Martha, Billy, Manuel, and Joe and of what they each need. A class is made up of individuals and it is impossible for a teacher to individualize instruction appropriately if observation skills are lacking.

---

[8]E. Gil Boyer, Anita Boyer, and Gail Karafin, eds., *Measures of Maturation: An Anthology of Early Childhood Observation Instruments* (Philadelphia: Humanizing Learning Program, Research for Better Schools, Inc., 1973).

[9]Anita Simon and E. Gil Boyer, *Mirrors for Behavior: An Anthology of Classroom Observation Instruments* (Philadelphia: Humanizing Learning Program, Research for Better Schools, Inc., 1967, 1969, 1970). ERIC Accession No. ED 029 833.

[10]R. Brandt, *Studying Behavior in Natural Settings* (New York: Holt, Rinehart and Winston, 1972); Carol A. Cartwright and G. Phillip Cartwright, *Developing Observation Skills* (New York: McGraw-Hill, 1974); Gary Borich and Susan Madden, *Evaluating Classroom Instruction* (Menlo Park, Calif.: Addison-Wesley, 1977).

Review of Observation Systems

Systems 1 - 73	Facial Expressions	Body Activity	Level of Activity	Nervous Habits	Body Orientation	Sensory Perception	Caretaking of Self	Cognitive	Playing	Expressions of Affect	Personality Traits	Background Data	Number of Contacts	Duration of Contacts	Child to Child	Child to Adult	Adult to Child	Adult to Adult	Leadership/Followership	Affective Communication	Reinforcement Patterns	Caretaking of/by Others	Information Processing
	INDIVIDUAL CATEGORY / Psychomotor						Activity			Other			SOCIAL CONTACT CATEGORY / Time		Who is Contacted				Type of Contact				
1 Ainsworth		•	•		•	•				•			•						•	•	•	•	
2 Ainsworth-Bell-Stayton	•	•			•					•			•	•		•	•		•	•	•	•	
3 Anderson													•	•	•				•				
4 Arrington	•	•											•	•	•	•	•						
5 Barker		•							•				•	•		•	•		•				
6 Bee-Streissguth						•									•	•					•		•
7 Bell-Weller-Waldrop	•	•	•			•	•			•	•	•	•	•					•	•			
8 Berk-Jackson-Wolfson	•	•								•			•						•				•
9 Bing									•	•			•			•	•		•		•		•
10 Bishop									•	•			•	•		•	•		•		•		•
11 Blurton Jones-Leach	•	•				•				•			•	•		•	•		•			•	
12 Bobbitt-Jensen	•	•	•		•	•	•						•			•	•	•	•				
13 Boger-Cunningham		•	•			•		•	•	•			•						•	•			•
14 Bonney	•	•	•		•		•			•	•		•						•	•	•		•
15 Borke										•	•		•			•			•	•			
16 Bott	•	•		•		•				•			•			•	•		•	•			
17 Bowman													•	•		•			•	•		•	
18 Brody-Axelrad				•									•	•					•	•		•	
19 Caldwell-Honig		•	•	•		•	•		•	•		•	•	•		•	•		•	•	•	•	•
20 Coates-Anderson-Hartup	•	•				•							•										
21 Cohen-Stern	•	•	•			•				•			•			•	•		•	•			
22 Coller		•	•			•						•	•			•	•	•					
23 Danziger-Greenglass																•	•		•	•		•	
24 Dawe		•								•			•			•	•		•	•			
25 Ding	•	•								•			•			•	•		•				
26 DiNola-Kaminsky-Sternfeld (P)		•	•			•	•		•	•									•	•			
27 DiNola-Kaminsky-Sternfeld (Y)		•	•			•	•	•	•	•									•	•			
28 Dopyera	•	•	•	•		•	•			•	•			•		•	•	•	•		•	•	•
29 Gellert	•	•	•										•		•				•				•
30 Goodenough	•	•	•													•	•	•	•				•
31 Gordon-Jester													•			•	•	•	•	•	•	•	
32 Greenberg	•	•	•			•	•			•	•		•			•	•		•	•	•		
33 Hartup-Charlesworth	•					•				•	•		•			•	•		•	•	•	•	
34 Heathers										•			•			•	•		•				
35 Jack		•											•	•		•	•		•				
36 Jersild-Markey		•			•						•					•	•		•		•		•
37 Kagan																•	•		•				•
38 Katz		•	•		•	•	•		•	•			•			•	•	•	•	•			
39 Kaufman-Rosenblum	•	•		•	•	•	•			•			•	•		•	•		•	•	•	•	
40 Kogan-Wimberger	•	•	•		•	•							•	•		•	•		•				•
41 Lewis	•	•	•		•	•				•			•	•		•	•		•			•	
42 McGrew-McGrew	•	•		•	•	•					•		•										
43 Manwell-Mengert	•	•				•		•	•	•			•	•	•	•			•	•			
44 Marshall-McCandless						•				•			•	•	•	•			•				•
45 Mash-Terdal-Anderson		•	•		•	•	•			•		•	•	•		•	•	•	•	•	•	•	•
46 Medley, et al.	•	•			•								•	•		•			•				
47 Morgan-Ricciuti	•	•	•		•	•							•	•		•			•			•	
48 Moss-Robson	•	•	•			•							•			•	•		•				
49 Murphy	•	•				•				•	•		•			•	•		•	•			
50 Ogilvie-Shapiro		•								•	•		•	•		•			•	•		•	
51 Olmsted													•	•		•	•		•				
52 Olson	•	•		•									•	•		•	•	•	•		•		•
53 Parsons							•		•				•	•		•	•		•				
54 Parten																			•				
55 Ricketts	•	•				•				•			•			•	•		•	•	•		
56 Rosen-D'Andrade										•			•			•	•		•	•	•		•
57 Schaefer-Aaronson	•	•	•			•				•	•		•			•	•		•	•			
58 Schoggen													•	•		•	•		•	•			
59 Schroeer-Flapan												•	•	•					•	•			
60 Sears-Rau-Alpert (BUO)		•		•						•									•	•			
61 Sears-Rau-Alpert (DP)										•	•								•	•			
62 Soar-Soar-Ragosta	•	•				•				•			•			•	•		•	•			•
63 Spaulding						•				•			•	•					•	•			
64 Stallings		•				•	•		•	•			•		•	•	•	•	•	•		•	
65 Stover-Guerney-O'Connell						•													•	•		•	
66 Tulkin-Kagan	•	•			•	•				•	•		•	•		•	•		•	•	•		
67 Van Alstyne						•							•	•	•	•			•				
68 Walters-Pearce-Dahms	•	•			•							•	•			•	•		•	•		•	
69 Washburn		•	•																•				
70 Watts, et al.		•			•	•		•	•	•			•	•	•	•	•	•	•	•		•	
71 White-Kaban		•			•	•							•	•		•	•		•				•
72 Wright										•		•	•			•	•	•	•	•		•	
73 Yarrow, et al.		•	•			•		•	•	•	•		•			•	•	•	•		•		

Source: E. Gil Boyer, Anita Boyer, and Gail Karafin, eds., *Measures of Maturation: An Anthology of Early Childhood Observation Instruments.* (Philadelphia: Humanizing Learning Program, Research for Better Schools, Inc., 1973).

BIBLIOGRAPHY

Suggested Readings

Barker, Roger G., ed. *The Stream of Behavior*. New York: Appleton-Century-Crofts, 1963.

Beegle, Charles W., and Brandt, Richard M., eds. *Observational Methods in the Classroom*. Washington, D.C.: Association for Supervision and Curriculum Development, 1973.

Borich, Gary, and Madden, Susan. *Evaluating Classroom Instruction*. Menlo Park, Calif.: Addison-Wesley, 1977.

Boyer, E. Gil; Boyer, Anita; and Karafin, Gail, eds. *Measures of Maturation: An Anthology of Early Childhood Observation Instruments*. Philadelphia: Humanizing Learning Program, Research for Better Schools, Inc., 1973. A review of seventy-three observation systems for use with younger children.

Brandt, R. *Studying Behavior in Natural Settings*. New York: Holt, Rinehart and Winston, 1972. Reports on classroom observational studies and describes observation instruments for use in the classroom.

Caldwell, Betty E., and Honig, Alice S. *Approach: A Procedure for Patterning Responses of Adults and Children Coding Manual*. Little Rock, Ark.: University of Arkansas, 1971.

Cartwright, Carol A., and Cartwright, G. Phillip. *Developing Observation Skills*. New York: McGraw-Hill, 1974.

Flanders, Ned A. *Analyzing Teaching Behavior*. Reading, Mass: Addison-Wesley, 1970. Describes Flanders interaction observation system.

Kohn, Martin and Rosman, Bernice L. "A Social Competence Scale and Symptom Checklist for the Preschool Child: Factor Dimensions, Their Cross-Instrument Generality, and Longitudinal Persistence," *Developmental Psychology* 6, no. 3, (1972): 430-444.

Medley, D. M. "Observation Schedule and Record Form 5 Verbal (OScAR 5V)." Mimeographed. Charlottesville: University of Virginia, 1973.

Medley, Donald M., and Mitzel, Harold E. "Measuring Classroom Behavior by Systematic Observation." In *Handbook of Research on Teaching,* edited by N. L. Gage. Chicago: Rand McNally, 1963.

Prescott, Elizabeth. *Who Thrives In Group Day Care? Assessment of Child-Rearing Environments: An Ecological Approach*. Pasadena, Calif.: Pacific Oaks College, 1973. ERIC Accession No. ED 076 229.

Rist, R. C. "Race, Policy, and Schooling." In *The Use and Abuse of Social Science*, edited by Irving Louis Horowitz. New Brunswick, N. J.: Trans-Action Books, 1975.

Rosenshine, B., and Furst, N. "The Use of Direct Observation to Study Teaching." In *Second Handbook of Research on Teaching*, edited by Robert M. W. Travers. Chicago: Rand McNally, 1973.

Rowen, Betty. *The Children We See: An Observational Approach to Child Study*. New York: Holt, Rinehart and Winston, 1973.

Sears, Pauline S., and Sherman, Vivian S. *In Pursuit of Self-Esteem*. Belmont, Calif.: Wadsworth, 1966. An in-depth case study of eight fifth-grade children. Extensive narrative observations were collected and analyzed. The study was conducted over two years.

Simon, Anita, and Boyer, E. Gil. *Mirrors for Behavior: An Anthology of Classroom Observation Instruments*. Philadelphia: Humanizing Learning Program, Research for Better Schools, Inc., 1967, 1969, 1970. ERIC Accession No. ED 029 833. A review of 132 observation systems.

Soar, R. S.; Soar, R. M.; and Ragosta, M. "Florida Climate and Control System (FLACCS)." Gainesville, Fla.: Institute for Development of Human Resources, University of Florida, 1968.

Stallings, Jane, and Wilcox, Mary. "Report of the Field Testing of Instruments for the National Day Care Cost-Effects Study" (Prepared at Stanford Research Institute, Menlo Park, Calif., for the Department of Health, Education, and Welfare, Washington, D.C., 1976).

Tikunoff, William J.; Berliner, David C.; and Rist, Ray C. *An Ethnographic Study of the Fort Classrooms of the Beginning Teacher Evaluation Study Known Sample*. Technical Report No. 75-10-5. San Francisco, Calif.: Far West Laboratory for Educational Research and Development, 1975.

Chapter 2

Learning to Use the Observation System

OVERVIEW OF THE SRI SYSTEM

This chapter explains in detail an observation system developed by the author and staff members at Stanford Research Institute (SRI) to evaluate several educational programs in the Follow Through Planned Variation Project. The Follow Through Project was established by Congress in 1967 under the Office of Economic Opportunity to find a grade-school program that would reinforce and extend the academic gains made by economically disadvantaged children who had been enrolled in Head Start and similar preschool programs. The goal of the project was to develop and implement several programs based on different educational theories to see how these programs influenced the growth and development of children. The project began when the government funded 22 sponsored models to implement their own programs.

The purpose of the Follow Through classroom observation evaluation was twofold. First, it was meant to assess the implementation of several Follow Through sponsored models that had been selected for special study; and second, it was meant to examine the relationships between classroom instructional processes and child outcomes.

The programs selected for observation represented the entire range of innovative educational theories in Follow Through. They included behavior modification models based on the theory of B. F. Skinner; a model based on the theory of Jean Piaget; an open school model based on English infant school theory; and other models based on various combinations of the theories and practices of Jean Piaget, John Dewey, Carl Rogers, and the English infant schools.

Observation was the only way to see whether or not the Follow Through programs were successful in getting their ideas into the classrooms. We (the SRI staff) had to see if the materials specified in each program were being used; if children were grouped with classroom aides and teachers as specified; and if the verbal interactions of teachers and children were those specified by the sponsors of the models.

After studying the available observation systems, we found that none in existence at that time was broad enough or flexible enough to accommodate the wide range of programs in the Follow Through Project, thus we decided to develop our own. With assistance from representatives of eight Follow Through model sponsors, the SRI observation system was launched in December 1969.

The observation system consists of three instruments:

1. Physical Environment Information (PEI). This is filled out once a day and provides information on seating patterns and the presence and use of equipment and materials.

2. Classroom Check List (CCL). This is filled out four times an hour and provides information on the type of activities occurring in the classroom and on the grouping of children and the teaching staff.

3. Five-Minute Interaction (FMI). This is completed four times an hour, after each Check List is completed. It provides information about the type of interactions that occur in the classroom.

(See Appendix A for a copy of this observation system.)

The system was used four times from 1970 to 1973 to collect observation data for the Follow Through Project. Each year it was refined so that subtler teacher and child behaviors could be recorded. These refinements made the system more comprehensive and more complicated, and at present the SRI staff requires observers in our projects to attend a seven-day training session and pass a criterion test before they can collect data for us. For readers to use this system effectively, they should study the codes and complete the exercises in this book. They should also discuss examples with colleagues or instructors and practice using the system in classrooms.

Physical Environment

The physical environment of the classroom—its size, shape, lighting, ventilation, and noise level—was considered important to the process of educating children. We tried to record this kind of information during our first two years of observation but found it impossible to get observers to agree on what was "light enough" or "cool enough" or "quiet enough." (See Figure 2.1.) Therefore, since we could not establish reliability among observers, we deleted these items from subsequent observations.

The use of materials and equipment was very important to some educational models, so we developed instead a comprehensive checklist of equipment that allowed the observer to indicate whether the materials were present and/or used (see Figure 2.2). Seating patterns could also be recorded. This record was easy to complete and the findings were reliable—that is, observers agreed on the presence and usage of materials.

Activities and Groupings

Next we wanted to know what activities occurred in classrooms throughout the day. Some sponsors of models expected a variety of activities to occur simultaneously so that children could have a real choice as to what they wanted to do. Others directed teachers and aides to assign children to small groups and then spend much of their time teaching reading, writing, and arithmetic to these small groups. To record this kind of information we developed an activity checklist (see Figure 2.3). With this, each child and adult is marked on the grid in some activity. The possible activities are listed at the left of the table. The grouping of the children is indicated by the four columns. The letters to the left of each grouping column stand for teacher (T), aide (A), volunteer (V), and independent child (i). The numbers within each column allow the observer to record the fact that, for instance, more than one child is working on math alone. Look at Activity 6 on Figure 2.3. Two children were working together on math. Two aides were each working with a small group of children in math, and one teacher was working with a small group in math. Materials and equipment used in teaching

PHYSICAL ENVIRONMENT INFORMATION — Mark all that apply.

Playground Facilities/Use/Activities
- ○ Playground equipment in new condition.
- ○ Playground equipment in old condition.
- ○ Playground equipment seems to be used a lot.

Playground activity directed by adults:
- ○ Always
- ○ Sometimes
- ○ Never

Condition of Building

Yes No
○   ○ Is the school building in good condition?

Noise Level

Yes No
○   ○ Adults seem to have difficulty making themselves heard (have to repeat questions, ask the children to be quiet, etc.)
○   ○ Children are noticeably disturbed in their work by the noise level.

Lighting

Yes No
○   ○ Physical lighting seems adequate.
○   ○ Some areas of the room are noticeably lighter/darker than the rest.

Heating and Ventilating

Yes No
○   ○ Some areas of the classroom are noticeably warmer/cooler than the rest. (Direct sunlight, proximity to heating system, etc.)
○   ○ Classroom is comfortably heated.

Displays in Classroom

Yes No
○   ○ Children's own art on display.
○   ○ Photographs of the children on display.
○   ○ Pictures of various ethnic groups on display.
○   ○ Community events posted.
○   ○ Other (Specify) ————▶

NOTE: Do not write outside this box

Description of Classroom Space

Yes No
○   ○ Single contained classroom within a building.
○   ○ Open classrooms.
○   ○ Portable classrooms.

Space per Child

Yes No
○   ○ Does there seem to be adequate space per child?

Figure 2.1

Physical Environment Information
(Mark all that apply.)

For each of the items below, mark all that apply:

① Present
② Used today

Seating Patterns:
- ○ Movable tables and chairs for seating purposes.
- ○ Stationary desks in rows.
- ○ Assigned seating for at least part of the day.
- ○ Children select their own seating locations.
- ○ Teacher assigns children to groups.
- ○ Children select their own work groups.

GAMES, TOYS, PLAY EQUIPMENT
- ①② small toys (trucks, cars, dolls and accessories
- ①② puzzles, games
- ①② wheel toys
- ①② small play equipment (jumpropes, balls)
- ①② large play equipment (swings, jungle gym)
- ①② children's storybooks
- ①② animals, other nature objects
- ①② sandbox, water table
- ①② carpentry materials, large blocks
- ①② cooking and sewing supplies

INSTRUCTIONAL MATERIALS
- ①② Montessori, other educational toys
- ①② children's texts, workbooks
- ①② math/science equipment, concrete objects
- ①② instructional charts

AUDIO, VISUAL EQUIPMENT
- ①② television
- ①② record or tape player
- ①② audio-visual equipment

GENERAL EQUIPMENT, MATERIALS
- ①② children's own products on display
- ①② displays reflecting children's ethnicity
- ①② other displays especially for children
- ①② magazines
- ①② achievement charts
- ①② child-size sink
- ①② child-size table and chairs
- ①② child-size shelves
- ①② arts and crafts materials
- ①② blackboard, feltboard
- ①② child's own storage space
- ①② photographs of the children on display

OTHER
- ①② please specify . . . . . .

MAKE NO

STRAY MARKS

IN BLANK AREAS

Figure 2.2 Physical Environment Information

CLASSROOM OBSERVATION PROCEDURE

CLASSROOM CHECK LIST (be sure to code **EVERYONE** in the class)

	ONE CHILD	TWO CHILDREN	SMALL GROUPS	LARGE GROUPS
1. Snack, lunch	T ①②③ A ①②③ v ①②③ i ①②③	T ①②③ A ①②③ v ①②③ i ①②③	T ①②③④ A ①②③④ v ①②③④ i ①②③④	T ①② A ①② v ①② i ①②
2. Group time	T ①②③ A ①②③ v ①②③ i ①②③	T ①②③ A ①②③ v ①②③ i ①②③	T ①②③④ A ①②③④ v ①②③④ i ①②③④	T ①② A ①② v ①② i ①②
Story **3. Music** Dancing	T ①②③ A ①②③ v ①②③ i ①②③	T ①②③ A ①②③ v ①②③ i ①②③	T ①②③④ A ①②③④ v ①②③④ i ①②③④	T ①② A ①② v ①② i ①②
4. Arts, Crafts	T ①②③ A ①②③ v ①②③ i ①②③	T ①②③ A ①②③ v ①②③ i ①②③	T ①②③④ A ①②③④ v ①②③④ i ①②③④	T ①② A ①② v ①② i ①②
Guessing Games **5. Table Games** Puzzles	T ①②③ A ①②③ v ①②③ i ①②③	T ①②③ A ①②③ v ①②③ i ①②③	T ①②③④ A ①②③④ v ①②③④ i ①②③④	T ①② A ①② v ①② i ①②
Numbers **6. Math** Arithmetic	T ①②③ A ①②③ v ①②③ i ①②③	T ①②③ A ①②③ v ①②③ i ●②③	T ●②③④ A ①●③④ v ①②③④ i ①②③④	T ①② A ①② v ①② i ①②
Reading **7. Alphabet** Lang. Development	T ①②③ A ①②③ v ①②③ i ①②③	T ①②③ A ①②③ v ①②③ i ①②③	T ①②③④ A ①②③④ v ①②③④ i ①②③④	T ①② A ①② v ①② i ①②
Social Studies **8. Geography**	T ①②③ A ①②③ v ①②③ i ①②③	T ①②③ A ①②③ v ①②③ i ①②③	T ①②③④ A ①②③④ v ①②③④ i ①②③④	T ①② A ①② v ①② i ①②
Science **9. Natural World**	T ①②③ A ①②③ v ①②③ i ①②③	T ①②③ A ①②③ v ①②③ i ①②③	T ①②③④ A ①②③④ v ①②③④ i ①②③④	T ①② A ①② v ①② i ①②
Sewing Cooking **10. Pounding** Sawing	T ①②③ A ①②③ v ①②③ i ①②③	T ①②③ A ①②③ v ①②③ i ①②③	T ①②③④ A ①②③④ v ①②③④ i ①②③④	T ①② A ①② v ①② i ①②
Blocks **11. Trucks**	T ①②③ A ①②③ v ①②③ i ①②③	T ①②③ A ①②③ v ①②③ i ①②③	T ①②③④ A ①②③④ v ①②③④ i ①②③④	T ①② A ①② v ①② i ①②
Dramatic Play **12. Dress-Up**	T ①②③ A ①②③ v ①②③ i ①②③	T ①②③ A ①②③ v ①②③ i ①②③	T ①②③④ A ①②③④ v ①②③④ i ①②③④	T ①② A ①② v ①② i ①②
13. Active Play	T ①②③ A ①②③ v ①②③ i ①②③	T ①②③ A ①②③ v ①②③ i ①②③	T ①②③④ A ①②③④ v ①②③④ i ①②③④	T ①② A ①② v ①② i ①②
14. RELIABILITY SHEET ○				

Materials key (left column):

○ TV
○ Audio-Visual Materials
○ Exploratory Materials
○ Math and Science Equipment
● Texts, Workbooks
● Puzzles, Games

Figure 2.3 Classroom Observation Procedure

			ONE CHILD	TWO CHILDREN	SMALL GROUPS	LARGE GROUPS
15. Practical Skills Acquisition			T ①②③	T ①②③	T ①②③④	T ①②
			A ①②③	A ①②③	A ①②③④	A ①②
			v ①②③	v ①②③	v ①②③④	v ①②
			i ①②③	i ①②③	i ①②③④	i ①②
16. Observing			T ①②③	T ①②③	T ①②③④	T ①②
			A ①②③	A ①②③	A ①②③④	A ①②
			v ①②③	v ①②③	v ①②③④	v ①②
			i ①②③	i ①②③	i ①②③④	i ①②
17. Social Interaction	Ob [©②⑤]	T A V	T ①②③	T ①②③	T ①②③④	T ①②
			A ①②③	A ①②③	A ①②③④	A ①②
			v ①②③	v ①②③	v ①②③④	v ①②
			i ①②③	i ①②③	i ①②③④	i ①②
18. Unoccupied Child			T ①②③	T ①②③	T ①②③④	T ①②
			A ①②③	A ①②③	A ①②③④	A ①②
			v ①②③	v ①②③	v ①②③④	v ①②
			i ①②③	i ①②③	i ①②③④	i ①②
19. Discipline			T ①②③	T ①②③	T ①②③④	T ①②
			A ①②③	A ①②③	A ①②③④	A ①②
			v ①②③	v ①②③	v ①②③④	v ①②
			i ①②③	i ①②③	i ①②③④	i ①②
20. Transitional Activities		T A V	T ①②③	T ①②③	T ①②③④	T ①②
			A ①②③	A ①②③	A ①②③④	A ①②
			v ①②③	v ①②③	v ①②③④	v ①②
			i ①②③	i ①②③	i ①②③④	i ①②
21. Classroom Management		T A V	T ①②③	T ①②③	T ①②③④	T ①②
			A ①②③	A ①②③	A ①②③④	A ①②
			v ①②③	v ①②③	v ①②③④	v ①②
			i ①②③	i ①②③	i ①②③④	i ①②
22. Out of Room		T A V	T ①②③	T ①②③	T ①②③④	T ①②
			A ①②③	A ①②③	A ①②③④	A ①②
			v ①②③	v ①②③	v ①②③④	v ①②
			i ①②③	i ①②③	i ①②③④	i ①②

NUMBER OF ADULTS IN CLASSROOM ⓪ ① ② ● ④ ⑤ ⑥ ⑦ ⑧ ⑨ ⑩

can also be indicated—on the list left of the grid. Here we see that textbooks, workbooks, puzzles, or games are being used.

In the Follow Through study, children, teachers, and aides were placed on this grid four times an hour, five hours a day, for three days—sixty grids per classroom. Such a quantity of data gave us a good idea of what activities were occurring in the classroom and with what frequency. It also showed the responsibilities of teachers and aides and answered such questions as: Are aides a part of the instructional team? Are children receiving individual attention? Are children operating independently?

The grid is easy to fill out. Our observers were instructed to place everyone in the room on the grid once, starting from the door through which the observer entered and going clockwise around the room. Observer reliability was not difficult to gain once we had operationally defined each activity. Appendix B has a list of operational definitions for the activities in the Classroom Check List and an exercise for the reader to complete. Turn to Appendix B and study this now. When you have finished, do Exercise 2.1 and then check your answers against the correct ones given at the end of this chapter.

EXERCISE 2.1 Place each child and adult in the picture on the grid that follows.

CLASSROOM OBSERVATION PROCEDURE

CLASSROOM CHECK LIST (be sure to code **EVERYONE** in the class)

		ONE CHILD	TWO CHILDREN	SMALL GROUPS	LARGE GROUPS
1. Snack, lunch		T ① ② ③ A ① ② ③ v ① ② ③ i ① ② ③	T ① ② ③ A ① ② ③ v ① ② ③ i ① ② ③	T ① ② ③ ④ A ① ② ③ ④ v ① ② ③ ④ i ① ② ③ ④	T ① ② A ① ② v ① ② i ① ②
2. Group time		T ① ② ③ A ① ② ③ v ① ② ③ i ① ② ③	T ① ② ③ A ① ② ③ v ① ② ③ i ① ② ③	T ① ② ③ ④ A ① ② ③ ④ v ① ② ③ ④ i ① ② ③ ④	T ① ② A ① ② v ① ② i ① ②
3. Story / Music / Dancing		T ① ② ③ A ① ② ③ v ① ② ③ i ① ② ③	T ① ② ③ A ① ② ③ v ① ② ③ i ① ② ③	T ① ② ③ ④ A ① ② ③ ④ v ① ② ③ ④ i ① ② ③ ④	T ① ② A ① ② v ① ② i ① ②
4. Arts, Crafts		T ① ② ③ A ① ② ③ v ① ② ③ i ① ② ③	T ① ② ③ A ① ② ③ v ① ② ③ i ① ② ③	T ① ② ③ ④ A ① ② ③ ④ v ① ② ③ ④ i ① ② ③ ④	T ① ② A ① ② v ① ② i ① ②
5. Guessing Games / Table Games / Puzzles		T ① ② ③ A ① ② ③ v ① ② ③ i ① ② ③	T ① ② ③ A ① ② ③ v ① ② ③ i ① ② ③	T ① ② ③ ④ A ① ② ③ ④ v ① ② ③ ④ i ① ② ③ ④	T ① ② A ① ② v ① ② i ① ②
6. Math / Numbers / Arithmetic		T ① ② ③ A ① ② ③ v ① ② ③ i ① ② ③	T ① ② ③ A ① ② ③ v ① ② ③ i ① ② ③	T ① ② ③ ④ A ① ② ③ ④ v ① ② ③ ④ i ① ② ③ ④	T ① ② A ① ② v ① ② i ① ②
7. Reading / Alphabet / Lang. Development		T ① ② ③ A ① ② ③ v ① ② ③ i ① ② ③	T ① ② ③ A ① ② ③ v ① ② ③ i ① ② ③	T ① ② ③ ④ A ① ② ③ ④ v ① ② ③ ④ i ① ② ③ ④	T ① ② A ① ② v ① ② i ① ②
8. Social Studies / Geography		T ① ② ③ A ① ② ③ v ① ② ③ i ① ② ③	T ① ② ③ A ① ② ③ v ① ② ③ i ① ② ③	T ① ② ③ ④ A ① ② ③ ④ v ① ② ③ ④ i ① ② ③ ④	T ① ② A ① ② v ① ② i ① ②
9. Science / Natural World		T ① ② ③ A ① ② ③ v ① ② ③ i ① ② ③	T ① ② ③ A ① ② ③ v ① ② ③ i ① ② ③	T ① ② ③ ④ A ① ② ③ ④ v ① ② ③ ④ i ① ② ③ ④	T ① ② A ① ② v ① ② i ① ②
10. Sewing / Cooking / Pounding / Sawing		T ① ② ③ A ① ② ③ v ① ② ③ i ① ② ③	T ① ② ③ A ① ② ③ v ① ② ③ i ① ② ③	T ① ② ③ ④ A ① ② ③ ④ v ① ② ③ ④ i ① ② ③ ④	T ① ② A ① ② v ① ② i ① ②
11. Blocks / Trucks		T ① ② ③ A ① ② ③ v ① ② ③ i ① ② ③	T ① ② ③ A ① ② ③ v ① ② ③ i ① ② ③	T ① ② ③ ④ A ① ② ③ ④ v ① ② ③ ④ i ① ② ③ ④	T ① ② A ① ② v ① ② i ① ②
12. Dramatic Play / Dress-Up		T ① ② ③ A ① ② ③ v ① ② ③ i ① ② ③	T ① ② ③ A ① ② ③ v ① ② ③ i ① ② ③	T ① ② ③ ④ A ① ② ③ ④ v ① ② ③ ④ i ① ② ③ ④	T ① ② A ① ② v ① ② i ① ②
13. Active Play		T ① ② ③ A ① ② ③ v ① ② ③ i ① ② ③	T ① ② ③ A ① ② ③ v ① ② ③ i ① ② ③	T ① ② ③ ④ A ① ② ③ ④ v ① ② ③ ④ i ① ② ③ ④	T ① ② A ① ② v ① ② i ① ②
14. RELIABILITY SHEET	○				

Materials (checklist column):
- ○ TV
- ○ Audio-Visual Materials
- ○ Exploratory Materials
- ○ Math and Science Equipment
- ○ Texts, Workbooks
- ○ Puzzles, Games

Exercise 2.1   Classroom Observation Procedure

			ONE CHILD	TWO CHILDREN	SMALL GROUPS	LARGE GROUPS
15. Practical Skills Acquisition			T ①②③ A ①②③ v ①②③ i ①②③	T ①②③ A ①②③ v ①②③ i ①②③	T ①②③④ A ①②③④ v ①②③④ i ①②③④	T ①② A ①② v ①② i ①②
16. Observing			T ①②③ A ①②③ v ①②③ i ①②③	T ①②③ A ①②③ v ①②③ i ①②③	T ①②③④ A ①②③④ v ①②③④ i ①②③④	T ①② A ①② v ①② i ①②
17. Social Interaction	Ob [Ⓒ ② Ⓢ]	Ⓣ Ⓐ Ⓥ	T ①②③ A ①②③ v ①②③ i ①②③	T ①②③ A ①②③ v ①②③ i ①②③	T ①②③④ A ①②③④ v ①②③④ i ①②③④	T ①② A ①② v ①② i ①②
18. Unoccupied Child			T ①②③ A ①②③ v ①②③ i ①②③	T ①②③ A ①②③ v ①②③ i ①②③	T ①②③④ A ①②③④ v ①②③④ i ①②③④	T ①② A ①② v ①② i ①②
19. Discipline			T ①②③ A ①②③ v ①②③ i ①②③	T ①②③ A ①②③ v ①②③ i ①②③	T ①②③④ A ①②③④ v ①②③④ i ①②③④	T ①② A ①② v ①② i ①②
20. Transitional Activities		Ⓣ Ⓐ Ⓥ	T ①②③ A ①②③ v ①②③ i ①②③	T ①②③ A ①②③ v ①②③ i ①②③	T ①②③④ A ①②③④ v ①②③④ i ①②③④	T ①② A ①② v ①② i ①②
21. Classroom Management		Ⓣ Ⓐ Ⓥ	T ①②③ A ①②③ v ①②③ i ①②③	T ①②③ A ①②③ v ①②③ i ①②③	T ①②③④ A ①②③④ v ①②③④ i ①②③④	T ①② A ①② v ①② i ①②
22. Out of Room		Ⓣ Ⓐ Ⓥ	T ①②③ A ①②③ v ①②③ i ①②③	T ①②③ A ①②③ v ①②③ i ①②③	T ①②③④ A ①②③④ v ①②③④ i ①②③④	T ①② A ①② v ①② i ①②

NUMBER OF ADULTS IN CLASSROOM ⓪ ① ② ③ ④ ⑤ ⑥ ⑦ ⑧ ⑨ ⑩

Interaction Observations

Besides knowing what materials are used and what activities occur, it is important to know what happens between teachers and children in a classroom. To understand these interactions we constructed a coding system that could tell us (1) who the speaker was, (2) to whom he or she was speaking, (3) what the message was, and (4) how the message was given (or what its intention was). Figure 2.4 illustrates one interaction frame or sentence. Below this frame is a list of general code meanings (operational definitions are given in Appendix C). The column at the far left of the frame allows the observer to mark "R" when the entire preceding frame is repeated, "S" when there is simultaneous action, and "C" when a frame should be cancelled because of an error.

The system displayed here was built from the Flanders interaction system mentioned in the previous chapter. However, since the Flanders system is limited to assessing the teacher's behavior in a group discussion, we had to add a code to show movement in the classroom. We also developed a nonverbal code, since we saw that many important messages between people were sent nonverbally, through nodding, smiling, or grimacing, for example.

The focus person of the interaction observation can be the teacher, an aide, or a child; everything that a person says or does during the five-minute observation period is recorded on the form

using the specified coding system. Approximately seventy-two interaction frames can be recorded in five minutes.

In the Follow Through study, five-minute interaction observations were made for three days in each classroom, four times an hour
for five hours a day provided sixty interaction observations in each
classroom. From this great quantity of data, we could study, for example, teachers' questioning patterns, reinforcement methods, control systems, and positive and negative displays of emotions. Also,
the independence, task persistence, cooperativeness, and inquiry of
children in the different educational models could be assessed.

List of Codes

1	Who	To Whom	What	How
Ⓡ	Ⓣ Ⓐ Ⓥ	Ⓣ Ⓐ Ⓥ	① ② ③ ④ ⑤	Ⓗ Ⓤ Ⓝ Ⓣ
Ⓢ	Ⓒ Ⓓ ②	Ⓒ Ⓓ ②	⑥ ⑦ ⑧ ⑨ ⑩	Ⓠ Ⓖ Ⓟ
Ⓒ	Ⓢ Ⓛ Ⓐⁿ Ⓜ	Ⓢ Ⓛ Ⓐⁿ Ⓜ	⑪ ⑫ Ⓝⱽ Ⓧ	Ⓞ Ⓦ ᴰᴾ Ⓐ Ⓑ

Who/To Whom	What	How
T – Teacher	1 – Command or Request	H – Happy
A – Aide	2 – Open-ended Question	U – Unhappy
V – Volunteer	3 – Response	N – Negative
C – Child	4 – Instruction,	T – Touch
D – Different Child	Explanation	Q – Question
2 – Two Children	5 – Comments, Greetings;	G – Guide/Reason
S – Small Group (3-8)	General Action	P – Punish
L – Large Group (9 up)	6 – Task-related Statement	O – Object
An – Animal	7 – Acknowledge	W – Worth
M – Machine	8 – Praise	DP – Dramatic Play/Pretend
	9 – Corrective Feedback	A – Academic
	10 – No Response	B – Behavior
	11 – Waiting	
	12 – Observing, Listening	
	NV – Nonverbal	
	X – Movement	

R – Repeat the frame
S – Simultaneous action
C – Cancel the frame

Figure 2.4

USING AN OBSERVATION SYSTEM

All observation systems necessarily include some procedures for training observers. If data are to be useful, they must be gathered systematically and reliably; that is, two or more observers must record the same event in the same way. It is important to start with objective observations (events that can be seen, heard, and agreed upon by two or more people). Subjective events such as feelings or intuition should be avoided in systematic observation unless the observation team shares common assumptions and has spent a great deal of time rating similar events.

Observer training usually starts with an explanation of the observation instrument, including a list of codes with their operational definitions. An *operational definition* defines an idea, concept, term, or word by identifying precisely what you can see, feel, or touch, and gives many concrete examples of what the behavior is—as well as what it is *not*—so that inferences and assumptions are minimized. The operational definitions for a given system are important since two systems may use the same terms for different behaviors. For example, the PROSE system[1] defines "cooperation" as compliance with the teacher's request, while our system defines it as two or more children working together in a task. All SRI interaction code definitions are presented in Appendix C and should be studied at this time.

The first step toward using any observation instrument is to memorize the operational definitions. A set of flash cards is useful for memorization, and the last three pages of this book can be cut up into cards using the SRI system. The code is on one side and its definition is on the other. Work with these cards until you can recite the definitions automatically. That's the easy part.

Building a concept around the definition and recognizing events defined by the code is more difficult. For instance, in this observation system, an important difference among teaching styles can be identified by the types of questions teachers ask most often. The question coded as a "1Q" requires a child to respond with a single known answer, a question coded as "2Q" requires a more extended thought from the child. (Be sure you know and understand the codes given in Appendix C.) Trainee observers may memorize the operational definition of both codes, but will they be able to distinguish between "1Q" and "2Q" questions embedded in conversations? Try Exercise 2.2 to see if you can use the codes correctly. Remember that the correct answers are given at the end of the chapter.

EXERCISE 2.2 Code each sentence.

Situation: A third-grade class is discussing a movie called *Sounder*.

1. Teacher to large group: "Who saw the movie yesterday?"

1	Who	To Whom	What	How
	Ⓡ Ⓣ Ⓐ Ⓥ	Ⓣ Ⓐ Ⓥ	① ② ③ ④ ⑤	Ⓗ Ⓤ Ⓝ Ⓣ
	Ⓢ Ⓒ Ⓓ ②	Ⓒ Ⓓ ②	⑥ ⑦ ⑧ ⑨ ⑩	Ⓠ Ⓖ Ⓟ
	Ⓒ Ⓢ Ⓛ ⒶⓃ Ⓜ	Ⓢ Ⓛ ⒶⓃ Ⓜ	⑪ ⑫	Ⓝⱽ Ⓧ Ⓞ Ⓦ ᴼᴾ	Ⓐ Ⓑ

---

[1]Donald M. Medley *et al., The Personal Record of School Experiences: A Manual for PROSE Recorders* (Princeton, N.J.: Educational Testing Service, 1971). ERIC Accession No. ED 054 215.

2. Most of the group
   raise their hands.

2	Who	To Whom	What	How
	Ⓡ Ⓣ Ⓐ Ⓥ	Ⓣ Ⓐ Ⓥ	① ② ③ ④ ⑤	Ⓗ Ⓤ Ⓝ Ⓣ
	Ⓢ Ⓒ Ⓓ ②	Ⓒ Ⓓ ②	⑥ ⑦ ⑧ ⑨ ⑩	Ⓠ Ⓖ Ⓟ
	Ⓒ Ⓢ Ⓛ Ⓐ⒩ Ⓜ	Ⓢ Ⓛ Ⓐ⒩ Ⓜ	⑪ ⑫ ⒩⒱ Ⓧ	Ⓞ Ⓦ Ⓓ⒫ Ⓐ Ⓑ

3. Teacher: "Stanley, how
   many saw the movie?"

3	Who	To Whom	What	How
	Ⓡ Ⓣ Ⓐ Ⓥ	Ⓣ Ⓐ Ⓥ	① ② ③ ④ ⑤	Ⓗ Ⓤ Ⓝ Ⓣ
	Ⓢ Ⓒ Ⓓ ②	Ⓒ Ⓓ ②	⑥ ⑦ ⑧ ⑨ ⑩	Ⓠ Ⓖ Ⓟ
	Ⓒ Ⓢ Ⓛ Ⓐ⒩ Ⓜ	Ⓢ Ⓛ Ⓐ⒩ Ⓜ	⑪ ⑫ ⒩⒱ Ⓧ	Ⓞ Ⓦ Ⓓ⒫ Ⓐ Ⓑ

4. Stanley counts the hands
   and says: "Nineteen."

4	Who	To Whom	What	How
	Ⓡ Ⓣ Ⓐ Ⓥ	Ⓣ Ⓐ Ⓥ	① ② ③ ④ ⑤	Ⓗ Ⓤ Ⓝ Ⓣ
	Ⓢ Ⓒ Ⓓ ②	Ⓒ Ⓓ ②	⑥ ⑦ ⑧ ⑨ ⑩	Ⓠ Ⓖ Ⓟ
	Ⓒ Ⓢ Ⓛ Ⓐ⒩ Ⓜ	Ⓢ Ⓛ Ⓐ⒩ Ⓜ	⑪ ⑫ ⒩⒱ Ⓧ	Ⓞ Ⓦ Ⓓ⒫ Ⓐ Ⓑ

5. Teacher: "Which part made
   you laugh, Millie?"

5	Who	To Whom	What	How
	Ⓡ Ⓣ Ⓐ Ⓥ	Ⓣ Ⓐ Ⓥ	① ② ③ ④ ⑤	Ⓗ Ⓤ Ⓝ Ⓣ
	Ⓢ Ⓒ Ⓓ ②	Ⓒ Ⓓ ②	⑥ ⑦ ⑧ ⑨ ⑩	Ⓠ Ⓖ Ⓟ
	Ⓒ Ⓢ Ⓛ Ⓐ⒩ Ⓜ	Ⓢ Ⓛ Ⓐ⒩ Ⓜ	⑪ ⑫ ⒩⒱ Ⓧ	Ⓞ Ⓦ Ⓓ⒫ Ⓐ Ⓑ

6. Millie, laughing: "When
   the dog ran around and
   made people fall down."

6	Who	To Whom	What	How
	Ⓡ Ⓣ Ⓐ Ⓥ	Ⓣ Ⓐ Ⓥ	① ② ③ ④ ⑤	Ⓗ Ⓤ Ⓝ Ⓣ
	Ⓢ Ⓒ Ⓓ ②	Ⓒ Ⓓ ②	⑥ ⑦ ⑧ ⑨ ⑩	Ⓠ Ⓖ Ⓟ
	Ⓒ Ⓢ Ⓛ Ⓐ⒩ Ⓜ	Ⓢ Ⓛ Ⓐ⒩ Ⓜ	⑪ ⑫ ⒩⒱ Ⓧ	Ⓞ Ⓦ Ⓓ⒫ Ⓐ Ⓑ

7. Teacher to large group:
   "How did you feel when
   the sheriff took the
   daddy away?"

7	Who	To Whom	What	How
	Ⓡ Ⓣ Ⓐ Ⓥ	Ⓣ Ⓐ Ⓥ	① ② ③ ④ ⑤	Ⓗ Ⓤ Ⓝ Ⓣ
	Ⓢ Ⓒ Ⓓ ②	Ⓒ Ⓓ ②	⑥ ⑦ ⑧ ⑨ ⑩	Ⓠ Ⓖ Ⓟ
	Ⓒ Ⓢ Ⓛ Ⓐ⒩ Ⓜ	Ⓢ Ⓛ Ⓐ⒩ Ⓜ	⑪ ⑫ ⒩⒱ Ⓧ	Ⓞ Ⓦ Ⓓ⒫ Ⓐ Ⓑ

8. Three children: "Afraid,"
   "mad," "sad."

8	Who	To Whom	What	How
	Ⓡ Ⓣ Ⓐ Ⓥ	Ⓣ Ⓐ Ⓥ	① ② ③ ④ ⑤	Ⓗ Ⓤ Ⓝ Ⓣ
	Ⓢ Ⓒ Ⓓ ②	Ⓒ Ⓓ ②	⑥ ⑦ ⑧ ⑨ ⑩	Ⓠ Ⓖ Ⓟ
	Ⓒ Ⓢ Ⓛ Ⓐ⒩ Ⓜ	Ⓢ Ⓛ Ⓐ⒩ Ⓜ	⑪ ⑫ ⒩⒱ Ⓧ	Ⓞ Ⓦ Ⓓ⒫ Ⓐ Ⓑ

9. Stanley offers: "When my
   daddy had to go away to
   the Army, I felt really
   bad."

9	Who	To Whom	What	How
	Ⓡ Ⓣ Ⓐ Ⓥ	Ⓣ Ⓐ Ⓥ	① ② ③ ④ ⑤	Ⓗ Ⓤ Ⓝ Ⓣ
	Ⓢ Ⓒ Ⓓ ②	Ⓒ Ⓓ ②	⑥ ⑦ ⑧ ⑨ ⑩	Ⓠ Ⓖ Ⓟ
	Ⓒ Ⓢ Ⓛ Ⓐ⒩ Ⓜ	Ⓢ Ⓛ Ⓐ⒩ Ⓜ	⑪ ⑫ ⒩⒱ Ⓧ	Ⓞ Ⓦ Ⓓ⒫ Ⓐ Ⓑ

This type of interaction can elicit children's feelings and ideas about human problems. It may also allow children to express feelings about their own problems. At the end of a day, an observer can see whether classroom discussions included questions about the children's feelings or ideas, as well as questions about the subject matter to be learned. The focused direct question is very useful in helping children learn specific subject matter, but the open-ended question can help them extend ideas. Classroom teachers would probably like to know if they shift from one type of question to the other as the focus of learning shifts.

HOW TO PRACTICE CODING

After memorizing the codes, the observer must listen to conversations and practice coding what is said. Television provides many situations that can be used to practice coding. However, the interactions are likely to be somewhat atypical. If the program is a western or detective show, for example, there are likely to be more punishing touches (hitting someone in anger) than are recorded in most classrooms, or most living rooms. And, of course, nothing can take the place of actual experience in observing classrooms. One technique that can be used to help trainees is to have one group role-play a classroom situation and the rest code the interactions. Acting out situations reflected in the codes helps observers understand the definitions. It is also helpful to would-be observers to have each write several vignettes (sequences of interactions), demonstrating the codes and their use. These vignettes can then be discussed with the group to see if everyone agrees with the coding given.

Turn now to the exercises in Appendix C beginning on page XXX and complete them. Practice coding until all codes are understood and can be recorded correctly.

Developing reliability in coding is essential to collecting usable observation data. Reliability means that two or more people code the same event in the same way. It is developed through practice and through checking that observers are all coding the same way.[2]

---

[2]Three dimensions of reliability for this observation system have been examined in a report by Stallings and Kaskowitz (Jane A. Stallings and David Kaskowitz, *Follow Through Classroom Observation Evaluation* [Menlo Park, Calif.: Stanford Research Institute, 1974]): day-to-day stability of classroom processes, observer reliability, and confusability of the operational definitions of the observation codes. Classrooms were found to be acceptably stable on observed variables from one day to another. Observers were found to be acceptably reliable 70 percent or more of the time on all codes at the end of training or they were not allowed to observe. Observers were also examined two weeks after they started collecting data. Any codes found to be unreliable were omitted from further study. Anomalies in the data were deleted where unwarranted; for example, if the teacher went home sick in the middle of the morning, that day's observation was deleted.

MODIFYING AN OBSERVATION SYSTEM

If you do not find the observation system that you need, you may have to modify an existing one. For example, in a recent study of bilingual education programs, we used the interaction-frame instrument shown in Figure 2.4. Because of the nature of the programs, we found it necessary to record whether Spanish or English was being used at the time of an observation. To do this, we came up with the rather simple idea of redefining the "S" in the first column as "Spanish" (replacing "Simultaneous") and directing observers to mark it whenever Spanish was being used. Thus, the language being used was identified for each recorded sentence.

Exercise 2.3 is an interaction conducted in Spanish.

EXERCISE 2.3 Fill in the correct coding for each sentence.

Situation: In a bilingual second-grade classroom, the teacher is working with one child:

1. Teacher: "Teresa, what is ten plus five plus five?"

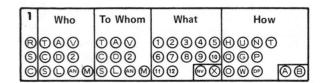

2. Teresa: "Viente."

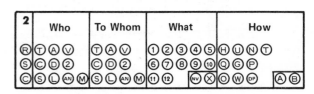

3. Teacher: "Muy bien, Teresa."

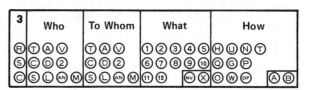

We modified our system in several other instances also. In a study of reading in Teacher Corps classrooms, for example, we found that not all of our checklist activities were needed and that more specific reading activities were needed. Figure 2.5 shows the form that was finally used for the study.

In another instance, a National Day Care Cost-Effects Study needed an observation instrument to record the teacher and child behaviors found in many day-care centers. While the procedures for recording information stayed the same, the materials, activities, groupings, and interaction codes were modified to fit a study of three- and four-year-olds in day-care centers. A similar instrument was developed for use in junior high and high schools. The operational definitions were changed but the system stayed the same.[3]

---

[3]These instruments are available from Stanford Research Institute, Menlo Park, CA 94025.

CLASSROOM CHECK LIST (be sure to code **EVERYONE** in the class)

		(1) ONE CHILD	(2) TWO CHILDREN	(3) SMALL GROUPS	(4) LARGE GROUPS
1. Reading Silently	1–	T ①②③	T ①②③	T ①②③④	T ①②
	2–	A ①②③	A ①②③	A ①②③④	A ①②
		V ①②③	V ①②③	V ①②③④	V ①②
	3–	i ①②③	i ①②③	i ①②③④	i ①②
2. Spelling, Writing, Language Structure	1–	T ①②③	T ①②③	T ①②③④	T ①②
	2–	A ①②③	A ①②③	A ①②③④	A ①②
		V ①②③	V ①②③	V ①②③④	V ①②
	3–	i ①②③	i ①②③	i ①②③④	i ①②
3. Reading Comprehension	1–	T ①②③	T ①②③	T ①②③④	T ①②
	2–	A ①②③	A ①②③	A ①②③④	A ①②
		V ①②③	V ①②③	V ①②③④	V ①②
	3–	i ①②③	i ①②③	i ①②③④	i ①②
4. Pronunciation, Word Recognition, Listening	1–	T ①②③	T ①②③	T ①②③④	T ①②
	2–	A ①②③	A ①②③	A ①②③④	A ①②
		V ①②③	V ①②③	V ①②③④	V ①②
	3–	i ①②③	i ①②③	i ①②③④	i ①②
5. Arithmetic Drill	1–	T ①②③	T ①②③	T ①②③④	T ①②
	2–	A ①②③	A ①②③	A ①②③④	A ①②
		V ①②③	V ①②③	V ①②③④	V ①②
	3–	i ①②③	i ①②③	i ①②③④	i ①②
6. Number Concepts, Puzzles, Logic Games	1–	T ①②③	T ①②③	T ①②③④	T ①②
	2–	A ①②③	A ①②③	A ①②③④	A ①②
		V ①②③	V ①②③	V ①②③④	V ①②
	3–	i ①②③	i ①②③	i ①②③④	i ①②
7. Finding Out About People and How They Live	1–	T ①②③	T ①②③	T ①②③④	T ①②
	2–	A ①②③	A ①②③	A ①②③④	A ①②
		V ①②③	V ①②③	V ①②③④	V ①②
	3–	i ①②③	i ①②③	i ①②③④	i ①②
8. Finding Out About the Natural World	1–	T ①②③	T ①②③	T ①②③④	T ①②
	2–	A ①②③	A ①②③	A ①②③④	A ①②
		V ①②③	V ①②③	V ①②③④	V ①②
	3–	i ①②③	i ①②③	i ①②③④	i ①②
9. Group Time, Sharing, Singing, Dancing	1–	T ①②③	T ①②③	T ①②③④	T ①②
	2–	A ①②③	A ①②③	A ①②③④	A ①②
		V ①②③	V ①②③	V ①②③④	V ①②
	3–	i ①②③	i ①②③	i ①②③④	i ①②
10. Arts, Crafts, Constructing Things	1–	T ①②③	T ①②③	T ①②③④	T ①②
	2–	A ①②③	A ①②③	A ①②③④	A ①②
		V ①②③	V ①②③	V ①②③④	V ①②
	3–	i ①②③	i ①②③	i ①②③④	i ①②
11. Transition, Classroom Management, Other	1–	T ①②③	T ①②③	T ①②③④	T ①②
	2–	A ①②③	A ①②③	A ①②③④	A ①②
		V ①②③	V ①②③	V ①②③④	V ①②
	3–	i ①②③	i ①②③	i ①②③④	i ①②

Observer Number 70 71	Activity 72 73	Focus Person 74	① Child ② Teacher

Number of Children 75	① ② ⑤ ⓛ

Adult 76	Directing ① Observing ③	Participating ② Not Involved ④	TIME STARTED

TIME STARTED

Hour	Minute
⑧ ⑨ ⑩ ⑪ ⑫	① ② | ① ② ③ ④
① ② ③ ④ ⑤	③ ④ ⑤ | ⑤ ⑥ ⑦ ⑧ ⑨

Figure 2.5

PLANNING YOUR OBSERVATION

When you have selected an observation system and learned the codes so that you can record reliably, it is time to plan your observations.

If you are a student teacher, plan well in advance. If a teacher has been recommended to you for observation, call and ask permission to come in on a particular day. Make sure there are no special events planned for that day, such as field trips, parties, or special assemblies, for you will probably want to observe as typical a day as possible. Ask the principal's permission, too, and when the day for observation arrives, be sure to stop at the office to let people know you are present in the school. The observation is likely to proceed more smoothly if you arrive at the classroom ten to twenty minutes before the class begins. This will allow the teacher time to ask you about the observation. You do not need to go into great detail about the coding system, but you can reveal the purpose of the observation and reassure the teacher that you have come to learn and not to judge.

If you are a classroom teacher and want to improve your teaching or observe a particular child, you will most likely need to find a volunteer or hire an observer. Sometimes a classroom assistant may be able to take charge while you observe a child. Even a short period of systematic observations each day can become a useful study over several weeks. Where two or more teachers are assigned to a classroom, they may wish to take turns observing each other.

If you are a school administrator and want to observe teachers systematically and in a nonthreatening manner, show them the observation instrument beforehand. You may even want them to help select it, so it will evaluate more clearly their own classroom goals and objectives. But whether or not they see the instrument beforehand, classroom teachers are likely to feel apprehensive at being observed if they think their position will be threatened by the resulting evaluation. School administrators can relieve some apprehension if they always use observation as a feedback mechanism to help teachers. Together, they can analyze the observation record and discuss changes that will benefit the children.

BEING AN UNOBTRUSIVE OBSERVER

People often ask, "But doesn't the presence of an observer change the character of the classroom? Teachers and children must certainly behave differently if they know they are being observed." And indeed, that is probably true although available data do suggest that the observer's impact is minimal after the first half hour (that is, the behavior of teachers and students pretty much returns to normal). Nevertheless, the observer must be as unobtrusive as possible; the following rules should help:

1. Wear quiet colors. Flamboyant clothes can be distracting.

2. Try not to disturb the class in any way. If possible, carry a small classroom chair with you as you move about the room. Get only as close as necessary and sit down as soon as possible. An adult towering over a child is likely to be not merely distracting but overwhelming.

3. Avoid eye contact with the person you are observing. Eye contact is distracting for both of you.

4. Try not to respond to students while you are coding. This may seem unfriendly or harsh, but it is the simplest way to discourage attention, and they are more likely to behave as though you were not there.

5. Keep conversations with teachers as short as possible without being rude. You might suggest continuing the conversation later.

ANALYZING THE DATA

Plan how you want to analyze the observational data before you collect it. The simplest way to analyze data is to count the occurrences of events you selected for observation, that is, that you designated as important. How many times during the day, outside of the formal reading period, were children reading? How often did the teacher work with individual children? How often did a teacher praise or correct a student's behavior? The list of variables, or events you select to study, can be formed by the codes you used to record information in the classroom. In our system, for example, if we want to know how many direct questions (1Q) a teacher (T) asked a child (C), we count the number of TC1Qs on the observation form. If we want to see how many times a teacher (T) asked a child (C) an open-ended question (2Q), we count all the frames with a TC2Q in them. And if we want to see how often children in academic (A) situations respond to questions (3), we count the CT3A frames.

Most analyses, of course, go beyond simple counting. How would you analyze teacher behavior? Since no standard measure of teacher behavior has been developed yet, you might make comparisons among teachers. Finding that Teacher A asked ten thought-provoking questions during the observation period tells you little unless you also know that Teacher B asked none at all and Teacher C asked twenty. Teachers analyzing their own behavior individually might compare the number of thought-provoking questions to the number of single-answer questions they asked. Or, they might compare the number of positive expressions they made to the number of negative expressions. A school administrator or a student teacher might compare teachers on such variables as how much attention they gave individual children, how often they worked with small groups or with the total group.

Classroom teachers can also analyze children's behavior. They can compare observations of individual children to see the range of behavior in their rooms. How often does Child A lead (or follow) compared to Children B, C, and D? How often does Child A ask questions or work independently compared to others? Or they can compare observations of one child to get a pattern of individual behavior.

Observational data can also be used to correlate classroom instructional processes with specific elements in child growth and school achievement. For example, you can analyze the correlation between individual attention, independent reading, and teachers' praise, and success on reading achievement tests. This type of analysis, of course, requires observational and test data from at least four classrooms so that comparisons can be made.

In our recent study of 108 first-grade and 58 third-grade classrooms in the Follow Through Project, we found that:

1. Classroom instructional practices can contribute to higher test scores, desirable behavior, and lower absence rates.

2. Highly controlled classroom environments, in which teachers
   used systematic instruction and a high rate of positive reinforcement, contributed to higher scores in math and reading. Flexible classroom environments, which provided more
   exploratory materials and allowed children more choice, contributed to higher scores on a test of nonverbal reasoning,
   as well as lower absence rates, and a willingness on the
   part of children to work independently.[4]

These findings strongly suggest that what teachers do in classrooms
does make a difference in the growth and development of children.

The remaining chapters will describe the philosophy, teaching
practices, and predicted results of five educational models. The
models will be described largely in terms of what can be observed
and recorded on the SRI observation instruments so that you can get
practice in evaluating teaching methods in concrete operational
terms and so that you will gain a thorough understanding of at least
one observational system. On the basis of your experience with this
book, you should then be able to judge and effectively use other observational systems.

---

[4]Jane A. Stallings and David Kaskowitz, *Follow Through Classroom Observation Evaluation 1972-1973* (Menlo Park, Calif.: Stanford
Research Institute, 1974). ERIC Accession No. ED 104 969.

CLASSROOM CHECK LIST (be sure to code **EVERYONE** in the class)

		ONE CHILD	TWO CHILDREN	SMALL GROUPS	LARGE GROUPS
1. Snack, lunch		T ①②③ A ①②③ v ①②③ i ①②③	T ①②③ A ①②③ v ①②③ i ①②③	T ①②③④ A ①②③④ v ①②③④ i ①②③④	T ①② A ①② v ①② i ①②
2. Group time		T ①②③ A ①②③ v ①②③ i ①②③	T ①②③ A ①②③ v ①②③ i ①②③	T ①②③④ A ①②③④ v ①②③④ i ①②③④	T ①② A ①② v ①② i ①②
3. Story Music Dancing		T ①②③ A ①②③ v ①②③ i ①②③	T ①②③ A ①②③ v ①②③ i ①②③	T ①②③④ A ①②③④ v ①②③④ i ①②③④	T ①② A ①② v ①② i ①②
4. Arts, Crafts		T ①②③ A ①②③ v ①②③ i ①②③	T ①②③ A ①②③ v ①②③ i ●②③	T ①②③④ A ①②③④ v ①②③④ i ●②③④	T ①② A ①② v ①② i ①②
5. Guessing Games Table Games Puzzles		T ①②③ A ①②③ v ①②③ i ①②③	T ①②③ A ①②③ v ①②③ i ①②③	T ①②③④ A ①②③④ v ①②③④ i ①②③④	T ①② A ①② v ①② i ①②
6. Math	Numbers Arithmetic	T ①②③ A ①②③ v ①②③ i ①②③	T ①②③ A ①②③ v ①②③ i ①②③	T ①②③④ A ①②③④ v ①②③④ i ①②③④	T ①② A ①② v ①② i ①②
7. Alphabet	Reading Lang. Development	T ①②③ A ①②③ v ①②③ i ●②③	T ①②③ A ①②③ v ①②③ i ①②③	T ①②③④ A ①②③④ v ①②③④ i ●②③④	T ①② A ①② v ①② i ①②
8.	Social Studies Geography	T ①②③ A ①②③ v ①②③ i ①②③	T ①②③ A ①②③ v ①②③ i ①②③	T ①②③④ A ①②③④ v ①②③④ i ①②③④	T ①② A ①② v ①② i ①②
9.	Science Natural World	T ①②③ A ①②③ v ①②③ i ●②③	T ①②③ A ①②③ v ①②③ i ①②③	T ①②③④ A ①②③④ v ①②③④ i ①②③④	T ①② A ①② v ①② i ①②
10. Sewing Cooking Pounding Sawing		T ①②③ A ①②③ v ①②③ i ①②③	T ①②③ A ①②③ v ①②③ i ①②③	T ①②③④ A ①②③④ v ①②③④ i ①②③④	T ①② A ①② v ①② i ①②
11. Blocks Trucks		T ①②③ A ①②③ v ①②③ i ①②③	T ①②③ A ①②③ v ①②③ i ①②③	T ①②③④ A ①②③④ v ①②③④ i ①②③④	T ①② A ①② v ①② i ①②
12. Dramatic Play Dress-Up		T ①②③ A ①②③ v ①②③ i ①②③	T ①②③ A ①②③ v ①②③ i ●②③	T ①②③④ A ①②③④ v ①②③④ i ①②③④	T ①② A ①② v ①② i ①②
13. Active Play		T ①②③ A ①②③ v ①②③ i ①②③	T ①②③ A ①②③ v ①②③ i ①②③	T ①②③④ A ①②③④ v ①②③④ i ①②③④	T ①② A ①② v ①② i ①②
14. RELIABILITY SHEET	○				

Materials (left column, items 6–9 group):

○ TV
● Audio-Visual Materials
● Exploratory Materials
● Math and Science Equipment
○ Texts, Workbooks
○ Puzzles, Games

			ONE CHILD	TWO CHILDREN	SMALL GROUPS	LARGE GROUPS
15. Practical Skills Acquisition			T ①②③ A ①②③ v ①②③ i ①②③	T ①②③ A ①②③ v ①②③ i ①②③	T ①②③④ A ①②③④ v ①②③④ i ①②③④	T ①② A ①② v ①② i ①②
16. Observing			T ①②③ A ①②③ v ①②③ i ①②③	T ①②③ A ①②③ v ①②③ i ①②③	T ①②③④ A ①②③④ v ①②③④ i ①②③④	T ●② A ①② v ①② i ①②
17. Social Interaction	Ob	Ⓒ②Ⓢ	Ⓣ T ①②③ Ⓐ A ①②③ Ⓥ v ①②③ i ①②③	T ①②③ A ①②③ v ①②③ i ①②③	T ①②③④ A ①②③④ v ①②③④ i ①②③④	T ①② A ①② v ①② i ①②
18. Unoccupied Child			T ①②③ A ①②③ v ①②③ i ①②③	T ①②③ A ①②③ v ①②③ i ①②③	T ①②③④ A ①②③④ v ①②③④ i ①②③④	T ①② A ①② v ①② i ①②
19. Discipline			T ①②③ A ①②③ v ①②③ i ①②③	T ①②③ A ①②③ v ①②③ i ①②③	T ①②③④ A ①②③④ v ①②③④ i ①②③④	T ①② A·①② v ①② i ①②
20. Transitional Activities		Ⓣ Ⓐ Ⓥ	T ①②③ A ①②③ v ①②③ i ①②③	T ①②③ A ①②③ v ①②③ i ①②③	T ①②③④ A ①②③④ v ①②③④ i ①②③④	T ①② A ①② v ①② i ①②
21. Classroom Management		Ⓣ Ⓐ Ⓥ	T ①②③ A ①②③ v ①②③ i ①②③	T ①②③ A ①②③ v ①②③ i ①②③	T ①②③④ A ①②③④ v ①②③④ i ①②③④	T ①② A ①② v ①② i ①②
22. Out of Room		Ⓣ ● Ⓥ	T ①②③ A ①②③ v ①②③ i ①②③	T ①②③ A ①②③ v ①②③ i ①②③	T ①②③④ A ①②③④ v ①②③④ i ①②③④	T ①② A ①② v ①② i ①②

NUMBER OF ADULTS IN CLASSROOM ⓪ ① ● ③ ④ ⑤ ⑥ ⑦ ⑧ ⑨ ⑩

ANSWERS: CORRECT CODING FOR EXERCISE 2.2

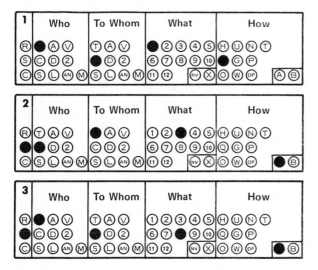

ANSWERS: CORRECT CODING FOR EXERCISE 2.3

Chapter 3

Points of View

There are many points of view about what education ought to be. The extremes are based on individual developmental theory at one end and on behavior modification theory at the other. There are advocates of each extreme and of more moderate views, but all parties share the goal of providing the best possible education for children. What is considered the best education for children changes as the needs of society change.

Throughout the history of education, the pendulum has swung continually. Schools of the 1930s that practiced John Dewey's theory of learning by doing or experiencing education seem very similar to many current open education schools. Present-day basic fundamentals schools can be traced back to the beginning of public education. Chapters 4-9 describe five models of education that range in theory and practice from one extreme to the other.

OPEN EDUCATION

Open education theory is based on the notion that each person should have a program of education tailored to his or her own specific needs, because people learn not only at different rates, but in different ways. Some people learn best by seeing, some by hearing, and others by touching. Others learn best when given small bits of information that they can link together to form a total word, idea, or concept. Open education respects these different learning styles, and although there are many models and a variety of names for open education programs, all value the individual and try to aid the individual to develop his or her potential in his or her own way and time.

Open education is an outgrowth of the recent popularity with the middle class of clinical and developmental psychology and their focus on developing individual awareness. The values of clinical psychology—that people can increase their self-awareness, be open in expressing their feelings, be free to test new ideas—found their way into the classroom, and now open education models have sprung up in almost every community. The ideas of many clinical psychologists have been adapted to educational programs. The Lestershire County Schools in England and A. S. Neill's Summerhill School have been especially influential.[1]

---

[1]See William Glasser, *Schools Without Failure* (New York: Harper & Row, 1969); Abraham Maslow, *Toward a Psychology of Being* (Princeton, N.J.: Van Nostrand Reinhold, 1962); A. S. Neill, *Summerhill: A Radical Approach to Child Rearing* (New York: Hart, 1960); Frederick S. Perls, *Gestalt Therapy Verbatim* (Lafayette, Calif.: Real People

Open education is based on the assumption that children are individuals—each develops in a unique way and each has unique problems. Because of this assumption, advocates believe that a supportive environment—one that supports each child's uniqueness and allows for individual differences—is more important than planned programs and fixed patterns of development.

There are innumerable ways an open education classroom can be arranged and managed, yet have some things in common. All have learning centers arranged throughout the classroom. There is usually a center for math, science, arts and crafts, language development, reading, and writing. Within these centers children may be playing blackjack, dominoes, measuring liquids, weighing equal volumes of sugar and flour, making puppets, painting, sculpturing, learning another language, or listening to their voices on a tape recorder. Other areas in the room may be designated for music, dance, and drama. Also in open classrooms, the student learner is the focus of the instruction. The table on page 51 compares the goals and activities of student-centered programs with instructor-centered programs.

Each classroom will differ considerably, however, in how much freedom of choice children have and how the teachers moderate and guide the progress of the children. In some classrooms, children are allowed to choose their own work groups. They start and end projects when they wish. In other classrooms, teachers assign children to reading and math groups according to a diagnosis of learning styles or learning problems. The progress of children in the latter classrooms is carefully monitored and lessons are prescribed on a daily basis. Such open classrooms require teachers to organize their schedules carefully.

Contrary to some beliefs, the concept of open education does not imply minimizing basic skills. Open education is not only a program that encourages and supports basic skills but also uses them meaningfully.

> Open education does not ignore "basic skills" or achievements such as reading and math, but interprets them and gives them meaning within a broader context. Reading is not conceived as a set of overt responses to be shaped up in the youngster, but rather as a holistic activity involving thinking processes, reflection, emotions, awareness, creative experiences and sense of self. Open education does not ask how much of a given educational objective a child achieves, nor does it set arbitrary levels of achievement to be attained by children at fixed points in their environment. Open education assumes that all children are naturally curious explorers of the world, and that a school environment which is emotionally supportive, which provides a variety of interesting options, and which encourages the children's choices produces the motivation for self-directed learning.[2]

([1]continued) Press, 1969); Carl R. Rogers, *Freedom to Learn* (Columbus, Ohio: Charles E. Merrill, 1969); William Schutz, *Joy: Expanding Human Awareness* (New York: Grove Press, 1967); Bruce Joyce and Marsha Weil, *Models of Teaching* (Englewood Cliffs, N.J.: Prentice-Hall, 1972).

[2]Bernice J. Wolfson and Kenneth H. Wodtke, "What Can We Evaluate in Open Classrooms?" *Educating Children: Early and Middle Years* 20, no. 3 (1975): p. 20. Reprinted by permission of the American Association of Elementary, Kindergarten, and Nursery Educators.

Goals and Classroom Activities of Student-Centered and Instructor-Centered Programs

	Student Centered	Instructor Centered
Goals	Determined by group.	Determined by instructor.
	Emphasis upon affective and attitudinal changes.	Emphasis upon intellectual changes.
	Attempts to develop group cohesiveness.	No attempt to develop group cohesiveness.
Classroom Activities	Much student participation.	Much instructor participation.
	Student-student interaction.	Instructor-student interaction.
	Instructor accepts erroneous or irrelevant student contributions.	Instructor corrects, criticizes, or rejects erroneous or irrelevant student contributions.
	Group decides upon own activities.	Instructor determines activities.
	Discussion of students' personal experiences encouraged.	Discussion kept on course materials.
	Deemphasis of tests and grades.	Traditional use of tests and grades.
	Students share responsibility for evaluation.	
	Instructor interprets feelings and ideas of class member when necessary for class progress.	Instructor avoids interpretation of feelings.
	Reaction reports.	No reaction reports.

Source: W. J. McKeachie, "Research on Teaching at the College and University Level," in *Handbook of Research on Teaching*, ed. N. L. Gage (Chicago: Rand McNally, 1963), p. 1,134. Copyright 1963, American Educational Research Association, Washington, D.C.

The expected outcome for children in open education classrooms is very similar regardless of the variations in the programs. Objectives for children in holistic programs include the ability to resist what does not make sense, openness to different points of view, confidence to speak one's mind, alertness in putting things together, confidence to think things out, and curiosity with initiative in pursuing curiosities. "If intelligence develops as a whole by the child's own construction, then what makes this construction possible is the child's own curiosity, interest, alertness, desire to communicate and exchange points of view and a desire to make sense out of it all."[3] Open education advocates believe that these abilities are more likely to develop in holistic approaches to education.

In the following chapters, three models of open education are described: an exploratory model, a group process model, and a developmental cognitive model. They all have open space and learning centers, but each is organized in its own way and has its own objectives.

---

[3]Constance Kamii, "One Intelligence Indivisible," *Young Children* 30 (May 1975), pp. 228-238.

Advocates of these models would most likely agree that the goals of education in a democratic society should assist students to become individuals:

who are able to take self-initiated action and to be responsible for those actions;

who are capable of intelligent choice and self-direction;

who are critical learners, able to evaluate the contributions made by others;

who have acquired knowledge relevant to the solution of problems;

who, even more importantly, are able to adapt flexibly and intelligently to new problem situations;

who have internalized an adaptive mode of approach to problems utilizing all pertinent experience freely and creatively;

who are able to cooperate effectively with others in these various activities;

who work, not for the approval of others, but in terms of their own socialized purposes.[4]

BACK TO BASICS

In response to plummeting test scores recently reported by State and Federal Departments of Education, a counterrevolution against permissiveness in education has started. The powerful movement toward child-centered, open classroom schools, which gained momentum in the restless sixties, may have reached its peak.

Achievement test scores increased steadily from the 1940s and 1950s to the mid-1960s. Since then, however, many test scores have dropped. "The reported test score decline is more dramatic in recent years and most evident for higher grades. They are especially pronounced in verbal tests, but hold for nearly all tested areas."[5] Figure 3.1 illustrates this trend for college-bound seniors. The alarming drop in reading scores from the third to the eighth grade is shown in Figure 3.2.

The cause of the drop in test scores is not clear. Inadequate tests, television, broken families, working mothers, and increased use of drugs have been suggested; however, most of the blame is directed toward current educational programs and trends.

---

[4]Carl R. Rogers, *Client Centered Therapy* (Boston: Houghton Mifflin, 1951), pp. 387-388.
[5]Annegret Harnischfeger and David E. Wiley, *Achievement Test Score Decline: Do We Need to Worry?* (Chicago: ML Group for Policy Studies in Education, CEMREL, Inc., 1975).

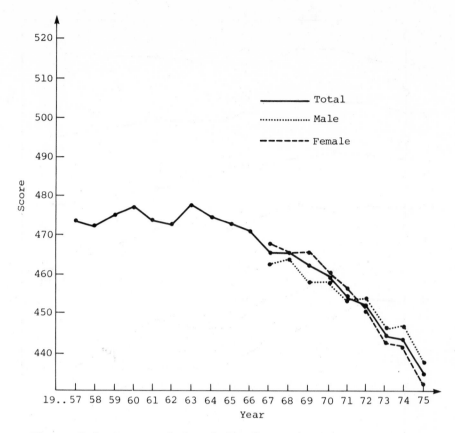

Figure 3.1 Mean Verbal Scholastic Aptitude Test Scores for College-Bound Seniors, 1957-1975.

Source: Annegret Harnischfeger, and David E. Wiley, *Achievement Test Score Decline: Do We Need to Worry?* (Chicago: ML Group for Policy Studies in Education, CEMREL, Inc., 1975).

In reaction to open education, where the teacher keeps a low profile and the students learn by discovering in their own way at their own pace, parents and educators in many communities are demanding education programs devoted to developing basic skills. Research by Wright, Soar, Soar, and Ragosta, and Stallings[6] suggests that children achieve higher scores in reading and math when they are enrolled in carefully structured classrooms. In these classrooms teachers focus the student's attention on academic subjects for longer periods of time, and they provide immediate feedback to the children's academic efforts.

Many communities are now experimenting anew with old Fundamental School programs. In these schools, most of the time is devoted to teaching reading, writing, spelling, grammar, and arithmetic. Students are expected to be quiet, courteous, and studious. Some communities never tried open education, so Fundamental Schools are

---

[6]Robert J. Wright, "The Affective and Cognitive Consequences of an Open Education Elementary School," *American Education Research Journal* 12 (Fall 1975): 449-465; R. S. Soar, R. M. Soar, and M. Ragosta, "Florida Climate and Control System (FLACCS)" (Gainesville, Fla.: Institute for Development of Human Resources, University of Florida, 1968); Jane Stallings, "Implementation and Child Effects of Teaching Practices in Follow Through Classrooms," *Monographs of the Society for Research in Child Development* 40 (1975): 1-133.

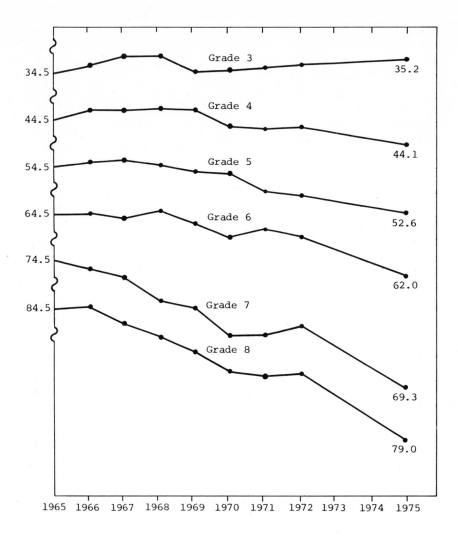

*Figure 3.2   Trends in Third- Through Eighth-Grade Student
ITBS Reading Test Scores from 1965-1975 (Expressed in 1965
Base-Year Grade Equivalents on the Iowa Reading Subtest)*

Source: Annegret Harnischfeger, and David E. Wiley, *Achievement Test
Score Decline: Do We Need to Worry*? (Chicago: ML Group for Policy
Studies in Education, CEMREL, Inc., 1975).

what they have always had. The Fundamental School Model is described
in Chapter 8.

Developing basic skills is also the main concern of three Follow Through models, which use behavior modification techniques to do
so. A behavior modification model is described in Chapter 7 as the
Programmed Model.

BIBLIOGRAPHY

Suggested Readings

Open Education

Barth, Roland S. *Open Education and the American School*. New York: Agathon Press, 1972.

Berlak, Ann C., et al. "Teaching and Learning in English Primary Schools." *School Review* 83 (February 1975): 215-243.

Blackie, John. *Inside the Primary School*. New York: Schocken Books, 1972.

Clegg, Sir Alec. "Revolution in the English Elementary Schools." Washington, D.C.: *National Association of Elementary School Principals* (September 1969): 23-32.

Combs, Arthur W. *Educational Accountability: Beyond Behavioral Objectives*. Washington, D.C.: Association for Supervision and Curriculum Development, 1972. ERIC Accession No. ED 067 381.

Devaney, Kathleen. *Developing Open Education in America*. Washington, D.C.: National Association for the Development of Young Children, 1974.

Eisner, Elliot W. *English Primary Schools: Some Observations and Assessments*. Stanford, Calif.: Stanford University Press, 1973.

Evans, Judith T. *Characteristics of Open Education: Results from a Classroom Observation Rating Scale and a Teacher Questionnaire*. Newton, Mass.: Education Development Center, Inc., 1971. ERIC Accession No. ED 058 160.

Frazier, Alexander. *Open Schools for Children*. Washington, D.C.: Association for Supervision and Curriculum Development, 1972.

Hein, G. *An Open Education Perspective of Evaluation*. Grand Forks: North Dakota Study Group on Evaluation, 1975.

Howes, V. M. *Informal Teaching in the Open Classroom*. New York: Macmillan, 1974.

Kamii, Constance. "One Intelligence Indivisible." *Young Children* 30 (May 1975): 228-238.

Macdonald, James, and Wolfson, B. J. "A Case against Behavioral Objectives." *The Elementary School Journal* 71 (December 1970): 119-128.

Rathbone, Charles H., ed. *Open Education: The Informal Classroom*. New York: Citation Press, 1971.

Rogers, Vincent R., and Church, Bud, eds. *Open Education: Critique and Assessment*. Washington, D.C.: Association for Supervision and Curriculum Development, 1975. ERIC Accession No. ED 112 495.

Silberman, Charles E. *Crisis in the Classroom: The Remaking in American Education*. New York: Random House, 1970.

Silberman, Charles W., ed. *The Open Classroom Reader*. New York: Random House, 1973.

Spodek, Bernard, and Walberg, Herbert, eds. *Studies in Open Education*. New York: Agathon Press, 1975.

Walberg, H., and Thomas, S. *Characteristics of Open Education: Toward an Operation Definition*. Newton, Mass.: TDR Associates, 1971.

Weber, Lillian. *English Infant School and Informal Education*. Engle-wood Cliffs, N.J.: Prentice-Hall, 1971.

Basic Education

Brophy, J., and Good, T. *Teacher-Student Relationship: Causes and Consequences*. New York: Holt, Rinehart and Winston, 1974.

Farr, Roger; Tunman, J.; and Rowles, M. *Reading Achievement in the United States: Then and Now*. Bloomington: Indiana University, 1974. ERIC Accession No. ED 109 595.

Harnischfeger, A., and Wiley, D. E. *Achievement Test Score Decline: Do We Need to Worry*? Chicago: ML Group for Policy Studies in Education, 1975.

Lutz, Frank W., and Ramsey, Margaret A. "The Use of Anthropological Field Methods in Education." *Educational Researcher* 3 (November 1974): 5-9.

Skinner, B. F. "The Free and Happy Student." *Phi Delta Kappan 55* (September 1973): 13-16.

Stallings, Jane A. "How Instructional Processes Relate to Child Out-comes in a National Study of Follow Through." *Journal of Teach-er Education* 27 (Spring 1976): 43-47.

_____. "Implementation and Child Effects of Teaching Practices in Follow Through Classrooms." *Monographs of the Society for Re-search in Child Development* 40 (1975): 1-133.

Wiley, David E., and Harnischfeger, Annegret, "Explosion of a Myth: Quantity of Schooling and Exposure to Instruction, Major Edu-cational Vehicles." *Educational Researcher* 3 (April 1974): 7-12.

Wolynski, Mara. "Confessions of a Misspent Youth." *Newsweek*, 30 August, 1976, p. 11.

Wright, Robert J. "The Affective and Cognitive Consequences of an Open Education Elementary School." *American Education Research Journal* 12 (Fall 1975): 449-465.

Chapter 4

Educational Theory and Expected Child Development

Teacher Responsibilities

Schedule

Physical Environment

Interaction Patterns

Handling Misbehavior

A Contextual View

Classroom Requirements

Research Findings on How Children Grow and Develop

Observable Components

    Materials

    Activities and Groupings

    Interaction Observations

Importance of Teacher Observation

Summary of Components

Bibliography

    Where Components of the Exploratory Type Models Can Be Seen

    Suggested Readings

    Commercially Available Materials

    Research Findings

Exploratory Model

"Teacher, look-it! See how tall this block tower is? It's taller than I ever made it before."

"It is tall, Curt," said Ms. Bronsky. "What did you do to be able to build it so tall?"

"It's bigger at the bottom. It has to be big at the bottom if you want to build tall towers. The others fell down."

EDUCATIONAL THEORY AND EXPECTED CHILD DEVELOPMENT

This is a typical conversation between a child and a kindergarten teacher in the Exploratory Model of education. Here, children are given the opportunity to discover things for themselves. Teachers respond to children rather than having children respond to them. Teachers encourage children to experiment and to think through a problem and gain the satisfaction that comes from solving it. The advocates of this model think that children learn best in an environment where they can try things out, ask questions, make guesses, risk failure, and make discoveries. Children are expected to be more creative in their problem solving when left to their own devices.

This model is based on the belief that people (and especially children) are inherently curious and are intrinsically motivated. An intrinsic motive is described as the energy aroused by curiosity that leads to a satisfying behavior; for example, when children work on a puzzle for the satisfaction of doing it, they are intrinsically motivated. When adults seek new experiences—when they take flying lessons, for example, just for the satisfaction of it—they are intrinsically motivated. In a discussion of intrinsic motives, Hugh Perkins stated:

Organisms appear to seek not just any kind of environmental stimulation, but some degree of novelty and change in what they see, hear, feel, and touch. Novel stimuli arouse curiosity in animals, children and adults. An individual manifests curiosity when he avoids familiar aspects of the environment; seeks new experiences; approaches and investigates new, ambiguous, or incongruous aspects of the environment; or asks for information from other people. Children show curiosity when they examine and manipulate toys, puzzles, or mechanical gadgets, when they explore woods, dumps, caves or beaches, or when they ask questions about events or ideas that appear to be incomplete or incongruous.[1]

The theory of learning on which the model is based assumes that cognitive processes, insight, intelligence, and organization are the fundamental characteristics of human response.

> Human actions are marked by quality of intelligence and the capacity to perceive and to create relationships. This understanding of relationships steers man's actions. His responses are shaped by his purposes, cognition, and anticipation. Man is also an adaptive creature who organizes each subsequent response in the light of his prior experience. In each new perception the object or event is seen differently, because the cognitive structure has been reorganized by each prior perception. Sometimes this reorganization takes place in such a fashion as to create an illusion of intuition or a sudden insight. In this interaction of response and stimulus, a new mode of perception and essentially a new reality is created. Man learns only through his own responses: in part by reacting to selectively organized stimuli (*Gestalten*), and in part by creating new organized wholes. Man is not passive in the face of external stimuli but is an active agent who creates his own "phenomenal" world. Learning is essentially an active process of selecting and organizing.[2]

Since the Exploratory Model is based on the theory that children are inherently curious and that they learn from their explorations in a responsive environment, the physical arrangement of the classroom is very important. In this model, learning centers are set up around the room and provided with a variety of materials and equipment. Here children can tinker with objects and materials, developing their own questions and searching for solutions in their own way. All of the materials and equipment related to a particular skill or subject, such as music or science, are located in one center, which is often separated from the room by low dividers. New materials are added to the centers as teachers perceive that the children need new challenges. The children themselves are free to explore, to choose from the many possible activities offered within the carefully controlled environment, and to work at their own pace. Nicholas Rayder suggests further that this type of environment allows children to see immediately the consequences of their actions and to make full use of their capacities for discovering relationships. In such an environment a learner is likely to make a series of interconnected discoveries about the physical, cultural, and social world.[3]

---

[1]Hugh V. Perkins, *Human Development and Learning*, 2d ed. (Belmont, Calif.: Wadsworth, 1974), pp. 62-63.

[2]Hilda Taba, *Curriculum Development: Theory and Practice* (New York: Harcourt Brace Jovanovich, 1962) pp. 80-81.

Although little research has been done on this theory, for some discussion, see K. Kofka, *Principles of Gestalt Psychology* (New York: Harcourt Brace and World, 1935) and Jerome S. Bruner, *Toward a Theory of Instruction* (Cambridge, Mass.: Harvard University Press, 1966).

[3]Nicholas F. Rayder, Pierina Ng, and Anne Rhodes, *Implementation of the Responsive Program: A Report on Four Planned Variation*

In the Exploratory Model, as children progress through school, they are expected to spend some part of the day in activities promoting reading and computation skills, the basic skills. Reading materials include language experience charts, programmed materials, standard basic readers, and many storybooks. Math materials include weights and measures, counting blocks, and sticks. Learning materials are assigned according to each child's needs, and a trained adult (teacher, classroom aide, or volunteer) works with one child or a small group of children to help them. A great effort is made to help the children become self-motivated and to feel the subject intrinsically rewarding so that they pursue reading and problem-solving activities on their own. The model expects to help children develop intellectual abilities and a healthy self-concept.

The expected outcome of this environmental approach is children who are self-motivated and who not only succeed in their efforts to solve problems but also recognize their own success—that is, they are self-motivated, self-directing, and self-evaluating. They explore or play the game because it is self-rewarding, not because it pleases the teacher.

Advocates also believe that children learn to solve cognitive and social problems through the experience of solving cognitive and social problems. In this model, children are allowed to experience dissonance and conflict and are encouraged to search for alternate solutions. They are allowed to risk failure and learn from the consequences of actions. Advocates of the Exploratory Model envision a citizenry that is independent in judgment, creative in problem solving, and socially responsible.

TEACHER RESPONSIBILITIES

For this model to work, the adults must carefully plan and prepare the environment. First, the level of social, emotional, and cognitive development of each child must be diagnosed. Then, appropriate materials and experiences for the optimum continued development of each child must be prescribed. This is done through staff discussions and, to some extent, diagnostic tests. The following are examples of the kinds of materials a teacher might provide and the sequence in which they might be introduced. Remember that selection and use are based on children's developmental needs.

In a kindergarten math learning center, the materials might be food items and measuring equipment. The children might first make Jello by measuring one cup of hot water into the Jello and then adding one cup of cold water. Next they might make Kool-Aid, using two quarts of water, one cup of sugar, and one package of Kool-Aid. When the children are able to use these measuring tools successfully and understand the relationships between them, the next project might be to make biscuits. This would require measuring cups of flour, tablespoons of shortening, and teaspoons of baking powder and salt. Learning the relationships among cups, quarts, teaspoons and tablespoons would be part of the math program. Reading the recipe would be part of the reading program.

([3]continued) *Communities* (San Francisco: Far West Laboratory for Educational Research and Development, 1973), p. 8. ERIC Accession No. ED 085 102.

In the science learning center of a more advanced class, the teacher might provide a battery, copper wire, and a flashlight bulb. When the children have discovered the relationship among these three items, the teacher might place more wire and a bell in the center. Eventually, the teacher might add a small generator and even a solar cell. The children would learn about the relationships among these items by manipulating them and asking questions.

In a kindergarten or first-grade learning center, the teacher might provide lotto and bingo games to teach the alphabet and sounds. Audiovisual equipment, such as the reading master, filmstrips, and audiotapes, might be made available for the same purpose. After the children have mastered these prereading skills, they could use this equipment to learn whole words and develop a reading vocabulary. The teacher must be sure, however, that the equipment and materials are both easy enough and challenging enough for the children's level of development.

In this model adults must be good observers of children and aware of their developmental needs. Adults should provide a stimulating environment, be good listeners and responders, and ask questions that extend children's thinking. They should support children as they pursue their own learning and encourage them to become self-motivated.

Essentially, the teacher is responsible for the following:

1. Evaluating the total social, emotional, and academic growth and development of each child;

2. Establishing social, emotional, and academic goals for each child;

3. Diagnosing the cause for lack of progress in any area;

4. Planning the environment so specific child growth will be facilitated.

SCHEDULE

The following is a typical schedule for a second-grade class using the Exploratory Model.

8:00 Teachers place new materials in the learning centers.

8:30 Children enter the classroom and go to learning centers.

8:45 The roll is called and announcements are made. All children sit on a rug. This is a time for group sharing—children share their ideas and experiences with the group. Children are asked what center they want to work in first. A limit is set on the number in each center.

9:00 Children choose a learning center: arts and crafts, science, reading, or math. A teacher or aide assists the children in reading and math. They keep records of each child's daily progress.

10:15 Recess—teachers and aides check to see which children need individual help during the next period.

10:30 Children may choose a different learning center. Teachers or aides may call particular children to them to do some reading, writing, or math. This work will be closely associated with the child's most current interests.

12:00 Lunch—teachers and aides find which children have not yet had assistance in reading, writing, or math. An attempt is made to spend some time in these subjects each day with each child.

1:00 A story is read to the total group.

1:30 Children go to learning centers. One aide is in the art center with a special project. Children can either do this project or choose some other art project.

2:30 Group games.

3:00 Dismissal.

PHYSICAL ENVIRONMENT

A large room is best for implementing this model, but any size room will work if it is arranged properly. A large central space is needed for group discussions; this is often identified by a large rug where all the children can sit comfortably. Here, the group shares important happenings and discusses group problems. Furniture must be movable so all spaces can be made larger or smaller. Furniture includes movable bookshelves or screens made of heavy corrugated paper. These can be used to divide the classroom into separate learning centers. At the same time, they can be brightly painted and used for murals or bulletin boards to display the children's art or stories.

One learning center should allow children to learn to use a tape recorder, a language master, film strips, a record player, and earphones. After they have learned how to operate it, the children should be free to use all this equipment. The equipment selected should be responsive; that is, when a child starts a machine, the machine should respond with information or with a learning activity that involves a particular skill or concept. Teachers select the level of audiovisual materials appropriate for the age group.

Another learning center should contain a variety of games and materials that will help children develop math concepts. Children are expected to learn mathematical relationships, for example, by manipulating Cuisenaire rods or weights and measures, and these items should be included in the center. The math corner should also have an oven and a hot plate for cooking. Cooking equipment is important since many mathematical relationships can be discovered while preparing food.

In the science learning center, a wide variety of exploratory materials should be available. These materials will vary not only according to the children's developmental level, but also according to the season of the year. In the spring, for example, third- or fourth-grade children might find in the science center a microscope, pond water, and polliwogs collected on a field trip. After some instructions on how to use a microscope, the children could discover the living organisms in the pond water. They could also observe the development of the polliwogs.

An art center should provide paints, clay, crayons, and collage materials. Here, the children could illustrate stories, develop art projects, or collaborate on a mural.

A quiet area should also be designated. Here children could read, rest, or meditate and not be bothered by the running or loud voices of others. The area should contain comfortable furniture—a rug, couch, or rocking chair. An adult or a child might also read quietly to another child in this corner.

INTERACTION PATTERNS

In the Exploratory Model, a typical day in a kindergarten classroom, starts with the children entering the classroom, disposing of coats and belongings, and going to one of the learning centers. The kindergarten teacher welcomes each child by name and listens to comments regarding home events. The teacher then responds to the child in a way that extends rather than stops his or her use of language. The teacher does this by asking open-ended, thought-provoking questions that extend the child's use of language rather than questions requiring simple yes-or-no responses.

Using the SRI coding system, see if you can complete Exercise 4.1, which asks you to code a typical Exploratory Model interaction. The answers to the exercise can be found at the end of the chapter.

EXERCISE 4.1   Code the following Exploratory Model interaction on the frames given.

Situation: A first-grade teacher is speaking with a child.

1. Child: "Hey, Teacher! I got a Ho-Ho for lunch."

1	Who	To Whom	What	How
	Ⓡ Ⓣ Ⓐ Ⓥ	Ⓣ Ⓐ Ⓥ	① ② ③ ④ ⑤ Ⓗ Ⓤ Ⓝ Ⓣ	
	Ⓢ Ⓒ Ⓓ ②	Ⓒ Ⓓ ②	⑥ ⑦ ⑧ ⑨ ⑩ Ⓠ Ⓖ Ⓟ	
	Ⓒ Ⓢ Ⓛ ⒶⓃ Ⓜ	Ⓢ Ⓛ ⒶⓃ Ⓜ	⑪ ⑫	Ⓝⓥ Ⓧ Ⓞ Ⓦ ⒹⓅ Ⓐ Ⓑ

2. Teacher: "A Ho-Ho! What in the world is a Ho-Ho?"

2	Who	To Whom	What	How
	Ⓡ Ⓣ Ⓐ Ⓥ	Ⓣ Ⓐ Ⓥ	① ② ③ ④ ⑤ Ⓗ Ⓤ Ⓝ Ⓣ	
	Ⓢ Ⓒ Ⓓ ②	Ⓒ Ⓓ ②	⑥ ⑦ ⑧ ⑨ ⑩ Ⓠ Ⓖ Ⓟ	
	Ⓒ Ⓢ Ⓛ ⒶⓃ Ⓜ	Ⓢ Ⓛ ⒶⓃ Ⓜ	⑪ ⑫	Ⓝⓥ Ⓧ Ⓞ Ⓦ ⒹⓅ Ⓐ Ⓑ

3. Child, laughing: "It's a little round chocolate cake with white stuff inside."

3	Who	To Whom	What	How
	Ⓡ Ⓣ Ⓐ Ⓥ	Ⓣ Ⓐ Ⓥ	① ② ③ ④ ⑤ Ⓗ Ⓤ Ⓝ Ⓣ	
	Ⓢ Ⓒ Ⓓ ②	Ⓒ Ⓓ ②	⑥ ⑦ ⑧ ⑨ ⑩ Ⓠ Ⓖ Ⓟ	
	Ⓒ Ⓢ Ⓛ ⒶⓃ Ⓜ	Ⓢ Ⓛ ⒶⓃ Ⓜ	⑪ ⑫	Ⓝⓥ Ⓧ Ⓞ Ⓦ ⒹⓅ Ⓐ Ⓑ

4. Teacher, kiddingly: "What is the white stuff? Paste?"

4	Who	To Whom	What	How
	Ⓡ Ⓣ Ⓐ Ⓥ	Ⓣ Ⓐ Ⓥ	① ② ③ ④ ⑤ Ⓗ Ⓤ Ⓝ Ⓣ	
	Ⓢ Ⓒ Ⓓ ②	Ⓒ Ⓓ ②	⑥ ⑦ ⑧ ⑨ ⑩ Ⓠ Ⓖ Ⓟ	
	Ⓒ Ⓢ Ⓛ ⒶⓃ Ⓜ	Ⓢ Ⓛ ⒶⓃ Ⓜ	⑪ ⑫	Ⓝⓥ Ⓧ Ⓞ Ⓦ ⒹⓅ Ⓐ Ⓑ

5. Child, laughing: "No, it's sweet, like frosting."

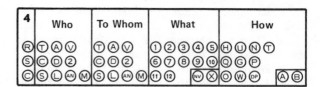

6. Teacher, with interest: "How does the frosting get inside?"

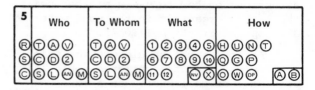

64   Chapter 4

7. As the teacher waits, the
   child looks pensive:
   "Maybe they have a
   squirter, . . . "

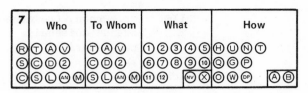

8. ". . . you know, like a
   water pistol, and they
   squirt it like this."
   Child motions with her
   finger in a trigger action.

To the child's initial statement regarding the Ho-Ho,
the teacher could have said "How nice," or "That sounds
good," or "Is it the first time you've had those?" Then, the
child would not have been required to extend her language or
think of a solution to a problem as she did in the exchange.

EXERCISE 4.2   See if you can write a vignette using thought-provoking questions.

Situation: A first-grade class is discussing a problem that occurred on
the playground.

Teacher: What rules can you make so that everyone who wants a turn can
         swing during recess?

Child: _____

Teacher: _____

Child: _____

Teacher: _____

Child: _____

EXERCISE 4.3   See if you can write a vignette where the child initiates the conversation
and the teacher responds with a question.

Situation: A fourth-grade child is weighing in a balance scale two white
mice that are on different controlled diets.

Child: Mr. Brown, the mouse eating cake and cookies weighs exactly five orange Cuisenaire rods.[4] The other mouse weighs five orange and two red rods.

Teacher: _____

Child: _____

Teacher: _____

Child: _____

Teacher: _____

HANDLING MISBEHAVIOR

During recess, Lewis comes running up to Ms. Henry. "Ms. Henry, Tony and Sally are fighting!" shouts Lewis. "What do you think the problem is?" asks Ms. Henry as they walk across the playground.

"They both wanted to be up at bat," offers Lewis.

As they approach the two children who are struggling over the bat, Ms. Henry commands, "Hey, you two. Come on, let's talk this over." The children continue to struggle over the bat. Ms. Henry takes each firmly by the shoulder and leads them toward the classroom.

Sally says tearfully, "Everyday Tony's up at bat first. He always yells, 'First one there is first at bat,' and just because he can run fastest he is *always* first."

"Yeah! Yeah!" chime in several other children.

"How does it seem to you, Tony?" asks Ms. Henry. "Well, first one there ought to be first," says Tony defensively.

"OK, we'll start our own game and you can be first all by yourself," retorts Lewis. "Right, Right," echo several other children. "Yeah, let's start our own game and each day someone different can be first." The group moves off to start another game, leaving Tony with Ms. Henry. Tony looks crestfallen. He bats the ball against the fence.

"Did you get what you want, Tony?" asks Ms. Henry as she tosses the ball back to him.

"No."

"What do you want?"

"To play ball with the kids."

---

[4]Cuisenaire Rods are blocks of wood whose size and weight are based on metric measurements. One white cube is exactly 1 cubic centimeter. It weighs exactly 1 gram. A red rod equals the length of two white cubes and weighs 2 grams. The rods are graduated in length and coded by color. Ten white cubes laid side by side are the same length as one orange rod; they also weigh the same as one orange rod.

"Can you think of a way that you might get to do that?"

"Yeah." Tony runs off and joins the outfield.

Advocates of the Exploratory Model want children to learn from conflicts with others. They want children to experience the consequences of their actions. Teachers, in this model, should neither moralize about the right solution nor ignore the problem. They should ask the children involved what they think and feel and, as much as possible, let the children resolve the problem. The expectation is that the experience itself will do the teaching. (Teachers would, of course, step into a situation where children might endanger themselves or others.)

A CONTEXTUAL VIEW

The following is an example of the situation in a typical first-grade classroom based on the Exploratory Model early in the spring, near the end of the school year. Many children are independently engaged in a wide variety of activities, either by themselves or in small groups. Two children are sitting in a rocking chair in the book corner; one child is reading to the other. Three other children are sitting on a rug reading to themselves. Occasionally, one child asks the next person, "What's that word?," gets the needed help, and continues. Seated at a small table nearby, three children are playing a word-letter game with a classroom aide. Four children are working together at the back of the room on a mural of a zoo. Two other children are making small clay animals.

In the science center one child is measuring her bean sprout to see how much it grew over the weekend. She has made a bar chart of colored paper showing each day's growth. She noticed there was twice as much growth on the weekend as on other days of the week. Another child is watering the seedlings. He gets too much water in the tray. A child wails, "You've drowned them! They're floating on top." The teacher, who is working with four children on a science project, hears the disruption and asks, "How can you get some of the water out?" Four children offer solutions: "With a spoon," "A cup," "A paper towel," "My daddy uses a hose to get gas out of the truck for his motorcycle."

The teacher in this situation has followed the strategy advocated by this model—he asked for and received a number of solutions. Now he will encourage the children to try their solutions and discover what works best. Figure 4.1 shows how the adults and children in this classroom would be coded on the Classroom Check List of activities and groupings.

Now try Exercise 4.4. The answers are at the end of the chapter.

CLASSROOM OBSERVATION PROCEDURE

CLASSROOM CHECK LIST (be sure to code **EVERYONE** in the class)

		ONE CHILD	TWO CHILDREN	SMALL GROUPS	LARGE GROUPS
1. Snack, lunch		T ①②③ / A ①②③ / V ①②③ / i ①②③	T ①②③ / A ①②③ / V ①②③ / i ①②③	T ①②③④ / A ①②③④ / V ①②③④ / i ①②③④	T ①② / A ①② / V ①② / i ①②
2. Group time		T ①②③ / A ①②③ / V ①②③ / i ①②③	T ①②③ / A ①②③ / V ①②③ / i ①②③	T ①②③④ / A ①②③④ / V ①②③④ / i ①②③④	T ①② / A ①② / V ①② / i ①②
3. Story / Music / Dancing		T ①②③ / A ①②③ / V ①②③ / i ①②③	T ①②③ / A ①②③ / V ①②③ / i ①②③	T ①②③④ / A ①②③④ / V ①②③④ / i ①②③④	T ①② / A ①② / V ①② / i ①②
4. Arts, Crafts		T ①②③ / A ①②③ / V ①②③ / i ①**●**③	T ①②③ / A ①②③ / V ①②③ / i ①②③	T ①②③④ / A ①②③④ / V ①②③④ / i **●**②③④	T ①② / A ①② / V ①② / i ①②
5. Guessing Games / Table Games / Puzzles		T ①②③ / A ①②③ / V ①②③ / i ①②③	T ①②③ / A ①②③ / V ①②③ / i ①②③	T ①②③④ / A ①②③④ / V ①②③④ / i ①②③④	T ①② / A ①② / V ①② / i ①②
○ TV ○ Audio-Visual Materials ● Exploratory Materials ○ Math and Science Equipment ○ Texts, Workbooks ○ Puzzles, Games	**6. Math** Numbers / Arithmetic	T ①②③ / A ①②③ / V ①②③ / i ①②③	T ①②③ / A ①②③ / V ①②③ / i ①②③	T ①②③④ / A ①②③④ / V ①②③④ / i ①②③④	T ①② / A ①② / V ①② / i ①②
	7. Alphabet Reading / Lang. Development	T ①②③ / A ①②③ / V ①②③ / i ①②**●**	T ①②③ / A ①②③ / V ①②③ / i **●**②③	T ①②③④ / A **●**②③④ / V ①②③④ / i ①②③④	T ①② / A ①② / V ①② / i ①②
	8. Social Studies / Geography	T ①②③ / A ①②③ / V ①②③ / i ①②③	T ①②③ / A ①②③ / V ①②③ / i ①②③	T ①②③④ / A ①②③④ / V ①②③④ / i ①②③④	T ①② / A ①② / V ①② / i ①②
	9. Science / Natural World	T ①②③ / A ①②③ / V ①②③ / i **●●**③	T ①②③ / A ①②③ / V ①②③ / i ①②③	T **●**②③④ / A ①②③④ / V ①②③④ / i ①②③④	T ①② / A ①② / V ①② / i ①②
10. Sewing / Cooking / Pounding / Sawing		T ①②③ / A ①②③ / V ①②③ / i ①②③	T ①②③ / A ①②③ / V ①②③ / i ①②③	T ①②③④ / A ①②③④ / V ①②③④ / i ①②③④	T ①② / A ①② / V ①② / i ①②
11. Blocks / Trucks		T ①②③ / A ①②③ / V ①②③ / i ①②③	T ①②③ / A ①②③ / V ①②③ / i ①②③	T ①②③④ / A ①②③④ / V ①②③④ / i ①②③④	T ①② / A ①② / V ①② / i ①②
12. Dramatic Play / Dress-Up		T ①②③ / A ①②③ / V ①②③ / i ①②③	T ①②③ / A ①②③ / V ①②③ / i ①②③	T ①②③④ / A ①②③④ / V ①②③④ / i ①②③④	T ①② / A ①② / V ①② / i ①②
13. Active Play		T ①②③ / A ①②③ / V ①②③ / i ①②③	T ①②③ / A ①②③ / V ①②③ / i ①②③	T ①②③④ / A ①②③④ / V ①②③④ / i ①②③④	T ①② / A ①② / V ①② / i ①②

14. RELIABILITY SHEET ○

Figure 4.1 Classroom Observation Procedure

			ONE CHILD	TWO CHILDREN	SMALL GROUPS	LARGE GROUPS
15. Practical Skills Acquisition			T ①②③ A ①②③ v ①②③ i ①②③	T ①②③ A ①②③ v ①②③ i ①②③	T ①②③④ A ①②③④ v ①②③④ i ①②③④	T ①② A ①② v ①② i ①②
16. Observing			T ①②③ A ①②③ v ①②③ i ①②③	T ①②③ A ①②③ v ①②③ i ①②③	T ①②③④ A ①②③④ v ①②③④ i ①②③④	T ①② A ①② v ①② i ①②
17. Social Interaction	Ob [©②⑤]	Ⓣ Ⓐ Ⓥ	T ①②③ A ①②③ v ①②③ i ①②③	T ①②③ A ①②③ v ①②③ i ①②③	T ①②③④ A ①②③④ v ①②③④ i ①②③④	T ①② A ①② v ①② i ①②
18. Unoccupied Child			T ①②③ A ①②③ v ①②③ i ①②③	T ①②③ A ①②③ v ①②③ i ①②③	T ①②③④ A ①②③④ v ①②③④ i ①②③④	T ①② A ①② v ①② i ①②
19. Discipline			T ①②③ A ①②③ v ①②③ i ①②③	T ①②③ A ①②③ v ①②③ i ①②③	T ①②③④ A ①②③④ v ①②③④ i ①②③④	T ①② A ①② v ①② i ①②
20. Transitional Activities		Ⓣ Ⓐ Ⓥ	T ①②③ A ①②③ v ①②③ i ①②③	T ①②③ A ①②③ v ①②③ i ①②③	T ①②③④ A ①②③④ v ①②③④ i ①②③④	T ①② A ①② v ①② i ①②
21. Classroom Management		Ⓣ Ⓐ Ⓥ	T ①②③ A ①②③ v ①②③ i ①②③	T ①②③ A ①②③ v ①②③ i ①②③	T ①②③④ A ①②③④ v ①②③④ i ①②③④	T ①② A ①② v ①② i ①②
22. Out of Room		Ⓣ Ⓐ Ⓥ	T ①②③ A ①②③ v ①②③ i ①②③	T ①②③ A ①②③ v ①②③ i ①②③	T ①②③④ A ①②③④ v ①②③④ i ①②③④	T ①② A ①② v ①② i ①②

NUMBER OF ADULTS IN CLASSROOM   ⓪ ① ● ③ ④ ⑤ ⑥ ⑦ ⑧ ⑨ ⑩

EXERCISE 4.4   Code each person in the situation below on the CCL.

Situation: In an exploratory first-grade classroom, a volunteer is helping a child place a card in the language master. They listen to the words being spoken and then repeat the words. Four children using earphones are listening to a recorded story. A classroom aide is writing down a story that a child is dictating to her. She reads what has been written. The child makes some corrections and then reads his own story. Four other children are writing stories at this table, referring to the eye-level alphabet cards pinned on the partition around the learning center. Stories from previous days are also on display on these partitions for the children to read. Two other children are drawing pictures to accompany their stories.

The teacher is discussing a construction problem with four children. They are figuring out how much wood they will need to build a counter for their classroom store. "How high do you want the counter of the store?" "About this high," two children say, indicating a height with their hands. "How can we know how high that is?" "Measure it with a string," offers Cynthia. "No," says Doris as she gets the yardstick and measures from the floor to Pete's rigid hand held in space. "Twenty-eight inches," she announces. "Twenty-eight inches," repeats the teacher. "Now you measure it with your string, Cynthia. How long is it?" Cynthia measures it on the yardstick. "Twenty-eight inches," she replies. "How many twenty-eight-inch pieces will you need to hold up the counter?" The teacher continues to ask questions, bringing up one by one the problems that need to be solved, until the children are ready to order their wood.

CLASSROOM OBSERVATION PROCEDURE

CLASSROOM CHECK LIST (be sure to code **EVERYONE** in the class)

	ONE CHILD	TWO CHILDREN	SMALL GROUPS	LARGE GROUPS
1. Snack, lunch	T ①②③ A ①②③ v ①②③ i ①②③	T ①②③ A ①②③ v ①②③ i ①②③	T ①②③④ A ①②③④ v ①②③④ i ①②③④	T ①② A ①② v ①② i ①②
2. Group time	T ①②③ A ①②③ v ①②③ i ①②③	T ①②③ A ①②③ v ①②③ i ①②③	T ①②③④ A ①②③④ v ①②③④ i ①②③④	T ①② A ①② v ①② i ①②
Story **3. Music** Dancing	T ①②③ A ①②③ v ①②③ i ①②③	T ①②③ A ①②③ v ①②③ i ①②③	T ①②③④ A ①②③④ v ①②③④ i ①②③④	T ①② A ①② v ①② i ①②
4. Arts, Crafts	T ①②③ A ①②③ v ①②③ i ①②③	T ①②③ A ①②③ v ①②③ i ①②③	T ①②③④ A ①②③④ v ①②③④ i ①②③④	T ①② A ①② v ①② i ①②
Guessing Games **5. Table Games** Puzzles	T ①②③ A ①②③ v ①②③ i ①②③	T ①②③ A ①②③ v ①②③ i ①②③	T ①②③④ A ①②③④ v ①②③④ i ①②③④	T ①② A ①② v ①② i ①②
Numbers **6. Math** Arithmetic	T ①②③ A ①②③ v ①②③ i ①②③	T ①②③ A ①②③ v ①②③ i ①②③	T ①②③④ A ①②③④ v ①②③④ i ①②③④	T ①② A ①② v ①② i ①②
Reading **7. Alphabet** Lang. Development	T ①②③ A ①②③ v ①②③ i ①②③	T ①②③ A ①②③ v ①②③ i ①②③	T ①②③④ A ①②③④ v ①②③④ i ①②③④	T ①② A ①② v ①② i ①②
8. Social Studies Geography	T ①②③ A ①②③ v ①②③ i ①②③	T ①②③ A ①②③ v ①②③ i ①②③	T ①②③④ A ①②③④ v ①②③④ i ①②③④	T ①② A ①② v ①② i ①②
9. Science Natural World	T ①②③ A ①②③ v ①②③ i ①②③	T ①②③ A ①②③ v ①②③ i ①②③	T ①②③④ A ①②③④ v ①②③④ i ①②③④	T ①② A ①② v ①② i ①②
Sewing Cooking **10. Pounding** Sawing	T ①②③ A ①②③ v ①②③ i ①②③	T ①②③ A ①②③ v ①②③ i ①②③	T ①②③④ A ①②③④ v ①②③④ i ①②③④	T ①② A ①② v ①② i ①②
11. Blocks Trucks	T ①②③ A ①②③ v ①②③ i ①②③	T ①②③ A ①②③ v ①②③ i ①②③	T ①②③④ A ①②③④ v ①②③④ i ①②③④	T ①② A ①② v ①② i ①②
12. Dramatic Play Dress-Up	T ①②③ A ①②③ v ①②③ i ①②③	T ①②③ A ①②③ v ①②③ i ①②③	T ①②③④ A ①②③④ v ①②③④ i ①②③④	T ①② A ①② v ①② i ①②
13. Active Play	T ①②③ A ①②③ v ①②③ i ①②③	T ①②③ A ①②③ v ①②③ i ①②③	T ①②③④ A ①②③④ v ①②③④ i ①②③④	T ①② A ①② v ①② i ①②
14. RELIABILITY SHEET ○				

Materials checklist (left column):

○ TV
○ Audio-Visual Materials
○ Exploratory Materials
○ Math and Science Equipment
○ Texts, Workbooks
○ Puzzles, Games

Exercise 4.4

			ONE CHILD	TWO CHILDREN	SMALL GROUPS	LARGE GROUPS
15. Practical Skills Acquisition			T ①②③	T ①②③	T ①②③④	T ①②
			A ①②③	A ①②③	A ①②③④	A ①②
			v ①②③	v ①②③	v ①②③④	v ①②
			i ①②③	i ①②③	i ①②③④	i ①②
16. Observing			T ①②③	T ①②③	T ①②③④	T ①②
			A ①②③	A ①②③	A ①②③④	A ①②
			v ①②③	v ①②③	v ①②③④	v ①②
			i ①②③	i ①②③	i ①②③④	i ①②
17. Social Interaction	Ob [©②⑤]	ⓣⒶⓥ	T ①②③	T ①②③	T ①②③④	T ①②
			A ①②③	A ①②③	A ①②③④	A ①②
			v ①②③	v ①②③	v ①②③④	v ①②
			i ①②③	i ①②③	i ①②③④	i ①②
18. Unoccupied Child			T ①②③	T ①②③	T ①②③④	T ①②
			A ①②③	A ①②③	A ①②③④	A ①②
			v ①②③	v ①②③	v ①②③④	v ①②
			i ①②③	i ①②③	i ①②③④	i ①②
19. Discipline			T ①②③	T ①②③	T ①②③④	T ①②
			A ①②③	A ①②③	A ①②③④	A ①②
			v ①②③	v ①②③	v ①②③④	v ①②
			i ①②③	i ①②③	i ①②③④	i ①②
20. Transitional Activities		ⓣⒶⓥ	T ①②③	T ①②③	T ①②③④	T ①②
			A ①②③	A ①②③	A ①②③④	A ①②
			v ①②③	v ①②③	v ①②③④	v ①②
			i ①②③	i ①②③	i ①②③④	i ①②
21. Classroom Management		ⓣⒶⓥ	T ①②③	T ①②③	T ①②③④	T ①②
			A ①②③	A ①②③	A ①②③④	A ①②
			v ①②③	v ①②③	v ①②③④	v ①②
			i ①②③	i ①②③	i ①②③④	i ①②
22. Out of Room		ⓣⒶⓥ	T ①②③	T ①②③	T ①②③④	T ①②
			A ①②③	A ①②③	A ①②③④	A ①②
			v ①②③	v ①②③	v ①②③④	v ①②
			i ①②③	i ①②③	i ①②③④	i ①②

NUMBER OF ADULTS IN CLASSROOM ⓪ ① ② ③ ④ ⑤ ⑥ ⑦ ⑧ ⑨ ⑩

A typical second- or third-grade classroom based on the Exploratory Model would have a similar room organization. The materials and equipment in the learning centers, as well as the activities, would be more advanced, however, and the amount of scheduling would be greater. Whereas younger children are allowed their choice of activity during most of the day, older children are guided into reading or math activities. Some teachers handle this by allowing the children to make contractual agreements regarding what work they will accomplish each day. As the children gain these basic reading and computation skills, they use them to solve problems and to learn more about their own culture and community.

One spring, all the activities of one third-grade class centered about a field trip they were making to the state capital. Reading revolved around the state flower, the state bird, and state heroes. Maps were on display and discussions took place regarding the number of miles between each of the towns they would pass through. Several different routes were suggested and the mileage compared for each route. Rest stops along the way were considered. At the conclusion of the discussion, one girl offered to talk with the bus driver and see which route he thought best. Two boys offered to make a list of all the items each child would need to take on the trip. Another group offered to write a letter to the school paper announcing their trip. The children appeared to be self-motivated, highly involved, and certainly competent enough to think through the problems involved in such a trip.

CLASSROOM REQUIREMENTS

The Exploratory Model has several classroom requirements. First, as we mentioned previously, the classroom must have movable furniture. The movable tables and chairs can be placed in the various learning centers as they are required. Seats in rows fastened on the floor would prohibit the functioning of this model.

Second, it requires a wide variety of materials. Small items like games and exploratory materials can be purchased or collected. The electric and electronic equipment often used in this model is, however, likely to place a strain on some school budgets. If that's the case, teachers might be able to check such equipment as the hot plate and portable oven, the record player and earphones, language master, filmstrip, or camera out of a central office. Of course, it's best if each classroom has its own equipment since the intent is to allow children many choices of activities and use of equipment throughout the day.

Third, the model requires that several adults be present—at least, it functions best when there are since greater personal attention can be paid to the children. If aides are not available, teachers may wish to train volunteers, perhaps parents or older students. Volunteers should understand both the philosophy of the model and the expected benefits for children. Teachers and volunteers should help each other become better listeners and responders instead of talkers and tellers. They must take time before or after class to discuss the progress of each child and make plans to rearrange the environment as necessary. Training volunteers is time consuming, but the result is personal attention for the children and opportunities for them to become independent, self-motivated problem solvers.

RESEARCH FINDINGS ON HOW CHILDREN GROW AND DEVELOP

Observation studies of the Follow Through Planned Variation Project made by Stallings and Kaskowitz[5] indicate that children in the first and third grades of the Exploratory Model work independently in a wide variety of activities more often than children in other, more teacher-directed educational models. They ask more questions, take greater initiative in starting conversations, work together more often, and cooperate more with each other in performing joint tasks than do children in other models.

Most outstanding were their scores on the Raven's Coloured Progressive Matrices test[6] (a test of nonverbal reasoning or problem solving, developed by J. C. Raven in 1956), which were higher than those of children in more teacher-directed or traditional classrooms. The test has eighteen matrices or designs, progressing from simple to complex. Each matrix has a part missing. The child is instructed to select the correct design to fit into the empty spot from six possible choices.

---

[5]Jane A. Stallings and David Kaskowitz, *Follow Through Classroom Observation Evaluation 1972-1973* (Menlo Park, Calif.: Stanford Research Institute, 1974), pp. 106-117. ERIC Accession No. ED 104 969.

[6]See J. C. Raven, "Raven's Coloured Progressive Matrices" (New York: Psychological Corp., 1956, 1962) and *Guide to Using the Coloured Progressive Matrices* (London: H. K. Lewis, 1965).

It is important to note that in this model, children in both first and third grades were absent less frequently than the children in more strictly controlled classrooms. This may mean that they enjoy school more, since children who like school want to be there whether they are sick or not; children who don't like school may plead to stay home, using any slight injury or ache, or the prospect of one, as an excuse.

There are some limitations in this model. The children from this model who were tested in the Follow Through evaluation did not score highest in reading and mathematical skills. The data indicated that in order to develop proficiency in reading and math, children must devote a large proportion of school time to those subjects. Where the instruction of reading and math was carefully programmed and feedback from the teachers was systematic, children had higher scores. Apparently, self-motivation, without specific direction from adults or carefully programmed materials, is not enough for children to develop excellence in reading and math skills in the early grades. Unfortunately, the study could not assess whether or not the children in the exploratory environment enjoy reading as much as children in traditional classes or whether they use reading skills to solve problems outside of school. These are important aspects of reading that a teacher, a student teacher, or a parent could discover by seeing how children spend their leisure time. My hunch is that they do enjoy reading and do use this skill in practical ways, for example, in reading rules for games or following directions to build models.

Test scores on the Intellectual Achievement Responsibility (IAR)[7] scale indicate that children in models similar to the Exploratory Model accept responsibility for their own success in academic achievement. One item on the scale asks, "If something is easy to learn at school it is because (A) You pay attention or (B) The teacher gives you lots of help." Children in models similar to the Exploratory Model are more likely to check the A answer, indicating that they accept responsibility for their success in learning. However, on test items examining attitudes toward failure, these children are likely to blame factors outside of themselves for any failure. On the test item "If you don't do as well as usual in something at school it would be because (A) You didn't do your work or (B) Someone bothered you," children in models similar to the Exploratory Model more frequently choose the B answer.

OBSERVABLE COMPONENTS

The SRI observation system cannot, of course, record all of the important elements of the Exploratory Model. For instance, it cannot record that a child is intrinsically motivated. It can only record whether or not children were involved with exploratory materials and that they were asking questions. Several other observation instruments are available that can assess the more complex adult and child behaviors found in the Exploratory Model. Some of these are: the Prescott Observation System described in Chapter 1; Analysis of Communication in Education, developed by Garda W. Bowman at Bank Street

---

[7]See Virginia C. Crandall, Walter Katkovsky, and Vaughn J. Crandall, *Child Development* (Chicago: University of Chicago Press, 1965), pp. 91-109.

College, and The Responsive Classroom Observation Schedule, developed at Far West Laboratory by Nicholas F. Rayder.[8]

The materials being used, the activities occurring, and interactions between adults and children can be observed and recorded using the SRI instrument.

Materials

When used with the Exploratory Model, the Physical Environment Information form would have a wide variety of materials marked in both the Present column and the Used Today column. Movable tables and chairs would also be indicated. And the items indicating that children select their own seats and groups would be marked (see Figure 4.2).

Activities and Groupings

Since many activities occur simultaneously, the Classroom Check List would have many activities marked on each grid. The adults would be most usually marked in the One Child, Two Children, or Small Groups columns. Many children would be marked in the independent row of the various activities, and independent children may be marked in all columns. Most of the categories in the materials column would also be marked (see Figure 4.3).

---

[8]Elizabeth Prescott, *Who Thrives in Group Day Care? Assessment of Child-Rearing Environments: An Ecological Approach* (Pasadena, Calif.: Pacific Oaks College, 1973). ERIC Accession No. ED 076 229; Garda W. Bowman, "Analysis of Communication in Education" (New York: Bank Street College of Education, 1972); Nicholas F. Rayder, Pierina Ng, and Anne Rhodes, *The Responsive Classroom Observation Schedule— Background and Development* (San Francisco, Calif.: Far West Laboratory for Educational Research and Development, 1974). ERIC Accession No. ED 107 375.

Physical Environment Information
(Mark all that apply.)

For each of the items below, mark all that apply:

① Present
② Used today

Seating Patterns:
● Movable tables and chairs for seating purposes.
○ Stationary desks in rows.
○ Assigned seating for at least part of the day.
● Children select their own seating locations.
○ Teacher assigns children to groups.
● Children select their own work groups.

GAMES, TOYS, PLAY EQUIPMENT
●● small toys (trucks, cars, dolls and accessories
●● puzzles, games
①② wheel toys
●② small play equipment (jumpropes, balls)
①② large play equipment (swings, jungle gym)
●● children's storybooks
●② animals, other nature objects
①② sandbox, water table
●● carpentry materials, large blocks
●● cooking and sewing supplies

INSTRUCTIONAL MATERIALS
①② Montessori, other educational toys
●● children's texts, workbooks
●● math/science equipment, concrete objects
●● instructional charts

AUDIO, VISUAL EQUIPMENT
●● television
●● record or tape player
●● audio-visual equipment

GENERAL EQUIPMENT, MATERIALS
●② children's own products on display
●② displays reflecting children's ethnicity
●② other displays especially for children
●② magazines
①② achievement charts
①② child-size sink
●② child-size table and chairs
●② child-size shelves
●② arts and crafts materials
●② blackboard, feltboard
①② child's own storage space
●② photographs of the children on display

OTHER
①② please specify . . . . . .

MAKE NO

STRAY MARKS

IN BLANK AREAS

Figure 4.2

CLASSROOM OBSERVATION PROCEDURE

CLASSROOM CHECK LIST (be sure to code **EVERYONE** in the class)

		ONE CHILD	TWO CHILDREN	SMALL GROUPS	LARGE GROUPS
1. Snack, lunch		T ①②③ A ①②③ v ①②③ i ①②③	T ①②③ A ①②③ v ①②③ i ①②③	T ①②③④ A ①②③④ v ①②③④ i ①②③④	T ①② A ①② v ①② i ①②
2. Group time		T ①②③ A ①②③ v ①②③ i ①②③	T ①②③ A ①②③ v ①②③ i ①②③	T ①②③④ A ①②③④ v ①②③④ i ①②③④	T ①② A ①② v ①② i ①②
3. Music	Story Dancing	T ①②③ A ①②③ v ①②③ i ①②③	T ①②③ A ①②③ v ①②③ i ●②③	T ①②③④ A ①②③④ v ①②③④ i ①②③④	T ①② A ①② v ①② i ①②
4. Arts, Crafts		T ①②③ A ①②③ v ①②③ i ①②③	T ①②③ A ①②③ v ①②③ i ①②③	T ①②③④ A ①②③④ v ①②③④ i ●②③④	T ①② A ①② v ①② i ①②
5. Table Games	Guessing Games Puzzles	T ①②③ A ①②③ v ①②③ i ①②③	T ①②③ A ①②③ v ①②③ i ①②③	T ①②③④ A ①②③④ v ①②③④ i ①②③④	T ①② A ①② v ①② i ①②
6. Math	Numbers Arithmetic	T ①②③ A ●②③ v ①②③ i ①②③	T ①②③ A ①②③ v ①②③ i ●②③	T ①②③④ A ①②③④ v ①②③④ i ①②③④	T ①② A ①② v ①② i ①②
7. Alphabet	Reading Lang. Development	T ●②③ A ①②③ v ●②③ i ①②③	T ①②③ A ①②③ v ①②③ i ①②③	T ①②③④ A ①②③④ v ①②③④ i ●②③④	T ①② A ①② v ①② i ①②
8.	Social Studies Geography	T ①②③ A ①②③ v ①②③ i ①②③	T ①②③ A ①②③ v ①②③ i ①②③	T ①②③④ A ①②③④ v ①②③④ i ●②③④	T ①② A ①② v ①② i ①②
9.	Science Natural World	T ①②③ A ①②③ v ①②③ i ①②③	T ①②③ A ①②③ v ①②③ i ①②③	T ①②③④ A ①②③④ v ①②③④ i ●②③④	T ①② A ①② v ①② i ①②
10.	Sewing Cooking Pounding Sawing	T ①②③ A ①②③ v ①②③ i ①②③	T ①②③ A ①②③ v ①②③ i ①②③	T ①②③④ A ①②③④ v ①②③④ i ①②③④	T ①② A ①② v ①② i ①②
11.	Blocks Trucks	T ①②③ A ①②③ v ①②③ i ①②③	T ①②③ A ①②③ v ①②③ i ①②③	T ①②③④ A ①②③④ v ①②③④ i ①②③④	T ①② A ①② v ①② i ①②
12.	Dramatic Play Dress-Up	T ①②③ A ①②③ v ①②③ i ①②③	T ①②③ A ①②③ v ①②③ i ①②③	T ①②③④ A ①②③④ v ①②③④ i ①②③④	T ①② A ①② v ①② i ①②
13. Active Play		T ①②③ A ①②③ v ①②③ i ①②③	T ①②③ A ①②③ v ①②③ i ①②③	T ①②③④ A ①②③④ v ①②③④ i ①②③④	T ①② A ①② v ①② i ①②
14. RELIABILITY SHEET	○				

Left sidebar (materials, items 6–9):

○ TV
● Audio-Visual Materials
● Exploratory Materials
● Math and Science Equipment
● Texts, Workbooks
● Puzzles, Games

Figure 4.3

	ONE CHILD	TWO CHILDREN	SMALL GROUPS	LARGE GROUPS
15. Practical Skills Acquisition	T ①②③ A ①②③ v ①②③ i ①②③	T ①②③ A ①②③ v ①②③ i ①②③	T ①②③④ A ①②③④ v ①②③④ i ①②③④	T ①② A ①② v ①② i ①②
16. Observing	T ①②③ A ①②③ v ①②③ i ①②③	T ①②③ A ①②③ v ①②③ i ①②③	T ①②③④ A ①②③④ v ①②③④ i ①②③④	T ①② A ①② v ①② i ①②
17. Social Interaction Ob [©/②/Ⓢ] Ⓣ Ⓐ Ⓥ	T ①②③ A ①②③ v ①②③ i ①②③	T ①②③ A ①②③ v ①②③ i ●②③	T ①②③④ A ①②③④ v ①②③④ i ①②③④	T ①② A ①② v ①② i ①②
18. Unoccupied Child	T ①②③ A ①②③ v ①②③ i ①②③	T ①②③ A ①②③ v ①②③ i ①②③	T ①②③④ A ①②③④ v ①②③④ i ①②③④	T ①② A ①② v ①② i ①②
19. Discipline	T ①②③ A ①②③ v ①②③ i ①②③	T ①②③ A ①②③ v ①②③ i ①②③	T ①②③④ A ①②③④ v ①②③④ i ①②③④	T ①② A ①② v ①② i ①②
20. Transitional Activities Ⓣ Ⓐ Ⓥ	T ①②③ A ①②③ v ①②③ i ①②③	T ①②③ A ①②③ v ①②③ i ①②③	T ①②③④ A ①②③④ v ①②③④ i ①②③④	T ①② A ①② v ①② i ①②
21. Classroom Management Ⓣ Ⓐ Ⓥ	T ①②③ A ①②③ v ①②③ i ①②③	T ①②③ A ①②③ v ①②③ i ①②③	T ①②③④ A ①②③④ v ①②③④ i ①②③④	T ①② A ①② v ①② i ①②
22. Out of Room Ⓣ Ⓐ Ⓥ	T ①②③ A ①②③ v ①②③ i ①②③	T ①②③ A ①②③ v ①②③ i ①②③	T ①②③④ A ①②③④ v ①②③④ i ①②③④	T ①② A ①② v ①② i ①②

NUMBER OF ADULTS IN CLASSROOM ⓪ ① ② ③ ● ⑤ ⑥ ⑦ ⑧ ⑨ ⑩

Interaction Observations

Many of the interactions between adults and children would be recorded as task-related, for example, "That seedling is growing very tall, John" (TC6). Many would be social comments about home life or daily non-task events: "My baby brother can walk now" (TC5). The adults' questions would be directed toward individual children rather than the group, and the questions would attempt to elicit a descriptive answer from the child. This type of question is coded as a thought-provoking one (TC2). Adults would be supportive and acknowledge a child's achievement, but they are not likely to heap praise on a child. Their support would come in the form of a nod of the head (TC7NV), a smile (TC7NVH), a pat on the shoulder or a hug (TC7NVT), or a mild "OK" or "All right" (TC7).

Children in the Exploratory Model often work together and instruct each other in playing games. Therefore, a number of "child (C) instructing (4) a different child (D) using objects (O)" interactions may be recorded (CD4O). Children can be expected to initiate conversations with adults by asking questions about a task or a problem to be solved. (CT1Q). Adults are expected to respond to a child's questions with another question, thus extending the child's thinking rather than giving the child an answer (TC1Q or TC2).

The following is a coded typical interaction in an Exploratory classroom.

Situation: A teacher is discussing a problem with a second-grade child.

1. Child: Teacher, how can I make this wire stay on the battery?

2. Teacher: What do we have here that can make one thing stick to another thing?

3. Child: Paste.

4. Teacher: Try it.

5. Child: It won't stick.

6. Teacher: What else do we have?

7. Child: Scotch tape.

8. Teacher: Try it.

9. Child: It works.

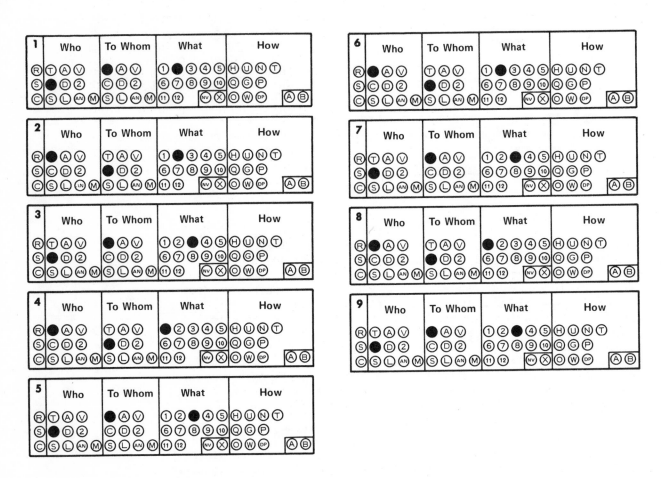

Figure 4.4 Coded Interaction of an Exploratory Model Classroom

IMPORTANCE OF TEACHER OBSERVATION

The primary reason for observing or being observed is to learn more about classroom instructional processes. If teachers observe each other, the teacher doing the observing learns more about how the other teacher teaches; the teacher being observed can receive immediate feedback by reading the observation record. Being observed allows teachers to evaluate themselves to see if goals they have set are being achieved.

Teachers using the Exploratory Model should periodically examine observation records of their own classroom performance. If the records show a high rate of TL4 (teacher instructing large group) or TL1QA (teacher questioning large group on academic subject matter), the teacher will need to reduce the amount of large group instruction to conform to the model's goal of individualized instruction.

SUMMARY OF COMPONENTS

Theorist or theory: Gestalt Dewey, Taba

Oriented toward: Self-motivation

Goals: To develop creativity and independence

Stress: Inquiring skills

Structure: Student-centered

Grouping patterns: Individual student

Materials: Teaching machines and exploratory materials

Where to teach: Learning centers

Who initiates: Child

Questioning strategy: Open-ended

Feedback from: Materials

Who evaluates: Student

Evaluation tools: Problem-solving tests, locus of control
                  tests (IAR), child observations

BIBLIOGRAPHY

The Exploratory Model is based in part on the work of Glen Nimnicht and the staff at the Far West Laboratory. They developed a Responsive Educational model for the Follow Through program. Other components come from the Follow Through model developed at the University of Arizona by Marie Hughes, and from the Follow Through model developed in Cambridge at the Educational Development Center.

Where Components of the Exploratory Type Models Can Be Seen

Interested readers should contact the Follow Through offices in the school districts of the cities listed.

Education Development Center model

Laurel, Delaware	Philadelphia, Pennsylvania
Washington, D.C.	Scranton, Pennsylvania
Chicago, Illinois	Rosebud, Texas
Paterson, New Jersey	Burlington, Vermont
Smithfield, North Carolina	

Far West Laboratory model

Berkeley, California	Buffalo, New York
Fresno, California	Salt Lake City, Utah
Duluth, Minnesota	Tacoma, Washington
St. Louis, Missouri	

University of Arizona model

Des Moines, Iowa	Lakewood, New Jersey
Wichita, Kansas	Newark, New Jersey
Lincoln, Nebraska	Chickasha, Oklahoma

Suggested Readings

Theory of the Exploratory Model

Bruner, Jerome S. *Toward a Theory of Instruction*. Cambridge, Mass.: Harvard University Press, 1966.

Dewey, John. *How We Think: A Restatement of the Relation of Reflective Thinking to the Educative Process*, rev. ed. Boston: Heath, 1933.

Hein, George. "An Open Education Perspective on Evaluation." North Dakota Study Group on Evaluation, Grand Forks, 1975.

Neill, A. S. *Summerhill: A Radical Approach to Child Rearing*. New York: Hart, 1960.

Rogers, Carl R. "The Facilitation of Significant Learning." In *Contemporary Theories of Instruction*, edited by Laurence Siegel. Philadelphia: Chandler, 1951.

————. "Toward a Theory of Creativity." In *Creativity and Its Cultivation,* edited by Harold H. Anderson. New York: Harper & Row, 1959, pp. 69-82.

Taba, Hilda. *Curriculum Development: Theory and Practice*. New York: Harcourt Brace Jovanovich, 1962.

Torrance, Ellis. *Guiding Creative Talent*. Englewood Cliffs, N.J.: Prentice-Hall, 1962.

Implementing the Exploratory Model

Gordon, William J. *Synectics: The Development of Creative Capacity*. New York: Harper & Row, 1961.

Hawkins, David. "Messing About in Science." *Science and Children* 2 (1965), pp. 5-9.

Maccoby, Eleanor E., and Zellner, Miriam. *Experiments in Primary Education: Aspects of Project Follow-Through*. New York: Harcourt Brace Jovanovich, 1970, pp. 17-18.

Nimnicht, Glen. *Handbook for Teacher Assistants: A Guide to the Use of Specific Responsive Activities for Children*. Morristown, N.J.: General Learning Corporation, 1971.

————. *Inservice Teacher Training in the Use of the Responsive Program* (with film overview of inservice training). Morristown, N.J.: General Learning Corporation, 1971.

Rayder, Nicholas F.; Ng, Pierina; Rhodes, Anne. *The Responsive Classroom Observation Schedule—Background and Development*. San Francisco, Calif.: Far West Laboratory for Educational Research and Development, 1974.

Silberman, Charles E., ed. *The Open Classroom Reader*. New York: Random House, 1973, pp. 485-789.

Stallings, Jane A., and Kaskowitz, David. *Follow Through Classroom Observation Evaluation 1972-1973*. Menlo Park, Calif.: Stanford Research Institute, 1974, pp. 106-117. ERIC Accession No. ED 104 969.

Commercially Available Materials

Big Rock Candy Mountain: An anthology of educational materials available to classroom teachers from K-12. (Portola Institute, 558 Santa Cruz Avenue, Menlo Park, CA 94025.)

Cuisenaire Rods: A set of color-coded wooden blocks graduated in size from 1 centimeter to 10 centimeters. (Cuisenaire Company of America, 12 Church Street, New Rochelle, NY 10805.)

Developmental Mathematics Processes: A basal math series for grades K-6. Materials include games, activity cards, as well as the usual pupil workbooks. Complete K-6 math program, based on the measurement approach to learning math. Developed in the context of Individually Guided Instruction. Designed to be compatible with I.G.E. (Research and Development Center, University of Wisconsin, Madison, WI 53706.)

Language Experience in Reading: Guide to developing reading by using the children's experiences. (Encyclopaedia Britannica Education Corporation, 425 North Michigan, Chicago, IL 60611.)

Mathematics Workshop Series: Guides to teachers on helping students learn logical relationships. (Encyclopaedia Britannica Education Corporation, 425 North Michigan, Chicago, IL 60611).

Phonics Practice Program: Workbooks that extend phonetic practice through games and exercises. (Durrell-Murphy Phonics, Harcourt Brace Jovanovich, Polk and Geary, San Francisco, CA 94109).

Science: A Process Approach: Students learn by doing experiments. (Xerox Educational Division, 1200 High Ridge Park, Stamford, CT 06904).

SCIS Elementary Science Program: An innovative program using student manuals and a teacher's guide (but no textbook) that covers both the physical and life sciences. Thirteen kits are available, two each for grades 1-6 and one for kindergarten. Children work through the kits at their own pace and conduct their own investigations while receiving guidance from the teacher. (Rand McNally, P.O. Box 7600, Chicago, IL 60680).

Research Findings

Crandall, Virginia C.; Katkovsky, Walter; and Crandall, Vaughn J. "Children's Beliefs in Their Own Control of Reinforcements in Intellectual-Academic Achievement Situations." *Child Development*. (March 1965): 91-106.

Hamby, Trudy M. "An Investigation of the Relationship between Teacher Structuring and Change in Children's Creative Performance and Self-Ideal Self Reports." Unpublished doctoral dissertation, University of Maryland, 1966.

Mendel, Gisela. "Children's Preferences for Differing Degrees of Novelty." *Child Development* 36 (June 1965): 453-465.

Minuchin, Patricia P. "Curiosity and Exploratory Behavior in Disadvantaged Children: A Follow-Up Study." Urbana: University of Illinois, 1971. ERIC Accession No. ED 056 747.

Raven, J. C. *Guide to Using the Coloured Progressive Matrices*. London: H. K. Lewis, 1965.

————. "Raven's Coloured Progressive Matrices." New York: Psychological Corp., 1956, 1962.

Rayder, Nicholas F.; Ng, Pierina; and Rhodes, Anne. *Implementation of the Responsive Program: A Report on Four Communities*. San Francisco: Far West Laboratory for Educational Research and Development, 1971.

————. "Research on the Responsive Model Childhood Educational Program," *California Journal of Educational Research* 22 (1972).

Stallings, Jane A. *Follow Through Program Classroom Observation Evaluation 1971-1972*. Menlo Park, Calif.: Stanford Research Institute, 1973. ERIC Accession No. ED 085 100.

Stallings, Jane A., and Kaskowitz, David. *Follow Through Classroom Observation Evaluation 1972-1973*. SRI Project URU-7370. Menlo Park, Calif.: Stanford Research Institute, 1974. ERIC Accession No. ED 104 969.

1

Who	To Whom	What	How
Ⓡ Ⓣ Ⓐ Ⓥ	● Ⓐ Ⓥ	① ② ③ ④ ●	Ⓗ Ⓤ Ⓝ Ⓣ
Ⓢ ● Ⓓ ②	Ⓒ Ⓓ ②	⑥ ⑦ ⑧ ⑨ ⑩	Ⓠ Ⓖ Ⓟ
Ⓒ Ⓢ Ⓛ ⒶⓃ Ⓜ	Ⓢ Ⓛ ⒶⓃ Ⓜ	⑪ ⑫	ⓃⓋ ⓧ Ⓞ Ⓦ ⓄⓅ Ⓐ Ⓑ

2

Who	To Whom	What	How
Ⓡ ● Ⓐ Ⓥ	Ⓣ Ⓐ Ⓥ	① ● ③ ④ ⑤	Ⓗ Ⓤ Ⓝ Ⓣ
Ⓢ Ⓒ Ⓓ ②	● Ⓓ ②	⑥ ⑦ ⑧ ⑨ ⑩	Ⓠ Ⓖ Ⓟ
Ⓒ Ⓢ Ⓛ ⒶⓃ Ⓜ	Ⓢ Ⓛ ⒶⓃ Ⓜ	⑪ ⑫	ⓃⓋ ⓧ Ⓞ Ⓦ ⓄⓅ Ⓐ Ⓑ

3

Who	To Whom	What	How
Ⓡ Ⓣ Ⓐ Ⓥ	● Ⓐ Ⓥ	① ② ● ④ ⑤ ●	Ⓤ Ⓝ Ⓣ
Ⓢ ● Ⓓ ②	Ⓒ Ⓓ ②	⑥ ⑦ ⑧ ⑨ ⑩	Ⓠ Ⓖ Ⓟ
Ⓒ Ⓢ Ⓛ ⒶⓃ Ⓜ	Ⓢ Ⓛ ⒶⓃ Ⓜ	⑪ ⑫	ⓃⓋ ⓧ Ⓞ Ⓦ ⓄⓅ Ⓐ Ⓑ

4

Who	To Whom	What	How
Ⓡ ● Ⓐ Ⓥ	Ⓣ Ⓐ Ⓥ	① ● ③ ④ ⑤	Ⓗ Ⓤ Ⓝ Ⓣ
Ⓢ Ⓒ Ⓓ ②	● Ⓓ ②	⑥ ⑦ ⑧ ⑨ ⑩	Ⓠ Ⓖ Ⓟ
Ⓒ Ⓢ Ⓛ ⒶⓃ Ⓜ	Ⓢ Ⓛ ⒶⓃ Ⓜ	⑪ ⑫	ⓃⓋ ⓧ Ⓞ Ⓦ ⓄⓅ Ⓐ Ⓑ

5

Who	To Whom	What	How
Ⓡ Ⓣ Ⓐ Ⓥ	● Ⓐ Ⓥ	① ② ● ④ ⑤ ●	Ⓤ Ⓝ Ⓣ
Ⓢ ● Ⓓ ②	Ⓒ Ⓓ ②	⑥ ⑦ ⑧ ⑨ ⑩	Ⓠ Ⓖ Ⓟ
Ⓒ Ⓢ Ⓛ ⒶⓃ Ⓜ	Ⓢ Ⓛ ⒶⓃ Ⓜ	⑪ ⑫	ⓃⓋ ⓧ Ⓞ Ⓦ ⓄⓅ Ⓐ Ⓑ

6

Who	To Whom	What	How
Ⓡ ● Ⓐ Ⓥ	Ⓣ Ⓐ Ⓥ	① ● ③ ④ ⑤	Ⓗ Ⓤ Ⓝ Ⓣ
Ⓢ Ⓒ Ⓓ ②	● Ⓓ ②	⑥ ⑦ ⑧ ⑨ ⑩	Ⓠ Ⓖ Ⓟ
Ⓒ Ⓢ Ⓛ ⒶⓃ Ⓜ	Ⓢ Ⓛ ⒶⓃ Ⓜ	⑪ ⑫	ⓃⓋ ⓧ Ⓞ Ⓦ ⓄⓅ Ⓐ Ⓑ

7

Who	To Whom	What	How
Ⓡ Ⓣ Ⓐ Ⓥ	● Ⓐ Ⓥ	① ② ● ④ ⑤	Ⓗ Ⓤ Ⓝ Ⓣ
Ⓢ ● Ⓓ ②	Ⓒ Ⓓ ②	⑥ ⑦ ⑧ ⑨ ⑩	Ⓠ Ⓖ Ⓟ
Ⓒ Ⓢ Ⓛ ⒶⓃ Ⓜ	Ⓢ Ⓛ ⒶⓃ Ⓜ	⑪ ⑫	ⓃⓋ ⓧ Ⓞ Ⓦ ⓄⓅ Ⓐ Ⓑ

8

Who	To Whom	What	How
Ⓡ Ⓣ Ⓐ Ⓥ	● Ⓐ Ⓥ	① ② ③ ● ⑤	Ⓗ Ⓤ Ⓝ Ⓣ
Ⓢ ● Ⓓ ②	Ⓒ Ⓓ ②	⑥ ⑦ ⑧ ⑨ ⑩	Ⓠ Ⓖ Ⓟ
Ⓒ Ⓢ Ⓛ ⒶⓃ Ⓜ	Ⓢ Ⓛ ⒶⓃ Ⓜ	⑪ ⑫	ⓃⓋ ⓧ Ⓞ Ⓦ ⓄⓅ Ⓐ Ⓑ

CLASSROOM CHECK LIST (be sure to code **EVERYONE** in the class)

		ONE CHILD	TWO CHILDREN	SMALL GROUPS	LARGE GROUPS
1. Snack, lunch		T ①②③ / A ①②③ / v ①②③ / i ①②③	T ①②③ / A ①②③ / v ①②③ / i ①②③	T ①②③④ / A ①②③④ / v ①②③④ / i ①②③④	T ①② / A ①② / v ①② / i ①②
2. Group time		T ①②③ / A ①②③ / v ①②③ / i ①②③	T ①②③ / A ①②③ / v ①②③ / i ①②③	T ①②③④ / A ①②③④ / v ①②③④ / i ①②③④	T ①② / A ①② / v ①② / i ①②
3. Music	Story / Dancing	T ①②③ / A ①②③ / v ①②③ / i ①②③	T ①②③ / A ①②③ / v ①②③ / i ①②③	T ①②③④ / A ①②③④ / v ①②③④ / i ①②③④	T ①② / A ①② / v ①② / i ①②
4. Arts, Crafts		T ①②③ / A ①②③ / v ①②③ / i ①●③	T ①②③ / A ①②③ / v ①②③ / i ①②③	T ①②③④ / A ①②③④ / v ①②③④ / i ①②③④	T ①② / A ①② / v ①② / i ①②
5. Table Games	Guessing Games / Puzzles	T ①②③ / A ①②③ / v ①②③ / i ①②③	T ①②③ / A ①②③ / v ①②③ / i ①②③	T ①②③④ / A ①②③④ / v ①②③④ / i ①②③④	T ①② / A ①② / v ①② / i ①②
6. Math	Numbers / Arithmetic	T ①②③ / A ①②③ / v ①②③ / i ①②③	T ①②③ / A ①②③ / v ①②③ / i ①②③	T ●②③④ / A ①②③④ / v ①②③④ / i ①②③④	T ①② / A ①② / v ①② / i ①②
7. Alphabet	Reading / Lang. Development	T ①②③ / A ●②③ / v ●②③ / i ①②③	T ①②③ / A ①②③ / v ①②③ / i ①②③	T ①②③④ / A ①②③④ / v ①②③④ / i ●●③④	T ①② / A ①② / v ①② / i ①②
8. Geography	Social Studies	T ①②③ / A ①②③ / v ①②③ / i ①②③	T ①②③ / A ①②③ / v ①②③ / i ①②③	T ①②③④ / A ①②③④ / v ①②③④ / i ①②③④	T ①② / A ①② / v ①② / i ①②
9.	Science / Natural World	T ①②③ / A ①②③ / v ①②③ / i ①②③	T ①②③ / A ①②③ / v ①②③ / i ①②③	T ①②③④ / A ①②③④ / v ①②③④ / i ①②③④	T ①② / A ①② / v ①② / i ①②
10.	Sewing / Cooking / Pounding / Sawing	T ①②③ / A ①②③ / v ①②③ / i ①②③	T ①②③ / A ①②③ / v ①②③ / i ①②③	T ①②③④ / A ①②③④ / v ①②③④ / i ①②③④	T ①② / A ①② / v ①② / i ①②
11.	Blocks / Trucks	T ①②③ / A ①②③ / v ①②③ / i ①②③	T ①②③ / A ①②③ / v ①②③ / i ①②③	T ①②③④ / A ①②③④ / v ①②③④ / i ①②③④	T ①② / A ①② / v ①② / i ①②
12.	Dramatic Play / Dress-Up	T ①②③ / A ①②③ / v ①②③ / i ①②③	T ①②③ / A ①②③ / v ①②③ / i ①②③	T ①②③④ / A ①②③④ / v ①②③④ / i ①②③④	T ①② / A ①② / v ①② / i ①②
13. Active Play		T ①②③ / A ①②③ / v ①②③ / i ①②③	T ①②③ / A ①②③ / v ①②③ / i ①②③	T ①②③④ / A ①②③④ / v ①②③④ / i ①②③④	T ①② / A ①② / v ①② / i ①②
14. RELIABILITY SHEET	○				

Legend (left of items 6–9):
- ○ TV
- ● Audio-Visual Materials
- ○ Exploratory Materials
- ● Math and Science Equipment
- ○ Texts, Workbooks
- ○ Puzzles, Games

					ONE CHILD	TWO CHILDREN	SMALL GROUPS	LARGE GROUPS
				T	① ② ③	① ② ③	① ② ③ ④	① ②
15. Practical Skills Acquisition				A	① ② ③	① ② ③	① ② ③ ④	① ②
				V	① ② ③	① ② ③	① ② ③ ④	① ②
				i	① ② ③	① ② ③	① ② ③ ④	① ②
				T	① ② ③	① ② ③	① ② ③ ④	① ②
16. Observing				A	① ② ③	① ② ③	① ② ③ ④	① ②
				V	① ② ③	① ② ③	① ② ③ ④	① ②
				i	① ② ③	① ② ③	① ② ③ ④	① ②
	Ob	ⓒ ② ⓢ	Ⓣ	T	① ② ③	① ② ③	① ② ③ ④	① ②
17. Social Interaction			Ⓐ	A	① ② ③	① ② ③	① ② ③ ④	① ②
			Ⓥ	V	① ② ③	① ② ③	① ② ③ ④	① ②
				i	① ② ③	① ② ③	① ② ③ ④	① ②
				T	① ② ③	① ② ③	① ② ③ ④	① ②
18. Unoccupied Child				A	① ② ③	① ② ③	① ② ③ ④	① ②
				V	① ② ③	① ② ③	① ② ③ ④	① ②
				i	① ② ③	① ② ③	① ② ③ ④	① ②
				T	① ② ③	① ② ③	① ② ③ ④	① ②
19. Discipline				A	① ② ③	① ② ③	① ② ③ ④	① ②
				V	① ② ③	① ② ③	① ② ③ ④	① ②
				i	① ② ③	① ② ③	① ② ③ ④	① ②
			Ⓣ	T	① ② ③	① ② ③	① ② ③ ④	① ②
20. Transitional Activities			Ⓐ	A	① ② ③	① ② ③	① ② ③ ④	① ②
			Ⓥ	V	① ② ③	① ② ③	① ② ③ ④	① ②
				i	① ② ③	① ② ③	① ② ③ ④	① ②
			Ⓣ	T	① ② ③	① ② ③	① ② ③ ④	① ②
21. Classroom Management			Ⓐ	A	① ② ③	① ② ③	① ② ③ ④	① ②
			Ⓥ	V	① ② ③	① ② ③	① ② ③ ④	① ②
				i	① ② ③	① ② ③	① ② ③ ④	① ②
			Ⓣ	T	① ② ③	① ② ③	① ② ③ ④	① ②
22. Out of Room			Ⓐ	A	① ② ③	① ② ③	① ② ③ ④	① ②
			Ⓥ	V	① ② ③	① ② ③	① ② ③ ④	① ②
				i	① ② ③	① ② ③	① ② ③ ④	① ②

NUMBER OF ADULTS IN CLASSROOM ⓪ ① ② ③ ④ ⑤ ⑥ ⑦ ⑧ ⑨ ⑩

Chapter 5

Group Process Model

Situation: A meeting of the second-grade class is called by Angela just before the noon recess.

1. Angela: This room is too noisy, I can't read!

2. Sarah: Well, you help make the noise. You talk and talk to Christine.

3. Angela: Not all the time!

4. Mike: I think it's too noisy, too.

5. Julie: Yeah, some of us want it quieter.

6. Billy: Some of us were just reading out loud to our partner. We weren't goofing off.

7. Mike: Well, that still makes noise.

8. Billy: But, we need to practice reading.

9. Mike: You can do it some other place.

10. Billy: Where?

11. Angela: Maybe in the book room or right outside the glass door.

12. Billy: Can we read outside, Ms. Klein?

13. Ms. Klein: You can read outside if you read quietly and do not disturb the children next door.

14. Mario: What if it rains?

15. Julie: Yes, I think the book room is best. Behind the bookcases no one could hear you.

16. Billy: Well, Betty and me are reading outside. Ms. Klein said we could.

17. David: Mario and I will read in the back room.

18. Angela: Good, then it will be quiet in here.

19. Sarah: Yeah, if you didn't talk.

20. Julie: She won't. She's the one who called this meeting about being quiet.

This vignette is coded on Figure 5.1. Each child who contributes to the discussion is speaking to the total group. This is coded CL6, a task-related statement to the large group. DL6 indicates that a different child has made a task-related statement to the large group. Sarah's personal critical statements to Angela are coded DC9NB since she is criticizing Angela's behavior in a negative way.

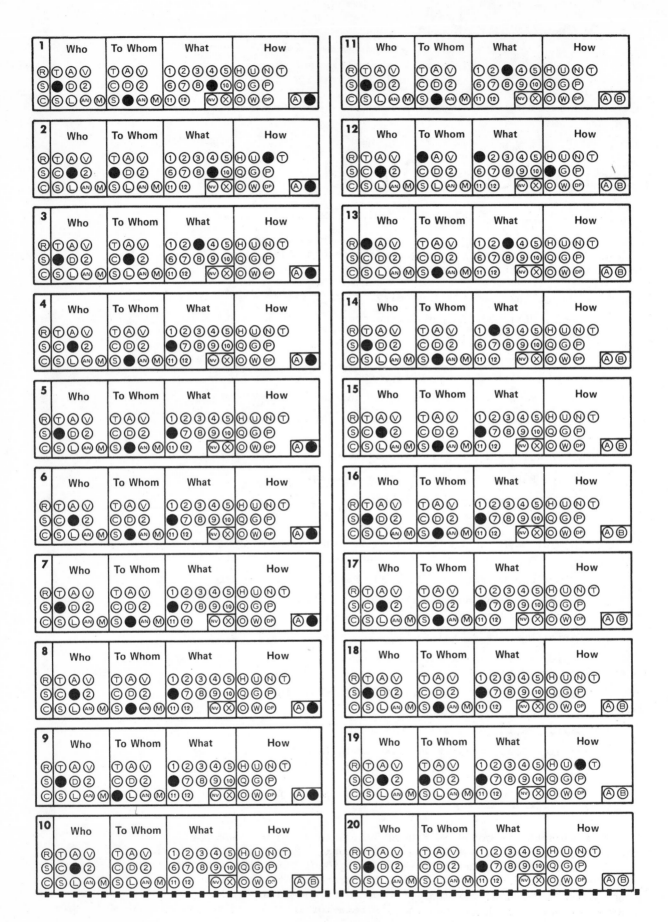

Figure 5.1

EDUCATIONAL THEORY AND EXPECTED CHILD DEVELOPMENT

This discussion took place in an open education classroom where
the Group Process Model is used. These are twenty-five second-grade
children who are two months into the school year. The Group Process
Model is based on field theory formulated by Lewin.[1] Field theory
states that behavior is the function of the present life space, and
learning is a change in the way of perceiving events. The change in
how we perceive events is brought about by experiences. The concept
of "wholeness" of the learning situation is central to this theory.
"Wholeness" means that all of the cognitive, emotional, and physical
input a person receives affects learning.

To learn, an organism must interact with others. For this
reason, provision for group work and interaction, such as discussion, is an important element of curriculum planning. Individual differences are crucial. Because each individual has a
unique sequence of experiences and therefore selects different
stimuli to respond to and organizes his responses differently
from every other individual, provision for idiosyncratic responses is essential in curriculum planning. Each current experience is colored by and so can build on the preceding ones.
This continuity of learning is essential to maturing; therefore, a curriculum is effective to the extent that it incorpo-
rates the idea of cumulative learning and plans for accumula-
tive sequences of learning.[2]

The Group Process Model has many of the components of William
Glasser's Classroom Meeting Model, described in *Schools Without
Failure*.[3] Glasser's model is based on the three basic constructs of
his Reality Therapy: reality, responsibility, and right.[4] Glasser
believes that performance is raised and basic needs such as love and
self-worth are met by doing what's real, responsible, and right. He
defines reality as what is relevant right now, and responsibility as
the ability to fulfill one's needs in a way that does not deprive
others of their ability to fulfill their needs. Glasser does not
back away from moral issues as do many theorists and educators.
Glasser feels that conforming to societal standards of behavior is
related to a person's feelings of self-worth. Persons who do not do
"right" according to societal standards—who cheat, lie, steal, hurt
other people—are not likely to have good feelings of self-worth.

How Glasser's ideas are put into practice in a social problem-
solving meeting is described by Joyce and Weil:

Education for social responsibility involves thinking,
problem-solving, and decision-making, as individuals and
groups, about subjects of concern to the students. This can be

---

[1]Kurt Lewin, "Lewin's Field Theory," in *Theories of Person-
ality: Primary Sources and Research*, eds. Gardner Lindzey and Calvin
S. Hall (New York: John Wiley and Sons, 1970).
[2]Hilda Taba, *Curriculum Development: Theory and Practice* (New
York: Harcourt Brace Jovanovich, 1962), p. 82.
[3]William Glasser, *Schools Without Failure* (New York: Harper &
Row, 1969).
[4]William Glasser, *Reality Therapy* (New York: Harper & Row,
1965).

accomplished through the mechanism of the daily (preferably), open-ended, non-judgmental Classroom Meeting in which students and/or teacher can introduce for discussion behavioral problems, personal problems, or academic or curriculum issues. . . . The Social Problem-Solving Meeting usually concerns itself with behavioral and social problems. However, other possible subjects include friendship, loneliness, vocational choice, etc. Students attempt to share the responsibility for learning and behaving by resolving their problems within the classroom. The orientation of the meeting is always positive, that is, toward a solution rather than fault-finding. Obviously many problems don't have a single answer. For example, in the case of coping with a "bully," the solution is often in the discussion itself, which serves to decrease the intimidation of. other students and increase their strength. If this is the case, further discussion of the "bully" should be avoided unless he does something constructive. In Glasser's opinion, the whole disciplinary structure of the school should revolve around the Classroom Meeting.[5]

Theoretically, children in the Group Process Model could be expected to develop an ability to govern themselves and express their ideas and feelings. They would listen to the ideas of other people and judge the merit of the ideas. Members of the group would generate several solutions to problems, and through discussion foresee consequences of possible actions. Because they learn to listen to each other, the children would develop empathy for others (the ability to put themselves in another's shoes). Because they deal fairly with each other, they would feel self-worth and would gain experience in giving and receiving love.

TEACHER RESPONSIBILITIES

Teachers in the Group Process Model must value the benefits children gain from the group process and devote a portion of each day to group meetings. These should be scheduled for a regular time but allowed to occur as needed to solve immediate problems. Also, teachers must be willing to risk not always being in control of these meetings. They must sometimes allow events to take their course and allow children to experience and express their feelings of loneliness, frustration, anger, fear, and joy.

It is important that teachers in this model allow children to role-play and learn leadership skills. For example, the teacher may read a story with a moral dilemma and stop before the end, asking, "What happens next?" The children are asked to offer endings to the story. Several solutions are always possible. In one of Fannie and George Shaftel's stories,[6] a group of children can win a paper drive contest if they place pieces of metal inside their paper stacks so the stacks will weigh more. Some feel justified in doing this because they hear their competition from another school is wetting the inside papers. Other children feel guilty at winning unfairly. At

---

[5]Bruce Joyce and Marsha Weil, *Models of Teaching* (Englewood Cliffs, N.J.: Prentice-Hall, 1972), p. 227.

[6]Fannie R. Shaftel and George Shaftel, *Role-Playing for Social Values: Decision-Making in the Social Studies* (Englewood Cliffs, N.J.: Prentice-Hall, 1967).

this point, the teacher stops and asks, "What should happen next?" Children who offer a solution are asked to role-play the ending of the story as they see it. At the completion, the teacher asks, "How did you feel playing the bully? or the cheater? or the fair play guy? or the person being cheated?" The children share their feelings about the roles they were playing and most likely suggest other solutions. Fannie and George Shaftel's *Role Playing for Social Values*[7] offers many unfinished problem stories and a step-by-step procedure for conducting role-playing sessions.

Another book that will be useful to teachers interested in the Group Process Model is *The Child Within the Group* by Marion E. Turner.[8] Turner offers a detailed account of the growth and development of several children as recorded while they were taking part in the group process. The reader is also guided to the case studies of Frank in Chapter 1 and Marcy in Appendix D for illustrations of how the group process helped reveal the emotional, social, and cognitive development of children.

Teachers must gain an in-depth knowledge of the children in their group in order to guide the discussions appropriately. They must be willing to listen to children, encourage them to express ideas, and, in general, allow them every opportunity to interact and solve personal and classroom problems.

One technique for gaining knowledge early in the year will also help identify isolates in the class. On a questionnaire, the children are asked:

1. Who are two children you would like to sit by?

2. Who would make a good leader of group meetings?

3. Who are four people you like to play with most?

Children not selected in the third question are most likely isolated in the group. These children can be worked into it slowly by asking their opinion or asking them to play a role in some problem story.

The group process is a means of managing the classroom. In the vignette on page 89 the children arrived at a solution to get a quieter room during the reading period. The following vignette illustrates how children can guide curriculum activities.

EXERCISE 5.1   Code the following vignette.

Situation: A third-grade group of children are discussing their social studies project.

1. Student Chairperson: "Does anyone have anything they want to talk about today for the Bay Project?"

1	Who	To Whom	What	How
	Ⓡ Ⓣ Ⓐ Ⓥ	Ⓣ Ⓐ Ⓥ	① ② ③ ④ ⑤ Ⓗ Ⓤ Ⓝ Ⓣ	
	Ⓢ Ⓒ Ⓓ ②	Ⓒ Ⓓ ②	⑥ ⑦ ⑧ ⑨ ⑩ Ⓠ Ⓖ Ⓟ	
	Ⓒ Ⓢ Ⓛ ⒜ Ⓜ	Ⓢ Ⓛ ⒜ Ⓜ	⑪ ⑫ Ⓝⓥ Ⓧ Ⓞ Ⓦ ⒹⓅ Ⓐ Ⓑ	

---

[7]Fannie R. Shaftel and George Shaftel, *Role-Playing for Social Values: Decision-Making in the Social Studies* (Englewood Cliffs, N.J.: Prentice-Hall, 1967).

[8]Marion E. Turner, *The Child Within the Group: An Experiment in Self-Government* (Stanford, Calif.: Stanford University Press, 1957).

2. Eugene: "I read that Indians used to put sticks in the mud flats on the bay and that when the water was down, they collected the sticks that were covered with salt."

2	Who	To Whom	What	How
	R T A V	T A V	1 2 3 4 5	H U N T
	S C D 2	C D 2	6 7 8 9 10	Q G P
	C S L AN M	S L AN M	11 12 NV X O W DP	A B

3. Julie: "I've been on a salt ship in Redwood City."

3	Who	To Whom	What	How
	R T A V	T A V	1 2 3 4 5	H U N T
	S C D 2	C D 2	6 7 8 9 10	Q G P
	C S L AN M	S L AN M	11 12 NV X O W DP	A B

4. Susan: "I've seen the salt flats where you go across the Dumbarton Bridge."

4	Who	To Whom	What	How
	R T A V	T A V	1 2 3 4 5	H U N T
	S C D 2	C D 2	6 7 8 9 10	Q G P
	C S L AN M	S L AN M	11 12 NV X O W DP	A B

5. Carla: "Some day we could go to the San Francisco Fun House. I like the slides."

5	Who	To Whom	What	How
	R T A V	T A V	1 2 3 4 5	H U N T
	S C D 2	C D 2	6 7 8 9 10	Q G P
	C S L AN M	S L AN M	11 12 NV X O W DP	A B

6. Eugene: "That's not what we're talking about, Carla. We're talking about salt."

6	Who	To Whom	What	How
	R T A V	T A V	1 2 3 4 5	H U N T
	S C D 2	C D 2	6 7 8 9 10	Q G P
	C S L AN M	S L AN M	11 12 NV X O W DP	A B

7. Chairperson: "Anybody have more to say about salt?"

7	Who	To Whom	What	How
	R T A V	T A V	1 2 3 4 5	H U N T
	S C D 2	C D 2	6 7 8 9 10	Q G P
	C S L AN M	S L AN M	11 12 NV X O W DP	A B

8. Eugene: "Let's see if we can get salt like the Indians did."

8	Who	To Whom	What	How
	R T A V	T A V	1 2 3 4 5	H U N T
	S C D 2	C D 2	6 7 8 9 10	Q G P
	C S L AN M	S L AN M	11 12 NV X O W DP	A B

9. Dale: "Yeah, we could put sticks with our names on them in the mud by the duck pond. That's all salt water around there."

9	Who	To Whom	What	How
	R T A V	T A V	1 2 3 4 5	H U N T
	S C D 2	C D 2	6 7 8 9 10	Q G P
	C S L AN M	S L AN M	11 12 NV X O W DP	A B

10. Chairperson: "How many want to do that?" (Ten hands go up.)

10	Who	To Whom	What	How
	R T A V	T A V	1 2 3 4 5	H U N T
	S C D 2	C D 2	6 7 8 9 10	Q G P
	C S L AN M	S L AN M	11 12 NV X O W DP	A B

11. Teacher: "Would you want to see if Monty, the science teacher, can take you in his van?"

11	Who	To Whom	What	How
	R T A V	T A V	1 2 3 4 5	H U N T
	S C D 2	C D 2	6 7 8 9 10	Q G P
	C S L AN M	S L AN M	11 12 NV X O W DP	A B

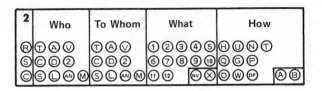

12. Children: (Nod yes.)

12	Who	To Whom	What	How
	R T A V	T A V	1 2 3 4 5	H U N T
	S C D 2	C D 2	6 7 8 9 10	Q G P
	C S L AN M	S L AN M	11 12	NV X O W DP	A B

13. Susan: "I would like to see inside that big salt factory by the bridge."

13	Who	To Whom	What	How
	R T A V	T A V	1 2 3 4 5	H U N T
	S C D 2	C D 2	6 7 8 9 10	Q G P
	C S L AN M	S L AN M	11 12	NV X O W DP	A B

14. Julia: "Yeah, how do they make salt white? It looks all gray and greenish by the bridge."

14	Who	To Whom	What	How
	R T A V	T A V	1 2 3 4 5	H U N T
	S C D 2	C D 2	6 7 8 9 10	Q G P
	C S L AN M	S L AN M	11 12	NV X O W DP	A B

15. Chairperson: "How many want to go to the salt factory?" (All hands go up.)

15	Who	To Whom	What	How
	R T A V	T A V	1 2 3 4 5	H U N T
	S C D 2	C D 2	6 7 8 9 10	Q G P
	C S L AN M	S L AN M	11 12	NV X O W DP	A B

16. Teacher: "That sounds like a good trip. We have time to go on Friday, if they will let us visit then. I'll call at recess."

16	Who	To Whom	What	How
	R T A V	T A V	1 2 3 4 5	H U N T
	S C D 2	C D 2	6 7 8 9 10	Q G P
	C S L AN M	S L AN M	11 12	NV X O W DP	A B

17. Teacher: "Let's each make a list of all the things we want to find out."

17	Who	To Whom	What	How
	R T A V	T A V	1 2 3 4 5	H U N T
	S C D 2	C D 2	6 7 8 9 10	Q G P
	C S L AN M	S L AN M	11 12	NV X O W DP	A B

18. Children: (Take out paper for writing the list.)

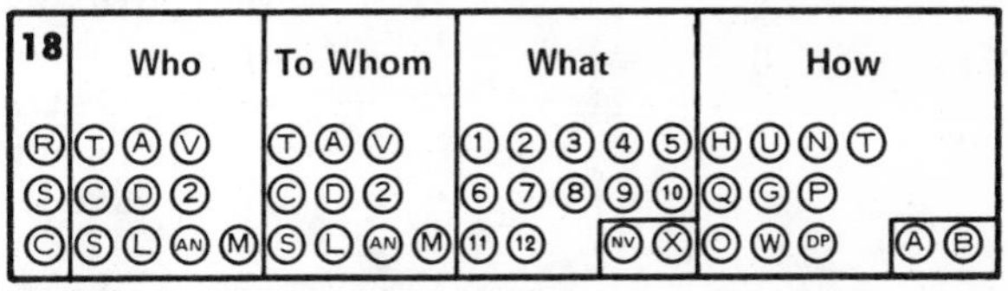

18	Who	To Whom	What	How
	R T A V	T A V	1 2 3 4 5	H U N T
	S C D 2	C D 2	6 7 8 9 10	Q G P
	C S L AN M	S L AN M	11 12	NV X O W DP	A B

19. Teacher: "Tonight ask if your parents would like to go with us. We'll need a few more drivers to take all of us."

19	Who	To Whom	What	How
	R T A V	T A V	1 2 3 4 5	H U N T
	S C D 2	C D 2	6 7 8 9 10	Q G P
	C S L AN M	S L AN M	11 12	NV X O W DP	A B

20. Max: "My mom can go."

20	Who	To Whom	What	How
	R T A V	T A V	1 2 3 4 5	H U N T
	S C D 2	C D 2	6 7 8 9 10	Q G P
	C S L AN M	S L AN M	11 12	NV X O W DP	A B

Each child who contributes to the discussion is speaking to the total group, so these interactions are coded CL6, task-related statements made to the large group. DL6 indicates that a different child has made a task-related statement to the total group. In this vignette one child corrects another child who gets off the subject (DC9B). Other answers are at the end of the chapter.

SCHEDULE

The following is a typical schedule for a second-grade class using the Group Process Model.

8:00 Teacher finishes preparing reading and math lessons for individuals. Children enter room and read, talk, or work at science table.

8:30 Chairperson calls meeting to order.

8:35 Roll chairperson takes roll. Chairperson asks for items to be discussed; secretary writes these on the board. Items can be suggestions for study, social events, outings; personal or group problems, or role playing.

9:30 Reading—each child has a reading program. Two or three children might be reading in the same book; they may sometimes read aloud to each other or work with a teacher. The teacher, assistant, and aide usually work with one or two children at a time. The teacher prepares written material for those having difficulty with reading. To increase motivation, the teacher uses subject matter of interest to the child. Reading problems are diagnosed weekly and the next week's lessons prepared.

10:30 Recess—children do not have to go outside. They may develop a play using available costumes or props. They may continue to read or some children may continue to work with a teacher on reading.

11:00 Handwriting—the teacher demonstrates how to form letters in cursive handwriting. Children practice from letters in copybooks.

11:10 Spelling—each child has a list to study that includes words the child misspelled in a story. A spelling workbook is also used.

11:20 Story writing—the teacher reads a short story or poem and points out how certain words create word pictures that can be seen in the mind. The children are asked to write a story that will give others mind pictures. The teacher and aides help children spell words in their stories and keep a spelling list for each child.

12:00 Lunch—children can eat inside or outside. After lunch, children can play in the room, making up dramatic plays, or working with exploratory materials, which are changed periodically so interest is kept high.

1:00 Math—verbal problems, requiring logic, are given to the whole group. Materials like Cuisenaire rods can be used to solve them. Children can make up problems for others to solve. They may also use programmed math books or materials prepared by the teacher.

2:00 Recess—children can be inside using science exploratory material if they wish.

2:30 Social studies and science activities—the children may join a group social studies unit, or work on individual projects. In one class, the group unit was a study of the San Francisco Bay. The children learned how the Costa Noan Indians had used the bay. They took trips to see the marshlands and salt flats, the shipping yards, and the fishing boats. The study was reflected in their art work, stories, and dramatic play. Out of this came an in-depth study of the Indians who had lived in this area.

3:30 Dismissal.

PHYSICAL ENVIRONMENT

Open space is important to a Group Process or any other open classroom model. Furniture must be movable—traditional desks and seats can be unbolted from the floor and moved as necessary. Closets might be converted to learning centers; a teacher's big desk might give way to a stage. (An open classroom teacher has little time to spend at his or her desk anyway.) Outdoor space, for climbing, digging, and planting seeds, is important also. The school gardener may welcome help in keeping a flower bed free from weeds and filled with growing things.

One open classroom teacher described her room in the following way:

From where I'm standing now, I can see out the large sliding glass doors into a child-filled sandbox. There are trees and bushes close around. I have the feeling of looking into a green and lively world (not well manicured, but alive). Beyond the sandbox is a twisty slide—a delight salvaged from a beer packing warehouse. The slide is about fifteen feet high and has three supporting poles to slide down. This structure serves as a space ship, monkey house, and is used for games of "Got you Last." Nearby are two tall trees in which houses were built, under the supervision of the school carpenter. Near the fence are excavations for cave houses and tunnels—also subject to inspection by the carpenter. Every construction is a lesson in math since the school carpenter is also a special math teacher. Some sixth-grade boys on the other side of the school yard have been constructing a geodesic dome with his help. Back of our building we have planted lettuce, spinach, and beans. I am told by the children that it takes too long for carrots; they wouldn't be ready before school is out. Beside the garden is an old-fashioned porch swing large enough for me and five children (two sitting on my lap). Here we sing songs, tell stories, and solve problems.

Inside, the room is arranged for our convenience. Each child has a desk for personal belongings. Desks are movable and we change their positions when we change activities. At present the room looks like this:

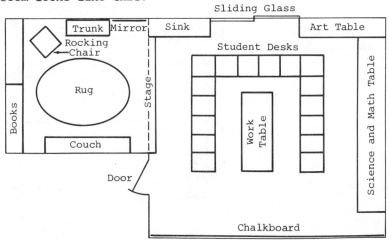

This arrangement is for activities such as reading, math, science, and social studies. If we want to dance, or have a play, we push all the furniture to one side. The backroom is a place where children read quietly or play quiet games during work times. At other times, it is the room where most of our dramatic productions are hatched. There is a large trunk filled with costumes and clothes, and a mirror where the children can examine their full effect. Children develop plays on their own. They evaluate and decide when they are ready for an audience. The audience is usually the carpenter, the principal, and the first grade next door. After each performance they give each other critical feedback aimed at making the next play better.

The room is dirtier than I would like it to be. But, with the sand and dirt right outside the door, it can't be kept very clean. The school maintenance committee considered putting asphalt in this area; it would be cleaner, but it also hurts more when a person falls down—and earth smells better. I guess I'll put up with the dirt. I think it is important for children to learn about their world through all the senses, including smell and touch—so it is important to provide a rich environment where they can experience water, earth, sky, height, and growing things in addition to materials usually found in classrooms.

INTERACTION PATTERNS

Within the Group Process Model, leadership is provided by the teacher, but the students also initiate discussions and find solutions to problems. The teacher elicits ideas during group meetings through open-ended questions, and thus must create a climate of openness where children can discuss freely and not feel defensive. The following exercise is an example of a group meeting interaction. The group has been having meetings each day to discuss projects and any problems that arise. Try doing the exercise now. The answers are at the end of the chapter.

EXERCISE 5.2   See if you can code these interactions. (Group discussions are coded CL6 or DL6.)

Situation: A group of second-grade students are discussing their group meetings.

1. Teacher: "How did you like the way Lee read the roll?"

2. Janet: "He read it clearly."

3. Nancy: "Lee told everyone to be quiet before
   he read the roll."

3	Who	To Whom	What	How
	Ⓡ Ⓣ Ⓐ Ⓥ	Ⓣ Ⓐ Ⓥ	① ② ③ ④ ⑤	Ⓗ Ⓤ Ⓝ Ⓣ
	Ⓢ Ⓒ Ⓓ ②	Ⓒ Ⓓ ②	⑥ ⑦ ⑧ ⑨ ⑩	Ⓠ Ⓖ Ⓟ
	Ⓒ Ⓢ Ⓛ ⒜ⓝ Ⓜ	Ⓢ Ⓛ ⒜ⓝ Ⓜ	⑪ ⑫	ⓃⓋ Ⓧ Ⓞ Ⓦ ⒹⓅ	Ⓐ Ⓑ

4. Hugh: "At the end he
   got silly, but he read
   it good."

4	Who	To Whom	What	How
	Ⓡ Ⓣ Ⓐ Ⓥ	Ⓣ Ⓐ Ⓥ	① ② ③ ④ ⑤	Ⓗ Ⓤ Ⓝ Ⓣ
	Ⓢ Ⓒ Ⓓ ②	Ⓒ Ⓓ ②	⑥ ⑦ ⑧ ⑨ ⑩	Ⓠ Ⓖ Ⓟ
	Ⓒ Ⓢ Ⓛ ⒜ⓝ Ⓜ	Ⓢ Ⓛ ⒜ⓝ Ⓜ	⑪ ⑫	ⓃⓋ Ⓧ Ⓞ Ⓦ ⒹⓅ	Ⓐ Ⓑ

5. Teacher: "Are there any
   other comments?"

5	Who	To Whom	What	How
	Ⓡ Ⓣ Ⓐ Ⓥ	Ⓣ Ⓐ Ⓥ	① ② ③ ④ ⑤	Ⓗ Ⓤ Ⓝ Ⓣ
	Ⓢ Ⓒ Ⓓ ②	Ⓒ Ⓓ ②	⑥ ⑦ ⑧ ⑨ ⑩	Ⓠ Ⓖ Ⓟ
	Ⓒ Ⓢ Ⓛ ⒜ⓝ Ⓜ	Ⓢ Ⓛ ⒜ⓝ Ⓜ	⑪ ⑫	ⓃⓋ Ⓧ Ⓞ Ⓦ ⒹⓅ	Ⓐ Ⓑ

6. Class: (No response)

6	Who	To Whom	What	How
	Ⓡ Ⓣ Ⓐ Ⓥ	Ⓣ Ⓐ Ⓥ	① ② ③ ④ ⑤	Ⓗ Ⓤ Ⓝ Ⓣ
	Ⓢ Ⓒ Ⓓ ②	Ⓒ Ⓓ ②	⑥ ⑦ ⑧ ⑨ ⑩	Ⓠ Ⓖ Ⓟ
	Ⓒ Ⓢ Ⓛ ⒜ⓝ Ⓜ	Ⓢ Ⓛ ⒜ⓝ Ⓜ	⑪ ⑫	ⓃⓋ Ⓧ Ⓞ Ⓦ ⒹⓅ	Ⓐ Ⓑ

7. Teacher: "You have been
   doing a good job of
   taking the roll this
   year."

7	Who	To Whom	What	How
	Ⓡ Ⓣ Ⓐ Ⓥ	Ⓣ Ⓐ Ⓥ	① ② ③ ④ ⑤	Ⓗ Ⓤ Ⓝ Ⓣ
	Ⓢ Ⓒ Ⓓ ②	Ⓒ Ⓓ ②	⑥ ⑦ ⑧ ⑨ ⑩	Ⓠ Ⓖ Ⓟ
	Ⓒ Ⓢ Ⓛ ⒜ⓝ Ⓜ	Ⓢ Ⓛ ⒜ⓝ Ⓜ	⑪ ⑫	ⓃⓋ Ⓧ Ⓞ Ⓦ ⒹⓅ	Ⓐ Ⓑ

8. Teacher: "Now I wonder
   if you might all like
   to have a chance to be
   the chairperson of our
   group meetings."

8	Who	To Whom	What	How
	Ⓡ Ⓣ Ⓐ Ⓥ	Ⓣ Ⓐ Ⓥ	① ② ③ ④ ⑤	Ⓗ Ⓤ Ⓝ Ⓣ
	Ⓢ Ⓒ Ⓓ ②	Ⓒ Ⓓ ②	⑥ ⑦ ⑧ ⑨ ⑩	Ⓠ Ⓖ Ⓟ
	Ⓒ Ⓢ Ⓛ ⒜ⓝ Ⓜ	Ⓢ Ⓛ ⒜ⓝ Ⓜ	⑪ ⑫	ⓃⓋ Ⓧ Ⓞ Ⓦ ⒹⓅ	Ⓐ Ⓑ

9. Class: "Yes!"

9	Who	To Whom	What	How
	Ⓡ Ⓣ Ⓐ Ⓥ	Ⓣ Ⓐ Ⓥ	① ② ③ ④ ⑤	Ⓗ Ⓤ Ⓝ Ⓣ
	Ⓢ Ⓒ Ⓓ ②	Ⓒ Ⓓ ②	⑥ ⑦ ⑧ ⑨ ⑩	Ⓠ Ⓖ Ⓟ
	Ⓒ Ⓢ Ⓛ ⒜ⓝ Ⓜ	Ⓢ Ⓛ ⒜ⓝ Ⓜ	⑪ ⑫	ⓃⓋ Ⓧ Ⓞ Ⓦ ⒹⓅ	Ⓐ Ⓑ

10. Hugh: "What is a chair-
    person?"

10	Who	To Whom	What	How
	Ⓡ Ⓣ Ⓐ Ⓥ	Ⓣ Ⓐ Ⓥ	① ② ③ ④ ⑤	Ⓗ Ⓤ Ⓝ Ⓣ
	Ⓢ Ⓒ Ⓓ ②	Ⓒ Ⓓ ②	⑥ ⑦ ⑧ ⑨ ⑩	Ⓠ Ⓖ Ⓟ
	Ⓒ Ⓢ Ⓛ ⒜ⓝ Ⓜ	Ⓢ Ⓛ ⒜ⓝ Ⓜ	⑪ ⑫	ⓃⓋ Ⓧ Ⓞ Ⓦ ⒹⓅ	Ⓐ Ⓑ

11. Lee: "The one who con-
    ducts meetings."

11	Who	To Whom	What	How
	Ⓡ Ⓣ Ⓐ Ⓥ	Ⓣ Ⓐ Ⓥ	① ② ③ ④ ⑤	Ⓗ Ⓤ Ⓝ Ⓣ
	Ⓢ Ⓒ Ⓓ ②	Ⓒ Ⓓ ②	⑥ ⑦ ⑧ ⑨ ⑩	Ⓠ Ⓖ Ⓟ
	Ⓒ Ⓢ Ⓛ ⒜ⓝ Ⓜ	Ⓢ Ⓛ ⒜ⓝ Ⓜ	⑪ ⑫	ⓃⓋ Ⓧ Ⓞ Ⓦ ⒹⓅ	Ⓐ Ⓑ

12. Teacher: "Who would
    like to be chair-
    person?"

12	Who	To Whom	What	How
	Ⓡ Ⓣ Ⓐ Ⓥ	Ⓣ Ⓐ Ⓥ	① ② ③ ④ ⑤	Ⓗ Ⓤ Ⓝ Ⓣ
	Ⓢ Ⓒ Ⓓ ②	Ⓒ Ⓓ ②	⑥ ⑦ ⑧ ⑨ ⑩	Ⓠ Ⓖ Ⓟ
	Ⓒ Ⓢ Ⓛ ⒜ⓝ Ⓜ	Ⓢ Ⓛ ⒜ⓝ Ⓜ	⑪ ⑫	ⓃⓋ Ⓧ Ⓞ Ⓦ ⒹⓅ	Ⓐ Ⓑ

13. Class: (Many hands go up.)

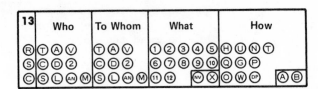

13	Who	To Whom	What	How
	R T A V	T A V	1 2 3 4 5	H U N T
	S C D 2	C D 2	6 7 8 9 10	Q G P
	C S L AN M	S L AN M	11 12 NV X	O W DP A B

14. Teacher: "How do we decide?"

14	Who	To Whom	What	How
	R T A V	T A V	1 2 3 4 5	H U N T
	S C D 2	C D 2	6 7 8 9 10	Q G P
	C S L AN M	S L AN M	11 12 NV X	O W DP A B

15. Lee: "Take a vote."

15	Who	To Whom	What	How
	R T A V	T A V	1 2 3 4 5	H U N T
	S C D 2	C D 2	6 7 8 9 10	Q G P
	C S L AN M	S L AN M	11 12 NV X	O W DP A B

16. Ralph: "I vote the same as Lee."

16	Who	To Whom	What	How
	R T A V	T A V	1 2 3 4 5	H U N T
	S C D 2	C D 2	6 7 8 9 10	Q G P
	C S L AN M	S L AN M	11 12 NV X	O W DP A B

17. Hugh: "Maybe everyone will vote for himself."

17	Who	To Whom	What	How
	R T A V	T A V	1 2 3 4 5	H U N T
	S C D 2	C D 2	6 7 8 9 10	Q G P
	C S L AN M	S L AN M	11 12 NV X	O W DP A B

18. Juanita: "Let's take turns."

18	Who	To Whom	What	How
	R T A V	T A V	1 2 3 4 5	H U N T
	S C D 2	C D 2	6 7 8 9 10	Q G P
	C S L AN M	S L AN M	11 12 NV X	O W DP A B

19. Lee: "That takes too long."

19	Who	To Whom	What	How
	R T A V	T A V	1 2 3 4 5	H U N T
	S C D 2	C D 2	6 7 8 9 10	Q G P
	C S L AN M	S L AN M	11 12 NV X	O W DP A B

20. Tony: "If we vote, maybe some people will get extra turns and some people won't get any turns."

20	Who	To Whom	What	How
	R T A V	T A V	1 2 3 4 5	H U N T
	S C D 2	C D 2	6 7 8 9 10	Q G P
	C S L AN M	S L AN M	11 12 NV X	O W DP A B

21. Wendy: "Let's take a vote on how to choose people."

21	Who	To Whom	What	How
	R T A V	T A V	1 2 3 4 5	H U N T
	S C D 2	C D 2	6 7 8 9 10	Q G P
	C S L AN M	S L AN M	11 12 NV X	O W DP A B

22. Alice: "We should pick people we can trust so we'll know that they'll do what we tell them and be fair."

22	Who	To Whom	What	How
	R T A V	T A V	1 2 3 4 5	H U N T
	S C D 2	C D 2	6 7 8 9 10	Q G P
	C S L AN M	S L AN M	11 12 NV X	O W DP A B

23. Marcy: "I'd like to go to the castle in the zoo."

23	Who	To Whom	What	How
	®ⓉⒶⓋ	ⓉⒶⓋ	①②③④⑤ⒽⓊⓃⓉ	
	ⓈⒸⒹ②	ⒸⒹ②	⑥⑦⑧⑨⑩ⓆⒼⓅ	
	ⒸⓈⓁⒶⓃⓂ	ⓈⓁⒶⓃⓂ	⑪⑫ ⓃⓥⓍⓄⓌⓄⓅ	ⒶⒺ

24. Beth: "We are not talking about that."

24	Who	To Whom	What	How
	®ⓉⒶⓋ	ⓉⒶⓋ	①②③④⑤ⒽⓊⓃⓉ	
	ⓈⒸⒹ②	ⒸⒹ②	⑥⑦⑧⑨⑩ⓆⒼⓅ	
	ⒸⓈⓁⒶⓃⓂ	ⓈⓁⒶⓃⓂ	⑪⑫ ⓃⓥⓍⓄⓌⓄⓅ	ⒶⒷ

25. Tony: "Juanita would make a good chairperson. She doesn't get into fights."

25	Who	To Whom	What	How
	®ⓉⒶⓋ	ⓉⒶⓋ	①②③④⑤ⒽⓊⓃⓉ	
	ⓈⒸⒹ②	ⒸⒹ②	⑥⑦⑧⑨⑩ⓆⒼⓅ	
	ⒸⓈⓁⒶⓃⓂ	ⓈⓁⒶⓃⓂ	⑪⑫ ⓃⓥⓍⓄⓌⓄⓅ	ⒶⒷ

26. Ralph: "Mike S. would be good. He doesn't cause trouble. He just does his regular work good. Both Mikes would make a good chairperson. They talk about problems. They don't just hit."

26	Who	To Whom	What	How
	®ⓉⒶⓋ	ⓉⒶⓋ	①②③④⑤ⒽⓊⓃⓉ	
	ⓈⒸⒹ②	ⒸⒹ②	⑥⑦⑧⑨⑩ⓆⒼⓅ	
	ⒸⓈⓁⒶⓃⓂ	ⓈⓁⒶⓃⓂ	⑪⑫ ⓃⓥⓍⓄⓌⓄⓅ	ⒶⒷ

27. Lee: "One thing that I don't like. They tackle each other. When Hugh tackles Mike K., Mike S. chases Hugh, too. Jane (teacher), you should be the chairperson." (Lee may be resisting the group because he has not yet been named, and he would enjoy the role of chairperson.)

27	Who	To Whom	What	How
	®ⓉⒶⓋ	ⓉⒶⓋ	①②③④⑤ⒽⓊⓃⓉ	
	ⓈⒸⒹ②	ⒸⒹ②	⑥⑦⑧⑨⑩ⓆⒼⓅ	
	ⒸⓈⓁⒶⓃⓂ	ⓈⓁⒶⓃⓂ	⑪⑫ ⓃⓥⓍⓄⓌⓄⓅ	ⒶⒷ

28. Mike S.: "That's dumb! What does chasing someone at recess have to do with being a good chairperson?"

28	Who	To Whom	What	How
	®ⓉⒶⓋ	ⓉⒶⓋ	①②③④⑤ⒽⓊⓃⓉ	
	ⓈⒸⒹ②	ⒸⒹ②	⑥⑦⑧⑨⑩ⓆⒼⓅ	
	ⒸⓈⓁⒶⓃⓂ	ⓈⓁⒶⓃⓂ	⑪⑫ ⓃⓥⓍⓄⓌⓄⓅ	ⒶⒷ

29. Lee: "A chairperson can't be silly. A chairperson would have to stop fights and start a meeting to talk about it. You know, help settle it."

29	Who	To Whom	What	How
	®ⓉⒶⓋ	ⓉⒶⓋ	①②③④⑤ⒽⓊⓃⓉ	
	ⓈⒸⒹ②	ⒸⒹ②	⑥⑦⑧⑨⑩ⓆⒼⓅ	
	ⒸⓈⓁⒶⓃⓂ	ⓈⓁⒶⓃⓂ	⑪⑫ ⓃⓥⓍⓄⓌⓄⓅ	ⒶⒷ

30. Frances: "The chairperson has to be fair."

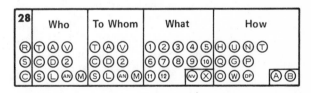

30	Who	To Whom	What	How
	®ⓉⒶⓋ	ⓉⒶⓋ	①②③④⑤ⒽⓊⓃⓉ	
	ⓈⒸⒹ②	ⒸⒹ②	⑥⑦⑧⑨⑩ⓆⒼⓅ	
	ⒸⓈⓁⒶⓃⓂ	ⓈⓁⒶⓃⓂ	⑪⑫ ⓃⓥⓍⓄⓌⓄⓅ	ⒶⒷ

31. Sam: "The chairperson has to be able to talk with someone. You know, like, go over and help if they are lonely."

31	Who	To Whom	What	How
	Ⓡ Ⓣ Ⓐ Ⓥ	Ⓣ Ⓐ Ⓥ	① ② ③ ④ ⑤	Ⓗ Ⓤ Ⓝ Ⓣ
	Ⓢ Ⓒ Ⓓ ②	Ⓒ Ⓓ ②	⑥ ⑦ ⑧ ⑨ ⑩	Ⓠ Ⓖ Ⓟ
	Ⓒ Ⓢ Ⓛ ⒶⓃ Ⓜ	Ⓢ Ⓛ ⒶⓃ Ⓜ	⑪ ⑫	ⓃⓋ Ⓧ Ⓞ Ⓦ ⒹⓅ Ⓐ Ⓑ

32. Lee: "Let's vote on whether to elect or take turns. I think it is more fair to take turns."

32	Who	To Whom	What	How
	Ⓡ Ⓣ Ⓐ Ⓥ	Ⓣ Ⓐ Ⓥ	① ② ③ ④ ⑤	Ⓗ Ⓤ Ⓝ Ⓣ
	Ⓢ Ⓒ Ⓓ ②	Ⓒ Ⓓ ②	⑥ ⑦ ⑧ ⑨ ⑩	Ⓠ Ⓖ Ⓟ
	Ⓒ Ⓢ Ⓛ ⒶⓃ Ⓜ	Ⓢ Ⓛ ⒶⓃ Ⓜ	⑪ ⑫	ⓃⓋ Ⓧ Ⓞ Ⓦ ⒹⓅ Ⓐ Ⓑ

33. Teacher: "Raise your hands if you want to take turns."

33	Who	To Whom	What	How
	Ⓡ Ⓣ Ⓐ Ⓥ	Ⓣ Ⓐ Ⓥ	① ② ③ ④ ⑤	Ⓗ Ⓤ Ⓝ Ⓣ
	Ⓢ Ⓒ Ⓓ ②	Ⓒ Ⓓ ②	⑥ ⑦ ⑧ ⑨ ⑩	Ⓠ Ⓖ Ⓟ
	Ⓒ Ⓢ Ⓛ ⒶⓃ Ⓜ	Ⓢ Ⓛ ⒶⓃ Ⓜ	⑪ ⑫	ⓃⓋ Ⓧ Ⓞ Ⓦ ⒹⓅ Ⓐ Ⓑ

34. Class: (Everyone votes for taking turns.)

34	Who	To Whom	What	How
	Ⓡ Ⓣ Ⓐ Ⓥ	Ⓣ Ⓐ Ⓥ	① ② ③ ④ ⑤	Ⓗ Ⓤ Ⓝ Ⓣ
	Ⓢ Ⓒ Ⓓ ②	Ⓒ Ⓓ ②	⑥ ⑦ ⑧ ⑨ ⑩	Ⓠ Ⓖ Ⓟ
	Ⓒ Ⓢ Ⓛ ⒶⓃ Ⓜ	Ⓢ Ⓛ ⒶⓃ Ⓜ	⑪ ⑫	ⓃⓋ Ⓧ Ⓞ Ⓦ ⒹⓅ Ⓐ Ⓑ

35. Teacher: "How long should one person be the chairperson? A week?"

35	Who	To Whom	What	How
	Ⓡ Ⓣ Ⓐ Ⓥ	Ⓣ Ⓐ Ⓥ	① ② ③ ④ ⑤	Ⓗ Ⓤ Ⓝ Ⓣ
	Ⓢ Ⓒ Ⓓ ②	Ⓒ Ⓓ ②	⑥ ⑦ ⑧ ⑨ ⑩	Ⓠ Ⓖ Ⓟ
	Ⓒ Ⓢ Ⓛ ⒶⓃ Ⓜ	Ⓢ Ⓛ ⒶⓃ Ⓜ	⑪ ⑫	ⓃⓋ Ⓧ Ⓞ Ⓦ ⒹⓅ Ⓐ Ⓑ

36. Lee: "A day. If it was a week, it would take too long to get your turn. Twenty weeks if you are the last one."

36	Who	To Whom	What	How
	Ⓡ Ⓣ Ⓐ Ⓥ	Ⓣ Ⓐ Ⓥ	① ② ③ ④ ⑤	Ⓗ Ⓤ Ⓝ Ⓣ
	Ⓢ Ⓒ Ⓓ ②	Ⓒ Ⓓ ②	⑥ ⑦ ⑧ ⑨ ⑩	Ⓠ Ⓖ Ⓟ
	Ⓒ Ⓢ Ⓛ ⒶⓃ Ⓜ	Ⓢ Ⓛ ⒶⓃ Ⓜ	⑪ ⑫	ⓃⓋ Ⓧ Ⓞ Ⓦ ⒹⓅ Ⓐ Ⓑ

37. Teacher: "If you think a person should be chairperson for a day, raise your hand."

37	Who	To Whom	What	How
	Ⓡ Ⓣ Ⓐ Ⓥ	Ⓣ Ⓐ Ⓥ	① ② ③ ④ ⑤	Ⓗ Ⓤ Ⓝ Ⓣ
	Ⓢ Ⓒ Ⓓ ②	Ⓒ Ⓓ ②	⑥ ⑦ ⑧ ⑨ ⑩	Ⓠ Ⓖ Ⓟ
	Ⓒ Ⓢ Ⓛ ⒶⓃ Ⓜ	Ⓢ Ⓛ ⒶⓃ Ⓜ	⑪ ⑫	ⓃⓋ Ⓧ Ⓞ Ⓦ ⒹⓅ Ⓐ Ⓑ

38. Class: (Over one half raise their hands.)

38	Who	To Whom	What	How
	Ⓡ Ⓣ Ⓐ Ⓥ	Ⓣ Ⓐ Ⓥ	① ② ③ ④ ⑤	Ⓗ Ⓤ Ⓝ Ⓣ
	Ⓢ Ⓒ Ⓓ ②	Ⓒ Ⓓ ②	⑥ ⑦ ⑧ ⑨ ⑩	Ⓠ Ⓖ Ⓟ
	Ⓒ Ⓢ Ⓛ ⒶⓃ Ⓜ	Ⓢ Ⓛ ⒶⓃ Ⓜ	⑪ ⑫	ⓃⓋ Ⓧ Ⓞ Ⓦ ⒹⓅ Ⓐ Ⓑ

39. Juanita: "Let's start from this side. The roll chairperson started from the other side."

39	Who	To Whom	What	How
	Ⓡ Ⓣ Ⓐ Ⓥ	Ⓣ Ⓐ Ⓥ	① ② ③ ④ ⑤	Ⓗ Ⓤ Ⓝ Ⓣ
	Ⓢ Ⓒ Ⓓ ②	Ⓒ Ⓓ ②	⑥ ⑦ ⑧ ⑨ ⑩	Ⓠ Ⓖ Ⓟ
	Ⓒ Ⓢ Ⓛ ⒶⓃ Ⓜ	Ⓢ Ⓛ ⒶⓃ Ⓜ	⑪ ⑫	ⓃⓋ Ⓧ Ⓞ Ⓦ ⒹⓅ Ⓐ Ⓑ

40. Teacher: "How many agree with Juanita's idea?"

40	Who	To Whom	What	How
	Ⓡ Ⓣ Ⓐ Ⓥ	Ⓣ Ⓐ Ⓥ	① ② ③ ④ ⑤	Ⓗ Ⓤ Ⓝ Ⓣ
	Ⓢ Ⓒ Ⓓ ②	Ⓒ Ⓓ ②	⑥ ⑦ ⑧ ⑨ ⑩	Ⓠ Ⓖ Ⓟ
	Ⓒ Ⓢ Ⓛ ⒶⓃ Ⓜ	Ⓢ Ⓛ ⒶⓃ Ⓜ	⑪ ⑫ ⓃⓋ Ⓧ	Ⓞ Ⓦ ⒹⓅ / Ⓐ Ⓑ

One pitfall for teachers implementing this model is the tendency to interfere in the group process before the children get really involved in it. In the preceding exercise, the teacher, in frame 35, starts to solve the problem instead of turning the problem back to the children to discuss and resolve.

HANDLING MISBEHAVIOR

Elizabeth comes into the classroom crying. "Karin and Natalie always get to be the princesses. I always have to be the maid. Everyday they say you can be a princess tomorrow, but it never happens!"

The teacher calls Karin, Natalie, Patty, Cindy Lou, and Elizabeth to come and sit down in a circle.

Teacher: Elizabeth has a complaint.

Elizabeth: Yeah, you guys always get to be the princess—I want to be sometimes.

Patty: I don't mind. I help them get dressed.

Cindy Lou: Well, I mind. I want to be a princess sometimes, too.

Karin: Well, you guys could, but you never get there first. Who ever gets the crown, gets to be princess.

Teacher: Karin, try to feel what it would be like if you never got to be a princess.

Karin: (Gets quiet.) Not so good.

Teacher: OK, let's all get quiet and think about what is most fair to each person and try to think how this game can be most fair and fun for everyone.

Children: (Quiet for several minutes.)

Teacher: Any ideas?

Natalie: We could sign up and take turns. Two different people could be princess each day.

Karin: We could make more crowns and then everyone could be a princess. (All agree this is a good idea.)

Cindy Lou: We need a prince so we can dance at the ball.

Patty: I'll be the prince.

Elizabeth: Let's get some boys to be in it.

Teacher: I know a story about twelve dancing princesses. They kept wearing their shoes out by dancing all night.

Natalie: Oh, tell it to us.

In this model, misbehavior is handled in a way that helps the children think about the consequences of their behavior and make plans to modify it. Children are asked to feel what it would be like to be the injured person. They are also asked to think of several solutions to the problem. If property has been destroyed, they are asked to think of ways to make retribution. Learning to understand how other people feel is an important part of developing a sense of responsibility to others. Fannie and George Shaftel's *Role Playing for Social Values*[9] provides specific instruction for helping children develop a feeling of empathy. In order to learn how other people feel, children must have experiences that provide opportunities to learn about feelings.

A CONTEXTUAL VIEW

The following is an example of the situation in a typical fourth-grade classroom based on the Group Process Model. Six children are shaping green salt dough around the edges of a map of the San Francisco Bay. The large map is glued to the table. They have salt ready to sprinkle into glue to make salt flats when they can see clearly where they go. Two other children are constructing school buildings and their homes of cardboard. Four children are making the bridges that span the bay. Each of the four has a picture of his or her bridge to guide the model. They are using tongue depressors, pipe cleaners, and string. Aretha is reading aloud statistics about the Golden Gate Bridge. She tells the others how many lives were lost building it. Kevin grabs his throat and says "Arg! I'll probably die making it." The teacher is copying a story that Manual is dictating about the class's trip to the Morton Salt Factory. Alex and Margaret are measuring level tablespoons into a cup of water to see how much salt will dissolve in a cup of water. They plan to pour the cup of salt water into a flat pan to see how long it takes to evaporate and to see if they can recover all the salt.

All of these class members have been coded on Figure 5.2. Note that since all of the art activities have to do with the bay project, the children working on them are placed in the social studies activity rather than the arts activity. The two children experimenting with salt are placed in a science activity since they are conducting an experiment rather than working out math problems. Now try Exercise 5.3. The answers are at the end of the chapter.

---

[9]Fannie R. Shaftel and George Shaftel, *Role-Playing for Social Values: Decision-Making in the Social Studies* (Englewood Cliffs, N.J.: Prentice-Hall, 1967).

CLASSROOM CHECK LIST (be sure to code **EVERYONE** in the class)

	ONE CHILD	TWO CHILDREN	SMALL GROUPS	LARGE GROUPS
1. Snack, lunch	T ①②③ A ①②③ v ①②③ i ①②③	T ①②③ A ①②③ v ①②③ i ①②③	T ①②③④ A ①②③④ v ①②③④ i ①②③④	T ①② A ①② v ①② i ①②
2. Group time	T ①②③ A ①②③ v ①②③ i ①②③	T ①②③ A ①②③ v ①②③ i ①②③	T ①②③④ A ①②③④ v ①②③④ i ①②③④	T ①② A ①② v ①② i ①②
3. Music — Story / Dancing	T ①②③ A ①②③ v ①②③ i ①②③	T ①②③ A ①②③ v ①②③ i ①②③	T ①②③④ A ①②③④ v ①②③④ i ①②③④	T ①② A ①② v ①② i ①②
4. Arts, Crafts	T ①②③ A ①②③ v ①②③ i ①②③	T ①②③ A ①②③ v ①②③ i ①②③	T ①②③④ A ①②③④ v ①②③④ i ①②③④	T ①② A ①② v ①② i ①②
5. Table Games — Guessing Games / Puzzles	T ①②③ A ①②③ v ①②③ i ①②③	T ①②③ A ①②③ v ①②③ i ①②③	T ①②③④ A ①②③④ v ①②③④ i ①②③④	T ①② A ①② v ①② i ①②
6. Math — Numbers / Arithmetic	T ①②③ A ①②③ v ①②③ i ①②③	T ①②③ A ①②③ v ①②③ i ①②③	T ①②③④ A ①②③④ v ①②③④ i ①②③④	T ①② A ①② v ①② i ①②
7. Reading — Alphabet / Lang. Development	T ●②③ A ①②③ v ①②③ i ●②③	T ①②③ A ①②③ v ①②③ i ①②③	T ①②③④ A ①②③④ v ①②③④ i ①②③④	T ①② A ①② v ①② i ①②
8. Social Studies — Geography	T ①②③ A ①②③ v ①②③ i ①②③	T ①②③ A ①②③ v ①②③ i ●②③	T ①②③④ A ①②③④ v ①②③④ i ●●③④	T ①② A ①② v ①② i ①②
9. Science — Natural World	T ①②③ A ①②③ v ①②③ i ①②③	T ①②③ A ①②③ v ①②③ i ●②③	T ①②③④ A ①②③④ v ①②③④ i ①②③④	T ①② A ①② v ①② i ①②
10. Sewing / Cooking / Pounding / Sawing	T ①②③ A ①②③ v ①②③ i ①②③	T ①②③ A ①②③ v ①②③ i ①②③	T ①②③④ A ①②③④ v ①②③④ i ①②③④	T ①② A ①② v ①② i ①②
11. Blocks / Trucks	T ①②③ A ①②③ v ①②③ i ①②③	T ①②③ A ①②③ v ①②③ i ①②③	T ①②③④ A ①②③④ v ①②③④ i ①②③④	T ①② A ①② v ①② i ①②
12. Dramatic Play / Dress-Up	T ①②③ A ①②③ v ①②③ i ①②③	T ①②③ A ①②③ v ①②③ i ①②③	T ①②③④ A ①②③④ v ①②③④ i ①②③④	T ①② A ①② v ①② i ①②
13. Active Play	T ①②③ A ①②③ v ①②③ i ①②③	T ①②③ A ①②③ v ①②③ i ①②③	T ①②③④ A ①②③④ v ①②③④ i ①②③④	T ①② A ①② v ①② i ①②
14. RELIABILITY SHEET	○			

Legend (for items 6–9):
○ TV
○ Audio-Visual Materials
● Exploratory Materials
● Math and Science Equipment
● Texts, Workbooks
○ Puzzles, Games

Figure 5.2

		ONE CHILD	TWO CHILDREN	SMALL GROUPS	LARGE GROUPS
15. Practical Skills Acquisition		T ①②③	T ①②③	T ①②③④	T ①②
		A ①②③	A ①②③	A ①②③④	A ①②
		v ①②③	v ①②③	v ①②③④	v ①②
		i ①②③	i ①②③	i ①②③④	i ①②
16. Observing		T ①②③	T ①②③	T ①②③④	T ①②
		A ①②③	A ①②③	A ①②③④	A ①②
		v ①②③	v ①②③	v ①②③④	v ①②
		i ①②③	i ①②③	i ①②③④	i ①②
17. Social Interaction Ob [Ⓒ ② Ⓢ]	Ⓣ Ⓐ Ⓥ	T ①②③	T ①②③	T ①②③④	T ①②
		A ①②③	A ①②③	A ①②③④	A ①②
		v ①②③	v ①②③	v ①②③④	v ①②
		i ①②③	i ①②③	i ①②③④	i ①②
18. Unoccupied Child		T ①②③	T ①②③	T ①②③④	T ①②
		A ①②③	A ①②③	A ①②③④	A ①②
		v ①②③	v ①②③	v ①②③④	v ①②
		i ①②③	i ①②③	i ①②③④	i ①②
19. Discipline		T ①②③	T ①②③	T ①②③④	T ①②
		A ①②③	A ①②③	A ①②③④	A ①②
		v ①②③	v ①②③	v ①②③④	v ①②
		i ①②③	i ①②③	i ①②③④	i ①②
20. Transitional Activities	Ⓣ Ⓐ Ⓥ	T ①②③	T ①②③	T ①②③④	T ①②
		A ①②③	A ①②③	A ①②③④	A ①②
		v ①②③	v ①②③	v ①②③④	v ①②
		i ①②③	i ①②③	i ①②③④	i ①②
21. Classroom Management	Ⓣ Ⓐ Ⓥ	T ①②③	T ①②③	T ①②③④	T ①②
		A ①②③	A ①②③	A ①②③④	A ①②
		v ①②③	v ①②③	v ①②③④	v ①②
		i ①②③	i ①②③	i ①②③④	i ①②
22. Out of Room	Ⓣ Ⓐ Ⓥ	T ①②③	T ①②③	T ①②③④	T ①②
		A ①②③	A ①②③	A ①②③④	A ①②
		v ①②③	v ①②③	v ①②③④	v ①②
		i ①②③	i ①②③	i ①②③④	i ①②

NUMBER OF ADULTS IN CLASSROOM ⓪ ① ② ③ ④ ⑤ ⑥ ⑦ ⑧ ⑨ ⑩

EXERCISE 5.3 Code each person in the situation below on the CCL.

Situation: During a morning session, three children are sitting on the couch reading to themselves. Five are doing lessons in reading workbooks. Three have completed their work and are exploring with batteries, wires, and light bulbs at the science table. The teacher is listening to one child read. The aide is helping two children with some writing. Four children are independently writing stories at their desks. Two children who have finished their assignments are painting at the easel.

CLASSROOM CHECK LIST (be sure to code **EVERYONE** in the class)

		ONE CHILD	TWO CHILDREN	SMALL GROUPS	LARGE GROUPS
1. Snack, lunch		T ① ② ③ A ① ② ③ V ① ② ③ i ① ② ③	T ① ② ③ A ① ② ③ V ① ② ③ i ① ② ③	T ① ② ③ ④ A ① ② ③ ④ V ① ② ③ ④ i ① ② ③ ④	T ① ② A ① ② V ① ② i ① ②
2. Group time		T ① ② ③ A ① ② ③ V ① ② ③ i ① ② ③	T ① ② ③ A ① ② ③ V ① ② ③ i ① ② ③	T ① ② ③ ④ A ① ② ③ ④ V ① ② ③ ④ i ① ② ③ ④	T ① ② A ① ② V ① ② i ① ②
3. Story **Music** Dancing		T ① ② ③ A ① ② ③ V ① ② ③ i ① ② ③	T ① ② ③ A ① ② ③ V ① ② ③ i ① ② ③	T ① ② ③ ④ A ① ② ③ ④ V ① ② ③ ④ i ① ② ③ ④	T ① ② A ① ② V ① ② i ① ②
4. Arts, Crafts		T ① ② ③ A ① ② ③ V ① ② ③ i ① ② ③	T ① ② ③ A ① ② ③ V ① ② ③ i ① ② ③	T ① ② ③ ④ A ① ② ③ ④ V ① ② ③ ④ i ① ② ③ ④	T ① ② A ① ② V ① ② i ① ②
5. Guessing Games **Table Games** Puzzles		T ① ② ③ A ① ② ③ V ① ② ③ i ① ② ③	T ① ② ③ A ① ② ③ V ① ② ③ i ① ② ③	T ① ② ③ ④ A ① ② ③ ④ V ① ② ③ ④ i ① ② ③ ④	T ① ② A ① ② V ① ② i ① ②

○ TV
 ○ Audio-Visual
    Materials
 ○ Exploratory
    Materials
 ○ Math and Science
    Equipment
 ○ Texts, Workbooks
 ○ Puzzles, Games
	Numbers
	 6. Math
	 Arithmetic
		T ① ② ③
		 A ① ② ③
		 V ① ② ③
		 i ① ② ③
			T ① ② ③
			 A ① ② ③
			 V ① ② ③
			 i ① ② ③
				T ① ② ③ ④
				 A ① ② ③ ④
				 V ① ② ③ ④
				 i ① ② ③ ④
					T ① ②
					 A ① ②
					 V ① ②
					 i ① ②

	Reading **7. Alphabet** Lang. Development	T ① ② ③ A ① ② ③ V ① ② ③ i ① ② ③	T ① ② ③ A ① ② ③ V ① ② ③ i ① ② ③	T ① ② ③ ④ A ① ② ③ ④ V ① ② ③ ④ i ① ② ③ ④	T ① ② A ① ② V ① ② i ① ②
	8. Social Studies Geography	T ① ② ③ A ① ② ③ V ① ② ③ i ① ② ③	T ① ② ③ A ① ② ③ V ① ② ③ i ① ② ③	T ① ② ③ ④ A ① ② ③ ④ V ① ② ③ ④ i ① ② ③ ④	T ① ② A ① ② V ① ② i ① ②
	9. Science Natural World	T ① ② ③ A ① ② ③ V ① ② ③ i ① ② ③	T ① ② ③ A ① ② ③ V ① ② ③ i ① ② ③	T ① ② ③ ④ A ① ② ③ ④ V ① ② ③ ④ i ① ② ③ ④	T ① ② A ① ② V ① ② i ① ②
10. Sewing Cooking Pounding Sawing		T ① ② ③ A ① ② ③ V ① ② ③ i ① ② ③	T ① ② ③ A ① ② ③ V ① ② ③ i ① ② ③	T ① ② ③ ④ A ① ② ③ ④ V ① ② ③ ④ i ① ② ③ ④	T ① ② A ① ② V ① ② i ① ②
11. Blocks Trucks		T ① ② ③ A ① ② ③ V ① ② ③ i ① ② ③	T ① ② ③ A ① ② ③ V ① ② ③ i ① ② ③	T ① ② ③ ④ A ① ② ③ ④ V ① ② ③ ④ i ① ② ③ ④	T ① ② A ① ② V ① ② i ① ②
12. Dramatic Play Dress-Up		T ① ② ③ A ① ② ③ V ① ② ③ i ① ② ③	T ① ② ③ A ① ② ③ V ① ② ③ i ① ② ③	T ① ② ③ ④ A ① ② ③ ④ V ① ② ③ ④ i ① ② ③ ④	T ① ② A ① ② V ① ② i ① ②
13. Active Play		T ① ② ③ A ① ② ③ V ① ② ③ i ① ② ③	T ① ② ③ A ① ② ③ V ① ② ③ i ① ② ③	T ① ② ③ ④ A ① ② ③ ④ V ① ② ③ ④ i ① ② ③ ④	T ① ② A ① ② V ① ② i ① ②
14. RELIABILITY SHEET ○					

Exercise 5.3

			ONE CHILD	TWO CHILDREN	SMALL GROUPS	LARGE GROUPS
15. Practical Skills Acquisition			T ①②③ A ①②③ v ①②③ i ①②③	T ①②③ A ①②③ v ①②③ i ①②③	T ①②③④ A ①②③④ v ①②③④ i ①②③④	T ①② A ①② v ①② i ①②
16. Observing			T ①②③ A ①②③ v ①②③ i ①②③	T ①②③ A ①②③ v ①②③ i ①②③	T ①②③④ A ①②③④ v ①②③④ i ①②③④	T ①② A ①② v ①② i ①②
17. Social Interaction	Ob [Ⓒ ② Ⓢ]	Ⓣ Ⓐ Ⓥ	T ①②③ A ①②③ v ①②③ i ①②③	T ①②③ A ①②③ v ①②③ i ①②③	T ①②③④ A ①②③④ v ①②③④ i ①②③④	T ①② A ①② v ①② i ①②
18. Unoccupied Child			T ①②③ A ①②③ v ①②③ i ①②③	T ①②③ A ①②③ v ①②③ i ①②③	T ①②③④ A ①②③④ v ①②③④ i ①②③④	T ①② A ①② v ①② i ①②
19. Discipline			T ①②③ A ①②③ v ①②③ i ①②③	T ①②③ A ①②③ v ①②③ i ①②③	T ①②③④ A ①②③④ v ①②③④ i ①②③④	T ①② A ①② v ①② i ①②
20. Transitional Activities		Ⓣ Ⓐ Ⓥ	T ①②③ A ①②③ v ①②③ i ①②③	T ①②③ A ①②③ v ①②③ i ①②③	T ①②③④ A ①②③④ v ①②③④ i ①②③④	T ①② A ①② v ①② i ①②
21. Classroom Management		Ⓣ Ⓐ Ⓥ	T ①②③ A ①②③ v ①②③ i ①②③	T ①②③ A ①②③ v ①②③ i ①②③	T ①②③④ A ①②③④ v ①②③④ i ①②③④	T ①② A ①② v ①② i ①②
22. Out of Room		Ⓣ Ⓐ Ⓥ	T ①②③ A ①②③ v ①②③ i ①②③	T ①②③ A ①②③ v ①②③ i ①②③	T ①②③④ A ①②③④ v ①②③④ i ①②③④	T ①② A ①② v ①② i ①②

NUMBER OF ADULTS IN CLASSROOM ⓪ ① ② ③ ④ ⑤ ⑥ ⑦ ⑧ ⑨ ⑩

CLASSROOM REQUIREMENTS

Flexible space is very important to this model. However, even more important is flexible timing. When problems arise, it is essential that the teacher call a group meeting and allow each person to express a point of view. The group process will work if the necessary time is allowed in the schedule. Also essential to the model is a teacher who is warm, supportive, and skilled in group discussion techniques. The teacher must be able to guide children into making commitments, evaluating their own behavior, and then changing that behavior as necessary. It helps if the teacher is flexible, and secure in the group process, where open discussions bring continuing change. Size of class is also important in this model. Small classes are best since it takes longer for all ideas to be expressed in large ones.

RESEARCH FINDINGS ON HOW CHILDREN GROW AND DEVELOP

Observation studies made during the evaluation of the Follow Through Planned Variation Project[10] indicate that children in an

---

[10]Jane A. Stallings and David Kaskowitz, *Follow Through Classroom Observation Evaluation 1972-1973* (Menlo Park, Calif.: Stanford Research Institute, 1974). ERIC Accession No. ED 104 969.

open education model similar to the Group Process Model take more responsibility for themselves, are more independent in their activities, and make more task-related comments than children in other models. Children in this model also cooperate with each other in joint projects more frequently than children in the programmed models.

Children in open education models are encouraged to say what they think and feel. We found that both adults and children expressed more positive feelings and more negative feelings than did participants in other models. There was, of course, considerably more joy expressed than anger and sorrow.

This Group Process Model is the only one in which the children's scores on the Intellectual Achievement Responsibility scale (IAR) were positive for accepting responsibility for both their success and their failure. Examples of the test items are given on page 73.

Children in open classroom models performed well in the Raven's Coloured Progressive Matrices test. Their scores were considerably higher than the scores of children in the programmed models and comparison classrooms. This test is described on page 72.

Overall, the outcomes for these children are very similar to those in the Exploratory Model. However, first-grade children in this model did better than the national norm in math. They had scores as high as those for children in the structured models.

OBSERVABLE COMPONENTS

The SRI observation system cannot record all of the important elements of the Group Process Model. It cannot record, for example, that children are examining their feelings and developing empathy for other people. The instrument could be modified, of course, so that one of the circles rarely used in the How section could be used to record instances when feelings are being discussed. Any sentence about feelings could then be modified to show the frequency that feelings were dealt with in classroom interactions. However, a coding system is limited in its ability to reflect the depth of the personal responsibility and personal relationships this model is trying to foster.

Yet, several important components of the Group Process Model, including materials being used, activities occurring, and interactions between adults and children can be observed and recorded using our instruments.

Materials

When used with the Group Process Model, the Physical Environment Information form would show many games, toys, and instructional materials marked in the Used Today column. A wide variety of general equipment would also be indicated. The desks and chairs would be movable and the children would have seats assigned for at least part of the day. Although children are not assigned to groups, they are given specific lessons to complete; they don't choose their own work groups (see Figure 5.3).

Physical Environment Information
(Mark all that apply.)

Seating Patterns:
● Movable tables and chairs for seating purposes.
○ Stationary desks in rows.
● Assigned seating for at least part of the day.
○ Children select their own seating locations.
● Teacher assigns children to groups.
○ Children select their own work groups.

For each of the items below, mark all that apply:

① Present
② Used today

GAMES, TOYS, PLAY EQUIPMENT
① ② small toys (trucks, cars, dolls and accessories
① ● puzzles, games
① ② wheel toys
① ② small play equipment (jumpropes, balls)
① ② large play equipment (swings, jungle gym)
① ● children's storybooks
① ● animals, other nature objects
① ● sandbox, water table
① ● carpentry materials, large blocks
① ● cooking and sewing supplies

INSTRUCTIONAL MATERIALS
① ② Montessori, other educational toys
① ● children's texts, workbooks
① ● math/science equipment, concrete objects
① ② instructional charts

AUDIO, VISUAL EQUIPMENT
① ② television
① ● record or tape player
① ② audio-visual equipment

GENERAL EQUIPMENT, MATERIALS
● ② children's own products on display
① ② displays reflecting children's ethnicity
● ② other displays especially for children
● ② magazines
① ② achievement charts
● ② child-size sink
● ② child-size table and chairs
● ② child-size shelves
● ② arts and crafts materials
● ② blackboard, feltboard
● ② child's own storage space
● ② photographs of the children on display

OTHER
① ② please specify . . . . . .

MAKE NO

STRAY MARKS

IN BLANK AREAS

Figure 5.3

Activities and Groupings

The Classroom Check List would be filled out differently for different parts of the day. When group meetings were being conducted, all teachers and children would be marked in activity 2 in the Large Group column. When reading period began, everyone would be marked in the reading activity. Most of the children would be coded as working independently; two or three would be coded as working with a teacher or aide. Toward the end of the reading period some children would have moved to other activities. At the end of the reading period, the grid might look like Figure 5.4. Here, two children are working at the easel. The teacher is reading with one child. The aide is reading with two children. Another aide is playing a word game with three children. Three children are reading alone. Four children are playing an alphabet game. Two children are finishing a bridge for their project, and two children are examining their hair through a microscope. Three children are developing a dramatic play. This model is unique from the others since each grid coded for it is likely to be different. Within other models the grids are similar.

Interaction Observations

Interactions during group meeting time would have many open-ended questions, for example, "How do you think the California Indians caught rabbits without using bows and arrows or guns?" (TC2) There would also be many task-related comments as each child contributed ideas to the discussion. Much more child talk would be recorded than teacher talk since the teacher acts more as a guide and a prober than as a dominant leader. The teacher asks for student ideas on how to solve problems and listens to their suggestions.

During reading time the teacher would make clear what was expected and be supportive in helping the child through the lesson.

The following is a typical interaction in a Group Process Model. The interaction is coded in Figure 5.5.

Situation: A teacher is helping a second-grade child with reading.

1. Teacher: Here is a story I think you will like.

2. Teacher: There are a few new words I'll tell you as we go along.

3. Teacher: Start right here.

4. Jim: Billy liked his Halloween costume; it was a Batman suit.

5. Teacher: Very good! You knew those new words.

6. Teacher: How did you figure out "Halloween" and "costume"?

7. Jim: You wrote "Halloween" on the board the other day and I sounded out "costume."

8. Jim: Did you write this story?

9. Teacher: Yes, because I knew you liked Batman.

10. Jim: Maybe I can write some more to the story when we finish.

11. Teacher: Good idea, Jim.

CLASSROOM CHECK LIST (be sure to code EVERYONE in the class)

	ONE CHILD	TWO CHILDREN	SMALL GROUPS	LARGE GROUPS
1. Snack, lunch	T ①②③ / A ①②③ / V ①②③ / i ①②③	T ①②③ / A ①②③ / V ①②③ / i ①②③	T ①②③④ / A ①②③④ / V ①②③④ / i ①②③④	T ①② / A ①② / V ①② / i ①②
2. Group time	T ①②③ / A ①②③ / V ①②③ / i ①②③	T ①②③ / A ①②③ / V ①②③ / i ①②③	T ①②③④ / A ①②③④ / V ①②③④ / i ①②③④	T ①② / A ①② / V ①② / i ①②
3. Story / Music / Dancing	T ①②③ / A ①②③ / V ①②③ / i ①②③	T ①②③ / A ①②③ / V ①②③ / i ①②③	T ①②③④ / A ①②③④ / V ①②③④ / i ①②③④	T ①② / A ①② / V ①② / i ①②
4. Arts, Crafts	T ①②③ / A ①②③ / V ①②③ / i ①●③	T ①②③ / A ①②③ / V ①②③ / i ①②③	T ①②③④ / A ①②③④ / V ①②③④ / i ①②③④	T ①② / A ①② / V ①② / i ①②
5. Guessing Games / Table Games / Puzzles	T ①②③ / A ①②③ / V ①②③ / i ①②③	T ①②③ / A ①②③ / V ①②③ / i ①②③	T ①②③④ / A ①②③④ / V ①②③④ / i ①②③④	T ①② / A ①② / V ①② / i ①②
6. Math — Numbers / Arithmetic	T ①②③ / A ①②③ / V ①②③ / i ①②③	T ①②③ / A ①②③ / V ①②③ / i ①②③	T ①②③④ / A ①②③④ / V ①②③④ / i ①②③④	T ①② / A ①② / V ①② / i ①②
7. Reading — Alphabet / Lang. Development	T ●②③ / A ①②③ / V ①②③ / i ①②●	T ①②③ / A ●②③ / V ①②③ / i ①②③	T ①②③④ / A ●②③④ / V ①②③④ / i ●②③④	T ①② / A ①② / V ①② / i ①②
8. Social Studies / Geography	T ①②③ / A ①②③ / V ①②③ / i ①②③	T ①②③ / A ①②③ / V ①②③ / i ●②③	T ①②③④ / A ①②③④ / V ①②③④ / i ①②③④	T ①② / A ①② / V ①② / i ①②
9. Science / Natural World	T ①②③ / A ①②③ / V ①②③ / i ①②③	T ①②③ / A ①②③ / V ①②③ / i ①②③	T ①②③④ / A ①②③④ / V ①②③④ / i ①②③④	T ①② / A ①② / V ①② / i ①②
10. Sewing / Cooking / Pounding / Sawing	T ①②③ / A ①②③ / V ①②③ / i ①②③	T ①②③ / A ①②③ / V ①②③ / i ①②③	T ①②③④ / A ①②③④ / V ①②③④ / i ①②③④	T ①② / A ①② / V ①② / i ①②
11. Blocks / Trucks	T ①②③ / A ①②③ / V ①②③ / i ①②③	T ①②③ / A ①②③ / V ①②③ / i ①②③	T ①②③④ / A ①②③④ / V ①②③④ / i ①②③④	T ①② / A ①② / V ①② / i ①②
12. Dramatic Play / Dress-Up	T ①②③ / A ①②③ / V ①②③ / i ①②③	T ①②③ / A ①②③ / V ①②③ / i ①②③	T ①②③④ / A ①②③④ / V ①②③④ / i ●②③④	T ①② / A ①② / V ①② / i ①②
13. Active Play	T ①②③ / A ①②③ / V ①②③ / i ①②③	T ①②③ / A ①②③ / V ①②③ / i ①②③	T ①②③④ / A ①②③④ / V ①②③④ / i ①②③④	T ①② / A ①② / V ①② / i ①②
14. RELIABILITY SHEET ○				

Legend (beside items 6–9):
○ TV
○ Audio-Visual Materials
● Exploratory Materials
● Math and Science Equipment
○ Texts, Workbooks
● Puzzles, Games

Figure 5.4

			ONE CHILD	TWO CHILDREN	SMALL GROUPS	LARGE GROUPS
15. Practical Skills Acquisition			T ①②③ A ①②③ v ①②③ i ①②③	T ①②③ A ①②③ v ①②③ i ①②③	T ①②③④ A ①②③④ v ①②③④ i ①②③④	T ①② A ①② v ①② i ①②
16. Observing			T ①②③ A ①②③ v ①②③ i ①②③	T ①②③ A ①②③ v ①②③ i ①②③	T ①②③④ A ①②③④ v ①②③④ i ①②③④	T ①② A ①② v ①② i ①②
17. Social Interaction	Ob Ⓒ ② Ⓢ	Ⓣ Ⓐ Ⓥ	T ①②③ A ①②③ v ①②③ i ①②③	T ①②③ A ①②③ v ①②③ i ①②③	T ①②③④ A ①②③④ v ①②③④ i ①②③④	T ①② A ①② v ①② i ①②
18. Unoccupied Child			T ①②③ A ①②③ v ①②③ i ①②③	T ①②③ A ①②③ v ①②③ i ①②③	T ①②③④ A ①②③④ v ①②③④ i ①②③④	T ①② A ①② v ①② i ①②
19. Discipline			T ①②③ A ①②③ v ①②③ i ①②③	T ①②③ A ①②③ v ①②③ i ①②③	T ①②③④ A ①②③④ v ①②③④ i ①②③④	T ①② A ①② v ①② i ①②
20. Transitional Activities		Ⓣ Ⓐ Ⓥ	T ①②③ A ①②③ v ①②③ i ①②③	T ①②③ A ①②③ v ①②③ i ①②③	T ①②③④ A ①②③④ v ①②③④ i ①②③④	T ①② A ①② v ①② i ①②
21. Classroom Management		Ⓣ Ⓐ Ⓥ	T ①②③ A ①②③ v ①②③ i ①②③	T ①②③ A ①②③ v ①②③ i ①②③	T ①②③④ A ①②③④ v ①②③④ i ①②③④	T ①② A ①② v ①② i ①②
22. Out of Room		Ⓣ Ⓐ Ⓥ	T ①②③ A ①②③ v ①②③ i ①②③	T ①②③ A ①②③ v ①②③ i ①②③	T ①②③④ A ①②③④ v ①②③④ i ①②③④	T ①② A ①② v ①② i ①②

NUMBER OF ADULTS IN CLASSROOM   ⓪ ① ② ③ ④ ⑤ ⑥ ⑦ ⑧ ⑨ ⑩

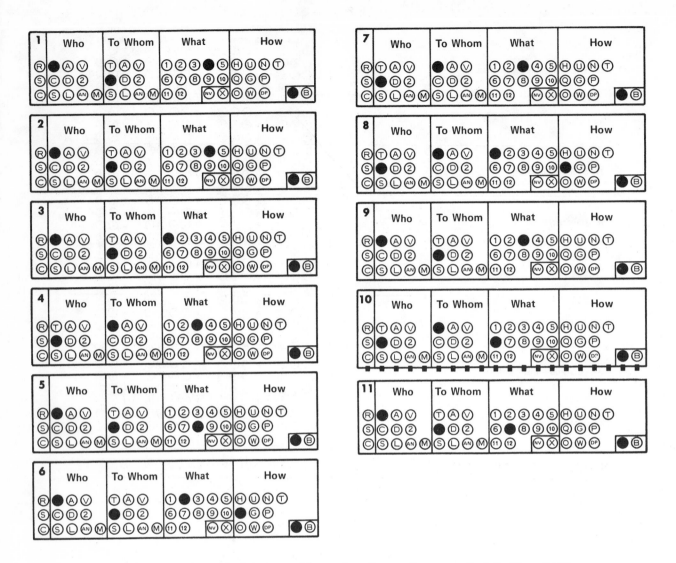

Figure 5.5   Coded Interaction of a Group Process Model Classroom

IMPORTANCE OF TEACHER OBSERVATION

To conduct a self-evaluation, teachers who use the Group Process Model need to examine several five-minute observation records of their classroom performance. If the records made during the class meeting time show a high rate of TL4 (teacher instructing large group), the teacher will probably want to become less obtrusive during group meetings—do more asking and less telling. Teachers can correct their own behavior through feedback from the observation record.

SUMMARY OF COMPONENTS

Theorist or theory: Lewin field theory, Glasser

Oriented toward: Social-emotional development

Goals: To develop self-awareness, responsibility, and cooperation

Stress: Social problem solving skills

Structure: Student-centered

Grouping patterns: Large group and individual student

Materials: Textbooks and exploratory materials

Where to teach: Large group circle or individual desks

Who initiates: Child

Questioning strategy: Open-ended

Feedback from: Other students and teacher

Who evaluates: Students and teacher

Evaluation tools: Problem-solving tests, achievement tests, child observations, locus of control (IAR) tests

BIBLIOGRAPHY

The Group Process Model described in this chapter is based primarily on the curriculum developed by the author at Peninsula School in Menlo Park, and curriculum developed by William Glasser.

Where Components of the Group Process Type Models Can Be Seen

Components of the Group Process Model might be seen in the Bank Street College Follow Through Model, the University of Arizona Follow Through Model, the Far West Follow Through Model, and the Education Development Center's Follow Through Model. Interested readers should contact the Follow Through offices in the school districts of the cities listed.

Bank Street College model

Tuskegee, Alabama	Philadelphia, Pennsylvania
Fall River, Massachusetts	Brattleboro, Vermont
New York City, New York	

Education Development Center models

Paterson, New Jersey	Rosebud, Texas
Smithfield, North Carolina	Burlington, Vermont
Philadelphia, Pennsylvania	

Far West Laboratories models

Berkeley, California	Salt Lake City, Utah
Duluth, Minnesota	Tacoma, Washington
Lebanon, New Hampshire	

Glasser's Classroom Meeting model

    Los Angeles, California   Palo Alto, California

Peninsula School
    Menlo Park, California

University of Arizona models

    Des Moines, Iowa   Lakewood, New Jersey

    Wichita, Kansas   Chickasha, Oklahoma

    Lincoln, Nebraska

Suggested Readings

Theory of the Group Process Model

Glasser, William. *Reality Therapy*. New York: Harper & Row, 1965.

Kelly, George A. *The Psychology of Personal Constructs*. New York: W. W. Norton, 1955.

Maslow, Abraham. *Toward a Psychology of Being*. Princeton, N.J.: Von Nostrand Reinhold, 1962.

Perls, Frederick; Hefferlin, Ralph; and Goodman, Paul. *Gestalt Therapy*. New York: Delta Books, 1965.

Rogers, Carl R. *Client-Centered Therapy*. Boston: Houghton Mifflin, 1951.

Schutz, William. *Joy: Expanding Human Awareness*. New York: Grove Press, 1967.

Implementing the Group Process Model

Baker, K., and Fane, X. *Understanding and Guiding Young Children*. Englewood Cliffs, N.J.: Prentice-Hall, 1967.

Glasser, William. *Schools Without Failure*. New York: Harper & Row, 1969.

Miller, S. *The Psychology of Play*. London: Cox and Wyman, Ltd., 1969.

Rath, L.; Jonas, A.; and Wasserman, S. *Teaching for Thinking*. Columbus, Ohio: Charles E. Merrill, 1967.

Rogers, Carl. *Freedom to Learn*. Columbus, Ohio: Charles E. Merrill, 1969.

Shaftel, Fannie R., and Shaftel, George. *Role-Playing for Social Values: Decision-Making in the Social Studies*. Englewood Cliffs, N.J.: Prentice-Hall, 1967.

Smith, James A. *Creative Teaching of Language Arts in the Elementary School*. 2d ed. Boston: Allyn and Bacon, 1973.

Torrance, Ellis P. *Guiding Creative Talent*. Englewood Cliffs, N.J.: Prentice-Hall, 1962.

Turner, Marion E. *The Child Within the Group: An Experiment in Self-Government*. Stanford, Calif.: Stanford University Press, 1957.

Commercially Available Materials

Cross-Number Puzzle-Story Problems: A curriculum kit of materials for use in developing the four basic mathematical functions plus fractions, decimals, and percents. (Science Research Association, 259 East Erie, Chicago, IL 60611)

Elementary Science Study: Fifty-six different modules, covering grades K-8, that deemphasize "book learning." Students learn from their own experiments working with everyday materials and simple scientific equipment. (Webster/McGraw-Hill, Princeton Road, Heightstown, NJ 08520)

SCIS Elementary Science Program: An innovative program using student manuals and a teacher's guide (but no textbook) that covers both the physical and life sciences. Thirteen kits are available, two each for grades 1-6 and one for kindergarten. Children work through the kits at their own pace and conduct their own investigations while receiving guidance from the teacher. (Rand McNally, P.O. Box 7600, Chicago, IL 60680)

Strange and Familiar: Two books, one centered around grade 3 and one around grade 6, covering math, science, social studies, art, and creative writing. Methods of creative problem solving are taught to help students make connections between what they are trying to learn and what they already know. (Synectics Education Systems, 121 Brattle Street, Cambridge, MA 02138)

Research Findings

Butler, A. "Current Research in Early Childhood and Education." Washington, D.C.: American Association of Elementary, Kindergarten, and Nursery Educators, 1970.

Johnson, David W., and Johnson, Roger T. *Learning Together and Alone: Cooperation, Competition, and Individualization.* Englewood Cliffs, N.J.: Prentice-Hall, 1975.

Perrone, Vito. *Testing and Evaluation: New Views.* Washington, D.C.: Association for Childhood Education International, 1975.

ANSWERS: CORRECT CODING FOR EXERCISE 5.1

ANSWERS: CORRECT CODING FOR EXERCISE 5.2

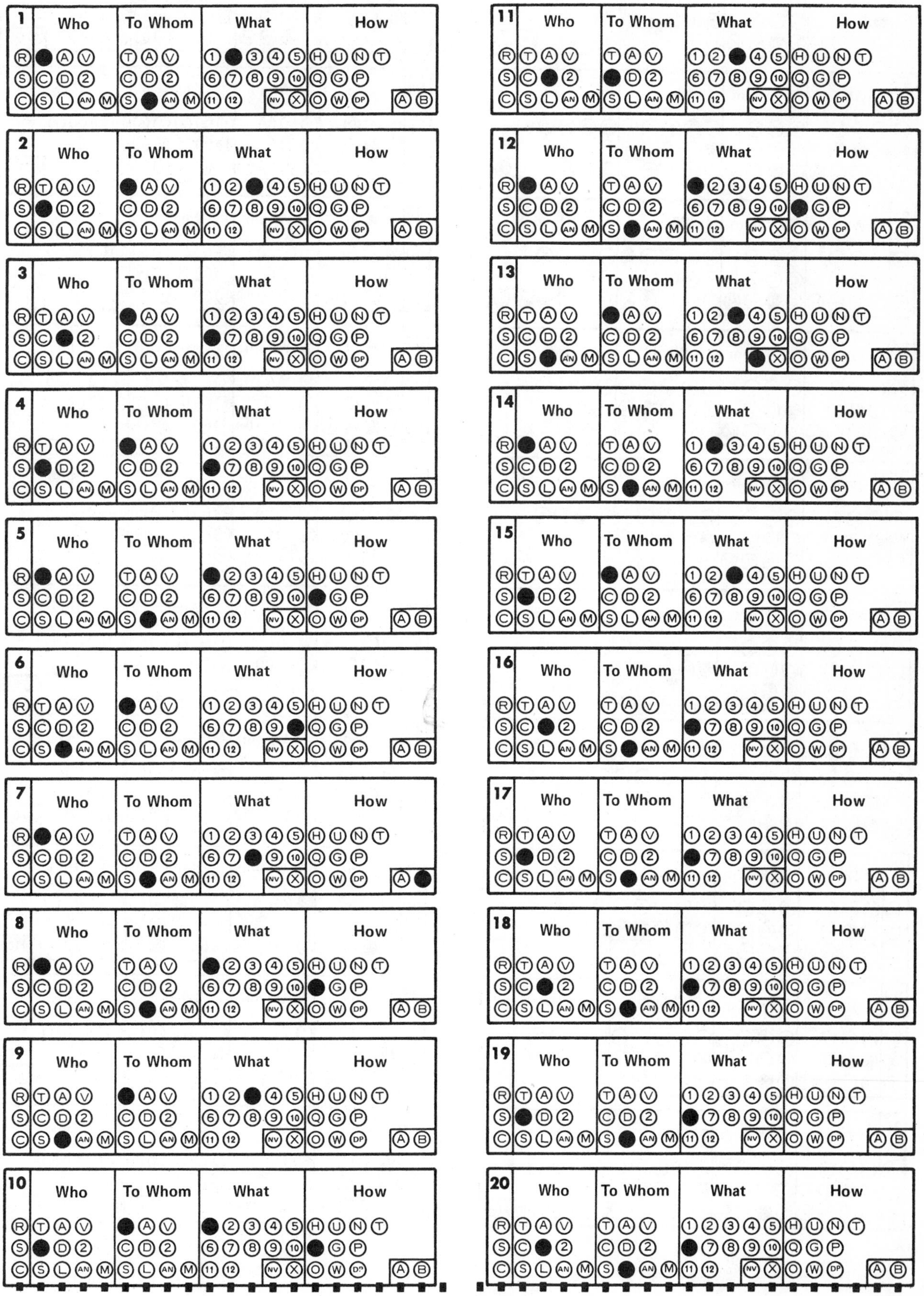
1 Who To Whom What How
2 Who To Whom What How
3 Who To Whom What How
4 Who To Whom What How
5 Who To Whom What How
6 Who To Whom What How
7 Who To Whom What How
8 Who To Whom What How
9 Who To Whom What How
10 Who To Whom What How
11 Who To Whom What How
12 Who To Whom What How
13 Who To Whom What How
14 Who To Whom What How
15 Who To Whom What How
16 Who To Whom What How
17 Who To Whom What How
18 Who To Whom What How
19 Who To Whom What How
20 Who To Whom What How

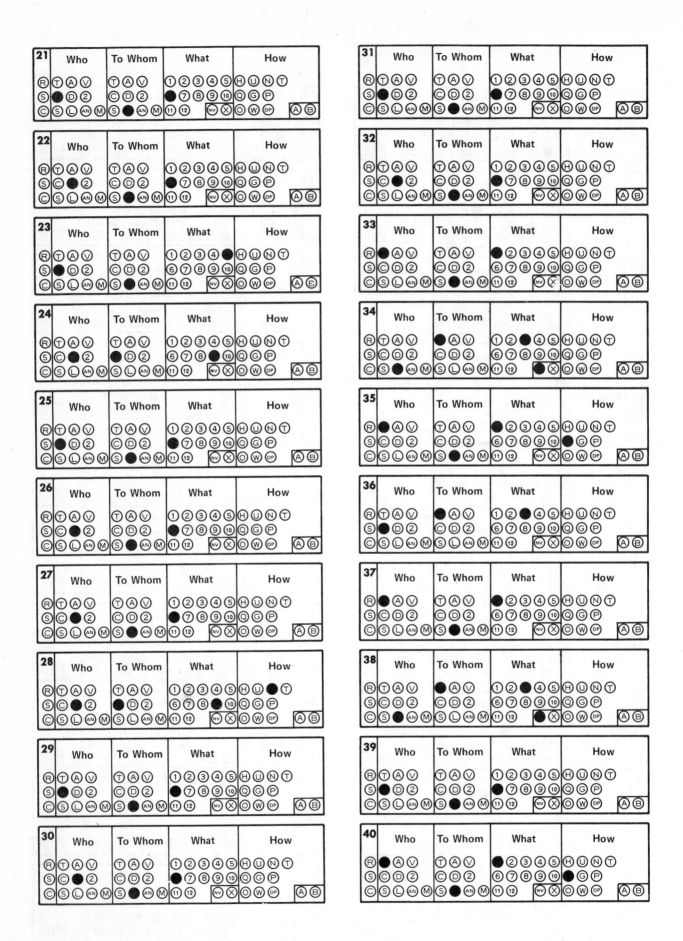

CLASSROOM CHECK LIST (be sure to code **EVERYONE** in the class)

		ONE CHILD	TWO CHILDREN	SMALL GROUPS	LARGE GROUPS
1. Snack, lunch	T	①②③	①②③	①②③④	①②
	A	①②③	①②③	①②③④	①②
	V	①②③	①②③	①②③④	①②
	i	①②③	①②③	①②③④	①②
2. Group time	T	①②③	①②③	①②③④	①②
	A	①②③	①②③	①②③④	①②
	V	①②③	①②③	①②③④	①②
	i	①②③	①②③	①②③④	①②
3. Story / Music / Dancing	T	①②③	①②③	①②③④	①②
	A	①②③	①②③	①②③④	①②
	V	①②③	①②③	①②③④	①②
	i	①②③	①②③	①②③④	①②
4. Arts, Crafts	T	①②③	①②③	①②③④	①②
	A	①②③	①②③	①②③④	①②
	V	①②③	①②③	①②③④	①②
	i	①●③	①②③	①②③④	①②
5. Guessing Games / Table Games / Puzzles	T	①②③	①②③	①②③④	①②
	A	①②③	①②③	①②③④	①②
	V	①②③	①②③	①②③④	①②
	i	①②③	①②③	①②③④	①②
6. Math / Numbers / Arithmetic	T	①②③	①②③	①②③④	①②
	A	①②③	①②③	①②③④	①②
	V	①②③	①②③	①②③④	①②
	i	①②③	①②③	①②③④	①②
7. Reading / Alphabet / Lang. Development	T	●②③	①②③	①②③④	①②
	A	①②③	●②③	①②③④	①②
	V	①②③	①②③	①②③④	①②
	i	①②●	①②③	●●③④	①②
8. Social Studies / Geography	T	①②③	①②③	①②③④	①②
	A	①②③	①②③	①②③④	①②
	V	①②③	①②③	①②③④	①②
	i	①②③	①②③	①②③④	①②
9. Science / Natural World	T	①②③	①②③	①②③④	①②
	A	①②③	①②③	①②③④	①②
	V	①②③	①②③	①②③④	①②
	i	①②③	①②③	●②③④	①②
10. Sewing / Cooking / Pounding / Sawing	T	①②③	①②③	①②③④	①②
	A	①②③	①②③	①②③④	①②
	V	①②③	①②③	①②③④	①②
	i	①②③	①②③	①②③④	①②
11. Blocks / Trucks	T	①②③	①②③	①②③④	①②
	A	①②③	①②③	①②③④	①②
	V	①②③	①②③	①②③④	①②
	i	①②③	①②③	①②③④	①②
12. Dramatic Play / Dress-Up	T	①②③	①②③	①②③④	①②
	A	①②③	①②③	①②③④	①②
	V	①②③	①②③	①②③④	①②
	i	①②③	①②③	①②③④	①②
13. Active Play	T	①②③	①②③	①②③④	①②
	A	①②③	①②③	①②③④	①②
	V	①②③	①②③	①②③④	①②
	i	①②③	①②③	①②③④	①②

14. RELIABILITY SHEET ○

Materials categories (beside items 6–8):

○ TV
○ Audio-Visual Materials
○ Exploratory Materials
● Math and Science Equipment
● Texts, Workbooks
○ Puzzles, Games

			ONE CHILD	TWO CHILDREN	SMALL GROUPS	LARGE GROUPS
15. Practical Skills Acquisition			T ①②③ A ①②③ v ①②③ i ①②③	T ①②③ A ①②③ v ①②③ i ①②③	T ①②③④ A ①②③④ v ①②③④ i ①②③④	T ①② A ①② v ①② i ①②
16. Observing			T ①②③ A ①②③ v ①②③ i ①②③	T ①②③ A ①②③ v ①②③ i ①②③	T ①②③④ A ①②③④ v ①②③④ i ①②③④	T ①② A ①② v ①② i ①②
17. Social Interaction	Ob [Ⓒ ② Ⓢ]	Ⓣ Ⓐ Ⓥ	T ①②③ A ①②③ v ①②③ i ①②③	T ①②③ A ①②③ v ①②③ i ①②③	T ①②③④ A ①②③④ v ①②③④ i ①②③④	T ①② A ①② v ①② i ①②
18. Unoccupied Child			T ①②③ A ①②③ v ①②③ i ①②③	T ①②③ A ①②③ v ①②③ i ①②③	T ①②③④ A ①②③④ v ①②③④ i ①②③④	T ①② A ①② v ①② i ①②
19. Discipline			T ①②③ A ①②③ v ①②③ i ①②③	T ①②③ A ①②③ v ①②③ i ①②③	T ①②③④ A ①②③④ v ①②③④ i ①②③④	T ①② A ①② v ①② i ①②
20. Transitional Activities		Ⓣ Ⓐ Ⓥ	T ①②③ A ①②③ v ①②③ i ①②③	T ①②③ A ①②③ v ①②③ i ①②③	T ①②③④ A ①②③④ v ①②③④ i ①②③④	T ①② A ①② v ①② i ①②
21. Classroom Management		Ⓣ Ⓐ Ⓥ	T ①②③ A ①②③ v ①②③ i ①②③	T ①②③ A ①②③ v ①②③ i ①②③	T ①②③④ A ①②③④ v ①②③④ i ①②③④	T ①② A ①② v ①② i ①②
22. Out of Room		Ⓣ Ⓐ Ⓥ	T ①②③ A ①②③ v ①②③ i ①②③	T ①②③ A ①②③ v ①②③ i ①②③	T ①②③④ A ①②③④ v ①②③④ i ①②③④	T ①② A ①② v ①② i ①②

NUMBER OF ADULTS IN CLASSROOM ⓪ ① ● ③ ④ ⑤ ⑥ ⑦ ⑧ ⑨ ⑩

Chapter 6

Educational Theory and Expected Child Development

Teacher Responsibilities

Schedule

Physical Environment

Interaction Patterns

Handling Misbehavior

A Contextual View

Classroom Requirements

Research Findings on How Children Grow and Develop

Observable Components

    Materials

    Activities and Groupings

    Interaction Observations

Importance of Teacher Observation

Summary of Components

Bibliography

    Where Components of the Developmental
      Cognitive Type Models Can Be Seen

    Suggested Readings

    Commercially Available Materials

    Research Findings

    Films Available

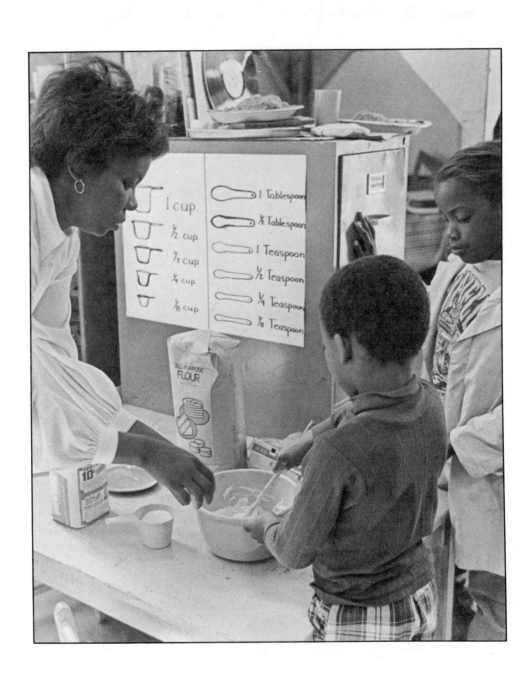

Developmental Cognitive Model

Situation: A teacher is sitting at a table with seven second-grade children. The children each have a small pine bough on the table in front of them.

1. Mr. Brown: What is this Anthony?

2. Anthony: A pine bough.

3. Mr. Brown: What else can you tell me about it, Shirley?

4. Shirley: It came from a Christmas tree like ours.

5. Mr. Brown: Is there something else you can say about it, Judi?

6. Judi: It smells strong like medicine.

7. Mr. Brown: OK, what else about it, Shaun?

8. Shaun: It feels sticky when you rub your hands on it backwards.

9. Mr. Brown: Sticky—like honey?

10. Shaun: No, it sticks like needles.

11. Shirley: Mine is sticky like gum on the end here.

12. Mr. Brown: What is that, Josh? The sticky stuff on the end?

13. Josh: Pine gum. You know, sap from inside the tree.

14. Mr. Brown: How does the gum taste, Josh?

15. Josh: (Putting his tongue on it) Not sweet.

16. Mr. Brown: How does it taste to you, Shirley?

17. Shirley: Kinda bitter.

18. Mr. Brown: When I was little, we chewed pine gum.

19. Children: (Laugh and wrinkle their faces.)

20. Mr. Brown: How could the pine bough you have be used, Judi?

21. Judi: For a decoration. Like put a ribbon on it.

22. Lisa: For a duster. We could wipe off the shelves.

23. Children: (Laugh.)

24. Mr. Brown: How is this pine bough like this red ball, Larkin?

25-27. Larkin: They aren't alike. One is red; one is green. One is round and smooth. The other is long and sticky.

28. Mr. Brown: Larkin told us how they are different.

29. Mr. Brown: How are they the same, Lisa?

30. Lisa: They are both Christmas decorations.

31. Mr. Brown: Right, Lisa.

This is a typical interaction pattern in the Developmental Cognitive Model. The interaction is coded in Figure 6.1.

EDUCATIONAL THEORY AND EXPECTED CHILD DEVELOPMENT

The preceding interaction might take place in a classroom where the Developmental Cognitive Model is used. The teacher asks the children questions about an item. The questions prompt the children to think about various attributes of the item—how it looks, smells, feels, tastes, and how it can be used. The teacher asks children to compare items for similarities and differences. When the teacher's question has only one correct answer it is coded 1Q, when the question calls for opinion or one of several ideas it is coded 2. The extended answers of the children are coded CT3 (response) followed by CT4 (inform).

The Developmental Cognitive Model is based primarily on the theory of Jean Piaget. Piaget's work indicates that a child's intelligence or logical thinking develops in stages according to the child's age and experience. Each stage is built on the previous one and requires that a new set of abilities be developed. Piaget believes the order of stages holds true for all children, but that the ages at which children progress through them depend on the children's physical and social environment.

Primary to Piaget's theory is the notion that a child learns through involvement in and manipulation of the environment. This is the process by which the child develops knowledge about self and objects, learns about relationships among objects, and comes to categorize events in his or her life. Piaget suggests that at each stage of development the child has a characteristic way of looking at and thinking about the world. Donna McClelland[1] has summarized these stages in the following way:

Stage 1: Sensorimotor (0-2 years)

The child's actions, which are at first aimless (from the adult's point of view) begin to show purpose, and he develops the concept of the permanent character of objects and begins to recognize objects through senses other than sight. In this stage, the child forms mental images of the objects and persons in his environment.

Stage 2: Preoperational (2-7 years)

The child uses symbols but in a very crude way. He begins to use words to represent objects and actions. The child at this time is guided by how things look; he judges entirely by appearance. For example, in a typical experiment Piaget set out

---

[1]Donna McClelland, "The Cognitive Curriculum" Ypsilanti Preschool Curriculum Demonstration Project. (Ypsilanti, Mich.: High/Scope Educational Research Foundation, May 1970). ERIC Accession No. ED 049 832.

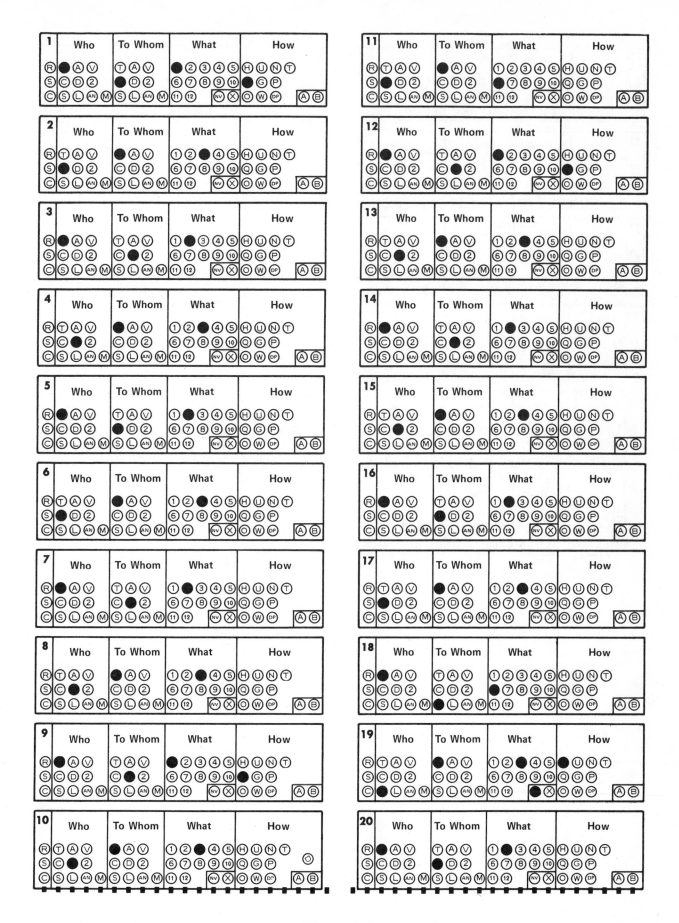

Figure 6.1

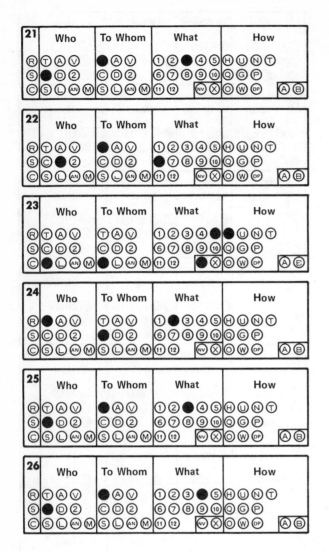

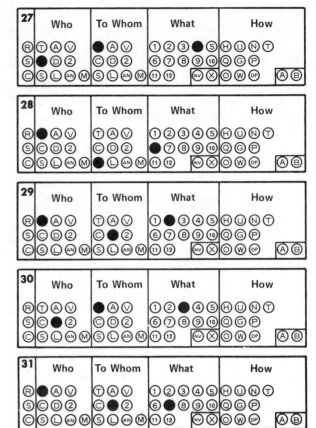

a row of cups and a basket of eggs. He asked the child to put
one egg in each cup. Then he asked, "Was there a cup for each
egg?" The child said yes. Then Piaget took all the eggs out of
the cups and put them in a bunch, leaving the row of cups. Then he
asked if there was still an egg for each cup. The child said no,
there were more cups. A child at this stage cannot understand that a
quantity remains the same when it is arranged differently. This is
called "conservation," and it is a key point in Piaget's theory.
Until a child has the ability to conserve, his thinking will be
governed to a great extent by how things look.

A child in the preoperational stage cannot put himself in
the position of another or take the point of view of another.
When he views an object from a changed perspective, the object
becomes a different thing to him because it looks different,
and only what the child sees at the moment is true for him.
Piaget's own small child was the subject of one of his most
famous observations on perspective. The child had a view of a
mountain from his window in their home in Geneva. One day,
Piaget and the child took a trip to the mountain in a car. When
they got to the base of the mountain, the child didn't recognize this as the same mountain he had seen from his window.
Later, when they drove around the mountain, the child still
couldn't understand that this was the same mountain. When the
perspective from which he views an object is changed (in this
case both the position and the distance were changed), the preoperational child cannot understand that the object remains the
same.

The preoperational child gives his attention only to one
characteristic of an object at a time. For example, in Piaget's
famous bead experiment, the child understands that all the
beads are wooden, that some are brown and some are white, but
he cannot reason about the whole (wooden beads) and a part
(brown beads) at the same time.

Gradually, in the preoperational stage, the child begins
to rely on his own action and thought and judge by what he
knows as well as by what he sees. He begins to understand that
certain characteristics of an object remain the same even
though the appearance of the object changes.

Stage 3: Concrete Operations (7-12 years)

The child begins to deal with his environment through
mental representations, or symbols, of actions and objects and
no longer needs to physically manipulate objects directly in
front of him to draw meaning from them. He can conserve quantity and can understand the relationship between the whole and
its parts. He begins to use logic to order the world, though he
does not generalize from one situation to another. At this
point, he is ready to learn to read and understand number and
is beginning to see the relation between cause and effect.

Stage 4: Formal Operations (12-17 years)

At this stage the child is capable of abstract thinking
and adult reasoning. He can think about the reality he sees,
and the possibilities he cannot see. He can survey a situation,
see alternatives, and select the one most suitable for solving
a problem.

The child's ability to think logically is developed gradually through the four stages, each stage building on the

previous stage, the child coordinating and integrating new knowledge with what he has learned in the past.

In his studies of children over many years, Piaget has accumulated a persuasive body of data to support his theory of stages in child development, but he has not attempted to implement his theory in school curriculum.

Some educators, however, have tried to put his theory into practice. Irving Siegel has translated some of Piaget's ideas into teaching strategies.[2] Siegel stipulates that children should have repeated experiences with objects. From experience with the object, the child learns that the object is permanent and becomes familiar with its various attributes. Children should also have many interactions with people. These interactions are expected to foster language development and a growing awareness of those around them. Since it is difficult for a teacher to know what concepts a child has developed, Siegel suggests that the teacher do some systematic questioning to identify steps in development, and thus learn which logical operations need strengthening. A teacher using such a strategy might conduct a class session similar to the one in Exercise 6.1 at the beginning of this chapter.

Dave Weikart and his staff have developed a comprehensive preschool and elementary school curriculum based on Piaget's theory.[3] They have focused their curriculum on developing an understanding of time, space, objects, and causality. Within the curriculum, children make and execute a plan and evaluate their work.

The elementary school children of concern in this work are in the preoperational and the concrete operations stages. If these children are in an environment suitable to their stage of development and if they engage in appropriate activities, they are expected to develop those abilities that will allow them to progress to the next stage.

TEACHER RESPONSIBILITIES

In the Developmental Cognitive Model, teachers are expected to understand Piaget's theory of development. They must learn a great deal about each child in order to understand how the child thinks about himself or herself and how he or she views the world. The teacher must decide what learning experiences should be provided at each point of the child's development. Activities should be provided that will help children learn how to classify objects (by size, color, material, shape, and so on) and to understand how objects are alike and different. Children also need to learn how to arrange objects in order—of size, quality, quantity. The goal is for children to learn relationships such as if A is bigger than B and B is bigger than C, then A is also bigger than C. This is called seriation. Understanding classifications and seriation is necessary for understanding number concepts.

---

[2]Irving Siegel, "The Piagetian System and the World of Education," in *Studies in Cognitive Development: Essays in Honor of Jean Piaget*, ed. David Elkind and John H. Flavell (New York: Oxford University Press, 1969).

[3]David Weikart, *Teacher Orientation Packet* (Ypsilanti, Mich.: High/Scope Educational Research Foundation, 1971).

Activities are also needed to help the child develop a sense of time or temporal relationships. Children can be helped to learn that time periods have a beginning and an end and that events can be sequenced. The teacher can do this by having clearly defined daily events with beginning and endings. Through planning sessions with the children, the teacher can help them develop concepts of yesterday, now, tomorrow, first, last, before, after, or next. Understanding temporal concepts is closely related to the ability to predict what happens if, for instance, I push this box, which is touching that board, which is against that block tower. As children explore the properties of objects and can predict the results of actions upon the objects, they come to understand cause and effect.

Teachers must also help children understand themselves in space. Games such as that for kindergarten in which children walk forward six steps, walk backward seven steps, turn to the left, and turn to the right may help them develop perspective. Children also need to develop concepts of objects in different perspectives. How does a block look when it is overhead, when it is on the floor, or when it is under another block and only partly visible?

Children must be helped, too, to develop their ability to represent things mentally. This ability develops through several levels, based on Piaget's stages. The first of these is the "Index Level," where the child develops the ability to construct the whole object mentally when only a part is seen; for example, from a hand and arm sticking out from behind a door, the child knows a whole person is there. Also in this level a child learns to identify objects or events through touch, smell, and hearing. Teachers can help develop this level through activities such as guessing games, where a child must discover what is in a sack or box only through feeling, smelling, or listening. J. Richard Suchman has developed an entire teaching program for using such an inquiry box.[4] In Suchman's program, the teacher uses very specific materials and questions to guide the child's thinking through logical problem-solving processes.

The second level of development is the "Symbol Level." At this level, representations are separate from the objects themselves. When children imitate a dog or make believe they are playing with elves, they are letting one thing or act stand for another—they are operating at the symbol level of representation. So too is a child who pretends that two crossed sticks are an airplane, or a child who makes three-dimensional clay models of animals or draws three-dimensional identifiable objects.

The third level of development is the "Sign Level." Children at this level are at the concrete operations stage described by Piaget. They understand that signs, or symbols, such as the alphabet, numerals, and words actually represent other things—things they do not in any way resemble. The teacher is responsible for developing or selecting appropriate experiences and materials that will help a child understand how a word can stand for an object or a concept. Beginning reading books start this process by showing a single word with a picture.

---

[4]J. Richard Suchman, *Inquiry Development Program* (Chicago: Science Research Associates, 1965).

SCHEDULE

The following is a typical schedule for any class in grades 1-6 using the Developmental Cognitive Model.

8:30 Roll is called and announcements made—groups are formed, each with an adult. Plans are made for reading and language development.

8:45 Teacher asks what each child did yesterday, and what each child plans to do today.

9:00 Children carry out plans—adults help as needed with reading, writing, and spelling.

11:00 Work is evaluated in small groups.

11:30 Lunch.

12:30 Teacher presents new concepts through materials and experiments. Plans are made for math and science projects in small groups.

12:45 Children carry out plans.

2:15 Work is evaluated in small groups.

2:30 Total group plays games, or teacher plays music or reads stories.

3:00 Dismissal.

PHYSICAL ENVIRONMENT

In the Developmental Cognitive Model, the structure of the physical environment provides a frame of reference for the children. This structure changes gradually through the course of the program to allow the children to encounter materials and develop new concepts when they are ready for them.

The room is divided into several interest centers. For kindergarten and first grade, there should be a large area for active group play, an art area, a construction area, a quiet area, a housekeeping area, and a language development area (with records, tapes, earphones, and so on). In the upper grades there should also be a science area and a math center. This arrangement permits children to use each area without interference from others.

Equipment is stored in the area where it is to be used and should be easily accessible to the children. Storage shelves and drawers should be arranged to teach classification—for example, similar items should be stored together (all big trucks should be stored on one shelf and all little trucks on another). For little children, shelves and drawers should have pictures or symbols on them to indicate the contents. At the end of a work session, children are expected to put all equipment back where it belongs—this gives them experience in classifying objects.

All bulletin boards, planning boards, pictures, and storage cabinets should be at the children's eye level. Bulletin boards should reflect the children's activities, written work, and art work. Planning boards should be maps of the room arrangement—and thus symbols of the room. They facilitate planning and keep areas from becoming overcrowded. Hooks are indicated in each work area of the planning board. The children could place their name tags on the hooks in the area where they plan to work. The number of hooks limits the number of children who can work in an area.

INTERACTION PATTERNS

A typical day would start with the children entering the classroom, greeting the teacher, and going to one of three assigned groups of approximately equal size. When all of the children had arrived, the teacher would meet with one group and two teaching aides would each meet with another. The adults would tell the children of any change in the schedule or of special events. This is a time when the children in each group would make their own plans for work time. Planning time is the cornerstone of the Developmental Cognitive Model. During this period, children gain experience in making a plan, sequencing events, carrying a task to completion, and evaluating the completed project. Teachers and aides use a questioning procedure to help them.

Exercise 6.1 is an example of a group planning the day's activities. Do the exercise now. The answers are at the end of the chapter.

EXERCISE 6.1 Using our coding system, see if you can code this interaction.

Situation: An aide and eight children are sitting on a rug in a kindergarten classroom, planning activities.

1. Aide: "Joseph, where did you work yesterday?"

1	Who	To Whom	What	How
	R T A V	T A V	1 2 3 4 5	H U N T
	S C D 2	C D 2	6 7 8 9 10	Q G P
	C S L AN M	S L AN M	11 12 NV X	O W DP A B

2. Joseph: "In the block area."

2	Who	To Whom	What	How
	R T A V	T A V	1 2 3 4 5	H U N T
	S C D 2	C D 2	6 7 8 9 10	Q G P
	C S L AN M	S L AN M	11 12 NV X	O W DP A B

3. Aide: "Where do you want to work today?"

3	Who	To Whom	What	How
	R T A V	T A V	1 2 3 4 5	H U N T
	S C D 2	C D 2	6 7 8 9 10	Q G P
	C S L AN M	S L AN M	11 12 NV X	O W DP A B

4. Joseph: "In the workshop."

4	Who	To Whom	What	How
	R T A V	T A V	1 2 3 4 5	H U N T
	S C D 2	C D 2	6 7 8 9 10	Q G P
	C S L AN M	S L AN M	11 12 NV X	O W DP A B

5. Aide: "What are you going to make, Joseph?"

5	Who	To Whom	What	How
	R T A V	T A V	1 2 3 4 5	H U N T
	S C D 2	C D 2	6 7 8 9 10	Q G P
	C S L AN M	S L AN M	11 12 NV X	O W DP A B

6. Joseph: "An airplane."

6	Who	To Whom	What	How
	Ⓡ Ⓣ Ⓐ Ⓥ	Ⓣ Ⓐ Ⓥ	① ② ③ ④ ⑤	Ⓗ Ⓤ Ⓝ Ⓣ
	Ⓢ Ⓒ Ⓓ ②	Ⓒ Ⓓ ②	⑥ ⑦ ⑧ ⑨ ⑩	Ⓠ Ⓖ Ⓟ
	Ⓒ Ⓢ Ⓛ ⒶⓃ Ⓜ	Ⓢ Ⓛ ⒶⓃ Ⓜ	⑪ ⑫ ⓃⓋ Ⓧ	Ⓞ Ⓦ ⓄⓅ Ⓐ Ⓑ

7. Aide: "What will you do first?"

7	Who	To Whom	What	How
	Ⓡ Ⓣ Ⓐ Ⓥ	Ⓣ Ⓐ Ⓥ	① ② ③ ④ ⑤	Ⓗ Ⓤ Ⓝ Ⓣ
	Ⓢ Ⓒ Ⓓ ②	Ⓒ Ⓓ ②	⑥ ⑦ ⑧ ⑨ ⑩	Ⓠ Ⓖ Ⓟ
	Ⓒ Ⓢ Ⓛ ⒶⓃ Ⓜ	Ⓢ Ⓛ ⒶⓃ Ⓜ	⑪ ⑫ ⓃⓋ Ⓧ	Ⓞ Ⓦ ⓄⓅ Ⓐ Ⓑ

8. Joseph: "I'll find two pieces of wood and nail them together in the center like this." (He crosses his index fingers.) "Then I'll find another little piece of wood for the propeller."

8	Who	To Whom	What	How
	Ⓡ Ⓣ Ⓐ Ⓥ	Ⓣ Ⓐ Ⓥ	① ② ③ ④ ⑤	Ⓗ Ⓤ Ⓝ Ⓣ
	Ⓢ Ⓒ Ⓓ ②	Ⓒ Ⓓ ②	⑥ ⑦ ⑧ ⑨ ⑩	Ⓠ Ⓖ Ⓟ
	Ⓒ Ⓢ Ⓛ ⒶⓃ Ⓜ	Ⓢ Ⓛ ⒶⓃ Ⓜ	⑪ ⑫ ⓃⓋ Ⓧ	Ⓞ Ⓦ ⓄⓅ Ⓐ Ⓑ

9. Aide: "That's a good plan, Joseph."

9	Who	To Whom	What	How
	Ⓡ Ⓣ Ⓐ Ⓥ	Ⓣ Ⓐ Ⓥ	① ② ③ ④ ⑤	Ⓗ Ⓤ Ⓝ Ⓣ
	Ⓢ Ⓒ Ⓓ ②	Ⓒ Ⓓ ②	⑥ ⑦ ⑧ ⑨ ⑩	Ⓠ Ⓖ Ⓟ
	Ⓒ Ⓢ Ⓛ ⒶⓃ Ⓜ	Ⓢ Ⓛ ⒶⓃ Ⓜ	⑪ ⑫ ⓃⓋ Ⓧ	Ⓞ Ⓦ ⓄⓅ Ⓐ Ⓑ

By her questioning procedure, the aide in the preceding exercise is helping the children develop a sense of time (yesterday-today) and the ability to make a plan. Joseph has been encouraged to think ahead about what he will do in the carpentry area.

EXERCISE 6.2   See if you can write a vignette.

Situation: A planning session, with seven first-grade children led by a first-grade teacher.

Teacher: _____

Child: _____

Teacher: _____

Child: _____

Teacher: _____

Child: _____

Teacher: _____

Child: _____

Teacher: _____

In all grades there is a daily planning session for work, a work session, and an evaluation session of the work that was accomplished. The following exercise is an example of an evaluation session. Do the exercise now.

EXERCISE 6.3   Code the following interaction.

Situation: A teacher is conducting an evaluation session with seven sixth-grade children.

1. Teacher: "Helen, what did you do today?"

1	Who	To Whom	What	How
	Ⓡ Ⓣ Ⓐ Ⓥ	Ⓣ Ⓐ Ⓥ	① ② ③ ④ ⑤	Ⓗ Ⓤ Ⓝ Ⓣ
	Ⓢ Ⓒ Ⓓ ②	Ⓒ Ⓓ ②	⑥ ⑦ ⑧ ⑨ ⑩	Ⓠ Ⓖ Ⓟ
	Ⓒ Ⓢ Ⓛ ⒶⓃ Ⓜ	Ⓢ Ⓛ ⒶⓃ Ⓜ	⑪ ⑫	ⓃⓋ Ⓧ Ⓞ Ⓦ ᴅᴘ Ⓐ Ⓑ

2. Helen: "I wrote an article for the school paper about the trip we're planning to take to the state capital."

2	Who	To Whom	What	How
	Ⓡ Ⓣ Ⓐ Ⓥ	Ⓣ Ⓐ Ⓥ	① ② ③ ④ ⑤	Ⓗ Ⓤ Ⓝ Ⓣ
	Ⓢ Ⓒ Ⓓ ②	Ⓒ Ⓓ ②	⑥ ⑦ ⑧ ⑨ ⑩	Ⓠ Ⓖ Ⓟ
	Ⓒ Ⓢ Ⓛ ⒶⓃ Ⓜ	Ⓢ Ⓛ ⒶⓃ Ⓜ	⑪ ⑫	ⓃⓋ Ⓧ Ⓞ Ⓦ ᴅᴘ Ⓐ Ⓑ

3. Teacher: "What do you think of it? Did you do a good job?"

3	Who	To Whom	What	How
	Ⓡ Ⓣ Ⓐ Ⓥ	Ⓣ Ⓐ Ⓥ	① ② ③ ④ ⑤	Ⓗ Ⓤ Ⓝ Ⓣ
	Ⓢ Ⓒ Ⓓ ②	Ⓒ Ⓓ ②	⑥ ⑦ ⑧ ⑨ ⑩	Ⓠ Ⓖ Ⓟ
	Ⓒ Ⓢ Ⓛ ⒶⓃ Ⓜ	Ⓢ Ⓛ ⒶⓃ Ⓜ	⑪ ⑫	ⓃⓋ Ⓧ Ⓞ Ⓦ ᴅᴘ Ⓐ Ⓑ

4-6. Helen: "Well, the beginning is OK, but in the middle I just keep listing things we're going to see. It's boring. I'd like to know what you other guys think."

4	Who	To Whom	What	How
	Ⓡ Ⓣ Ⓐ Ⓥ	Ⓣ Ⓐ Ⓥ	① ② ③ ④ ⑤	Ⓗ Ⓤ Ⓝ Ⓣ
	Ⓢ Ⓒ Ⓓ ②	Ⓒ Ⓓ ②	⑥ ⑦ ⑧ ⑨ ⑩	Ⓠ Ⓖ Ⓟ
	Ⓒ Ⓢ Ⓛ ⒶⓃ Ⓜ	Ⓢ Ⓛ ⒶⓃ Ⓜ	⑪ ⑫	ⓃⓋ Ⓧ Ⓞ Ⓦ ᴅᴘ Ⓐ Ⓑ

5	Who	To Whom	What	How
	Ⓡ Ⓣ Ⓐ Ⓥ	Ⓣ Ⓐ Ⓥ	① ② ③ ④ ⑤	Ⓗ Ⓤ Ⓝ Ⓣ
	Ⓢ Ⓒ Ⓓ ②	Ⓒ Ⓓ ②	⑥ ⑦ ⑧ ⑨ ⑩	Ⓠ Ⓖ Ⓟ
	Ⓒ Ⓢ Ⓛ ⒶⓃ Ⓜ	Ⓢ Ⓛ ⒶⓃ Ⓜ	⑪ ⑫	ⓃⓋ Ⓧ Ⓞ Ⓦ ᴅᴘ Ⓐ Ⓑ

6	Who	To Whom	What	How
	Ⓡ Ⓣ Ⓐ Ⓥ	Ⓣ Ⓐ Ⓥ	① ② ③ ④ ⑤	Ⓗ Ⓤ Ⓝ Ⓣ
	Ⓢ Ⓒ Ⓓ ②	Ⓒ Ⓓ ②	⑥ ⑦ ⑧ ⑨ ⑩	Ⓠ Ⓖ Ⓟ
	Ⓒ Ⓢ Ⓛ ⒶⓃ Ⓜ	Ⓢ Ⓛ ⒶⓃ Ⓜ	⑪ ⑫	ⓃⓋ Ⓧ Ⓞ Ⓦ ᴅᴘ Ⓐ Ⓑ

7. Teacher: "What do you plan to do next?"

7	Who	To Whom	What	How
	Ⓡ Ⓣ Ⓐ Ⓥ	Ⓣ Ⓐ Ⓥ	① ② ③ ④ ⑤	Ⓗ Ⓤ Ⓝ Ⓣ
	Ⓢ Ⓒ Ⓓ ②	Ⓒ Ⓓ ②	⑥ ⑦ ⑧ ⑨ ⑩	Ⓠ Ⓖ Ⓟ
	Ⓒ Ⓢ Ⓛ ⒶⓃ Ⓜ	Ⓢ Ⓛ ⒶⓃ Ⓜ	⑪ ⑫	ⓃⓋ Ⓧ Ⓞ Ⓦ ᴅᴘ Ⓐ Ⓑ

8. Helen: "I'll make some copies and ask Jerry, Mark, and Sally to give me suggestions."

8	Who	To Whom	What	How
	Ⓡ Ⓣ Ⓐ Ⓥ	Ⓣ Ⓐ Ⓥ	① ② ③ ④ ⑤	Ⓗ Ⓤ Ⓝ Ⓣ
	Ⓢ Ⓒ Ⓓ ②	Ⓒ Ⓓ ②	⑥ ⑦ ⑧ ⑨ ⑩	Ⓠ Ⓖ Ⓟ
	Ⓒ Ⓢ Ⓛ ⒶⓃ Ⓜ	Ⓢ Ⓛ ⒶⓃ Ⓜ	⑪ ⑫	ⓃⓋ Ⓧ Ⓞ Ⓦ ᴅᴘ Ⓐ Ⓑ

EXERCISE 6.4   Write a vignette.

Situation: Fourth-grade students are evaluating a mural they are doing on the westward movement.

Teacher: _____

Child: _____

Teacher: _____

Child: _____

Teacher: _____

Child: _____

Teacher: _____

Child: _____

Teacher: _____

Teachers in this model also conduct lessons that will develop the cognitive skills identified with Piaget's stages of development. Such a lesson might illustrate how objects can be classified according to size, shape, material, color, texture, or smell. The following exercise is an example of this. Using our coding system, complete the exercise now.

EXERCISE 6.5   Code the following interaction.

Situation: A teacher is helping his kindergarten class learn how objects can be classified.

1. Teacher: "What do I have, Wilma?"

2. Wilma: "A spoon and a fork."

3. Teacher: "How are they different, Ted?"

4. Ted: "The fork is longer."

4	Who	To Whom	What	How
	Ⓡ Ⓣ Ⓐ Ⓥ	Ⓣ Ⓐ Ⓥ	① ② ③ ④ ⑤	Ⓗ Ⓤ Ⓝ Ⓣ
	Ⓢ Ⓒ Ⓓ ②	Ⓒ Ⓓ ②	⑥ ⑦ ⑧ ⑨ ⑩	Ⓠ Ⓖ Ⓟ
	Ⓒ Ⓢ Ⓛ ⒜ Ⓜ	Ⓢ Ⓛ ⒜ Ⓜ	⑪ ⑫ ⓝⓥ Ⓧ	Ⓞ Ⓦ ⒟ⓟ Ⓐ Ⓑ

5. Teacher: "What other way are they different, Fred?"

5	Who	To Whom	What	How
	Ⓡ Ⓣ Ⓐ Ⓥ	Ⓣ Ⓐ Ⓥ	① ② ③ ④ ⑤	Ⓗ Ⓤ Ⓝ Ⓣ
	Ⓢ Ⓒ Ⓓ ②	Ⓒ Ⓓ ②	⑥ ⑦ ⑧ ⑨ ⑩	Ⓠ Ⓖ Ⓟ
	Ⓒ Ⓢ Ⓛ ⒜ Ⓜ	Ⓢ Ⓛ ⒜ Ⓜ	⑪ ⑫ ⓝⓥ Ⓧ	Ⓞ Ⓦ ⒟ⓟ Ⓐ Ⓑ

6. Fred: "The fork has four points at the ends and the spoon is round."

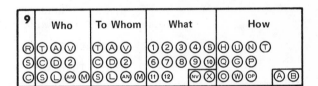

6	Who	To Whom	What	How
	Ⓡ Ⓣ Ⓐ Ⓥ	Ⓣ Ⓐ Ⓥ	① ② ③ ④ ⑤	Ⓗ Ⓤ Ⓝ Ⓣ
	Ⓢ Ⓒ Ⓓ ②	Ⓒ Ⓓ ②	⑥ ⑦ ⑧ ⑨ ⑩	Ⓠ Ⓖ Ⓟ
	Ⓒ Ⓢ Ⓛ ⒜ Ⓜ	Ⓢ Ⓛ ⒜ Ⓜ	⑪ ⑫ ⓝⓥ Ⓧ	Ⓞ Ⓦ ⒟ⓟ Ⓐ Ⓑ

7. Teacher: "In what way are they the same, Wilma?"

7	Who	To Whom	What	How
	Ⓡ Ⓣ Ⓐ Ⓥ	Ⓣ Ⓐ Ⓥ	① ② ③ ④ ⑤	Ⓗ Ⓤ Ⓝ Ⓣ
	Ⓢ Ⓒ Ⓓ ②	Ⓒ Ⓓ ②	⑥ ⑦ ⑧ ⑨ ⑩	Ⓠ Ⓖ Ⓟ
	Ⓒ Ⓢ Ⓛ ⒜ Ⓜ	Ⓢ Ⓛ ⒜ Ⓜ	⑪ ⑫ ⓝⓥ Ⓧ	Ⓞ Ⓦ ⒟ⓟ Ⓐ Ⓑ

8. Wilma: "They are both used for eating."

8	Who	To Whom	What	How
	Ⓡ Ⓣ Ⓐ Ⓥ	Ⓣ Ⓐ Ⓥ	① ② ③ ④ ⑤	Ⓗ Ⓤ Ⓝ Ⓣ
	Ⓢ Ⓒ Ⓓ ②	Ⓒ Ⓓ ②	⑥ ⑦ ⑧ ⑨ ⑩	Ⓠ Ⓖ Ⓟ
	Ⓒ Ⓢ Ⓛ ⒜ Ⓜ	Ⓢ Ⓛ ⒜ Ⓜ	⑪ ⑫ ⓝⓥ Ⓧ	Ⓞ Ⓦ ⒟ⓟ Ⓐ Ⓑ

9. Teacher: "What is another way they are the same, Lucas?"

9	Who	To Whom	What	How
	Ⓡ Ⓣ Ⓐ Ⓥ	Ⓣ Ⓐ Ⓥ	① ② ③ ④ ⑤	Ⓗ Ⓤ Ⓝ Ⓣ
	Ⓢ Ⓒ Ⓓ ②	Ⓒ Ⓓ ②	⑥ ⑦ ⑧ ⑨ ⑩	Ⓠ Ⓖ Ⓟ
	Ⓒ Ⓢ Ⓛ ⒜ Ⓜ	Ⓢ Ⓛ ⒜ Ⓜ	⑪ ⑫ ⓝⓥ Ⓧ	Ⓞ Ⓦ ⒟ⓟ Ⓐ Ⓑ

10. Lucas: "I don't know."

10	Who	To Whom	What	How
	Ⓡ Ⓣ Ⓐ Ⓥ	Ⓣ Ⓐ Ⓥ	① ② ③ ④ ⑤	Ⓗ Ⓤ Ⓝ Ⓣ
	Ⓢ Ⓒ Ⓓ ②	Ⓒ Ⓓ ②	⑥ ⑦ ⑧ ⑨ ⑩	Ⓠ Ⓖ Ⓟ
	Ⓒ Ⓢ Ⓛ ⒜ Ⓜ	Ⓢ Ⓛ ⒜ Ⓜ	⑪ ⑫ ⓝⓥ Ⓧ	Ⓞ Ⓦ ⒟ⓟ Ⓐ Ⓑ

11. Teacher: "What are they both made from?"

11	Who	To Whom	What	How
	Ⓡ Ⓣ Ⓐ Ⓥ	Ⓣ Ⓐ Ⓥ	① ② ③ ④ ⑤	Ⓗ Ⓤ Ⓝ Ⓣ
	Ⓢ Ⓒ Ⓓ ②	Ⓒ Ⓓ ②	⑥ ⑦ ⑧ ⑨ ⑩	Ⓠ Ⓖ Ⓟ
	Ⓒ Ⓢ Ⓛ ⒜ Ⓜ	Ⓢ Ⓛ ⒜ Ⓜ	⑪ ⑫ ⓝⓥ Ⓧ	Ⓞ Ⓦ ⒟ⓟ Ⓐ Ⓑ

12. Lucas: "Metal."

12	Who	To Whom	What	How
	Ⓡ Ⓣ Ⓐ Ⓥ	Ⓣ Ⓐ Ⓥ	① ② ③ ④ ⑤	Ⓗ Ⓤ Ⓝ Ⓣ
	Ⓢ Ⓒ Ⓓ ②	Ⓒ Ⓓ ②	⑥ ⑦ ⑧ ⑨ ⑩	Ⓠ Ⓖ Ⓟ
	Ⓒ Ⓢ Ⓛ ⒜ Ⓜ	Ⓢ Ⓛ ⒜ Ⓜ	⑪ ⑫ ⓝⓥ Ⓧ	Ⓞ Ⓦ ⒟ⓟ Ⓐ Ⓑ

HANDLING MISBEHAVIOR

Four children in a third-grade classroom are working in the construction area. The quiet working hum of the room is suddenly broken by angry shouts.

Brad: Take your hands off this hammer!

Dick: It's my turn!

Tom: I'm not finished!

Both boys pull on the hammer, shoving each other with their other hand. The teacher walks over, puts out her hand for the hammer.

Teacher: I want you each to think of at least one better way to decide who gets to use the hammer.

Dick: He's had it this whole work period!

Teacher: Is that a suggestion of how to solve the problem?

Dick: No. Maybe we could toss a coin. Heads I get to use it, tails he gets to keep it.

Brad: But I'm almost finished with my puppet stage.

Teacher: What other work could you do on the puppet stage if you were not using the hammer?

Brad (looks thoughtful): I could string the rope to pull the curtains.

Teacher: Dick thinks we could flip a coin to decide who uses the hammer. What do you think, Brad?

Brad: I think we need another hammer, but I guess we could each use it half the work time.

Teacher: What if some other person wants to use it?

Brad: Then we'll all get one-third of the work time.

Teacher: OK, who gets the hammer now?

Brad (shrugging his shoulders): Dick does.

Dick: I only have to pound about six nails to hold the shelves in the store. Then you can have it back.

Teacher: When you guys give yourselves a chance, you think really well about solving problems. You both had a reasonable solution. Dick said flip a coin and Tom said take turns by amount of time.

In the Developmental Cognitive Model, teachers ask the children to think of better ways to solve problems. As examples, when they solve problems, teachers are encouraged to use rational words. If a classroom is too noisy as students clean up for lunch, the teacher might say, "When everyone is quiet, then we will be excused for the lunch period." This approach differs from that of a teacher who shouts, "Be quiet!" or threatens, "If you don't get quiet you won't go to lunch." Teachers also encourage children to label feelings. "How did you feel when Bill knocked over your block tower?" "Can you think of another way to tell Bill you don't want him to knock down your tower besides hitting him?"

In the Developmental Cognitive Model, teachers verbalize extensively and try to get children to verbalize also. The children are often asked what they are doing or feeling in the midst of a problem. In this theory, a person who can verbalize a problem or a feeling can come to a more logical solution to it.

A CONTEXTUAL VIEW

The following exercises involve typical classrooms based on the Developmental Cognitive Model. Do the exercises now. The answers are at the end of the chapter.

EXERCISE 6.6 Code each person in the situation below on the CCL.

Situation: In a first-grade classroom during work period, the children are scattered about the room. Four children are in the quiet area, sitting on the rug reading books. Two children are painting at an easel, and near them three other children are shaping animals from clay. Four children are building boats in the carpentry area, while in the cooking center, five children are cutting cookies from rolled-out dough. At a desk, one child is dictating a story about his new dog to an aide. At another, the teacher is helping two children print their names. Another aide is showing three children how to make puppets from paper bags.

CLASSROOM CHECK LIST (be sure to code **EVERYONE** in the class)

	ONE CHILD	TWO CHILDREN	SMALL GROUPS	LARGE GROUPS
1. Snack, lunch	T ①②③ / A ①②③ / V ①②③ / i ①②③	T ①②③ / A ①②③ / V ①②③ / i ①②③	T ①②③④ / A ①②③④ / V ①②③④ / i ①②③④	T ①② / A ①② / V ①② / i ①②
2. Group time	T ①②③ / A ①②③ / V ①②③ / i ①②③	T ①②③ / A ①②③ / V ①②③ / i ①②③	T ①②③④ / A ①②③④ / V ①②③④ / i ①②③④	T ①② / A ①② / V ①② / i ①②
Story / **3. Music** / Dancing	T ①②③ / A ①②③ / V ①②③ / i ①②③	T ①②③ / A ①②③ / V ①②③ / i ①②③	T ①②③④ / A ①②③④ / V ①②③④ / i ①②③④	T ①② / A ①② / V ①② / i ①②
4. Arts, Crafts	T ①②③ / A ①②③ / V ①②③ / i ①②③	T ①②③ / A ①②③ / V ①②③ / i ①②③	T ①②③④ / A ①②③④ / V ①②③④ / i ①②③④	T ①② / A ①② / V ①② / i ①②
Guessing Games / **5. Table Games** / Puzzles	T ①②③ / A ①②③ / V ①②③ / i ①②③	T ①②③ / A ①②③ / V ①②③ / i ①②③	T ①②③④ / A ①②③④ / V ①②③④ / i ①②③④	T ①② / A ①② / V ①② / i ①②
Numbers / **6. Math** / Arithmetic	T ①②③ / A ①②③ / V ①②③ / i ①②③	T ①②③ / A ①②③ / V ①②③ / i ①②③	T ①②③④ / A ①②③④ / V ①②③④ / i ①②③④	T ①② / A ①② / V ①② / i ①②
Reading / **7. Alphabet** / Lang. Development	T ①②③ / A ①②③ / V ①②③ / i ①②③	T ①②③ / A ①②③ / V ①②③ / i ①②③	T ①②③④ / A ①②③④ / V ①②③④ / i ①②③④	T ①② / A ①② / V ①② / i ①②
8. Social Studies / Geography	T ①②③ / A ①②③ / V ①②③ / i ①②③	T ①②③ / A ①②③ / V ①②③ / i ①②③	T ①②③④ / A ①②③④ / V ①②③④ / i ①②③④	T ①② / A ①② / V ①② / i ①②
9. Science / Natural World	T ①②③ / A ①②③ / V ①②③ / i ①②③	T ①②③ / A ①②③ / V ①②③ / i ①②③	T ①②③④ / A ①②③④ / V ①②③④ / i ①②③④	T ①② / A ①② / V ①② / i ①②
Sewing / Cooking / **10.** Pounding / Sawing	T ①②③ / A ①②③ / V ①②③ / i ①②③	T ①②③ / A ①②③ / V ①②③ / i ①②③	T ①②③④ / A ①②③④ / V ①②③④ / i ①②③④	T ①② / A ①② / V ①② / i ①②
11. Blocks / Trucks	T ①②③ / A ①②③ / V ①②③ / i ①②③	T ①②③ / A ①②③ / V ①②③ / i ①②③	T ①②③④ / A ①②③④ / V ①②③④ / i ①②③④	T ①② / A ①② / V ①② / i ①②
12. Dramatic Play / Dress-Up	T ①②③ / A ①②③ / V ①②③ / i ①②③	T ①②③ / A ①②③ / V ①②③ / i ①②③	T ①②③④ / A ①②③④ / V ①②③④ / i ①②③④	T ①② / A ①② / V ①② / i ①②
13. Active Play	T ①②③ / A ①②③ / V ①②③ / i ①②③	T ①②③ / A ①②③ / V ①②③ / i ①②③	T ①②③④ / A ①②③④ / V ①②③④ / i ①②③④	T ①② / A ①② / V ①② / i ①②
14. RELIABILITY SHEET ○				

Categories listed beside items 6–9:

○ TV
○ Audio-Visual Materials
○ Exploratory Materials
○ Math and Science Equipment
○ Texts, Workbooks
○ Puzzles, Games

Exercise 6.6

		ONE CHILD	TWO CHILDREN	SMALL GROUPS	LARGE GROUPS
15. Practical Skills Acquisition		T ①②③	T ①②③	T ①②③④	T ①②
		A ①②③	A ①②③	A ①②③④	A ①②
		v ①②③	v ①②③	v ①②③④	v ①②
		i ①②③	i ①②③	i ①②③④	i ①②
16. Observing		T ①②③	T ①②③	T ①②③④	T ①②
		A ①②③	A ①②③	A ①②③④	A ①②
		v ①②③	v ①②③	v ①②③④	v ①②
		i ①②③	i ①②③	i ①②③④	i ①②
17. Social Interaction Ob [ⓒ ② ⓢ]	Ⓣ Ⓐ Ⓥ	T ①②③	T ①②③	T ①②③④	T ①②
		A ①②③	A ①②③	A ①②③④	A ①②
		v ①②③	v ①②③	v ①②③④	v ①②
		i ①②③	i ①②③	i ①②③④	i ①②
18. Unoccupied Child		T ①②③	T ①②③	T ①②③④	T ①②
		A ①②③	A ①②③	A ①②③④	A ①②
		v ①②③	v ①②③	v ①②③④	v ①②
		i ①②③	i ①②③	i ①②③④	i ①②
19. Discipline		T ①②③	T ①②③	T ①②③④	T ①②
		A ①②③	A ①②③	A ①②③④	A ①②
		v ①②③	v ①②③	v ①②③④	v ①②
		i ①②③	i ①②③	i ①②③④	i ①②
20. Transitional Activities	Ⓣ Ⓐ Ⓥ	T ①②③	T ①②③	T ①②③④	T ①②
		A ①②③	A ①②③	A ①②③④	A ①②
		v ①②③	v ①②③	v ①②③④	v ①②
		i ①②③	i ①②③	i ①②③④	i ①②
21. Classroom Management	Ⓣ Ⓐ Ⓥ	T ①②③	T ①②③	T ①②③④	T ①②
		A ①②③	A ①②③	A ①②③④	A ①②
		v ①②③	v ①②③	v ①②③④	v ①②
		i ①②③	i ①②③	i ①②③④	i ①②
22. Out of Room	Ⓣ Ⓐ Ⓥ	T ①②③	T ①②③	T ①②③④	T ①②
		A ①②③	A ①②③	A ①②③④	A ①②
		v ①②③	v ①②③	v ①②③④	v ①②
		i ①②③	i ①②③	i ①②③④	i ①②

NUMBER OF ADULTS IN CLASSROOM   ⓪ ① ② ③ ④ ⑤ ⑥ ⑦ ⑧ ⑨ ⑩

EXERCISE 6.7   Code each person in the situation below on the CCL.

Situation: In a second-grade classroom the teacher is working with seven children in a language development activity. She is saying, "Pick out one piece of fruit in the basket that feels furry. Pick one fruit that feels smooth." An aide is working with eight children in a math lesson. Each child has a set of Cuisenaire rods. She asks, "How many red rods are equal to an orange rod?" The children start stacking the red rods end to end next to an orange rod. Another group of eight children are writing stories about a trip they took to the local airport. An aide moves from child to child and assists when they ask how to spell a word. As they complete them, the aide listens to the children read their stories.

CLASSROOM CHECK LIST (be sure to code **EVERYONE** in the class)

Activity		ONE CHILD	TWO CHILDREN	SMALL GROUPS	LARGE GROUPS
1. Snack, lunch		T ①②③ / A ①②③ / v ①②③ / i ①②③	T ①②③ / A ①②③ / v ①②③ / i ①②③	T ①②③④ / A ①②③④ / v ①②③④ / i ①②③④	T ①② / A ①② / v ①② / i ①②
2. Group time		T ①②③ / A ①②③ / v ①②③ / i ①②③	T ①②③ / A ①②③ / v ①②③ / i ①②③	T ①②③④ / A ①②③④ / v ①②③④ / i ①②③④	T ①② / A ①② / v ①② / i ①②
3. Story / Music / Dancing		T ①②③ / A ①②③ / v ①②③ / i ①②③	T ①②③ / A ①②③ / v ①②③ / i ①②③	T ①②③④ / A ①②③④ / v ①②③④ / i ①②③④	T ①② / A ①② / v ①② / i ①②
4. Arts, Crafts		T ①②③ / A ①②③ / v ①②③ / i ①②③	T ①②③ / A ①②③ / v ①②③ / i ①②③	T ①②③④ / A ①②③④ / v ①②③④ / i ①②③④	T ①② / A ①② / v ①② / i ①②
5. Guessing Games / Table Games / Puzzles		T ①②③ / A ①②③ / v ①②③ / i ①②③	T ①②③ / A ①②③ / v ①②③ / i ①②③	T ①②③④ / A ①②③④ / v ①②③④ / i ①②③④	T ①② / A ①② / v ①② / i ①②
○ TV ○ Audio-Visual Materials ○ Exploratory Materials ○ Math and Science Equipment ○ Texts, Workbooks ○ Puzzles, Games	**6. Math** Numbers / Arithmetic	T ①②③ / A ①②③ / v ①②③ / i ①②③	T ①②③ / A ①②③ / v ①②③ / i ①②③	T ①②③④ / A ①②③④ / v ①②③④ / i ①②③④	T ①② / A ①② / v ①② / i ①②
	7. Reading / Alphabet / Lang. Development	T ①②③ / A ①②③ / v ①②③ / i ①②③	T ①②③ / A ①②③ / v ①②③ / i ①②③	T ①②③④ / A ①②③④ / v ①②③④ / i ①②③④	T ①② / A ①② / v ①② / i ①②
	8. Social Studies / Geography	T ①②③ / A ①②③ / v ①②③ / i ①②③	T ①②③ / A ①②③ / v ①②③ / i ①②③	T ①②③④ / A ①②③④ / v ①②③④ / i ①②③④	T ①② / A ①② / v ①② / i ①②
	9. Science / Natural World	T ①②③ / A ①②③ / v ①②③ / i ①②③	T ①②③ / A ①②③ / v ①②③ / i ①②③	T ①②③④ / A ①②③④ / v ①②③④ / i ①②③④	T ①② / A ①② / v ①② / i ①②
10. Sewing / Cooking / Pounding / Sawing		T ①②③ / A ①②③ / v ①②③ / i ①②③	T ①②③ / A ①②③ / v ①②③ / i ①②③	T ①②③④ / A ①②③④ / v ①②③④ / i ①②③④	T ①② / A ①② / v ①② / i ①②
11. Blocks / Trucks		T ①②③ / A ①②③ / v ①②③ / i ①②③	T ①②③ / A ①②③ / v ①②③ / i ①②③	T ①②③④ / A ①②③④ / v ①②③④ / i ①②③④	T ①② / A ①② / v ①② / i ①②
12. Dramatic Play / Dress-Up		T ①②③ / A ①②③ / v ①②③ / i ①②③	T ①②③ / A ①②③ / v ①②③ / i ①②③	T ①②③④ / A ①②③④ / v ①②③④ / i ①②③④	T ①② / A ①② / v ①② / i ①②
13. Active Play		T ①②③ / A ①②③ / v ①②③ / i ①②③	T ①②③ / A ①②③ / v ①②③ / i ①②③	T ①②③④ / A ①②③④ / v ①②③④ / i ①②③④	T ①② / A ①② / v ①② / i ①②
14. RELIABILITY SHEET ○					

Exercise 6.7

			ONE CHILD	TWO CHILDREN	SMALL GROUPS	LARGE GROUPS
15. Practical Skills Acquisition			T ①②③ A ①②③ v ①②③ i ①②③	T ①②③ A ①②③ v ①②③ i ①②③	T ①②③④ A ①②③④ v ①②③④ i ①②③④	T ①② A ①② v ①② i ①②
16. Observing			T ①②③ A ①②③ v ①②③ i ①②③	T ①②③ A ①②③ v ①②③ i ①②③	T ①②③④ A ①②③④ v ①②③④ i ①②③④	T ①② A ①② v ①② i ①②
17. Social Interaction	Ob [Ⓒ ② Ⓢ]	Ⓣ Ⓐ Ⓥ	T ①②③ A ①②③ v ①②③ i ①②③	T ①②③ A ①②③ v ①②③ i ①②③	T ①②③④ A ①②③④ v ①②③④ i ①②③④	T ①② A ①② v ①② i ①②
18. Unoccupied Child			T ①②③ A ①②③ v ①②③ i ①②③	T ①②③ A ①②③ v ①②③ i ①②③	T ①②③④ A ①②③④ v ①②③④ i ①②③④	T ①② A ①② v ①② i ①②
19. Discipline			T ①②③ A ①②③ v ①②③ i ①②③	T ①②③ A ①②③ v ①②③ i ①②③	T ①②③④ A ①②③④ v ①②③④ i ①②③④	T ①② A ①② v ①② i ①②
20. Transitional Activities		Ⓣ Ⓐ Ⓥ	T ①②③ A ①②③ v ①②③ i ①②③	T ①②③ A ①②③ v ①②③ i ①②③	T ①②③④ A ①②③④ v ①②③④ i ①②③④	T ①② A ①② v ①② i ①②
21. Classroom Management		Ⓣ Ⓐ Ⓥ	T ①②③ A ①②③ v ①②③ i ①②③	T ①②③ A ①②③ v ①②③ i ①②③	T ①②③④ A ①②③④ v ①②③④ i ①②③④	T ①② A ①② v ①② i ①②
22. Out of Room		Ⓣ Ⓐ Ⓥ	T ①②③ A ①②③ v ①②③ i ①②③	T ①②③ A ①②③ v ①②③ i ①②③	T ①②③④ A ①②③④ v ①②③④ i ①②③④	T ①② A ①② v ①② i ①②

NUMBER OF ADULTS IN CLASSROOM   ⓪ ① ② ③ ④ ⑤ ⑥ ⑦ ⑧ ⑨ ⑩

Students in the Developmental Cognitive Model continue to learn skills through experience. Over time, the skills become more practical for functioning successfully in adult life. Algebraic and geometric principles, for example, are applied to actual construction so that the relationships are clearly understood, not just memorized. Exercise 6.8 is an example of students learning skills through experience. Complete it now.

EXERCISE 6.8 Code each person in the situation below on the CCL.

Situation: In a sixth-grade classroom, six students, with the help of the math teacher, are designing a tree house. They are using an algebraic formula to figure what size wood they need to order for the floor joists. Another group of five students is designing a cable-hung footbridge to get to the tree house. A local bridge contractor is helping them understand the geometric relationships between the arches formed by the cables, the poles, and the tree so they'll see how the weight will be distributed. Another group of five children is discussing safety factors and trying to decide how high the tree house should be from the ground and how high the railing should be. Five other students are making bread. They are discussing the chemical properties of yeast with a dietician. The discussion centers about the differences and preferability of dry yeast, cake yeast, or yeast passed from one generation to another. Two other students are taking body measurements as they prepare to make dresses for themselves.

CLASSROOM CHECK LIST (be sure to code **EVERYONE** in the class)

		ONE CHILD	TWO CHILDREN	SMALL GROUPS	LARGE GROUPS
1. Snack, lunch		T ①②③ / A ①②③ / v ①②③ / i ①②③	T ①②③ / A ①②③ / v ①②③ / i ①②③	T ①②③④ / A ①②③④ / v ①②③④ / i ①②③④	T ①② / A ①② / v ①② / i ①②
2. Group time		T ①②③ / A ①②③ / v ①②③ / i ①②③	T ①②③ / A ①②③ / v ①②③ / i ①②③	T ①②③④ / A ①②③④ / v ①②③④ / i ①②③④	T ①② / A ①② / v ①② / i ①②
3. Story / Music / Dancing		T ①②③ / A ①②③ / v ①②③ / i ①②③	T ①②③ / A ①②③ / v ①②③ / i ①②③	T ①②③④ / A ①②③④ / v ①②③④ / i ①②③④	T ①② / A ①② / v ①② / i ①②
4. Arts, Crafts		T ①②③ / A ①②③ / v ①②③ / i ①②③	T ①②③ / A ①②③ / v ①②③ / i ①②③	T ①②③④ / A ①②③④ / v ①②③④ / i ①②③④	T ①② / A ①② / v ①② / i ①②
5. Guessing Games / Table Games / Puzzles		T ①②③ / A ①②③ / v ①②③ / i ①②③	T ①②③ / A ①②③ / v ①②③ / i ①②③	T ①②③④ / A ①②③④ / v ①②③④ / i ①②③④	T ①② / A ①② / v ①② / i ①②
○ TV ○ Audio-Visual Materials ○ Exploratory Materials ○ Math and Science Equipment ○ Texts, Workbooks ○ Puzzles, Games	6. Math: Numbers / Arithmetic	T ①②③ / A ①②③ / v ①②③ / i ①②③	T ①②③ / A ①②③ / v ①②③ / i ①②③	T ①②③④ / A ①②③④ / v ①②③④ / i ①②③④	T ①② / A ①② / v ①② / i ①②
	7. Reading / Alphabet / Lang. Development	T ①②③ / A ①②③ / v ①②③ / i ①②③	T ①②③ / A ①②③ / v ①②③ / i ①②③	T ①②③④ / A ①②③④ / v ①②③④ / i ①②③④	T ①② / A ①② / v ①② / i ①②
	8. Social Studies / Geography	T ①②③ / A ①②③ / v ①②③ / i ①②③	T ①②③ / A ①②③ / v ①②③ / i ①②③	T ①②③④ / A ①②③④ / v ①②③④ / i ①②③④	T ①② / A ①② / v ①② / i ①②
	9. Science / Natural World	T ①②③ / A ①②③ / v ①②③ / i ①②③	T ①②③ / A ①②③ / v ①②③ / i ①②③	T ①②③④ / A ①②③④ / v ①②③④ / i ①②③④	T ①② / A ①② / v ①② / i ①②
10. Sewing / Cooking / Pounding / Sawing		T ①②③ / A ①②③ / v ①②③ / i ①②③	T ①②③ / A ①②③ / v ①②③ / i ①②③	T ①②③④ / A ①②③④ / v ①②③④ / i ①②③④	T ①② / A ①② / v ①② / i ①②
11. Blocks / Trucks		T ①②③ / A ①②③ / v ①②③ / i ①②③	T ①②③ / A ①②③ / v ①②③ / i ①②③	T ①②③④ / A ①②③④ / v ①②③④ / i ①②③④	T ①② / A ①② / v ①② / i ①②
12. Dramatic Play / Dress-Up		T ①②③ / A ①②③ / v ①②③ / i ①②③	T ①②③ / A ①②③ / v ①②③ / i ①②③	T ①②③④ / A ①②③④ / v ①②③④ / i ①②③④	T ①② / A ①② / v ①② / i ①②
13. Active Play		T ①②③ / A ①②③ / v ①②③ / i ①②③	T ①②③ / A ①②③ / v ①②③ / i ①②③	T ①②③④ / A ①②③④ / v ①②③④ / i ①②③④	T ①② / A ①② / v ①② / i ①②
14. RELIABILITY SHEET	○				

Exercise 6.8

			ONE CHILD	TWO CHILDREN	SMALL GROUPS	LARGE GROUPS
15. Practical Skills Acquisition			T ①②③	T ①②③	T ①②③④	T ①②
			A ①②③	A ①②③	A ①②③④	A ①②
			v ①②③	v ①②③	v ①②③④	v ①②
			i ①②③	i ①②③	i ①②③④	i ①②
16. Observing			T ①②③	T ①②③	T ①②③④	T ①②
			A ①②③	A ①②③	A ①②③④	A ①②
			v ①②③	v ①②③	v ①②③④	v ①②
			i ①②③	i ①②③	i ①②③④	i ①②
17. Social Interaction	Ob [Ⓒ②Ⓢ]	Ⓣ	T ①②③	T ①②③	T ①②③④	T ①②
		Ⓐ	A ①②③	A ①②③	A ①②③④	A ①②
		Ⓥ	v ①②③	v ①②③	v ①②③④	v ①②
			i ①②③	i ①②③	i ①②③④	i ①②
18. Unoccupied Child			T ①②③	T ①②③	T ①②③④	T ①②
			A ①②③	A ①②③	A ①②③④	A ①②
			v ①②③	v ①②③	v ①②③④	v ①②
			i ①②③	i ①②③	i ①②③④	i ①②
19. Discipline			T ①②③	T ①②③	T ①②③④	T ①②
			A ①②③	A ①②③	A ①②③④	A ①②
			v ①②③	v ①②③	v ①②③④	v ①②
			i ①②③	i ①②③	i ①②③④	i ①②
20. Transitional Activities		Ⓣ	T ①②③	T ①②③	T ①②③④	T ①②
		Ⓐ	A ①②③	A ①②③	A ①②③④	A ①②
		Ⓥ	v ①②③	v ①②③	v ①②③④	v ①②
			i ①②③	i ①②③	i ①②③④	i ①②
21. Classroom Management		Ⓣ	T ①②③	T ①②③	T ①②③④	T ①②
		Ⓐ	A ①②③	A ①②③	A ①②③④	A ①②
		Ⓥ	v ①②③	v ①②③	v ①②③④	v ①②
			i ①②③	i ①②③	i ①②③④	i ①②
22. Out of Room		Ⓣ	T ①②③	T ①②③	T ①②③④	T ①②
		Ⓐ	A ①②③	A ①②③	A ①②③④	A ①②
		Ⓥ	v ①②③	v ①②③	v ①②③④	v ①②
			i ①②③	i ①②③	i ①②③④	i ①②

NUMBER OF ADULTS IN CLASSROOM ⓪ ① ② ③ ④ ⑤ ⑥ ⑦ ⑧ ⑨ ⑩

CLASSROOM REQUIREMENTS

To implement this model, it is essential that the room be arranged into several learning centers and that a wide variety of materials be made available to the children. The materials and equipment can be ordinary, routine items—they need not be purchased. For instance, a teacher might take the children on a scavenger hunt across the schoolyard. The children would fill their bags with items they found along the way: seeds, gum wrappers, sucker sticks, paper clips, a leaf, a button, safety pins, stones. Back in the classroom, the children could each arrange or classify their findings into categories according to color, shape, or whatever. Then they could play "What's My Set?" In this game the children take turns guessing by what rule the others classified their objects.

In this model it is also important that a daily schedule be followed. Children must know what to expect. Each day there should be a planning session; a work period to carry out the plans; a clean-up time when materials are returned to permanent storage areas; an evaluation period in which small groups of children discuss their accomplishments with teachers and aides; and an activity time during which the total group engages in some vigorous play such as ball games, circle games, or relays. Toward the end of the day the entire group should gather for a story or a preplanned activity that will demonstrate a concept. This latter might be a game in which children classify items. For example, the teacher of a kindergarten class might have many different spoons—large, small, wooden, plastic, metal. In an effort to build classification skills, the teacher might ask, "How are these items alike? How are they different? Pick the largest. Now pick the smallest."

Also, the teacher must be aware of the stages of growth Piaget has identified, and select or create activities that will provide children with the necessary experience to progress through each stage. This requires that teachers know the children and their needs very well. Since the teacher most often works with an individual child during work time and can observe his or her behavior, the teacher can make knowledgeable decisions in preparing the environment for the child. It also requires that teachers help children in their learning rather than direct them. The teacher can ask questions that help the children understand relationships among items. They can also use concrete objects to help children understand new concepts. Not until the upper grades, when children are in the symbol stage, should they present abstract concepts.

RESEARCH FINDINGS ON HOW CHILDREN GROW AND DEVELOP

Observation studies made during the evaluation of the Follow Through Planned Variation Project[5] indicate that children in Developmental Cognitive Model classrooms use concrete objects in their learning activities more often than children in other educational models. Objects such as weights, measures, and games are used when the children work by themselves to carry out their work plans.

Compared to children in the Programmed Model, children in the Developmental Cognitive Model initiate conversations with adults more often, ask more questions, and make more statements to adults regarding their work. Also, their scores on the Raven's Coloured Progressive Matrices test (a test of nonverbal problem-solving ability described on page 72) were higher than those of children in the Programmed Model classrooms. These higher scores on the Raven's reflect this model's environment, where children learn relationships between items through the manipulation of materials. The children in the Developmental Cognitive Model classrooms are also absent less frequently than children in the Programmed Model.

Overall, the growth patterns of children in this model are similar to those of children in the Exploratory Model. Unfortunately, concepts that are unique to this model (time, space, seriation, and classification) are not easily measured. Hence, important expected outcomes for children in this model have not been examined. However, educational theorists expect that children trained in this model will be self-directed and will understand logical relationships; therefore, once basic skills are mastered, the children will be able to use them in meaningful ways.

Current test results indicate that at the end of third grade, children in the Developmental Cognitive model are not scoring as high on achievement tests of reading and mathematics as children in the Programmed Model. If teachers and parents are primarily interested in having children do well on these tests in the early grades, they may not choose the Developmental Cognitive Model.

---

[5]Jane A. Stallings and David Kaskowitz, *Follow Through Classroom Observation Evaluation 1972-1973* (Menlo Park, Calif.: Stanford Research Institute, 1974). ERIC Accession No. ED 104 969.

The reader will find in the following chapters that in order to do well on achievement tests, children apparently need to spend a large amount of time drilling and practicing on carefully programmed materials with adults who provide immediate feedback. The teachers in the Developmental Cognitive model do not provide this type of systematic stimulus or feedback: They expect children to provide their own stimulus through establishing a work plan, and provide their own feedback through self-evaluation. Since abilities like self-motivation and self-evaluation are important to success in adult life, the Developmental Cognitive Model can only be fully evaluated at a later date with other outcome measures.

OBSERVABLE COMPONENTS

Some important components of this model, such as the fact that the teacher asked a question about spatial or temporal concepts, or that the children planned their activities and evaluated their work, cannot be observed on the SRI observation system. David Weikart's staff has developed an observation instrument that is more sensitive than the SRI system in observing these dimensions. However, we can record on our instrument whether, for example, small-group discussions were conducted or whether open-ended, thought-provoking questions were asked. The Developmental Cognitive Model would be recorded on the SRI instrument in the following way.

Materials

The Physical Environment Information form would have a wide range of materials marked in the Used Today column. The items indicating that the children selected their own seats and groups would also be checked. In its use of materials, the Developmental Cognitive Model would appear similar to the Exploratory Model, and different from the Programmed Model (see Figure 6.2). There would probably be less use of learning machines since the emphasis would be on learning the relationships among items by handling or manipulating them. The machine would be useful only if the children were to take it apart to study the relationships among its parts.

Activities and Groupings

In the Developmental Cognitive Model two major groupings would occur. During the planning and evaluation periods, the teacher and aides would be coded in the Small Group column for activity 2, group time (see Figure 6.3). No other marks would be made on the grid. The model differs in this way from the two models previously discussed. During work time, the children and teaching personnel would be scattered throughout the learning centers (see Figure 6.4), and the grid would be similar to that of the Exploratory Model. Children would be working independently in many activities, and the adults would be working with one or two children or a small group.

Physical Environment Information
(Mark all that apply.)

For each of the items below, mark all that apply:

① Present
② Used today

Seating Patterns:
- ● Movable tables and chairs for seating purposes.
- ○ Stationary desks in rows.
- ○ Assigned seating for at least part of the day.
- ● Children select their own seating locations.
- ○ Teacher assigns children to groups.
- ● Children select their own work groups.

GAMES, TOYS, PLAY EQUIPMENT
- ①② small toys (trucks, cars, dolls and accessories
- ●● puzzles, games
- ●● wheel toys
- ●● small play equipment (jumpropes, balls)
- ●● large play equipment (swings, jungle gym)
- ●● children's storybooks
- ●● animals, other nature objects
- ●② sandbox, water table
- ●● carpentry materials, large blocks
- ●● cooking and sewing supplies

INSTRUCTIONAL MATERIALS
- ●● Montessori, other educational toys
- ●● children's texts, workbooks
- ●● math/science equipment, concrete objects
- ①② instructional charts

AUDIO, VISUAL EQUIPMENT
- ①② television
- ①② record or tape player
- ①② audio-visual equipment

GENERAL EQUIPMENT, MATERIALS
- ●② children's own products on display
- ●② displays reflecting children's ethnicity
- ●② other displays especially for children
- ●② magazines
- ①② achievement charts
- ●② child-size sink
- ●② child-size table and chairs
- ●② child-size shelves
- ●● arts and crafts materials
- ●② blackboard, feltboard
- ①② child's own storage space
- ●② photographs of the children on display

OTHER
- ①② please specify . . . . . .

MAKE NO

STRAY MARKS

IN BLANK AREAS

Figure 6.2

CLASSROOM CHECK LIST (be sure to code **EVERYONE** in the class)

		ONE CHILD	TWO CHILDREN	SMALL GROUPS	LARGE GROUPS
1. Snack, lunch	T	①②③	①②③	①②③④	①②
	A	①②③	①②③	①②③④	①②
	V	①②③	①②③	①②③④	①②
	i	①②③	①②③	①②③④	①②
2. Group time	T	①②③	①②③	●②③④	①②
	A	①②③	①②③	①●③④	①②
	V	①②③	①②③	①②③④	①②
	i	①②③	①②③	①②③④	①②
3. Story / Music / Dancing	T	①②③	①②③	①②③④	①②
	A	①②③	①②③	①②③④	①②
	V	①②③	①②③	①②③④	①②
	i	①②③	①②③	①②③④	①②
4. Arts, Crafts	T	①②③	①②③	①②③④	①②
	A	①②③	①②③	①②③④	①②
	V	①②③	①②③	①②③④	①②
	i	①②③	①②③	①②③④	①②
5. Guessing Games / Table Games / Puzzles	T	①②③	①②③	①②③④	①②
	A	①②③	①②③	①②③④	①②
	V	①②③	①②③	①②③④	①②
	i	①②③	①②③	①②③④	①②
6. Math — Numbers / Arithmetic	T	①②③	①②③	①②③④	①②
	A	①②③	①②③	①②③④	①②
	V	①②③	①②③	①②③④	①②
	i	①②③	①②③	①②③④	①②
7. Reading / Alphabet / Lang. Development	T	①②③	①②③	①②③④	①②
	A	①②③	①②③	①②③④	①②
	V	①②③	①②③	①②③④	①②
	i	①②③	①②③	①②③④	①②
8. Social Studies / Geography	T	①②③	①②③	①②③④	①②
	A	①②③	①②③	①②③④	①②
	V	①②③	①②③	①②③④	①②
	i	①②③	①②③	①②③④	①②
9. Science / Natural World	T	①②③	①②③	①②③④	①②
	A	①②③	①②③	①②③④	①②
	V	①②③	①②③	①②③④	①②
	i	①②③	①②③	①②③④	①②
10. Sewing / Cooking / Pounding / Sawing	T	①②③	①②③	①②③④	①②
	A	①②③	①②③	①②③④	①②
	V	①②③	①②③	①②③④	①②
	i	①②③	①②③	①②③④	①②
11. Blocks / Trucks	T	①②③	①②③	①②③④	①②
	A	①②③	①②③	①②③④	①②
	V	①②③	①②③	①②③④	①②
	i	①②③	①②③	①②③④	①②
12. Dramatic Play / Dress-Up	T	①②③	①②③	①②③④	①②
	A	①②③	①②③	①②③④	①②
	V	①②③	①②③	①②③④	①②
	i	①②③	①②③	①②③④	①②
13. Active Play	T	①②③	①②③	①②③④	①②
	A	①②③	①②③	①②③④	①②
	V	①②③	①②③	①②③④	①②
	i	①②③	①②③	①②③④	①②
14. RELIABILITY SHEET	○				

Materials list (associated with items 6–9):

○ TV
○ Audio-Visual Materials
○ Exploratory Materials
○ Math and Science Equipment
○ Texts, Workbooks
○ Puzzles, Games

Figure 6.3

Developmental Cognitive Model   149

		ONE CHILD	TWO CHILDREN	SMALL GROUPS	LARGE GROUPS
15. Practical Skills Acquisition		T ①②③	T ①②③	T ①②③④	T ①②
		A ①②③	A ①②③	A ①②③④	A ①②
		v ①②③	v ①②③	v ①②③④	v ①②
		i ①②③	i ①②③	i ①②③④	i ①②
16. Observing		T ①②③	T ①②③	T ①②③④	T ①②
		A ①②③	A ①②③	A ①②③④	A ①②
		v ①②③	v ①②③	v ①②③④	v ①②
		i ①②③	i ①②③	i ①②③④	i ①②
17. Social Interaction Ob [ⓒ ② Ⓢ]	Ⓣ Ⓐ Ⓥ	T ①②③	T ①②③	T ①②③④	T ①②
		A ①②③	A ①②③	A ①②③④	A ①②
		v ①②③	v ①②③	v ①②③④	v ①②
		i ①②③	i ①②③	i ①②③④	i ①②
18. Unoccupied Child		T ①②③	T ①②③	T ①②③④	T ①②
		A ①②③	A ①②③	A ①②③④	A ①②
		v ①②③	v ①②③	v ①②③④	v ①②
		i ①②③	i ①②③	i ①②③④	i ①②
19. Discipline		T ①②③	T ①②③	T ①②③④	T ①②
		A ①②③	A ①②③	A ①②③④	A ①②
		v ①②③	v ①②③	v ①②③④	v ①②
		i ①②③	i ①②③	i ①②③④	i ①②
20. Transitional Activities	Ⓣ Ⓐ Ⓥ	T ①②③	T ①②③	T ①②③④	T ①②
		A ①②③	A ①②③	A ①②③④	A ①②
		v ①②③	v ①②③	v ①②③④	v ①②
		i ①②③	i ①②③	i ①②③④	i ①②
21. Classroom Management	Ⓣ Ⓐ Ⓥ	T ①②③	T ①②③	T ①②③④	T ①②
		A ①②③	A ①②③	A ①②③④	A ①②
		v ①②③	v ①②③	v ①②③④	v ①②
		i ①②③	i ①②③	i ①②③④	i ①②
22. Out of Room	Ⓣ Ⓐ Ⓥ	T ①②③	T ①②③	T ①②③④	T ①②
		A ①②③	A ①②③	A ①②③④	A ①②
		v ①②③	v ①②③	v ①②③④	v ①②
		i ①②③	i ①②③	i ①②③④	i ①②

NUMBER OF ADULTS IN CLASSROOM   ⓪ ① ② ● ④ ⑤ ⑥ ⑦ ⑧ ⑨ ⑩

CLASSROOM CHECK LIST (be sure to code **EVERYONE** in the class)

	ONE CHILD	TWO CHILDREN	SMALL GROUPS	LARGE GROUPS
1. Snack, lunch	T ①②③	T ①②③	T ①②③④	T ①②
	A ①②③	A ①②③	A ①②③④	A ①②
	v ①②③	v ①②③	v ①②③④	v ①②
	i ①②③	i ①②③	i ①②③④	i ①②
2. Group time	T ①②③	T ①②③	T ①②③④	T ①②
	A ①②③	A ①②③	A ①②③④	A ①②
	v ①②③	v ①②③	v ①②③④	v ①②
	i ①②③	i ①②③	i ①②③④	i ①②
3. Story / Music / Dancing	T ①②③	T ①②③	T ①②③④	T ①②
	A ①②③	A ①②③	A ①②③④	A ①②
	v ①②③	v ①②③	v ①②③④	v ①②
	i ①②③	i ①●③	i ①②③④	i ①②
4. Arts, Crafts	T ①②③	T ①②③	T ①②③④	T ①②
	A ①②③	A ①②③	A ①②③④	A ①②
	v ①②③	v ①②③	v ①②③④	v ①②
	i ①②③	i ●②③	i ①②③④	i ①②
5. Guessing Games / Table Games / Puzzles	T ①②③	T ①②③	T ①②③④	T ①②
	A ①②③	A ①②③	A ●②③④	A ①②
	v ①②③	v ①②③	v ①②③④	v ①②
	i ①②③	i ①②③	i ①②③④	i ①②
6. Math / Numbers / Arithmetic	T ①②③	T ①②③	T ①②③④	T ①②
	A ①②③	A ①②③	A ①②③④	A ①②
	v ①②③	v ①②③	v ①②③④	v ①②
	i ①②③	i ①②③	i ①②③④	i ①②
7. Reading / Alphabet / Lang. Development	T ●②③	T ①②③	T ①②③④	T ①②
	A ①②③	A ●②③	A ①②③④	A ①②
	v ①②③	v ①②③	v ①②③④	v ①②
	i ①②③	i ①②③	i ①②③④	i ①②
8. Social Studies / Geography	T ①②③	T ①②③	T ①②③④	T ①②
	A ①②③	A ①②③	A ①②③④	A ①②
	v ①②③	v ①②③	v ①②③④	v ①②
	i ①②③	i ①②③	i ①②③④	i ①②
9. Science / Natural World	T ①②③	T ①②③	T ①②③④	T ①②
	A ①②③	A ①②③	A ①②③④	A ①②
	v ①②③	v ①②③	v ①②③④	v ①②
	i ●②③	i ●②③	i ①②③④	i ①②
10. Sewing / Cooking / Pounding / Sawing	T ①②③	T ①②③	T ①②③④	T ①②
	A ①②③	A ①②③	A ①②③④	A ①②
	v ①②③	v ①②③	v ①②③④	v ①②
	i ①②③	i ●②③	i ●②③④	i ①②
11. Blocks / Trucks	T ①②③	T ①②③	T ①②③④	T ①②
	A ①②③	A ①②③	A ①②③④	A ①②
	v ①②③	v ①②③	v ①②③④	v ①②
	i ①②③	i ①●③	i ①②③④	i ①②
12. Dramatic Play / Dress-Up	T ①②③	T ①②③	T ①②③④	T ①②
	A ①②③	A ①②③	A ①②③④	A ①②
	v ①②③	v ①②③	v ①②③④	v ①②
	i ①②③	i ●②③	i ①②③④	i ①②
13. Active Play	T ①②③	T ①②③	T ①②③④	T ①②
	A ①②③	A ①②③	A ①②③④	A ①②
	v ①②③	v ①②③	v ①②③④	v ①②
	i ①②③	i ①②③	i ①②③④	i ①②

For items 6–9:
- ○ TV
- ○ Audio-Visual Materials
- ○ Exploratory Materials
- ○ Math and Science Equipment
- ○ Texts, Workbooks
- ○ Puzzles, Games

14. RELIABILITY SHEET ○

Figure 6.4

	ONE CHILD	TWO CHILDREN	SMALL GROUPS	LARGE GROUPS
15. Practical Skills Acquisition	T ①②③ A ①②③ v ①②③ i ①②③	T ①②③ A ①②③ v ①②③ i ①②③	T ①②③④ A ①②③④ v ①②③④ i ①②③④	T ①② A ①② v ①② i ①②
16. Observing	T ①②③ A ①②③ v ①②③ i ①②③	T ①②③ A ①②③ v ①②③ i ①②③	T ①②③④ A ①②③④ v ①②③④ i ①②③④	T ①② A ①② v ①② i ①②
17. Social Interaction Ob [ⓒ ② ⓢ] Ⓣ Ⓐ Ⓥ	T ①②③ A ①②③ v ①②③ i ①②③	T ①②③ A ①②③ v ①②③ i ①②③	T ①②③④ A ①②③④ v ①②③④ i ①②③④	T ①② A ①② v ①② i ①②
18. Unoccupied Child	T ①②③ A ①②③ v ①②③ i ①②③	T ①②③ A ①②③ v ①②③ i ①②③	T ①②③④ A ①②③④ v ①②③④ i ①②③④	T ①② A ①② v ①② i ①②
19. Discipline	T ①②③ A ①②③ v ①②③ i ①②③	T ①②③ A ①②③ v ①②③ i ①②③	T ①②③④ A ①②③④ v ①②③④ i ①②③④	T ①② A ①② v ①② i ①②
20. Transitional Activities Ⓣ Ⓐ Ⓥ	T ①②③ A ①②③ v ①②③ i ①②③	T ①②③ A ①②③ v ①②③ i ①②③	T ①②③④ A ①②③④ v ①②③④ i ①②③④	T ①② A ①② v ①② i ①②
21. Classroom Management Ⓣ Ⓐ Ⓥ	T ①②③ A ①②③ v ①②③ i ①②③	T ①②③ A ①②③ v ①②③ i ①②③	T ①②③④ A ①②③④ v ①②③④ i ①②③④	T ①② A ①② v ①② i ①②
22. Out of Room Ⓣ Ⓐ Ⓥ	T ①②③ A ①②③ v ①②③ i ①②③	T ①②③ A ①②③ v ①②③ i ①②③	T ①②③④ A ①②③④ v ①②③④ i ①②③④	T ①② A ①② v ①② i ①②

NUMBER OF ADULTS IN CLASSROOM ⓪ ① ② ● ④ ⑤ ⑥ ⑦ ⑧ ⑨ ⑩

Interaction Observations

During the planning and evaluation sessions, the teacher would ask many open-ended questions such as "What do you plan to do today, Ben?" (TC2), "How are these items alike?" (TC2). In the upper grades, the children's responses would be more detailed. The questions would always be directed to individual children rather than to the group. The adults would be supportive and acknowledge the children's good work. After hearing a child's plan, they would be likely to say, "You really have planned your work well today, John" (TC8). This differs from the Exploratory Model in that the praise would be direct, and differs from the Programmed Model in that the praise would not be for academic achievement. Misbehavior would be redirected (TC9GB).

The children would work together on projects. They would question each other (CD1Q) and give each other feedback (DC9G). A child's question to an adult would be answered with another question or the child would be guided to materials where she could discover her own solution. The following is a typical interaction of this sort. The interaction is coded in Figure 6.5.

Situation: Second-grade classroom during work period.

1. Child: Teacher, I am doubling this recipe.

2. Child: How much is 1 2/3 cups and 1 2/3 cups?

3. Teacher: There is a quart measuring bottle on the shelf with the other measuring tools.

4. Teacher: How could you find out how much milk it takes when you double the recipe?

5. Child: (Smiles and runs off to the baking center.)

6. Child: (Measures 1 2/3 cups of milk into the bottle twice.)

7. Child: Teacher, it comes up to 3 cups and 1/3.

8. Teacher: Is that more or less than 3 cups and 1/4?

9. Child: More!

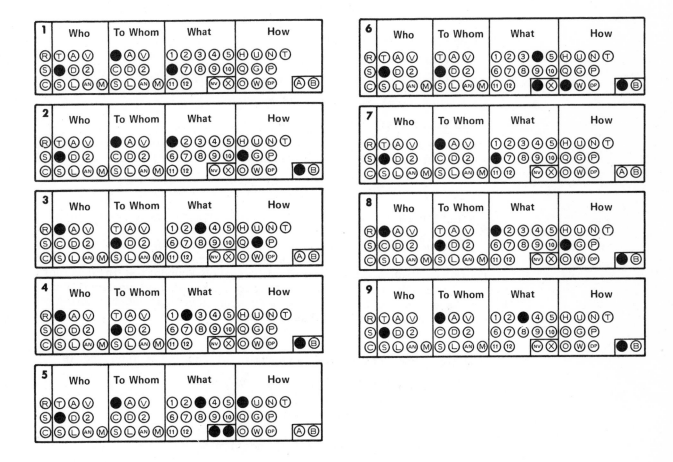

Figure 6.5 Coded Interaction of a Cognitive Model Classroom

IMPORTANCE OF TEACHER OBSERVATION

Being observed allows teachers to evaluate themselves to see if goals they have set are being achieved. They receive immediate feedback by reading the observation record. If teachers in the Developmental Cognitive Model find that they frequently answer children's questions (CT1Q-TC3), they must change, to conform to the model, and start redirecting children's questions more often by asking open-ended questions (CT1Q-TC2).

SUMMARY OF COMPONENTS

Theorist or theory: Piaget

Oriented toward: Cognitive growth

Goals: To develop cognitive skills

Stress: Classification, planning, and evaluation skills

Structure: Student-centered

Grouping patterns: Small group

Materials: Exploratory objects, building and cooking materials

Where to teach: Learning centers or around a table

Who initiates: Teacher and child

Questioning strategy: Open-ended and direct-answer questions

Feedback from: Materials and teacher

Who evaluates: Students and teacher

Evaluation tools: Problem-solving tests, cognitive tests, child observations, achievement tests

BIBLIOGRAPHY

The Developmental Cognitive Model described in this chapter is based primarily on the curriculum developed by David Weikart and the staff at the High/Scope Educational Research Foundation in Ypsilanti, Michigan. Some components of the Developmental Cognitive Model can also be seen in the Follow Through Program developed at the University of Arizona by Marie Hughes and staff.

Where Components of the Developmental Cognitive Type Models Can Be Seen

Interested readers should contact the Follow Through offices in the school districts of the cities listed.

High/Scope Educational Research Foundation model

Denver, Colorado	Ypsilanti, Michigan
Greeley, Colorado	New York City, New York
Okaloosa County, Florida	Seattle, Washington
Chicago V, Illinois	

University of Arizona model

Des Moines, Iowa	Lakewood, New Jersey
Wichita, Kansas	Newark, New Jersey
Lincoln, Nebraska	Chickasha, Oklahoma

Suggested Readings

Theory of the Developmental Cognitive Model

Almy, Millie; Chittenden, E.; and Miller, Paul A. *Young Children's Thinking: Studies of Some Aspects of Piaget's Theory*. New York: Teachers College Press, 1966.

Beard, Ruth M. *An Outline of Piaget's Developmental Psychology for Students and Teachers*. New York: Basic Books, 1972.

Brearley, Molly, and Hitchfield, Elizabeth. *A Guide to Reading Piaget*. New York: Schocken Books, 1967.

Elkind, David. "Children's Discovery of the Conservation of Mass, Weight, and Volume: Piaget Replication Study II." *Journal of Genetic Psychology* 98 (1961): 219-227.

_____. "The Development of Quantitative Thinking: A Systematic Replication of Piaget's Studies." *Journal of Genetic Psychology* 98 (1961): 37-46.

Flavell, John H. *The Development Psychology of Jean Piaget*. New York: Van Nostrand Reinhold, 1973.

Furth, Hans G. *Piaget and Knowledge: Theoretical Foundations*. Englewood Cliffs, N.J.: Prentice-Hall, 1969.

Gagné, Robert M. "The Learning of Concepts." In *Human Dynamics in Psychology and Education: Selected Readings*, edited by Don E. Hamachek, pp. 13-20. Boston: Allyn and Bacon, 1968.

Hunt, J. M. *Intelligence and Experience*. New York: Ronald Press, 1961, pp. 189-192.

Isaacs, Susan. *Intellectual Growth in Young Children*. New York: Schocken Books, 1966.

Kessen, William. "'Stage' and 'Structure' in the Study of Children." *Monographs of the Society for Research in Child Development*, vol. 27, no. 2, 1962.

Kessen, William, and Kuhlman, Clementina, eds. "Thought in the Young Child: Report of a Conference on the Intellective Development with Particular Attention to the Work of Jean Piaget." *Monographs of the Society for Research in Child Development*, vol. 27, no. 2, pp. 65-86, 1962.

Kohlberg, Lawrence. "Early Education: A Cognitive Developmental View." *Child Development*, 39 (1968): 1013-1062.

McClelland, Donna. "The Cognitive Curriculum." Ypsilanti Preschool Curriculum Demonstration Project. Ypsilanti, Mich.: High/Scope Educational Research Foundation, May 1970. ERIC Accession No. ED 049 832.

Piaget, Jean. *The Origins of Intelligence in Children*. Translated by Margaret Cook. New York: International Univ. Press, 1966.

———. *Play, Dreams, and Imitation in Childhood*. New York: W. W. Norton, 1962.

———. *The Psychology of Intelligence*. Paterson, N.J.: Littlefield, Adams, 1968.

———. *Six Psychological Studies*. Edited by David Elkind. Translated by A. Tenzer and David Elkind. New York: Random House, 1968.

Piaget, Jean, and Barbel Inhelder. *The Psychology of the Child*. Translated by Helen Weaver. New York: Basic Books, 1969.

Zimiles, Herbert. "A Note on Piaget's Concept of Conservation." *Child Development* 34 (1963): 691-695.

Implementing the Developmental Cognitive Model

Lalli, Richard. *An Introduction to the Cognitively Oriented Curriculum for Elementary Grades*. Ypsilanti, Mich.: High/Scope Educational Research Foundation, 1977.

Mainwaring, Sheila. *Teachers' Guide to the Daily Routine and Room Arrangement and Materials*. Ypsilanti, Mich.: High/Scope Educational Research Foundation, 1975.

Parker, Ronald K., et al. *An Overview of Cognitive and Language Programs for 3, 4, and 5 Year-Old Children*. Atlanta, Ga.: Southeastern Education Laboratory, 1970. ERIC Accession No. ED 045 209.

Seifert, Michael. *Recycling a Garage—The Story of the High/Scope Training and Development Center*. Ypsilanti, Mich.: High/Scope Educational Research Foundation, 1972.

Siegel, Irving. "The Piagetian System and the World of Education." In *Studies in Cognitive Development*, edited by David Elkind and John Flavell. New York: Oxford University Press, 1969.

Stallings, Jane, and Kaskowitz, David. *Follow Through Classroom Observation Evaluation 1972-1973*, Menlo Park, Calif.: Stanford Research Institute, 1974. ERIC Accession No. ED 104 969.

Suchman, J. Richard. *Inquiry Development Program*. Chicago: Science Research Associates, 1965.

Sullivan, Edmund. "Piaget and the School Curriculum: A Critical Appraisal." Ontario, Canada: Ontario Institute for Studies in Education, 1967. (Bulletin No. 2)

Commercially Available Materials

Churchill, Eileen M. *Counting and Measuring: Number Education in the Infant School*. Toronto: University of Toronto Press, 1961.

Hiatt, L.; Mainwaring, S.; and Weathers, T. *The Language Training Curriculum* (Ypsilanti, Mich.: High/Scope Educational Research Foundation, 1970). Detailed monthly reports by the teachers; key issues and sample lessons for this highly structured demonstration curriculum emphasize acquisition of academic skills through drill techniques.

Lindsey, Maria. *San Mateo County Reading Pak: Piaget Based Instruction and Assessment of Games and Activities for Early Childhood K-3 Teachers*. Redwood City, Calif.: San Mateo Office of Education, 1975.

Martin, Mary; Malte, Mary Lou; and Richardson, Joyce. *The Unit-Based Curriculum*. (Ypsilanti, Mich.: High/Scope Educational Research Foundation, 1970). A description of the traditional nursery-school program studied in the Curriculum Demonstration Project; written by the unit-based teachers, it includes program goals, units of activity, themes emphasized, teacher observations and particular problems encountered in this program emphasizing social and emotional growth.

Navarra, John G. *The Development of Scientific Concepts in a Young Child: A Case Study*. New York: Bureau of Publications, Teachers College, Columbia University, 1955.

Suppes, Patrick. *Sets and Numbers*. Stanford, Calif.: Stanford University, 1961.

Research Findings

Arthur, Grace. "A Non-Verbal Test of Logical Thinking." *Journal of Consulting Psychology* 8 (1944): 33-34.

Barker, Roger G., and Wright, Herbert F. *One Boy's Day: A Specimen Record of Behavior*. New York: Harper, 1951.

Beilin, Harry, and Franklin, Irene C. "Logical Operations in Area and Length Measurements: Age and Training Effects." *Child Development* 33 (1962): 607-618.

Couvares, Elizabeth, and Love, John. *Assessing the Writing of Elementary School Children: The Development of a Procedure and Preliminary Findings*. Ypsilanti, Mich.: High/Scope Educational Research Foundation, 1973.

Morris, Mary E., and Love, John. *Classroom Interactions in Four Follow-Through Sites*. Ypsilanti, Mich.: High/Scope Educational Research Foundation, 1973.

Smilansky, Sara. *The Effects of Sociodramatic Play of Disadvantaged Preschool Children*. New York: John Wiley and Sons, 1968.

Stallings, Jane A., and Kaskowitz, David. *Follow Through Classroom Observation Evaluation 1972-1973*. Menlo Park, Calif.: Stanford Research Institute, 1974. ERIC Accession No. ED 104 969.

Weikart, David P.; Deloria, Dennis J.; Lawser, Sarah A.; and Weigerink, Ronald. *The Cognitively Oriented Curriculum: A Framework for Preschool Teachers*. Final Report. Vol. 1 of 2 Vols. Ypsilanti, Mich.: High/Scope Educational Research Foundation, 1970. ERIC Accession No. ED 044 535.

Wheeler, Dorothy. "Studies in the Development of Reasoning in School Children: I. General Methods and Results." *British Journal of Statistical Psychology* 11 (1958): 137-159.

Films Available

These are available from High/Scope Educational Research Foundation, 600 North River Street, Ypsilanti, Mich. 48197.

The Cognitively Oriented Curriculum: A Framework for Education (19 min., 16 mm film).

The Daily Routine (30 min., 16 mm film).

Cognitive Development Series:
   Classification—A sequence of Exercises (25 min., 16 mm film).
   Seriation—A Sequence of Exercises (25 min., 16 mm film).
   Spatial Relations—A Sequence of Exercises (40 min., 16 mm film).
   Temporal Relations—A Sequence of Exercises (Part I, 39 min., 16 mm film; Part II, 15 min., 16 mm film).

Language in the Cognitively Oriented Curriculum:
   Language Case Study: A Day with Jeff - 5 years (21 min., video tape).
   Language Case Study: A Day with Timmy - 7 years (23 min., video tape).
   When Children are Involved in Personally Meaningful Activity . . . Language is an Important and Useful Tool (36 min., video tape).

Mathematics in the Cognitively Oriented Curriculum:
  Experiencing and Using the Concept of Number
    Part I. The Preoperational Stage (20 min., film strip).
    Part II. The Transitional Sub-stage (20 min., film strip).
    Part III. The Concrete Operational Stage (25 min., film strip).

  Experiencing and Using the Concept of Length
    Part I. The Preoperational Stage (film strip).
    Part II. The Transitional Sub-stage (film strip).
    Part III. The Concrete Operational Stage (film strip).

  Experiencing and Using the Concepts of Area, Volume, and Weight
    Part I. The Preoperational Stage (film strip).
    Part II. The Transitional Sub-stage (film strip).
    Part III. The Concrete Operational Stage (film strip).

  Three Mathematics Case Studies
    A Doll's House (film strip).
    Roger's Quilt (film strip).
    A Pound Cake (film strip).

Representation in the Cognitively Oriented Curriculum:
  Children Make Representations for Many Reasons (15 min., 16 mm film).
  Teachers Make Representing a Thinking Process (15 min., 16 mm film).
  Helping Children Represent: Strategies for Teachers (37 min., video tape).

ANSWERS: CORRECT CODING FOR EXERCISE 6.1

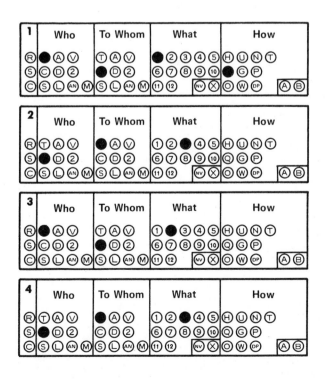

ANSWERS: CORRECT CODING FOR EXERCISE 6.3

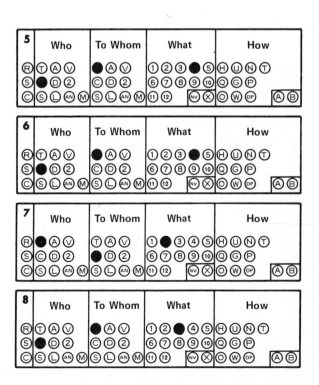

ANSWERS: CORRECT CODING FOR EXERCISE 6.5

1 | Who | To Whom | What | How

2 | Who | To Whom | What | How

3 | Who | To Whom | What | How

4 | Who | To Whom | What | How

5 | Who | To Whom | What | How

6 | Who | To Whom | What | How

7 | Who | To Whom | What | How

8 | Who | To Whom | What | How

9 | Who | To Whom | What | How

10 | Who | To Whom | What | How

11 | Who | To Whom | What | How

12 | Who | To Whom | What | How

CLASSROOM CHECK LIST (be sure to code **EVERYONE** in the class)

Activity	Code	ONE CHILD	TWO CHILDREN	SMALL GROUPS	LARGE GROUPS
1. Snack, lunch	T	①②③	①②③	①②③④	①②
	A	①②③	①②③	①②③④	①②
	V	①②③	①②③	①②③④	①②
	i	①②③	①②③	①②③④	①②
2. Group time	T	①②③	①②③	①②③④	①②
	A	①②③	①②③	①②③④	①②
	V	①②③	①②③	①②③④	①②
	i	①②③	①②③	①②③④	①②
3. Story / Music / Dancing	T	①②③	①②③	①②③④	①②
	A	①②③	①②③	①②③④	①②
	V	①②③	①②③	①②③④	①②
	i	①②③	①②③	①②③④	①②
4. Arts, Crafts	T	①②③	①②③	①②③④	①②
	A	①②③	①②③	●②③④	①②
	V	①②③	①②③	①②③④	①②
	i	①●③	①②③	●②③④	①②
5. Guessing Games / Table Games / Puzzles	T	①②③	①②③	①②③④	①②
	A	①②③	①②③	①②③④	①②
	V	①②③	①②③	①②③④	①②
	i	①②③	①②③	①②③④	①②
6. Math / Numbers / Arithmetic	T	①②③	①②③	①②③④	①②
	A	①②③	①②③	①②③④	①②
	V	①②③	①②③	①②③④	①②
	i	①②③	①②③	①②③④	①②
7. Reading / Alphabet / Lang. Development	T	①②③	●②③	①②③④	①②
	A	●②③	①②③	①②③④	①②
	V	①②③	①②③	①②③④	①②
	i	①②③	①②③	●②③④	①②
8. Social Studies / Geography	T	①②③	①②③	①②③④	①②
	A	①②③	①②③	①②③④	①②
	V	①②③	①②③	①②③④	①②
	i	①②③	①②③	①②③④	①②
9. Science / Natural World	T	①②③	①②③	①②③④	①②
	A	①②③	①②③	①②③④	①②
	V	①②③	①②③	①②③④	①②
	i	①②③	①②③	①②③④	①②
10. Sewing / Cooking / Pounding / Sawing	T	①②③	①②③	①②③④	①②
	A	①②③	①②③	①②③④	①②
	V	①②③	①②③	①②③④	①②
	i	①②③	①②③	●●③④	①②
11. Blocks / Trucks	T	①②③	①②③	①②③④	①②
	A	①②③	①②③	①②③④	①②
	V	①②③	①②③	①②③④	①②
	i	①②③	①②③	①②③④	①②
12. Dramatic Play / Dress-Up	T	①②③	①②③	①②③④	①②
	A	①②③	①②③	①②③④	①②
	V	①②③	①②③	①②③④	①②
	i	①②③	①②③	①②③④	①②
13. Active Play	T	①②③	①②③	①②③④	①②
	A	①②③	①②③	①②③④	①②
	V	①②③	①②③	①②③④	①②
	i	①②③	①②③	①②③④	①②

(Left-side list spanning items 6–9:)
○ TV
○ Audio-Visual Materials
○ Exploratory Materials
○ Math and Science Equipment
○ Texts, Workbooks
○ Puzzles, Games

14. RELIABILITY SHEET ○

		ONE CHILD	TWO CHILDREN	SMALL GROUPS	LARGE GROUPS
15. Practical Skills Acquisition		T ①②③ A ①②③ v ①②③ i ①②③	T ①②③ A ①②③ v ①②③ i ①②③	T ①②③④ A ①②③④ v ①②③④ i ①②③④	T ①② A ①② v ①② i ①②
16. Observing		T ①②③ A ①②③ v ①②③ i ①②③	T ①②③ A ①②③ v ①②③ i ①②③	T ①②③④ A ①②③④ v ①②③④ i ①②③④	T ①② A ①② v ①② i ①②
17. Social Interaction Ob [Ⓒ ② Ⓢ]	Ⓣ Ⓐ Ⓥ	T ①②③ A ①②③ v ①②③ i ①②③	T ①②③ A ①②③ v ①②③ i ①②③	T ①②③④ A ①②③④ v ①②③④ i ①②③④	T ①② A ①② v ①② i ①②
18. Unoccupied Child		T ①②③ A ①②③ v ①②③ i ①②③	T ①②③ A ①②③ v ①②③ i ①②③	T ①②③④ A ①②③④ v ①②③④ i ①②③④	T ①② A ①② v ①② i ①②
19. Discipline		T ①②③ A ①②③ v ①②③ i ①②③	T ①②③ A ①②③ v ①②③ i ①②③	T ①②③④ A ①②③④ v ①②③④ i ①②③④	T ①② A ①② v ①② i ①②
20. Transitional Activities	Ⓣ Ⓐ Ⓥ	T ①②③ A ①②③ v ①②③ i ①②③	T ①②③ A ①②③ v ①②③ i ①②③	T ①②③④ A ①②③④ v ①②③④ i ①②③④	T ①② A ①② v ①② i ①②
21. Classroom Management	Ⓣ Ⓐ Ⓥ	T ①②③ A ①②③ v ①②③ i ①②③	T ①②③ A ①②③ v ①②③ i ①②③	T ①②③④ A ①②③④ v ①②③④ i ①②③④	T ①② A ①② v ①② i ①②
22. Out of Room	Ⓣ Ⓐ Ⓥ	T ①②③ A ①②③ v ①②③ i ①②③	T ①②③ A ①②③ v ①②③ i ①②③	T ①②③④ A ①②③④ v ①②③④ i ①②③④	T ①② A ①② v ①② i ①②

NUMBER OF ADULTS IN CLASSROOM   ⓪ ① ② ③ ④ ⑤ ⑥ ⑦ ⑧ ⑨ ⑩

CLASSROOM CHECK LIST (be sure to code **EVERYONE** in the class)

		ONE CHILD	TWO CHILDREN	SMALL GROUPS	LARGE GROUPS
1. Snack, lunch		T ①②③ A ①②③ v ①②③ i ①②③	T ①②③ A ①②③ v ①②③ i ①②③	T ①②③④ A ①②③④ v ①②③④ i ①②③④	T ①② A ①② v ①② i ①②
2. Group time		T ①②③ A ①②③ v ①②③ i ①②③	T ①②③ A ①②③ v ①②③ i ①②③	T ①②③④ A ①②③④ v ①②③④ i ①②③④	T ①② A ①② v ①② i ①②
3. Music — Story / Music / Dancing		T ①②③ A ①②③ v ①②③ i ①②③	T ①②③ A ①②③ v ①②③ i ①②③	T ①②③④ A ①②③④ v ①②③④ i ①②③④	T ①② A ①② v ①② i ①②
4. Arts, Crafts		T ①②③ A ①②③ v ①②③ i ①②③	T ①②③ A ①②③ v ①②③ i ①②③	T ①②③④ A ①②③④ v ①②③④ i ①②③④	T ①② A ①② v ①② i ①②
5. Table Games — Guessing Games / Table Games / Puzzles		T ①②③ A ①②③ v ①②③ i ①②③	T ①②③ A ①②③ v ①②③ i ①②③	T ①②③④ A ①②③④ v ①②③④ i ①②③④	T ①② A ①② v ①② i ①②
○ TV ○ Audio-Visual Materials ○ Exploratory Materials ○ Math and Science Equipment ○ Texts, Workbooks ○ Puzzles, Games	**6. Math** — Numbers / Math / Arithmetic	T ①②③ A ①②③ v ①②③ i ①②③	T ①②③ A ①②③ v ①②③ i ①②③	T ①②③④ A ●②③④ v ①②③④ i ①②③④	T ①② A ①② v ①② i ①②
	7. Alphabet — Reading / Alphabet / Lang. Development	T ①②③ A ①②③ v ①②③ i ①②③	T ①②③ A ①②③ v ①②③ i ①②③	T ●②③④ A ●②③④ v ①②③④ i ①②③④	T ①② A ①② v ①② i ①②
	8. Geography — Social Studies / Geography	T ①②③ A ①②③ v ①②③ i ①②③	T ①②③ A ①②③ v ①②③ i ①②③	T ①②③④ A ①②③④ v ①②③④ i ①②③④	T ①② A ①② v ①② i ①②
	9. Science / Natural World	T ①②③ A ①②③ v ①②③ i ①②③	T ①②③ A ①②③ v ①②③ i ①②③	T ①②③④ A ①②③④ v ①②③④ i ①②③④	T ①② A ①② v ①② i ①②
10. Sewing / Cooking / Pounding / Sawing		T ①②③ A ①②③ v ①②③ i ①②③	T ①②③ A ①②③ v ①②③ i ①②③	T ①②③④ A ①②③④ v ①②③④ i ①②③④	T ①② A ①② v ①② i ①②
11. Blocks / Trucks		T ①②③ A ①②③ v ①②③ i ①②③	T ①②③ A ①②③ v ①②③ i ①②③	T ①②③④ A ①②③④ v ①②③④ i ①②③④	T ①② A ①② v ①② i ①②
12. Dramatic Play / Dress-Up		T ①②③ A ①②③ v ①②③ i ①②③	T ①②③ A ①②③ v ①②③ i ①②③	T ①②③④ A ①②③④ v ①②③④ i ①②③④	T ①② A ①② v ①② i ①②
13. Active Play		T ①②③ A ①②③ v ①②③ i ①②③	T ①②③ A ①②③ v ①②③ i ①②③	T ①②③④ A ①②③④ v ①②③④ i ①②③④	T ①② A ①② v ①② i ①②
14. RELIABILITY SHEET ○					

			ONE CHILD	TWO CHILDREN	SMALL GROUPS	LARGE GROUPS
15. Practical Skills Acquisition			T ①②③ A ①②③ V ①②③ i ①②③	T ①②③ A ①②③ V ①②③ i ①②③	T ①②③④ A ①②③④ V ①②③④ i ①②③④	T ①② A ①② V ①② i ①②
16. Observing			T ①②③ A ①②③ V ①②③ i ①②③	T ①②③ A ①②③ V ①②③ i ①②③	T ①②③④ A ①②③④ V ①②③④ i ①②③④	T ①② A ①② V ①② i ①②
17. Social Interaction	Ob [Ⓒ ② Ⓢ]	Ⓣ Ⓐ Ⓥ	T ①②③ A ①②③ V ①②③ i ①②③	T ①②③ A ①②③ V ①②③ i ①②③	T ①②③④ A ①②③④ V ①②③④ i ①②③④	T ①② A ①② V ①② i ①②
18. Unoccupied Child			T ①②③ A ①②③ V ①②③ i ①②③	T ①②③ A ①②③ V ①②③ i ①②③	T ①②③④ A ①②③④ V ①②③④ i ①②③④	T ①② A ①② V ①② i ①②
19. Discipline			T ①②③ A ①②③ V ①②③ i ①②③	T ①②③ A ①②③ V ①②③ i ①②③	T ①②③④ A ①②③④ V ①②③④ i ①②③④	T ①② A ①② V ①② i ①②
20. Transitional Activities		Ⓣ Ⓐ Ⓥ	T ①②③ A ①②③ V ①②③ i ①②③	T ①②③ A ①②③ V ①②③ i ①②③	T ①②③④ A ①②③④ V ①②③④ i ①②③④	T ①② A ①② V ①② i ①②
21. Classroom Management		Ⓣ Ⓐ Ⓥ	T ①②③ A ①②③ V ①②③ i ①②③	T ①②③ A ①②③ V ①②③ i ①②③	T ①②③④ A ①②③④ V ①②③④ i ①②③④	T ①② A ①② V ①② i ①②
22. Out of Room		Ⓣ Ⓐ Ⓥ	T ①②③ A ①②③ V ①②③ i ①②③	T ①②③ A ①②③ V ①②③ i ①②③	T ①②③④ A ①②③④ V ①②③④ i ①②③④	T ①② A ①② V ①② i ①②

NUMBER OF ADULTS IN CLASSROOM　　⓪ ① ② ③ ④ ⑤ ⑥ ⑦ ⑧ ⑨ ⑩

CLASSROOM CHECK LIST (be sure to code **EVERYONE** in the class)

		ONE CHILD	TWO CHILDREN	SMALL GROUPS	LARGE GROUPS
1. Snack, lunch		T ① ② ③	T ① ② ③	T ① ② ③ ④	T ① ②
		A ① ② ③	A ① ② ③	A ① ② ③ ④	A ① ②
		v ① ② ③	v ① ② ③	v ① ② ③ ④	v ① ②
		i ① ② ③	i ① ② ③	i ① ② ③ ④	i ① ②
2. Group time		T ① ② ③	T ① ② ③	T ① ② ③ ④	T ① ②
		A ① ② ③	A ① ② ③	A ① ② ③ ④	A ① ②
		v ① ② ③	v ① ② ③	v ① ② ③ ④	v ① ②
		i ① ② ③	i ① ② ③	i ① ② ③ ④	i ① ②
3. Music (Story, Dancing)		T ① ② ③	T ① ② ③	T ① ② ③ ④	T ① ②
		A ① ② ③	A ① ② ③	A ① ② ③ ④	A ① ②
		v ① ② ③	v ① ② ③	v ① ② ③ ④	v ① ②
		i ① ② ③	i ① ② ③	i ① ② ③ ④	i ① ②
4. Arts, Crafts		T ① ② ③	T ① ② ③	T ① ② ③ ④	T ① ②
		A ① ② ③	A ① ② ③	A ① ② ③ ④	A ① ②
		v ① ② ③	v ① ② ③	v ① ② ③ ④	v ① ②
		i ① ② ③	i ① ② ③	i ① ② ③ ④	i ① ②
5. Table Games (Guessing Games, Puzzles)		T ① ② ③	T ① ② ③	T ① ② ③ ④	T ① ②
		A ① ② ③	A ① ② ③	A ① ② ③ ④	A ① ②
		v ① ② ③	v ① ② ③	v ① ② ③ ④	v ① ②
		i ① ② ③	i ① ② ③	i ① ② ③ ④	i ① ②
○ TV	**6. Math** (Numbers, Arithmetic)	T ① ② ③	T ① ② ③	T ● ② ③ ④	T ① ②
○ Audio-Visual Materials		A ① ② ③	A ① ② ③	A ① ② ③ ④	A ① ②
○ Exploratory Materials		v ① ② ③	v ① ② ③	v ① ② ③ ④	v ① ②
● Math and Science Equipment		i ① ② ③	i ① ② ③	i ① ② ③ ④	i ① ②
○ Texts, Workbooks	**7. Alphabet** (Reading, Lang. Development)	T ① ② ③	T ① ② ③	T ① ② ③ ④	T ① ②
○ Puzzles, Games		A ① ② ③	A ① ② ③	A ① ② ③ ④	A ① ②
		v ① ② ③	v ① ② ③	v ① ② ③ ④	v ① ②
		i ① ② ③	i ① ② ③	i ① ② ③ ④	i ① ②
	8. Geography (Social Studies)	T ① ② ③	T ① ② ③	T ① ② ③ ④	T ① ②
		A ① ② ③	A ① ② ③	A ① ② ③ ④	A ① ②
		v ① ② ③	v ① ② ③	v ① ② ③ ④	v ① ②
		i ① ② ③	i ① ② ③	i ① ② ③ ④	i ① ②
	9. Natural World (Science, Health/Safety)	T ① ② ③	T ① ② ③	T ① ② ③ ④	T ① ②
		A ① ② ③	A ① ② ③	A ① ② ③ ④	A ① ②
		v ① ② ③	v ① ② ③	v ● ② ③ ④	v ① ②
		i ① ② ③	i ① ② ③	i ● ② ③ ④	i ① ②
10. Pounding (Sewing, Cooking, Sawing)		T ① ② ③	T ① ② ③	T ① ② ③ ④	T ① ②
		A ① ② ③	A ① ② ③	A ● ② ③ ④	A ① ②
		v ① ② ③	v ① ② ③	v ① ② ③ ④	v ① ②
		i ① ② ③	i ● ② ③	i ① ② ③ ④	i ① ②
11. Blocks (Trucks)		T ① ② ③	T ① ② ③	T ① ② ③ ④	T ① ②
		A ① ② ③	A ① ② ③	A ① ② ③ ④	A ① ②
		v ① ② ③	v ① ② ③	v ① ② ③ ④	v ① ②
		i ① ② ③	i ① ② ③	i ① ② ③ ④	i ① ②
12. Dramatic Play (Dress-Up)		T ① ② ③	T ① ② ③	T ① ② ③ ④	T ① ②
		A ① ② ③	A ① ② ③	A ① ② ③ ④	A ① ②
		v ① ② ③	v ① ② ③	v ① ② ③ ④	v ① ②
		i ① ② ③	i ① ② ③	i ① ② ③ ④	i ① ②
13. Active Play		T ① ② ③	T ① ② ③	T ① ② ③ ④	T ① ②
		A ① ② ③	A ① ② ③	A ① ② ③ ④	A ① ②
		v ① ② ③	v ① ② ③	v ① ② ③ ④	v ① ②
		i ① ② ③	i ① ② ③	i ① ② ③ ④	i ① ②
14. RELIABILITY SHEET ○					

	ONE CHILD	TWO CHILDREN	SMALL GROUPS	LARGE GROUPS
15. Practical Skills Acquisition	T ①②③ A ①②③ v ①②③ i ①②③	T ①②③ A ①②③ v ①②③ i ①②③	T ①②③④ A ①②③④ v ①②③④ i ①②③④	T ①② A ①② v ①② i ①②
16. Observing	T ①②③ A ①②③ v ①②③ i ①②③	T ①②③ A ①②③ v ①②③ i ①②③	T ①②③④ A ①②③④ v ①②③④ i ①②③④	T ①② A ①② v ①② i ①②
17. Social Interaction Ob [ⓒ②ⓢ] ⓣⓐⓥ	T ①②③ A ①②③ v ①②③ i ①②③	T ①②③ A ①②③ v ①②③ i ①②③	T ①②③④ A ①②③④ v ①②③④ i ①②③④	T ①② A ①② v ①② i ①②
18. Unoccupied Child	T ①②③ A ①②③ v ①②③ i ①②③	T ①②③ A ①②③ v ①②③ i ①②③	T ①②③④ A ①②③④ v ①②③④ i ①②③④	T ①② A ①② v ①② i ①②
19. Discipline	T ①②③ A ①②③ v ①②③ i ①②③	T ①②③ A ①②③ v ①②③ i ①②③	T ①②③④ A ①②③④ v ①②③④ i ①②③④	T ①② A ①② v ①② i ①②
20. Transitional Activities ⓣⓐⓥ	T ①②③ A ①②③ v ①②③ i ①②③	T ①②③ A ①②③ v ①②③ i ①②③	T ①②③④ A ①②③④ v ①②③④ i ①②③④	T ①② A ①② v ①② i ①②
21. Classroom Management ⓣⓐⓥ	T ①②③ A ①②③ v ①②③ i ①②③	T ①②③ A ①②③ v ①②③ i ①②③	T ①②③④ A ①②③④ v ①②③④ i ①②③④	T ①② A ①② v ①② i ①②
22. Out of Room ⓣⓐⓥ	T ①②③ A ①②③ v ①②③ i ①②③	T ①②③ A ①②③ v ①②③ i ①②③	T ①②③④ A ①②③④ v ①②③④ i ①②③④	T ①② A ①② v ①② i ①②

NUMBER OF ADULTS IN CLASSROOM ⓪ ① ② ● ④ ⑤ ⑥ ⑦ ⑧ ⑨ ⑩

Chapter 7

Programmed Model

"We are really going to have fun today," announces Ms. Day enthusiastically. "Each one of you is going to learn to read this book, *The Cat and the Rat*. Then you can take it home and read it to your mothers, or your brothers or sisters. On the first page there is a picture of a cat. The letters below the picture spell cat— C-A-T. Let's say the letters all together."

"C-A-T," respond the children.

"Very good spelling!" exclaims the teacher.

"Joyce, you spell it." "C-A-T," responds Joyce.

"Alonso, you spell it." "C-A-T," responds Alonso.

"Good spelling, Joyce. Good spelling, Alonso."

"What little word do you see in the word 'cat' that we learned yesterday?"

"At," shout the children.

"Oh, you are smart today. You really are smart," compliments Ms. Day with emphasis. The children smile, pleased with her praise.

EDUCATIONAL THEORY AND EXPECTED CHILD DEVELOPMENT

This is a typical interaction in a first-grade classroom where the teacher uses behavior modification techniques.

Behavior modification education models grew out of the learning theories of Pavlov and Skinner.[1] These theorists submit that any healthy animal or person can be taught to perform tasks successfully if the unit of learning is small enough and if the reinforcement offered is desired by the subject.

In education, most studies related to behavior shaping are based on B. F. Skinner's operant conditioning theory. Operant conditioning is a form of learning in which a designated behavioral act is reinforced in order to bring about its regular occurrence.

A description of operant condition is provided by Joyce and Weil[2]:

---

[1]Ivan P. Pavlov, *Conditioned Reflexes*, trans. G. V. Anrep (London: Oxford University Press, 1927); B. F. Skinner, *Technology of Teaching* (New York: Appleton-Century-Crofts, 1968).

[2]Bruce Joyce and Marsha Weil, *Models of Teaching* (Englewood Cliffs, N.J.: Prentice-Hall, 1972).

In *operant* conditioning the response (behavior) *operates* upon the environment to generate consequences. The consequences are contingent upon the emission of a response, and they are reinforcing. For example, the response "Pass the butter" operates upon the environment, another person, to obtain the butter. The response is reinforced by the receipt of *the butter*. In other words, the probability that a future desire for butter will elicit the same response is increased by its initial success. The introduction of an appropriate stimulus will also increase response probability. When a parent throws a small ball to a young child after he says "ball," the probability of the word "ball" being emitted is increased. In this case the physical object serves as a prior stimulus to the response "ball" which is reinforced by a mother's smile, nod or "That's right," and receiving the ball itself. These examples of operant conditioning may be represented by the following paradigm:

Stimulus → Response → Reinforcement

That is, behavior is modified because desired behavior is rewarded. For example, animals and people have been trained to perform certain acts by rewarding desired behavior with food, money, privileges, and so on.

There are several educational models based on behavior modification theory. Some models instruct teachers to reward acceptable behavior or responses with candies or tokens that can be exchanged for an opportunity to work at a preferred activity. Other models instruct teachers to reward correct behavior or responses with a great deal of praise. The Programmed Model described in this chapter is based on the assumption that since children seek praise and rewards, they will do what is necessary to gain them. However, this model recognizes that if children cannot get the praise, the positive attention, that they want, they will sometimes behave undesirably if these negative acts also lead to attention. Therefore, positive attention should be given when desired behavior occurs so that it will continue. In this model it is also important for a teacher to maximize the probability of a child's success, so that the child can be rewarded or positively reinforced.

Educational models based on behavior modification theory have carefully structured academic programs that depend on the premise that with proper instructional materials sequenced in small steps, and with consistent reinforcement, most children can master the skills necessary to read, use language, and compute at the level established by national norms for each grade level. While other subjects may be taught, the focus of the program is teaching the basic skills, and most of the time is devoted to this. Advocates believe that young children who can read and compute have the positive acclaim of their peers, parents, and teachers, and, consequently, feel good about themselves. They believe that these children will be able to use their skills to interpret information and solve complex problems.

The instructional materials in these programs consist of two necessary components: (1) programmed learning and (2) programmed teaching methods. The learning tasks are sequenced toward an increasing level of competence. When children succeed in a task, they progress to the next in the sequence—but not until then. The teaching methods are specific—they lead to concepts and skills required for mastering a subject.

It is possible for teachers to program their own materials for most school subjects by using the following procedure:

1. State the desired goal, or outcome behaviors, in terms that can be tested. Determine beforehand how you will know when the goal is reached.

2. Assess the child's relevant skills through tests or observations.

3. Arrange the instructional material in sequence, and identify the desired behavior to be reinforced at the completion of each sequence.

4. If the child learns slowly and needs more positive reinforcement, start the program with a unit in which the child can answer correctly at least 90 percent of the items; if the child learns more quickly, start with a unit in which the child answers 75 percent correctly. Follow a unit sequence that continues this success rate. This procedure allows the child to experience success before moving to something more difficult.

5. Develop a reinforcement schedule for each child to strengthen each behavior that builds toward the desired behavior.

6. Keep records of each child's progress and modify the program or reinforcement schedule accordingly. A child may need to go through a unit of work more than once to master the correct responses. Weekly tests will keep the teacher informed of each child's progress and help in planning for their needs.

These procedures are based on conversations with Wesley Becker at the University of Oregon.

In this model the teaching method is crucially important to the children's success. The teacher provides a stimulus by giving the children a small unit of information and then quickly asks a question about it. A child responds and the teacher provides immediate feedback as to whether the response was correct or incorrect. Correct responses are reinforced by praise and enthusiastic acknowledgment of the success. Incorrect responses are corrected and more drill and practice are provided. The teacher and students share the pleasure of each other's accomplishments. Unproductive or undesired behavior is ignored or stopped by a short reprimand.

Educators who have developed behavior modification models agree on the theory but differ in how they organize the instruction.[3] Lauren Resnick and Margaret Wang of the Learning Research and Development Center at the University of Pittsburgh developed a highly individualized approach. Children in this model are tested frequently to diagnose what material is needed for daily progress. At the start of school, each child receives a set of assignments for each basic skill based on the diagnosis. As a child completes an assignment, the teacher checks the work and provides feedback. The child then progresses to the next task. A comprehensive curriculum has been developed in small sequential steps so that the children can work independently most of the time.

The behavior analysis approach developed at the University of Kansas by Donald Bushell uses a token exchange system to provide positive reinforcement for desired behavior. The children are

---

[3]For more information on these models, refer to the bibliography at the end of this chapter.

organized according to ability into three groups. The groups rotate from one adult to another. The classroom teacher is responsible for the reading program; one full-time aide is responsible for the math program; two parent aides are responsible for spelling, handwriting, and tutoring. Within a group, each child is questioned and given tokens for correct responses. The tokens earned are later exchanged for activities in which the child wants to take part. Each child has a reinforcement schedule. If the child is doing poorly, the teacher will provide more opportunities for the child to succeed by asking questions he or she can answer. As the child becomes very successful, fewer tokens are provided, the assumption being that the child will become self-motivated as skills are developed and achievement brings pleasure.

The University of Oregon's model for direct instruction was developed by Siegfried Engelmann, Carl Bereiter, and Wesley Becker. It organizes a classroom of twenty-five to thirty children into small groups based on the children's ability in basic skills. The classroom teacher is responsible for the reading program; a full-time aide is responsible for the math program; and a second full-time aide is responsible for spelling and handwriting. In order for the children to receive maximum amounts of stimulation and praise during a learning session, the teacher works with eight to ten children at a time and addresses most questions and praise to the group. If each child were questioned separately, he or she would receive only one-fifth to one-eighth of the teacher's attention. By addressing the group, the teacher is attempting to keep all participants totally engaged all of the time. The teacher may rapidly question individuals to see if they have learned each step, but primarily the teacher addresses the entire group. Individual learning problems are diagnosed through weekly testing and each child then receives the drill and practice necessary to learn required skills. In this model, the teachers are the directors. They initiate each stimulus and quickly reinforce or modify each response. They control the students. Though students are expected to be task persistent, self-direction is not supported. The Programmed Model described in this chapter is based primarily but not solely on this University of Oregon model.

In behavior modification models, children are expected to thrive academically. By experiencing daily success in reading and math, they are also expected to develop positive self-images. The programs are set up so that children succeed approximately 90 percent of the time, so they are likely to feel successful and competent.

TEACHER RESPONSIBILITIES

In this model, the teacher and aides are responsible for teaching children basic skills in reading, writing, and computing. Other skills may be taught, but the primary focus is on the basic skills. Teachers must state specific goals, select or develop carefully sequenced programmed materials that will lead to their achievement, and establish means to determine when the goals have been reached. The teacher must test the children at least weekly to diagnose the level of their skill development, and separate them into three or four groups accordingly. The teacher selects the appropriate sequence of materials for each group and provides additional drill and practice for students who need it.

To function optimally, this model requires several adults. One is needed to teach reading, another to teach language development, and a third to teach math. If a fourth adult is available, that person assists individual children who need extra drill and practice. The teacher is responsible for training and supervising the aides in the proper use of sequenced materials. Specific sequenced verbal interactions are expected to take place between adults and children. The teachers and aides must learn how to give small units of information, how to ask precise, direct questions, and how to give children feedback. The adults are also responsible for generating enthusiasm for learning by praising the children a great deal and showing pleasure in their accomplishments. Teachers usually laugh, smile, and speak with emphasis when praising children.

Essentially, the teacher and aides must do the following daily:

1. Evaluate each student's progress in reading, math, handwriting, and spelling.

2. Diagnose the cause of errors.

3. Select materials that will provide drill and practice in areas where the child needs help.

4. Keep track of each student's progress through regular testing.

5. Select the appropriate materials in the learning sequence for each child.

SCHEDULE

The following is a typical schedule for a second-grade class using the Programmed Model.

8:00 Teachers select programmed materials for each group.

8:30 Greet children.

8:35 Take roll.

8:40 Make announcements, collect lunch money.

8:45 Separate into four groups:

Green birds to Ms. Ames for reading

Red birds to Mr. Celaya for spelling and handwriting

Blue birds to Ms. O'Connell for math

Yellow birds to seat work

9:30 Groups rotate.

10:15 Recess.

10:30 Groups rotate.

11:15 Groups rotate.

12:00 Lunch.

1:00 Programmed science, such as AAA3; aides help individuals with reading, math, or homework.

2:00 Recess.

2:15 Music (Monday and Wednesday); art (Tuesday and Thursday); story (Friday).

3:00 Dismissal.

PHYSICAL ENVIRONMENT

The Programmed Model requires space that can be divided among several small groups of children. Partitions are not necessary, but movable chairs are. The noise level is likely to be very high since each group will be enthusiastically shouting answers to teachers' questions. Neither audiovisual equipment nor materials such as paints, puzzles, trucks, blocks, or dolls are required for this model to function well. Bulletin boards, however, are used to display children's academic work and emphasize their progress and performance through graphs and charts.

INTERACTION PATTERNS

A typical day for a class at almost any grade level in the Programmed Model would start with the children entering the classroom and commenting enthusiastically to the adults present about the homework they had completed or about how they had read a whole book to some member of their family on the previous night. The adults would congratulate each child on these achievements. When it was time for the class to start working, the teacher would name and praise several children who had already gone to their seats and had started working on their assignments.

Teacher: I like the way Joan has started working already. And Leonard—he has started also. Why, this whole group by the window has started working! Aren't they grown up! They are going to learn so much today! OK, all of you, go quickly to your seats and take out your books! This whole class is so fantastic, you know just what to do when you come to school! Now, will Group 1 join Ms. DeStefano for math; Group 2 join Mr. Cleet for handwriting; Group 3 join me for reading; and Group 4 continue working on your assignments until it is time to rotate.

In the Programmed Model, all instructional interactions, regardless of grade level or subject matter, follow the same systematic format: the teacher informs the group; the teacher questions the group; the children respond to the teacher; and the teacher reinforces the children.

When the class is divided into small groups, each adult leader informs, questions, and praises the entire group, and the group responds as a group to the teacher. Look at the following situation. Since this is an arithmetic lesson, "A" is used at the end of the coding sequence to indicate that the content of the frame is academic. (If the content is behavioral, "B" is coded.) The interaction is coded in Figure 7.1.

Situation: A teacher is instructing a kindergarten group of six children in an arithmetic lesson.

1. Teacher: Group, I am going to count to five.

2. Teacher: What am I going to do?

3. Group: Count to five!

4. Teacher: You are listening very carefully today.

5. Teacher: Here I go: one, two, three, four, five.

6. Teacher: What did I do?

7. Group: Counted to five!

8. Teacher: Good answers!

9. Teacher: Now, you count to five.

10. Group: One, two, three, four, five!

11. Teacher: You are sharp today! You really are!
    (Teacher laughs.)

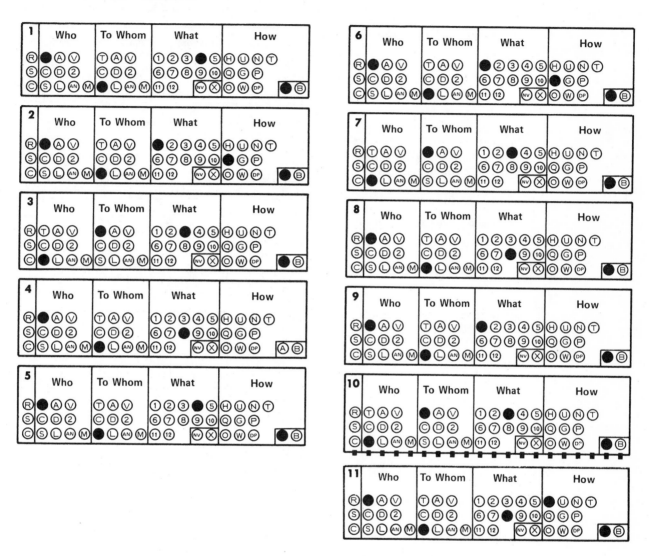

Figure 7.1

Now, try completing the following exercise. The answers are at
the end of the chapter.

EXERCISE 7.1 Using the SRI coding system, code the following interactions.

Situation: In a sixth-grade classroom, a group of seven children is
studying United States government. This group has just read a unit on the
Congress.

1. Teacher: "How many sena-
   tors are in the Congress?"

2. Group: "One hundred."

2	Who	To Whom	What	How
	Ⓡ Ⓣ Ⓐ Ⓥ	Ⓣ Ⓐ Ⓥ	① ② ③ ④ ⑤ Ⓗ Ⓤ Ⓝ Ⓣ	
	Ⓢ Ⓒ Ⓓ ②	Ⓒ Ⓓ ②	⑥ ⑦ ⑧ ⑨ ⑩ Ⓠ Ⓖ Ⓟ	
	Ⓒ Ⓢ Ⓛ ⒶⓃ Ⓜ	Ⓢ Ⓛ ⒶⓃ Ⓜ	⑪ ⑫ 〔NV〕Ⓧ Ⓞ Ⓦ ⒹⓅ	Ⓐ Ⓑ

3. Teacher: "Very good."

3	Who	To Whom	What	How
	Ⓡ Ⓣ Ⓐ Ⓥ	Ⓣ Ⓐ Ⓥ	① ② ③ ④ ⑤ Ⓗ Ⓤ Ⓝ Ⓣ	
	Ⓢ Ⓒ Ⓓ ②	Ⓒ Ⓓ ②	⑥ ⑦ ⑧ ⑨ ⑩ Ⓠ Ⓖ Ⓟ	
	Ⓒ Ⓢ Ⓛ ⒶⓃ Ⓜ	Ⓢ Ⓛ ⒶⓃ Ⓜ	⑪ ⑫ 〔NV〕Ⓧ Ⓞ Ⓦ ⒹⓅ	Ⓐ Ⓑ

4. Teacher: "How many representatives are there in
the United States House
of Representatives?"

4	Who	To Whom	What	How
	Ⓡ Ⓣ Ⓐ Ⓥ	Ⓣ Ⓐ Ⓥ	① ② ③ ④ ⑤ Ⓗ Ⓤ Ⓝ Ⓣ	
	Ⓢ Ⓒ Ⓓ ②	Ⓒ Ⓓ ②	⑥ ⑦ ⑧ ⑨ ⑩ Ⓠ Ⓖ Ⓟ	
	Ⓒ Ⓢ Ⓛ ⒶⓃ Ⓜ	Ⓢ Ⓛ ⒶⓃ Ⓜ	⑪ ⑫ 〔NV〕Ⓧ Ⓞ Ⓦ ⒹⓅ	Ⓐ Ⓑ

5. Group: (No response.)

5	Who	To Whom	What	How
	Ⓡ Ⓣ Ⓐ Ⓥ	Ⓣ Ⓐ Ⓥ	① ② ③ ④ ⑤ Ⓗ Ⓤ Ⓝ Ⓣ	
	Ⓢ Ⓒ Ⓓ ②	Ⓒ Ⓓ ②	⑥ ⑦ ⑧ ⑨ ⑩ Ⓠ Ⓖ Ⓟ	
	Ⓒ Ⓢ Ⓛ ⒶⓃ Ⓜ	Ⓢ Ⓛ ⒶⓃ Ⓜ	⑪ ⑫ 〔NV〕Ⓧ Ⓞ Ⓦ ⒹⓅ	Ⓐ Ⓑ

6. Teacher: "Look in your
text on page 117. Let's
read aloud."

6	Who	To Whom	What	How
	Ⓡ Ⓣ Ⓐ Ⓥ	Ⓣ Ⓐ Ⓥ	① ② ③ ④ ⑤ Ⓗ Ⓤ Ⓝ Ⓣ	
	Ⓢ Ⓒ Ⓓ ②	Ⓒ Ⓓ ②	⑥ ⑦ ⑧ ⑨ ⑩ Ⓠ Ⓖ Ⓟ	
	Ⓒ Ⓢ Ⓛ ⒶⓃ Ⓜ	Ⓢ Ⓛ ⒶⓃ Ⓜ	⑪ ⑫ 〔NV〕Ⓧ Ⓞ Ⓦ ⒹⓅ	Ⓐ Ⓑ

7. Group: (Reads in unison.)

7	Who	To Whom	What	How
	Ⓡ Ⓣ Ⓐ Ⓥ	Ⓣ Ⓐ Ⓥ	① ② ③ ④ ⑤ Ⓗ Ⓤ Ⓝ Ⓣ	
	Ⓢ Ⓒ Ⓓ ②	Ⓒ Ⓓ ②	⑥ ⑦ ⑧ ⑨ ⑩ Ⓠ Ⓖ Ⓟ	
	Ⓒ Ⓢ Ⓛ ⒶⓃ Ⓜ	Ⓢ Ⓛ ⒶⓃ Ⓜ	⑪ ⑫ 〔NV〕Ⓧ Ⓞ Ⓦ ⒹⓅ	Ⓐ Ⓑ

8. Teacher: "Good reading."

8	Who	To Whom	What	How
	Ⓡ Ⓣ Ⓐ Ⓥ	Ⓣ Ⓐ Ⓥ	① ② ③ ④ ⑤ Ⓗ Ⓤ Ⓝ Ⓣ	
	Ⓢ Ⓒ Ⓓ ②	Ⓒ Ⓓ ②	⑥ ⑦ ⑧ ⑨ ⑩ Ⓠ Ⓖ Ⓟ	
	Ⓒ Ⓢ Ⓛ ⒶⓃ Ⓜ	Ⓢ Ⓛ ⒶⓃ Ⓜ	⑪ ⑫ 〔NV〕Ⓧ Ⓞ Ⓦ ⒹⓅ	Ⓐ Ⓑ

9. Teacher: "How many representatives are there?"

9	Who	To Whom	What	How
	Ⓡ Ⓣ Ⓐ Ⓥ	Ⓣ Ⓐ Ⓥ	① ② ③ ④ ⑤ Ⓗ Ⓤ Ⓝ Ⓣ	
	Ⓢ Ⓒ Ⓓ ②	Ⓒ Ⓓ ②	⑥ ⑦ ⑧ ⑨ ⑩ Ⓠ Ⓖ Ⓟ	
	Ⓒ Ⓢ Ⓛ ⒶⓃ Ⓜ	Ⓢ Ⓛ ⒶⓃ Ⓜ	⑪ ⑫ 〔NV〕Ⓧ Ⓞ Ⓦ ⒹⓅ	Ⓐ Ⓑ

10. Group: "Four hundred and
thirty-five."

10	Who	To Whom	What	How
	Ⓡ Ⓣ Ⓐ Ⓥ	Ⓣ Ⓐ Ⓥ	① ② ③ ④ ⑤ Ⓗ Ⓤ Ⓝ Ⓣ	
	Ⓢ Ⓒ Ⓓ ②	Ⓒ Ⓓ ②	⑥ ⑦ ⑧ ⑨ ⑩ Ⓠ Ⓖ Ⓟ	
	Ⓒ Ⓢ Ⓛ ⒶⓃ Ⓜ	Ⓢ Ⓛ ⒶⓃ Ⓜ	⑪ ⑫ 〔NV〕Ⓧ Ⓞ Ⓦ ⒹⓅ	Ⓐ Ⓑ

11. Teacher: "Very good! Now you are really with it."

11	Who	To Whom	What	How
	Ⓡ Ⓣ Ⓐ Ⓥ	Ⓣ Ⓐ Ⓥ	① ② ③ ④ ⑤ Ⓗ Ⓤ Ⓝ Ⓣ	
	Ⓢ Ⓒ Ⓓ ②	Ⓒ Ⓓ ②	⑥ ⑦ ⑧ ⑨ ⑩ Ⓠ Ⓖ Ⓟ	
	Ⓒ Ⓢ Ⓛ ⒜ Ⓜ Ⓢ Ⓛ ⒜ Ⓜ	⑪ ⑫	ⓃⓋ Ⓧ Ⓞ Ⓦ ⓄⓅ	Ⓐ Ⓑ

EXERCISE 7.2 Complete the following vignette.

Situation: A first-grade class is learning a pattern of rhyming words.

Teacher: This word is "end." If I place an "s" before "end," the new word is "send." (TS4A)

Teacher: What is the new word? (TS1QA)

Group: _____

Teacher: _____

Teacher: _____

Group: _____

Teacher: _____

HANDLING MISBEHAVIOR

The children at a table are talking and laughing with each other instead of completing their lessons. The teacher, who is facing the entire class, is working with a group of ten children in the front of the room.

Teacher: I like the way Barbara is studying so quietly and the way Tom is working.

Children: (Stop talking.)

Teacher: If you are having trouble with your work, please skip ahead to the next question and do what you can until I can help you. We will finish here in five minutes.

At recess, Eddie comes running in to report that Carol and Greg are fighting. The teacher separates the children with a firm command and takes them both inside to sit out the rest of the recess. She does not lecture them or give them much attention for their bad behavior.

When the class lines up to enter the room, there is some pushing and shoving. The teacher says, "I like the way Amy is standing so quietly. Amy, can you lead us into the classroom?"

In each of the preceding instances, good behavior is rewarded and unacceptable behavior is ignored. Advocates of this model believe that behavior can be modified if the desired behavior is rewarded systematically. Human beings are thought to desire at-

tention, even negative attention. Calling attention to unacceptable behavior reinforces it and encourages it to continue. If
unacceptable behavior is ignored, it is more likely to be ex-
tinguished.

See if you can complete Exercise 7.3. Suggested interactions
for this vignette are given at the end of the chapter.

EXERCISE 7.3   Situation: A group of fourth-grade children are working in math workbooks.
One child is copying from a neighbor.

Teacher: _____

Teacher: _____

Child: _____

Teacher: _____

EXERCISE 7.4   This and the following exercises involve a typical first-grade classroom using the Programmed Model. Do the exercises and check your
answers at the end of the chapter.

Code each person in the situation below on the CCL.

Situation: The teacher is helping a group of five children with a reading
lesson. The teacher presents new words on a chart and the children find
the words in their workbooks. An aide is working with seven children. They
are counting pennies as they place them in a jar. Another aide is helping
a group of six children learn to write their first and last names. Six
other children are doing problems in a math workbook without the help of
an adult.

CLASSROOM CHECK LIST (be sure to code **EVERYONE** in the class)

Activity		ONE CHILD	TWO CHILDREN	SMALL GROUPS	LARGE GROUPS
1. Snack, lunch		T ①②③ / A ①②③ / v ①②③ / i ①②③	T ①②③ / A ①②③ / v ①②③ / i ①②③	T ①②③④ / A ①②③④ / v ①②③④ / i ①②③④	T ①② / A ①② / v ①② / i ①②
2. Group time		T ①②③ / A ①②③ / v ①②③ / i ①②③	T ①②③ / A ①②③ / v ①②③ / i ①②③	T ①②③④ / A ①②③④ / v ①②③④ / i ①②③④	T ①② / A ①② / v ①② / i ①②
3. Story / Music / Dancing		T ①②③ / A ①②③ / v ①②③ / i ①②③	T ①②③ / A ①②③ / v ①②③ / i ①②③	T ①②③④ / A ①②③④ / v ①②③④ / i ①②③④	T ①② / A ①② / v ①② / i ①②
4. Arts, Crafts		T ①②③ / A ①②③ / v ①②③ / i ①②③	T ①②③ / A ①②③ / v ①②③ / i ①②③	T ①②③④ / A ①②③④ / v ①②③④ / i ①②③④	T ①② / A ①② / v ①② / i ①②
5. Guessing Games / Table Games / Puzzles		T ①②③ / A ①②③ / v ①②③ / i ①②③	T ①②③ / A ①②③ / v ①②③ / i ①②③	T ①②③④ / A ①②③④ / v ①②③④ / i ①②③④	T ①② / A ①② / v ①② / i ①②
○ TV ○ Audio-Visual Materials ○ Exploratory Materials ○ Math and Science Equipment ○ Texts, Workbooks ○ Puzzles, Games	6. Math / Numbers / Arithmetic	T ①②③ / A ①②③ / v ①②③ / i ①②③	T ①②③ / A ①②③ / v ①②③ / i ①②③	T ①②③④ / A ①②③④ / v ①②③④ / i ①②③④	T ①② / A ①② / v ①② / i ①②
	7. Reading / Alphabet / Lang. Development	T ①②③ / A ①②③ / v ①②③ / i ①②③	T ①②③ / A ①②③ / v ①②③ / i ①②③	T ①②③④ / A ①②③④ / v ①②③④ / i ①②③④	T ①② / A ①② / v ①② / i ①②
	8. Social Studies / Geography	T ①②③ / A ①②③ / v ①②③ / i ①②③	T ①②③ / A ①②③ / v ①②③ / i ①②③	T ①②③④ / A ①②③④ / v ①②③④ / i ①②③④	T ①② / A ①② / v ①② / i ①②
	9. Science / Natural World	T ①②③ / A ①②③ / v ①②③ / i ①②③	T ①②③ / A ①②③ / v ①②③ / i ①②③	T ①②③④ / A ①②③④ / v ①②③④ / i ①②③④	T ①② / A ①② / v ①② / i ①②
10. Sewing / Cooking / Pounding / Sawing		T ①②③ / A ①②③ / v ①②③ / i ①②③	T ①②③ / A ①②③ / v ①②③ / i ①②③	T ①②③④ / A ①②③④ / v ①②③④ / i ①②③④	T ①② / A ①② / v ①② / i ①②
11. Blocks / Trucks		T ①②③ / A ①②③ / v ①②③ / i ①②③	T ①②③ / A ①②③ / v ①②③ / i ①②③	T ①②③④ / A ①②③④ / v ①②③④ / i ①②③④	T ①② / A ①② / v ①② / i ①②
12. Dramatic Play / Dress-Up		T ①②③ / A ①②③ / v ①②③ / i ①②③	T ①②③ / A ①②③ / v ①②③ / i ①②③	T ①②③④ / A ①②③④ / v ①②③④ / i ①②③④	T ①② / A ①② / v ①② / i ①②
13. Active Play		T ①②③ / A ①②③ / v ①②③ / i ①②③	T ①②③ / A ①②③ / v ①②③ / i ①②③	T ①②③④ / A ①②③④ / v ①②③④ / i ①②③④	T ①② / A ①② / v ①② / i ①②
14. RELIABILITY SHEET	○				

Exercise 7.4

		ONE CHILD	TWO CHILDREN	SMALL GROUPS	LARGE GROUPS
15. Practical Skills Acquisition		T ①②③ A ①②③ V ①②③ i ①②③	T ①②③ A ①②③ V ①②③ i ①②③	T ①②③④ A ①②③④ V ①②③④ i ①②③④	T ①② A ①② V ①② i ①②
16. Observing		T ①②③ A ①②③ V ①②③ i ①②③	T ①②③ A ①②③ V ①②③ i ①②③	T ①②③④ A ①②③④ V ①②③④ i ①②③④	T ①② A ①② V ①② i ①②
17. Social Interaction Ob [ⓒ ② Ⓢ]	Ⓣ Ⓐ Ⓥ	T ①②③ A ①②③ V ①②③ i ①②③	T ①②③ A ①②③ V ①②③ i ①②③	T ①②③④ A ①②③④ V ①②③④ i ①②③④	T ①② A ①② V ①② i ①②
18. Unoccupied Child		T ①②③ A ①②③ V ①②③ i ①②③	T ①②③ A ①②③ V ①②③ i ①②③	T ①②③④ A ①②③④ V ①②③④ i ①②③④	T ①② A ①② V ①② i ①②
19. Discipline		T ①②③ A ①②③ V ①②③ i ①②③	T ①②③ A ①②③ V ①②③ i ①②③	T ①②③④ A ①②③④ V ①②③④ i ①②③④	T ①② A ①② V ①② i ①②
20. Transitional Activities	Ⓣ Ⓐ Ⓥ	T ①②③ A ①②③ V ①②③ i ①②③	T ①②③ A ①②③ V ①②③ i ①②③	T ①②③④ A ①②③④ V ①②③④ i ①②③④	T ①② A ①② V ①② i ①②
21. Classroom Management	Ⓣ Ⓐ Ⓥ	T ①②③ A ①②③ V ①②③ i ①②③	T ①②③ A ①②③ V ①②③ i ①②③	T ①②③④ A ①②③④ V ①②③④ i ①②③④	T ①② A ①② V ①② i ①②
22. Out of Room	Ⓣ Ⓐ Ⓥ	T ①②③ A ①②③ V ①②③ i ①②③	T ①②③ A ①②③ V ①②③ i ①②③	T ①②③④ A ①②③④ V ①②③④ i ①②③④	T ①② A ①② V ①② i ①②

NUMBER OF ADULTS IN CLASSROOM   ⓪ ① ② ③ ④ ⑤ ⑥ ⑦ ⑧ ⑨ ⑩

EXERCISE 7.5   Code each person in the situation below on the CCL.

Situation: The teacher checks with her aides and decides these groups are finished. The teacher rings a bell and the groups rotate. The five children who were reading move to the aide who teaches math. The seven children who were counting pennies move to their seats and work in their math workbooks. The children who were working at their seats move to the aide who instructs handwriting. The children who were practicing writing move to the reading teacher.

CLASSROOM CHECK LIST (be sure to code **EVERYONE** in the class)

	ONE CHILD	TWO CHILDREN	SMALL GROUPS	LARGE GROUPS
1. Snack, lunch	T ①②③ A ①②③ v ①②③ i ①②③	T ①②③ A ①②③ v ①②③ i ①②③	T ①②③④ A ①②③④ v ①②③④ i ①②③④	T ①② A ①② v ①② i ①②
2. Group time	T ①②③ A ①②③ v ①②③ i ①②③	T ①②③ A ①②③ v ①②③ i ①②③	T ①②③④ A ①②③④ v ①②③④ i ①②③④	T ①② A ①② v ①② i ①②
Story **3. Music** Dancing	T ①②③ A ①②③ v ①②③ i ①②③	T ①②③ A ①②③ v ①②③ i ①②③	T ①②③④ A ①②③④ v ①②③④ i ①②③④	T ①② A ①② v ①② i ①②
4. Arts, Crafts	T ①②③ A ①②③ v ①②③ i ①②③	T ①②③ A ①②③ v ①②③ i ①②③	T ①②③④ A ①②③④ v ①②③④ i ①②③④	T ①② A ①② v ①② i ①②
Guessing Games **5. Table Games** Puzzles	T ①②③ A ①②③ v ①②③ i ①②③	T ①②③ A ①②③ v ①②③ i ①②③	T ①②③④ A ①②③④ v ①②③④ i ①②③④	T ①② A ①② v ①② i ①②
Numbers **6. Math** Arithmetic	T ①②③ A ①②③ v ①②③ i ①②③	T ①②③ A ①②③ v ①②③ i ①②③	T ①②③④ A ①②③④ v ①②③④ i ①②③④	T ①② A ①② v ①② i ①②
Reading **7. Alphabet** Lang. Development	T ①②③ A ①②③ v ①②③ i ①②③	T ①②③ A ①②③ v ①②③ i ①②③	T ①②③④ A ①②③④ v ①②③④ i ①②③④	T ①② A ①② v ①② i ①②
Social Studies **8.** Geography	T ①②③ A ①②③ v ①②③ i ①②③	T ①②③ A ①②③ v ①②③ i ①②③	T ①②③④ A ①②③④ v ①②③④ i ①②③④	T ①② A ①② v ①② i ①②
Science **9.** Natural World	T ①②③ A ①②③ v ①②③ i ①②③	T ①②③ A ①②③ v ①②③ i ①②③	T ①②③④ A ①②③④ v ①②③④ i ①②③④	T ①② A ①② v ①② i ①②
Sewing Cooking **10.** Pounding Sawing	T ①②③ A ①②③ v ①②③ i ①②③	T ①②③ A ①②③ v ①②③ i ①②③	T ①②③④ A ①②③④ v ①②③④ i ①②③④	T ①② A ①② v ①② i ①②
11. Blocks Trucks	T ①②③ A ①②③ v ①②③ i ①②③	T ①②③ A ①②③ v ①②③ i ①②③	T ①②③④ A ①②③④ v ①②③④ i ①②③④	T ①② A ①② v ①② i ①②
12. Dramatic Play Dress-Up	T ①②③ A ①②③ v ①②③ i ①②③	T ①②③ A ①②③ v ①②③ i ①②③	T ①②③④ A ①②③④ v ①②③④ i ①②③④	T ①② A ①② v ①② i ①②
13. Active Play	T ①②③ A ①②③ v ①②③ i ①②③	T ①②③ A ①②③ v ①②③ i ①②③	T ①②③④ A ①②③④ v ①②③④ i ①②③④	T ①② A ①② v ①② i ①②
14. RELIABILITY SHEET ○				

Associated with items 6–9:

○ TV
○ Audio-Visual Materials
○ Exploratory Materials
○ Math and Science Equipment
○ Texts, Workbooks
○ Puzzles, Games

Exercise 7.5

	ONE CHILD	TWO CHILDREN	SMALL GROUPS	LARGE GROUPS
15. Practical Skills Acquisition	T ①②③ A ①②③ v ①②③ i ①②③	T ①②③ A ①②③ v ①②③ i ①②③	T ①②③④ A ①②③④ v ①②③④ i ①②③④	T ①② A ①② v ①② i ①②
16. Observing	T ①②③ A ①②③ v ①②③ i ①②③	T ①②③ A ①②③ v ①②③ i ①②③	T ①②③④ A ①②③④ v ①②③④ i ①②③④	T ①② A ①② v ①② i ①②
17. Social Interaction Ob [ⓒ ② ⓢ] Ⓣ Ⓐ Ⓥ	T ①②③ A ①②③ v ①②③ i ①②③	T ①②③ A ①②③ v ①②③ i ①②③	T ①②③④ A ①②③④ v ①②③④ i ①②③④	T ①② A ①② v ①② i ①②
18. Unoccupied Child	T ①②③ A ①②③ v ①②③ i ①②③	T ①②③ A ①②③ v ①②③ i ①②③	T ①②③④ A ①②③④ v ①②③④ i ①②③④	T ①② A ①② v ①② i ①②
19. Discipline	T ①②③ A ①②③ v ①②③ i ①②③	T ①②③ A ①②③ v ①②③ i ①②③	T ①②③④ A ①②③④ v ①②③④ i ①②③④	T ①② A ①② v ①② i ①②
20. Transitional Activities Ⓣ Ⓐ Ⓥ	T ①②③ A ①②③ v ①②③ i ①②③	T ①②③ A ①②③ v ①②③ i ①②③	T ①②③④ A ①②③④ v ①②③④ i ①②③④	T ①② A ①② v ①② i ①②
21. Classroom Management Ⓣ Ⓐ Ⓥ	T ①②③ A ①②③ v ①②③ i ①②③	T ①②③ A ①②③ v ①②③ i ①②③	T ①②③④ A ①②③④ v ①②③④ i ①②③④	T ①② A ①② v ①② i ①②
22. Out of Room Ⓣ Ⓐ Ⓥ	T ①②③ A ①②③ v ①②③ i ①②③	T ①②③ A ①②③ v ①②③ i ①②③	T ①②③④ A ①②③④ v ①②③④ i ①②③④	T ①② A ①② v ①② i ①②

NUMBER OF ADULTS IN CLASSROOM   ⓪ ① ② ③ ④ ⑤ ⑥ ⑦ ⑧ ⑨ ⑩

The type of rotation illustrated in the exercises will continue until each group of children has worked with each adult. If the SRI Classroom Check List of activities (CCL) is recorded four times during the work periods, will each grid look exactly alike? Yes, since the teacher will always be working with a small group in reading, one aide with a small group in math, another aide with a small group in handwriting, and a group of children will always be working independently in math.

From kindergarten to third grade, the grouping of children and the rotation of groups from one adult to another is the same. The teacher usually teaches reading, one aide teaches math, and a second aide works with spelling and language development. When a volunteer is available, he or she helps children who need additional drill and practice in reading or math.

In the upper elementary grades, after the basic skills of reading, writing, and computing have been acceptably mastered, science and social studies are added to the curriculum. The same systematic, sequential manner is used to teach these subjects. The AAAS Science Program, developed by R. Gagné,[4] is a hierarchy of learning episodes, the type of science program that would be used in the Programmed Model. The teacher clearly states the problem to be solved; each child has a set of materials with which to find the correct answer. The correct solution is usually written down and the teacher

---

[4]Robert M. Gagné, "Science—A Process Approach: Commentary for Teachers," *Science Education News* 1, No. 11 (1963).

checks for correctness and provides the appropriate feedback. If the answer is correct, the child proceeds to the next unit of work; if the answer is incorrect, the child goes back through the learning unit.

In these higher grades also, an effort might be made to develop some student leaders who could occasionally be the teacher, following the instructional format and providing the necessary reinforcement.

CLASSROOM REQUIREMENTS

To implement this model, it is necessary to locate or develop carefully sequenced programmed materials for teaching reading, math, language, spelling, handwriting, and science. These materials and their systematic use are the cornerstone of this model. In every case, regardless of the subject matter, the instruction pattern takes the same form: a bit of information is given to the children; a question is asked about the information; feedback or reinforcement is given to the children's response. An example of this sequence is:

Teacher: Today we are going to learn about the several sounds a *g* can have. (Writes on the chalkboard.) *G* at the end of *tug* has a hard "ge" sound. The *g*'s in *George* have a "jă" sound, and when *g* is followed by *h*, there is an "f" sound. *Tough* is pronounced "tŭf." (Inform)

Teacher: (Writes *rough* on the chalkboard.) Bobby, how is *rough* pronounced? (Question)

Bobby: "Rŭf." (Response)

Teacher: Very good, Bobby. (Feedback)

Teacher: (Writes *enough* on the chalkboard.) Jean, what about this word? (Question)

Jean: "Ēnŭf." (Response)

Teacher: Excellent, Jean. (Feedback)

Teacher: Bill, can you think of other words that end in *gh* that have an "f" sound? (Question)

Bill: Well, *through* ends in *gh*, but it doesn't have an "f" sound. (Response)

Teacher: That's right, Bill. There are exceptions to most phonic rules. In the word *through*, the *g* and *h* are both silent. Only the "thrōō" is sounded. (Feedback)

The Programmed Model also requires three instructors. Two of these can be parent volunteers or older students. Sequenced materials and specific directions on how to carry out required verbal actions are necessary. The teacher can easily train the teaching assistants to use the materials correctly and to perform successfully in the classroom. In addition, all instructors must be enthusiastic and sincere in their praise of children's success. Enthusiastic praise reinforces and thus helps shape desired behavior.

RESEARCH FINDINGS ON HOW CHILDREN GROW AND DEVELOP

In classrooms where reading and math materials are carefully sequenced and teachers use reinforcement systematically, the children in these Follow Through models perform well on achievement tests. The children spend about 50 percent of their school time working in small reading and math groups and doing problems in workbooks. They are task persistent and request very little help with their seat work. When small groups of children work with adults, they are enthusiastically responsive to the adults' questions about their lessons. They are attentive and seldom misbehave. Their verbal interactions are primarily with adults rather than with each other. The children seem pleased with their accomplishments in learning to read and do problems in math. This pleasure is indicated by their smiles and enthusiasm during group instruction. They are eager to show their accomplishments to classroom visitors.

Although reading and math abilities in this model are superior to those in other educational models, there are some other, limiting factors. Children in this model did not perform very well on the Raven's Coloured Progressive Matrices test, a test of nonverbal problem-solving ability, described on page 72. Their poor performance on this test may be the result of their having few opportunities to explore with materials and discover the relationships between a whole and its parts, or among the parts of an object.

Children in the Programmed Model ask fewer questions and cooperate less often with classmates in working on tasks than children in more open classrooms. They are also absent more frequently.

On the Intellectual Achievement Responsibility scale (IAR), test findings indicate that if children in this model do poorly on academic tests, they accept the responsibility for their poor performance but apparently feel that any success they have in academic subjects is due to the teacher or other factors outside themselves. This model has a very strong teacher image and a child is likely to view this person as all-powerful—"If I do well, it is because the teacher is so good at teaching, but if I do poorly, it must be all my fault, because my teacher is so good."[5]

OBSERVABLE COMPONENTS

Some components of this model, such as the fact that each child has been tested and appropriate material selected, cannot be observed on the SRI observation system. Observation systems developed at the University of Pittsburgh, the University of Kansas, or the University of Oregon would be more appropriate for assessing whether children are receiving the prescribed amounts and kinds of attention. Also, our instrument can only reflect in a small way the great enthusiasm that teachers in these models bring to and sustain throughout learning episodes.

However, many other components, including materials being used, the activities occurring, and interactions between adults and children, can be systematically observed and recorded.

Materials

On the Physical Environment Information form, programmed workbooks and textbooks would be marked in both the Present and Used Today columns. Some art materials would also be coded. For math,

---

[5]Jane Stallings and David Kaskowitz, *Follow Through Classroom Observation Evaluation 1972-73*. (Menlo Park, Calif.: Stanford Research Institute, 1974.) ERIC Accession No. ED 104 969.

there would be items for counting, such as beads, marbles or coins (see Figure 7.2). Science materials, in the form of sequenced, programmed work units, would be offered in grades three, four, five, and six.

Activities and Groupings

On the Classroom Check List of activities, the adults and children would be marked in primarily two activities, reading and math. The three adults would be working with small groups (each composed of approximately one-fourth of the children enrolled). If a volunteer was present, that person would probably be working with an individual child on reading or math. Approximately one-fourth of the children would be working independently in reading or math workbooks (see Figure 7.3).

Interaction Observations

The interactions among the adults and children would have a systematic pattern. The adults would provide a discrete item of information to a small group of children (TS4A), then immediately ask a question about that information (TS1QA). The children would respond (ST3A). If they were correct, the adult would praise them (TS8A); if they were incorrect, the adult would guide them to another response (TS9GA). If the response indicated that the children had not understood the information, the adult would start the sequence over and continue to inform and question until it was clear that the child could respond correctly.

Physical Environment Information
(Mark all that apply.)

For each of the items below, mark all
that apply:

① Present
② Used today

Seating Patterns:
● Movable tables and chairs for seating
 purposes.
○ Stationary desks in rows.
● Assigned seating for at least part of
 the day.
○ Children select their own seating
 locations.
● Teacher assigns children to groups.
○ Children select their own work groups.

GAMES, TOYS, PLAY EQUIPMENT
①② small toys (trucks, cars, dolls and
   accessories
●● puzzles, games
①② wheel toys
①② small play equipment (jumpropes, balls)
①② large play equipment (swings, jungle gym)
①② children's storybooks
①② animals, other nature objects
①② sandbox, water table
①② carpentry materials, large blocks
①② cooking and sewing supplies

INSTRUCTIONAL MATERIALS
①② Montessori, other educational toys
●● children's texts, workbooks
●② math/science equipment, concrete objects
●● instructional charts

AUDIO, VISUAL EQUIPMENT
①② television
①② record or tape player
①② audio-visual equipment

GENERAL EQUIPMENT, MATERIALS
●② children's own products on display
①② displays reflecting children's ethnicity
①② other displays especially for children
①② magazines
●● achievement charts
①② child-size sink
①② child-size table and chairs
①② child-size shelves
●② arts and crafts materials
①② blackboard, feltboard
①② child's own storage space
①② photographs of the children on display

OTHER
①② please specify . . . . . .

MAKE NO

STRAY MARKS

IN BLANK AREAS

Figure 7.2

CLASSROOM CHECK LIST (be sure to code EVERYONE in the class)

		ONE CHILD	TWO CHILDREN	SMALL GROUPS	LARGE GROUPS
1. Snack, lunch		T ①②③ A ①②③ V ①②③ i ①②③	T ①②③ A ①②③ V ①②③ i ①②③	T ①②③④ A ①②③④ V ①②③④ i ①②③④	T ①② A ①② V ①② i ①②
2. Group time		T ①②③ A ①②③ V ①②③ i ①②③	T ①②③ A ①②③ V ①②③ i ①②③	T ①②③④ A ①②③④ V ①②③④ i ①②③④	T ①② A ①② V ①② i ①②
3. Story / Music / Dancing		T ①②③ A ①②③ V ①②③ i ①②③	T ①②③ A ①②③ V ①②③ i ①②③	T ①②③④ A ①②③④ V ①②③④ i ①②③④	T ①② A ①② V ①② i ①②
4. Arts, Crafts		T ①②③ A ①②③ V ①②③ i ①②③	T ①②③ A ①②③ V ①②③ i ①②③	T ①②③④ A ①②③④ V ①②③④ i ①②③④	T ①② A ①② V ①② i ①②
5. Guessing Games / Table Games / Puzzles		T ①②③ A ①②③ V ①②③ i ①②③	T ①②③ A ①②③ V ①②③ i ①②③	T ①②③④ A ①②③④ V ①②③④ i ①②③④	T ①② A ①② V ①② i ①②
○ TV ○ Audio-Visual Materials ○ Exploratory Materials ○ Math and Science Equipment ○ Texts, Workbooks ○ Puzzles, Games	6. Numbers / Math / Arithmetic	T ①②③ A ①②③ V ①②③ i ①②③	T ①②③ A ①②③ V ①②③ i ①②③	T ①②③④ A ●②③④ V ①②③④ i ●②③④	T ①② A ①② V ①② i ①②
	7. Reading / Alphabet / Lang. Development	T ①②③ A ①②③ V ①②③ i ①②③	T ①②③ A ①②③ V ①②③ i ①②③	T ●②③④ A ●②③④ V ①②③④ i ①②③④	T ①② A ①② V ①② i ①②
	8. Social Studies / Geography	T ①②③ A ①②③ V ①②③ i ①②③	T ①②③ A ①②③ V ①②③ i ①②③	T ①②③④ A ①②③④ V ①②③④ i ①②③④	T ①② A ①② V ①② i ①②
	9. Science / Natural World	T ①②③ A ①②③ V ①②③ i ①②③	T ①②③ A ①②③ V ①②③ i ①②③	T ①②③④ A ①②③④ V ①②③④ i ①②③④	T ①② A ①② V ①② i ①②
10. Sewing / Cooking / Pounding / Sawing		T ①②③ A ①②③ V ①②③ i ①②③	T ①②③ A ①②③ V ①②③ i ①②③	T ①②③④ A ①②③④ V ①②③④ i ①②③④	T ①② A ①② V ①② i ①②
11. Blocks / Trucks		T ①②③ A ①②③ V ①②③ i ①②③	T ①②③ A ①②③ V ①②③ i ①②③	T ①②③④ A ①②③④ V ①②③④ i ①②③④	T ①② A ①② V ①② i ①②
12. Dramatic Play / Dress-Up		T ①②③ A ①②③ V ①②③ i ①②③	T ①②③ A ①②③ V ①②③ i ①②③	T ①②③④ A ①②③④ V ①②③④ i ①②③④	T ①② A ①② V ①② i ①②
13. Active Play		T ①②③ A ①②③ V ①②③ i ①②③	T ①②③ A ①②③ V ①②③ i ①②③	T ①②③④ A ①②③④ V ①②③④ i ①②③④	T ①② A ①② V ①② i ①②
14. RELIABILITY SHEET	○				

Figure 7.3

			ONE CHILD	TWO CHILDREN	SMALL GROUPS	LARGE GROUPS
15. Practical Skills Acquisition			T ①②③	T ①②③	T ①②③④	T ①②
			A ①②③	A ①②③	A ①②③④	A ①②
			v ①②③	v ①②③	v ①②③④	v ①②
			i ①②③	i ①②③	i ①②③④	i ①②
16. Observing			T ①②③	T ①②③	T ①②③④	T ①②
			A ①②③	A ①②③	A ①②③④	A ①②
			v ①②③	v ①②③	v ①②③④	v ①②
			i ①②③	i ①②③	i ①②③④	i ①②
17. Social Interaction	Ob [ⓒ ② ⓢ]	ⓣ	T ①②③	T ①②③	T ①②③④	T ①②
		Ⓐ	A ①②③	A ①②③	A ①②③④	A ①②
		Ⓥ	v ①②③	v ①②③	v ①②③④	v ①②
			i ①②③	i ①②③	i ①②③④	i ①②
18. Unoccupied Child			T ①②③	T ①②③	T ①②③④	T ①②
			A ①②③	A ①②③	A ①②③④	A ①②
			v ①②③	v ①②③	v ①②③④	v ①②
			i ①②③	i ①②③	i ①②③④	i ①②
19. Discipline			T ①②③	T ①②③	T ①②③④	T ①②
			A ①②③	A ①②③	A ①②③④	A ①②
			v ①②③	v ①②③	v ①②③④	v ①②
			i ①②③	i ①②③	i ①②③④	i ①②
20. Transitional Activities		ⓣ	T ①②③	T ①②③	T ①②③④	T ①②
		Ⓐ	A ①②③	A ①②③	A ①②③④	A ①②
		Ⓥ	v ①②③	v ①②③	v ①②③④	v ①②
			i ①②③	i ①②③	i ①②③④	i ①②
21. Classroom Management		ⓣ	T ①②③	T ①②③	T ①②③④	T ①②
		Ⓐ	A ①②③	A ①②③	A ①②③④	A ①②
		Ⓥ	v ①②③	v ①②③	v ①②③④	v ①②
			i ①②③	i ①②③	i ①②③④	i ①②
22. Out of Room		ⓣ	T ①②③	T ①②③	T ①②③④	T ①②
		Ⓐ	A ①②③	A ①②③	A ①②③④	A ①②
		Ⓥ	v ①②③	v ①②③	v ①②③④	v ①②
			i ①②③	i ①②③	i ①②③④	i ①②

NUMBER OF ADULTS IN CLASSROOM　⓪ ① ② ③ ④ ⑤ ⑥ ⑦ ⑧ ⑨ ⑩

The following is a typical interaction in the Programmed Model. The interaction is coded in Figure 7.4. ("H" coded in a sequence would indicate pleasure.)

Situation: A kindergarten teacher with a small math group.

1. Teacher: There are five days in a week.

2. Teacher: How many days are in a week of school?

3. Group: Five! (Enthusiastically, gleefully)

4. Teacher: Very good! (Smiling)

5. Teacher: The first three school days are Monday, Tuesday, Wednesday.

6. Teacher: What are the first three school days?

7. Group: Monday, Tuesday (. . . Pause)

8. Teacher: The third day is Wednesday.

9. Teacher: What is the third day?

10. Group: Wednesday! (Enthusiastically)

11. Teacher: Very good! (Smiling)

12. Teacher: Now say all the days.

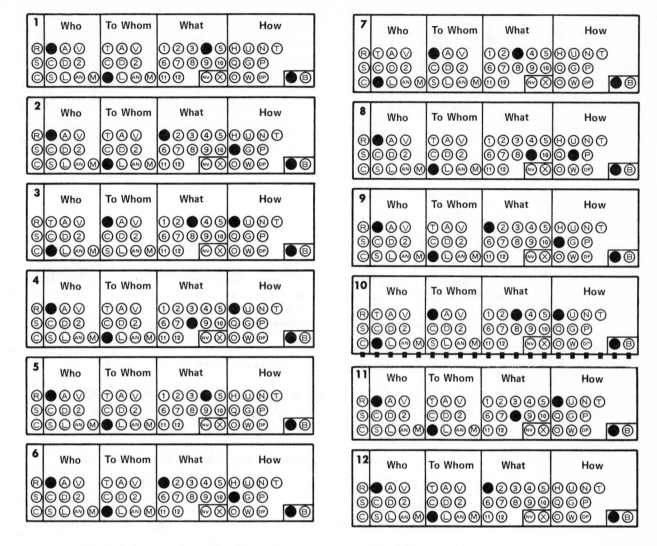

Figure 7.4 Coded Interaction of a Programmed Model Classroom

IMPORTANCE OF TEACHER OBSERVATION

Being observed gives teachers recorded data they can study,
and, if necessary, use to alter their behavior to match their goals.
Teachers looking at the observation records on Figures 7.2, 7.3, and
7.4 could see that the Programmed Model was being implemented faithfully. If the aide had been recorded as performing management activities rather than instructing math, the activities of the aide would
have to be changed to conform with model specifications. If the
teacher is recorded as carrying on social conversations during reading class instead of teaching reading, he or she would need to alter
that behavior.

SUMMARY OF COMPONENTS

Theorist or theory: Skinner

Oriented toward: Behavior modification

Goals: To develop basic skills

Stress: Drill, practice, and memory skills

Structure: Teacher-centered

Grouping patterns: Small group

Materials: Programmed workbooks

Where to teach: Small group of chairs in a half circle

Who initiates: Teacher

Questioning strategy: Direct single answers

Feedback from: Teacher and test scores

Who evaluates: Teacher

Evaluation tools: Achievement tests

BIBLIOGRAPHY

As previously stated, the Programmed Model is based primarily on the Follow Through model developed at the University of Oregon. However, some of the components may be seen in the Follow Through models of the University of Kansas and the University of Pittsburgh.

Where Components of the Programmed Type Models Can Be Seen

Interested readers should contact the Follow Through offices in the school districts of the cities listed.

University of Kansas model

Meridian Community, Illinois	New Madrid County, Missouri
Waukegan, Illinois	Trenton, New Jersey
Laurence, Kansas	New York City, PS-6, New York
Louisville, Kentucky	New York City, PS-77X, New York
Kansas City, Missouri	Philadelphia, Pennsylvania

University of Oregon model

Flippin, Arkansas	Eugene, Oregon
St. Louis, Illinois	Providence, Rhode Island
Flint, Michigan	Williamsburg, South Carolina
Grand Rapids, Michigan	Rosebud, South Dakota
West Iron County, Michigan	Todd County, South Dakota
Tupelo, Mississippi	Smithville, Tennessee
E. Las Vegas, New Mexico	Dimmitt, Texas
Brooklyn, New York	Uvalde, Texas
Cherokee, North Carolina	Racine, Wisconsin
Dayton, Ohio	Washington, D.C.

University of Pittsburgh model

Montevideo, Minnesota	Clinton County, Pennsylvania
Akron, Ohio	Pittsburgh, Pennsylvania

Suggested Readings

Theory of the Programmed Model

Becker, Wesley C., ed. *An Empirical Basis for Change in Education: Selections on Behavioral Psychology for Teachers*. Chicago: Science Research Associates, 1971.

Bereiter, Carl, and Engelmann, S. *Teaching Disadvantaged Children in the Preschool*. Englewood Cliffs, N.J.: Prentice-Hall, 1966.

Gagné, Robert M. *The Conditions of Learning*. 2d ed. New York: Holt, Rinehart and Winston, 1970.

Hilgard, Ernest R. "A Perspective on the Relationship between Learning Theory and Educational Practices." In *Theories of Learning and Instruction*, Sixty-third Yearbook. Edited by Ernest R. Hilgard. Chicago: National Society for the Study of Education, 1964, pp. 402-418.

Hunt, Joseph M. *Intelligence and Experience*. New York: Ronald Press, 1961, pp. 6, 106, 351.

Mager, Robert F. *Preparing Instructional Objectives*, 2d ed. Belmont, Calif.: Fearon Publications, 1975.

Schramm, Wilbur. *Programmed Instruction: Today and Tomorrow*. New York: The Fund for the Advancement of Education, 1962.

Skinner, B. F. *The Technology of Teaching*. New York: Appleton-Century-Crofts, 1968.

_____. *Verbal Behavior*. New York: Appleton-Century-Crofts, 1957.

_____. *Walden Two*. New York: Macmillan, 1948.

Taber, Julian I.; Glaser, Robert; and Schaeffer, Helmut. *Learning and Programmed Instruction*. Reading, Mass.: Addison-Wesley, 1965.

Implementing the Programmed Model

Becker, Wesley C.; Engelmann, Siegfried; Thomas, Donand R. *Teaching: A Course in Applied Psychology*. Chicago: Science Research Associates, 1971.

Becker, Wesley, C., and Osborn, Jean. *Teacher Training in the Engelmann-Becker Follow Through Model*. Washington, D.C.: U.S. Office of Education, 1970. Follow Through Library No. 7.10.

Bushell, Don, Jr., and Brigham, T. A. "Classroom Token Systems as Technology." *Educational Technology* 11 (1971): 14-17.

Glaser, Robert. *The Design and Programming of Instruction, the Schools, and the Challenge of Innovation*. Supplementary Paper No. 28. Pittsburgh, Pa.: Learning Research and Development Center, University of Pittsburgh, 1968: 156-215. ERIC Accession No. ED 031 939.

Lindvall, C. M., and Bolvin, J. O. "The Role of the Teacher in Individually Prescribed Instruction." *Educational Technology* 10 (February 1970):37-41.

Maccoby, Eleanor E., and Zellner, Miriam. *Experiments in Primary Education: Aspects of Project Follow-Through*. New York: Harcourt Brace Jovanovich, 1970.

Resnick, Lauren B. "Relations between Perceptual and Syntactic Control in Oral Reading." *Journal of Educational Psychology* 61 (October 1970): 382-385.

Resnick, Lauren B., and Wang, Margaret C. "Approaches to the Valida-
tion of Learning Hierarchies." Preprint 50. *Proceedings of the
18th Annual Western Regional Conference on Testing Problems*.
Pittsburgh, Pa.: Learning Research and Development Center,
University of Pittsburgh, 1969: 14-38. ERIC Accession No. ED
035 943.

Wang, Margaret C., ed. *The Use of Direct Observation to Study
Instructional-Learning Behaviors in School Settings*. Pittsburgh, Pa.: Learning Research and Development Center, University of Pittsburgh, 1974. ERIC Accession No. ED 100 798.

Weber, Evelyn. *Early Childhood Education: Perspectives on Change*
Worthington, Ohio: Charles A. Jones, 1970.

Commercially Available Materials

For materials used in the Engelmann-Becker Oregon model, see
Follow Through Materials Review (Portland, Ore.: Nero Associates).

Basic Goals in Spelling: A series of workbooks organized around the
sounds and structure of the language. The units introduce one
sound at a time (with spelling options), and then build on that
sound throughout the series. Reading and spelling skills are
developed together, and a comprehensive dictionary is refer-
enced throughout. (Webster Division, McGraw-Hill Book Co., Manchester Road, Manchester, MO 63011)

Criterion Reading and Individualized Learning Management Systems:
A set of criterion-referenced assessments that indicate whether
or not a child has mastered a specific reading skill. This series promotes individualized reading instruction by providing
a complete diagnostic profile for each child. For grades K-12.
(Random House School Division, 201 E. 50th Street, New York,
NY 10022)

Distar Instructional System for Reading, Mathematics, and Language:
The Distar System is based on the idea that every student can
learn if taught in the appropriate way. Distar programs are
carefully structured to focus on the students' response to a
question and the provision of immediate feedback; emphasis is
placed on the child's motivation to learn and on parental involvement in the learning process. Kits include storybooks and
take-home workbooks. For preschool to grade 3. (Science Research Associates, 259 East Erie Street, Chicago, IL 60611)

Let's Read: Leonard Bloomfield, and Clarence L. Barnhart, 1961. A
book describing "a way to teach reading based on entirely new
pedagogical principles," namely the application of phonemic
principles. Coauthored by a distinguished Professor of Lin-
guistics, this "linguistic approach" to the teaching of reading includes classroom exercises and lessons, teacher's guides
to the lessons, and essays introducing "the Bloomfield System."
(Wayne State University, 5980 Cass Avenue, Detroit, MI 48202)

Programmed Reading: A series of workbooks, related storybooks, film
strips, and achievement tests distinguished by a linguistic
approach to reading skills. The program format is individualized, allowing each student to progress at his or her own pace.
Grades K-3, but also used remedially as a corrective program
for middle and upper readers. (Webster Division, McGraw-Hill
Book Co., Manchester Road, Manchester, MO 63011)

Reading Laboratory Kits: Skill building materials for individualized
reading instruction, including student record books, power-
builder cards, and a teacher's handbook. Students begin at

their own level and progress as fast as their learning rate permits. "Power-builders" are drillable four-page reading selections on cards that develop comprehension, vocabulary, and word attack skills. Listening skill builders are read from the teacher's handbook. For grades 1-12. (Science Research Associates, 259 East Erie Street, Chicago, IL 60611)

Sets and Numbers: A modern elementary program utilizing a series of workbooks to stress the concepts, structure and logic of mathematics. Each concept is developed in such a way that pupils understand what they are doing and why they are doing it. Throughout the series, the set concept is used as a foundation for the four primary operators, and each book uses extensive color and illustrations to direct the child's thinking. (L. W. Singer, Inc., Random House, 201 E. 50th Street, New York, NY 10022)

Words and Patterns: A basic spelling program for grades 1-6. Answer strips below carefully sequenced exercises provide the immediate reinforcement or correction important in spelling. Full color illustrations, puzzles, and projects are included in both the case-bound or consumable text. (Science Research Associates, 259 East Erie Street, Chicago, IL 60611)

Research Findings

Becker, Wesley C., and Engelmann, Siegfried. *The Oregon Direct Instruction Model: A Summary of Nine Years of Work*. Eugene, Ore.: University of Oregon Follow Through Project, 1977.

_____. *Summary Analyses of Five-Year Data on Achievement and Teaching Progress with 14,000 Children in 20 Projects*. Technical Report 73-2. Eugene, Ore.: University of Oregon. ERIC Accession No. ED 096 781.

Briskin, Alan S., and Gardner, William I. "Social Reinforcement in Reducing Inappropriate Behavior." *Young Children*, 24, no. 2 (December 1968): 84-89.

Cooley, William W., and Leinhardt, Gaea. *The Application of a Model for Investigating Classroom Processes*. Pittsburgh, Pa.: Learning Research and Development Center, University of Pittsburgh, 1975. ERIC Accession No. ED 114 366.

Good, Thomas, and Brophy, Jere. *Looking in Classrooms*. New York: Harper & Row, 1973.

Madsen, C. H.; Becker, W. C.; and Thomas, D. R. "Rules, Praise and Ignoring: Elements of Classroom Control." *Journal of Applied Behavior Analysis* 1 (1968): 139-150.

Packard, R. G. "The Control of 'Classroom Attention': A Group Contingency for Complex Behavior." *Journal of Applied Psychology* 3 (1970): 13-28.

Stallings, Jane. *Follow Through Program Classroom Observation Evaluation 1971-72*. Menlo Park, Calif.: Stanford Research Institute, 1973, pp. 102-106. Exemplified by the Engelmann-Becker model at the University of Oregon. Funded by Department of HEW, Contract No. OEC-0-8522480-4633 (100).

Stallings, Jane, and Kaskowitz, David. *Follow Through Classroom Observation Evaluation 1972-73*. Menlo Park, Calif.: Stanford Research Institute, 1974, pp. 142-153, 233-303. Exemplified by the Engelmann-Becker model at the University of Oregon. Funded by Department of HEW, Contract No. OEC-0-8522480-4633 (100).

Wang, Margaret C., and Stiles, Billie. *An Investigation of Children's Concept of Self-Responsibility for Their School Learning*. Pittsburgh, Pa.: Learning Research and Development Center, University of Pittsburgh, 1975. ERIC Accession No. ED 116 815.

Film Available

Focus on Behavior: Learning about Learning (30 min; 16 mm, sound, black and white). Bloomington: Audio Visual Center, Indiana University. Describes the approaches used by Skinner, Harlow, and Spence in developing new theoretical concepts about man's ability to learn.

ANSWERS: CORRECT CODING FOR EXERCISE 7.1

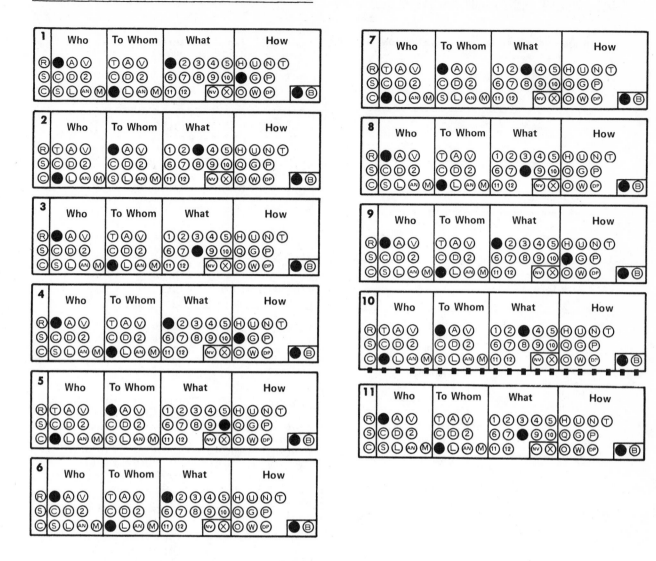

ANSWERS: EXERCISE 7.3

Situation: A group of fourth-grade children are working in math workbooks.
One child is copying from a neighbor.

Teacher: I like the way Gloria is doing her own work.

Teacher: I like the way Stephen and Joann are doing their own work.

Cindy: (Cindy is the child who has been copying. She looks at her own
workbook and starts working by herself.)

Teacher: I like the way Cindy is doing her own work.

CLASSROOM CHECK LIST (be sure to code **EVERYONE** in the class)

Activity		ONE CHILD	TWO CHILDREN	SMALL GROUPS	LARGE GROUPS
1. Snack, lunch		T ①②③ / A ①②③ / v ①②③ / i ①②③	T ①②③ / A ①②③ / v ①②③ / i ①②③	T ①②③④ / A ①②③④ / v ①②③④ / i ①②③④	T ①② / A ①② / v ①② / i ①②
2. Group time		T ①②③ / A ①②③ / v ①②③ / i ①②③	T ①②③ / A ①②③ / v ①②③ / i ①②③	T ①②③④ / A ①②③④ / v ①②③④ / i ①②③④	T ①② / A ①② / v ①② / i ①②
3. Story / Music / Dancing		T ①②③ / A ①②③ / v ①②③ / i ①②③	T ①②③ / A ①②③ / v ①②③ / i ①②③	T ①②③④ / A ①②③④ / v ①②③④ / i ①②③④	T ①② / A ①② / v ①② / i ①②
4. Arts, Crafts		T ①②③ / A ①②③ / v ①②③ / i ①②③	T ①②③ / A ①②③ / v ①②③ / i ①②③	T ①②③④ / A ①②③④ / v ①②③④ / i ①②③④	T ①② / A ①② / v ①② / i ①②
5. Guessing Games / Table Games / Puzzles		T ①②③ / A ①②③ / v ①②③ / i ①②③	T ①②③ / A ①②③ / v ①②③ / i ①②③	T ①②③④ / A ①②③④ / v ①②③④ / i ①②③④	T ①② / A ①② / v ①② / i ①②
6. Math	Numbers / Arithmetic	T ①②③ / A ①②③ / v ①②③ / i ①②③	T ①②③ / A ①②③ / v ①②③ / i ①②③	T ①②③④ / A ●②③④ / v ①②③④ / i ●②③④	T ①② / A ①② / v ①② / i ①②
7. Alphabet	Reading / Lang. Development	T ①②③ / A ①②③ / v ①②③ / i ①②③	T ①②③ / A ①②③ / v ①②③ / i ①②③	T ●②③④ / A ●②③④ / v ①②③④ / i ①②③④	T ①② / A ①② / v ①② / i ①②
8. Social Studies / Geography		T ①②③ / A ①②③ / v ①②③ / i ①②③	T ①②③ / A ①②③ / v ①②③ / i ①②③	T ①②③④ / A ①②③④ / v ①②③④ / i ①②③④	T ①② / A ①② / v ①② / i ①②
9. Science / Natural World		T ①②③ / A ①②③ / v ①②③ / i ①②③	T ①②③ / A ①②③ / v ①②③ / i ①②③	T ①②③④ / A ①②③④ / v ①②③④ / i ①②③④	T ①② / A ①② / v ①② / i ①②
10. Sewing / Cooking / Pounding / Sawing		T ①②③ / A ①②③ / v ①②③ / i ①②③	T ①②③ / A ①②③ / v ①②③ / i ①②③	T ①②③④ / A ①②③④ / v ①②③④ / i ①②③④	T ①② / A ①② / v ①② / i ①②
11. Blocks / Trucks		T ①②③ / A ①②③ / v ①②③ / i ①②③	T ①②③ / A ①②③ / v ①②③ / i ①②③	T ①②③④ / A ①②③④ / v ①②③④ / i ①②③④	T ①② / A ①② / v ①② / i ①②
12. Dramatic Play / Dress-Up		T ①②③ / A ①②③ / v ①②③ / i ①②③	T ①②③ / A ①②③ / v ①②③ / i ①②③	T ①②③④ / A ①②③④ / v ①②③④ / i ①②③④	T ①② / A ①② / v ①② / i ①②
13. Active Play		T ①②③ / A ①②③ / v ①②③ / i ①②③	T ①②③ / A ①②③ / v ①②③ / i ①②③	T ①②③④ / A ①②③④ / v ①②③④ / i ①②③④	T ①② / A ①② / v ①② / i ①②
14. RELIABILITY SHEET		○			

Legend (left column, beside items 6–9):

- ○ TV
- ○ Audio-Visual Materials
- ○ Exploratory Materials
- ○ Math and Science Equipment
- ● Texts, Workbooks
- ○ Puzzles, Games

		ONE CHILD	TWO CHILDREN	SMALL GROUPS	LARGE GROUPS
15. Practical Skills Acquisition		T ①②③	T ①②③	T ①②③④	T ①②
		A ①②③	A ①②③	A ①②③④	A ①②
		v ①②③	v ①②③	v ①②③④	v ①②
		i ①②③	i ①②③	i ①②③④	i ①②
16. Observing		T ①②③	T ①②③	T ①②③④	T ①②
		A ①②③	A ①②③	A ①②③④	A ①②
		v ①②③	v ①②③	v ①②③④	v ①②
		i ①②③	i ①②③	i ①②③④	i ①②
17. Social Interaction Ob [Ⓒ ② Ⓢ]	Ⓣ Ⓐ Ⓥ	T ①②③	T ①②③	T ①②③④	T ①②
		A ①②③	A ①②③	A ①②③④	A ①②
		v ①②③	v ①②③	v ①②③④	v ①②
		i ①②③	i ①②③	i ①②③④	i ①②
18. Unoccupied Child		T ①②③	T ①②③	T ①②③④	T ①②
		A ①②③	A ①②③	A ①②③④	A ①②
		v ①②③	v ①②③	v ①②③④	v ①②
		i ①②③	i ①②③	i ①②③④	i ①②
19. Discipline		T ①②③	T ①②③	T ①②③④	T ①②
		A ①②③	A ①②③	A ①②③④	A ①②
		v ①②③	v ①②③	v ①②③④	v ①②
		i ①②③	i ①②③	i ①②③④	i ①②
20. Transitional Activities	Ⓣ Ⓐ Ⓥ	T ①②③	T ①②③	T ①②③④	T ①②
		A ①②③	A ①②③	A ①②③④	A ①②
		v ①②③	v ①②③	v ①②③④	v ①②
		i ①②③	i ①②③	i ①②③④	i ①②
21. Classroom Management	Ⓣ Ⓐ Ⓥ	T ①②③	T ①②③	T ①②③④	T ①②
		A ①②③	A ①②③	A ①②③④	A ①②
		v ①②③	v ①②③	v ①②③④	v ①②
		i ①②③	i ①②③	i ①②③④	i ①②
22. Out of Room	Ⓣ Ⓐ Ⓥ	T ①②③	T ①②③	T ①②③④	T ①②
		A ①②③	A ①②③	A ①②③④	A ①②
		v ①②③	v ①②③	v ①②③④	v ①②
		i ①②③	i ①②③	i ①②③④	i ①②

NUMBER OF ADULTS IN CLASSROOM   ⓪ ① ② ● ④ ⑤ ⑥ ⑦ ⑧ ⑨ ⑩

CLASSROOM CHECK LIST (be sure to code **EVERYONE** in the class)

		ONE CHILD	TWO CHILDREN	SMALL GROUPS	LARGE GROUPS
1. Snack, lunch		T ①②③ / A ①②③ / v ①②③ / i ①②③	T ①②③ / A ①②③ / v ①②③ / i ①②③	T ①②③④ / A ①②③④ / v ①②③④ / i ①②③④	T ①② / A ①② / v ①② / i ①②
2. Group time		T ①②③ / A ①②③ / v ①②③ / i ①②③	T ①②③ / A ①②③ / v ①②③ / i ①②③	T ①②③④ / A ①②③④ / v ①②③④ / i ①②③④	T ①② / A ①② / v ①② / i ①②
3. Story, Music, Dancing		T ①②③ / A ①②③ / v ①②③ / i ①②③	T ①②③ / A ①②③ / v ①②③ / i ①②③	T ①②③④ / A ①②③④ / v ①②③④ / i ①②③④	T ①② / A ①② / v ①② / i ①②
4. Arts, Crafts		T ①②③ / A ①②③ / v ①②③ / i ①②③	T ①②③ / A ①②③ / v ①②③ / i ①②③	T ①②③④ / A ①②③④ / v ①②③④ / i ①②③④	T ①② / A ①② / v ①② / i ①②
5. Guessing Games, Table Games, Puzzles		T ①②③ / A ①②③ / v ①②③ / i ①②③	T ①②③ / A ①②③ / v ①②③ / i ①②③	T ①②③④ / A ①②③④ / v ①②③④ / i ①②③④	T ①② / A ①② / v ①② / i ①②
6. Math	Numbers / Arithmetic	T ①②③ / A ①②③ / v ①②③ / i ①②③	T ①②③ / A ①②③ / v ①②③ / i ①②③	T ①②③④ / A ●②③④ / v ①②③④ / i ●②③④	T ①② / A ①② / v ①② / i ①②
7. Alphabet	Reading / Lang. Development	T ①②③ / A ①②③ / v ①②③ / i ①②③	T ①②③ / A ①②③ / v ①②③ / i ①②③	T ●②③④ / A ●②③④ / v ①②③④ / i ①②③④	T ①② / A ①② / v ①② / i ①②
8.	Social Studies / Geography	T ①②③ / A ①②③ / v ①②③ / i ①②③	T ①②③ / A ①②③ / v ①②③ / i ①②③	T ①②③④ / A ①②③④ / v ①②③④ / i ①②③④	T ①② / A ①② / v ①② / i ①②
9.	Science / Natural World	T ①②③ / A ①②③ / v ①②③ / i ①②③	T ①②③ / A ①②③ / v ①②③ / i ①②③	T ①②③④ / A ①②③④ / v ①②③④ / i ①②③④	T ①② / A ①② / v ①② / i ①②
10. Sewing, Cooking, Pounding, Sawing		T ①②③ / A ①②③ / v ①②③ / i ①②③	T ①②③ / A ①②③ / v ①②③ / i ①②③	T ①②③④ / A ①②③④ / v ①②③④ / i ①②③④	T ①② / A ①② / v ①② / i ①②
11. Blocks, Trucks		T ①②③ / A ①②③ / v ①②③ / i ①②③	T ①②③ / A ①②③ / v ①②③ / i ①②③	T ①②③④ / A ①②③④ / v ①②③④ / i ①②③④	T ①② / A ①② / v ①② / i ①②
12. Dramatic Play, Dress-Up		T ①②③ / A ①②③ / v ①②③ / i ①②③	T ①②③ / A ①②③ / v ①②③ / i ①②③	T ①②③④ / A ①②③④ / v ①②③④ / i ①②③④	T ①② / A ①② / v ①② / i ①②
13. Active Play		T ①②③ / A ①②③ / v ①②③ / i ①②③	T ①②③ / A ①②③ / v ①②③ / i ①②③	T ①②③④ / A ①②③④ / v ①②③④ / i ①②③④	T ①② / A ①② / v ①② / i ①②
14. RELIABILITY SHEET	○				

Left-side category list (spanning sections 6–9):

○ TV
○ Audio-Visual Materials
○ Exploratory Materials
○ Math and Science Equipment
● Texts, Workbooks
○ Puzzles, Games

		ONE CHILD	TWO CHILDREN	SMALL GROUPS	LARGE GROUPS
15. Practical Skills Acquisition		T ①②③ A ①②③ V ①②③ i ①②③	T ①②③ A ①②③ V ①②③ i ①②③	T ①②③④ A ①②③④ V ①②③④ i ①②③④	T ①② A ①② V ①② i ①②
16. Observing		T ①②③ A ①②③ V ①②③ i ①②③	T ①②③ A ①②③ V ①②③ i ①②③	T ①②③④ A ①②③④ V ①②③④ i ①②③④	T ①② A ①② V ①② i ①②
17. Social Interaction Ob [©②Ⓢ]	Ⓣ Ⓐ Ⓥ	T ①②③ A ①②③ V ①②③ i ①②③	T ①②③ A ①②③ V ①②③ i ①②③	T ①②③④ A ①②③④ V ①②③④ i ①②③④	T ①② A ①② V ①② i ①②
18. Unoccupied Child		T ①②③ A ①②③ V ①②③ i ①②③	T ①②③ A ①②③ V ①②③ i ①②③	T ①②③④ A ①②③④ V ①②③④ i ①②③④	T ①② A ①② V ①② i ①②
19. Discipline		T ①②③ A ①②③ V ①②③ i ①②③	T ①②③ A ①②③ V ①②③ i ①②③	T ①②③④ A ①②③④ V ①②③④ i ①②③④	T ①② A ①② V ①② i ①②
20. Transitional Activities	Ⓣ Ⓐ Ⓥ	T ①②③ A ①②③ V ①②③ i ①②③	T ①②③ A ①②③ V ①②③ i ①②③	T ①②③④ A ①②③④ V ①②③④ i ①②③④	T ①② A ①② V ①② i ①②
21. Classroom Management	Ⓣ Ⓐ Ⓥ	T ①②③ A ①②③ V ①②③ i ①②③	T ①②③ A ①②③ V ①②③ i ①②③	T ①②③④ A ①②③④ V ①②③④ i ①②③④	T ①② A ①② V ①② i ①②
22. Out of Room	Ⓣ Ⓐ Ⓥ	T ①②③ A ①②③ V ①②③ i ①②③	T ①②③ A ①②③ V ①②③ i ①②③	T ①②③④ A ①②③④ V ①②③④ i ①②③④	T ①② A ①② V ①② i ①②

NUMBER OF ADULTS IN CLASSROOM   ⓪ ① ② ● ④ ⑤ ⑥ ⑦ ⑧ ⑨ ⑩

Chapter 8

Educational Theory and Expected Child Development

Teacher Responsibilities

Schedule

Physical Environment

Interaction Patterns

Handling Misbehavior

    Standards for Students

A Contextual View

Classroom Requirements

Research on How Children Grow and Develop

Observable Components

    Materials

    Activities and Groupings

    Interaction Observations

Importance of Teacher Observation

Summary of Components

Bibliography

    Where Fundamental School Models Can Be Seen

    Suggested Readings

    Commercially Available Materials

    Research Findings

Fundamental School Model

Situation: A second-grade class is being taught vowel sounds.

1-8. Teacher: Today we will be studying long vowel sounds, and we will start with *a*. The long vowel sound is the sound of the name of the letter. The long vowel sound for the *a* is *a*. Words are pronounced with a long vowel sound when a silent *e* comes after the consonant following the vowel. For example, the word *can* has a short *a* vowel sound, but when we place an *e* after the *n*, the word is pronounced *cāne*. In the same way, *cap* is pronounced *cāpe* when the *e* is added, and *Dan* becomes *Dāne*, and *plan* becomes *plāne*. The same thing happens with the other vowels. *Pin* becomes *pīne*, mop becomes *mōpe*, *tub* becomes *tūbe*, *pet* becomes *Pēte*.

9. Teacher: If we add an *e* to *mat* what do we have?

10. Class: (All raise hands.)

11. Teacher: What do we have, Bill?

12. Bill: *Mate*.

13. Teacher: (Nods, right.)

14. Teacher: If we add an *e* to *cub*, what do we have?

15. Class: (All raise hands.)

16. Teacher: Sarah?

17. Sarah: *Cube*.

18. Teacher: Very good.

19. Teacher: All right, take out your phonics books and turn to page 28. Do the exercises on pages 28 to 32.

20. Class: (Goes quickly and quietly to work.)

This is a typical instruction pattern in a second-grade classroom in the Fundamental School Model. It is coded in Figure 8.1.

EDUCATIONAL THEORY AND EXPECTED CHILD DEVELOPMENT

The theory at the heart of the Fundamental School Model is that children learn best in quiet and orderly classrooms where the teachers are responsible for administering carefully structured educational programs. Fundamental educators believe that children should spend most of their time at school studying and improving their basic skills. They feel that if children are expected to develop basic skills, then they should spend a lot of time doing just that.

The ability of children to study and understand is thought to be governed in part by how quiet and orderly the classroom is.

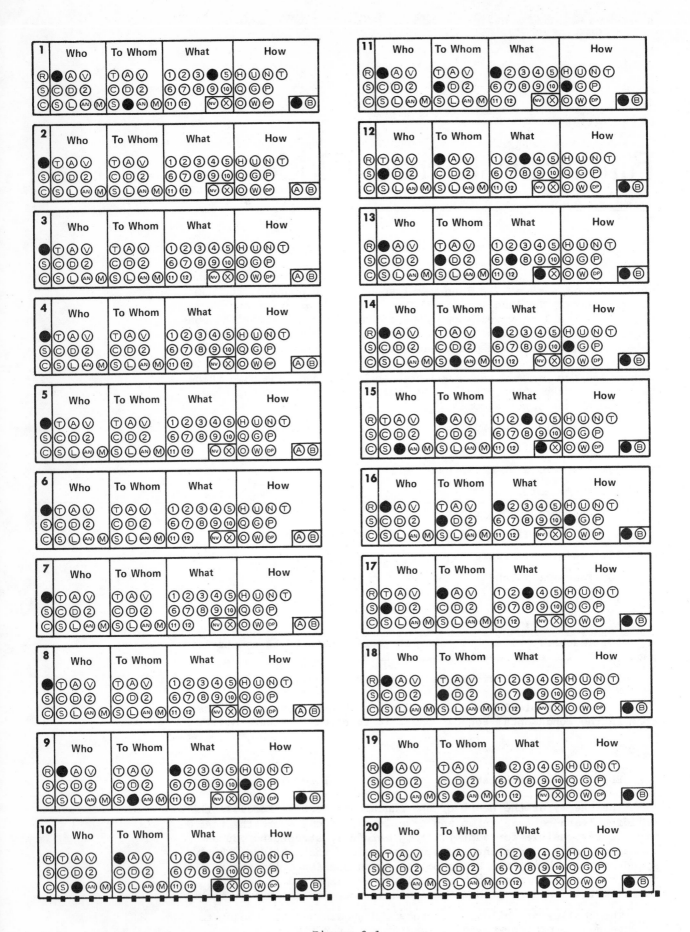

Figure 8.1

Therefore, student behavior is carefully controlled; rules are clearly stated, and discipline is consistently enforced. In order to enforce discipline, some fundamental schools allow spanking, others detain children after school. Whatever the punishment, there is a no-nonsense approach to breaking rules. Advocates consider this approach to be healthier for guiding young children than one that is not clear or consistent or that allows children to expend energy testing rules and discovering consequences.

Respect and courtesy are also believed to contribute to an orderly school atmosphere. Teachers and children are expected to speak politely to each other. Foul language is not tolerated. Personal dress is also thought to contribute to the atmosphere of the school; therefore, dress codes for teachers and students are strictly enforced.

In this kind of atmosphere, children are expected to establish good study habits, to develop an excellence in basic skills, to develop manners and respect for other people and property, and to develop a good self-image.

The Fundamental School Model has been developed in response to requests by parents for schools that focus on teaching basic skills. Most of the recently formed fundamental schools have come about in communities where there are open education schools. Parents who feel their children are not reading, writing, or computing as well as might be expected, have requested their boards of education to form another education alternative—a school devoted to teaching basic skills.

Carl Hansen, former superintendent of schools in the District of Columbia, developed, in the Amidon Elementary School[1] in the late 1950s and early 1960s, a model for rigorous education. However, the model was not diffused on any wide scale—at that time, national test scores were still reasonably high and people were interested in developing educational programs designed to promote individualism, problem-solving abilities, and creativity.

The fundamental schools springing up in the mid-1970s have goals and methods very similar to those advocated by Hansen. Fewer than three dozen of these new fundamental schools are known to exist as of this writing, but the entire school community is watching these with interest. Each fundamental school principal contacted reported receiving thousands of inquiries from all states in the nation. These schools incorporate trends—the move to a basic curriculum, the greater impact of parents on school policy—that may have broad implications for American schools. Importantly, advocates of fundamental schools are not recommending that open education be abolished. More reasonably, they are asking simply that another educational alternative be offered within the school system.

TEACHER RESPONSIBILITIES

Fundamental schools have a single graded, self-contained classroom organization plan: one grade to one classroom. Some have programs for kindergarten through sixth grade; others for kindergarten through twelfth. Classroom activities are initiated, directed, and supervised by the teacher.

---

[1]Carl F. Hansen, *The Amidon Elementary School: A Successful Demonstration in Basic Education* (Englewood Cliffs, N.J.: Prentice-Hall, 1962).

The curriculum follows a definite, progressive pattern, building on the skills and abilities—reading, handwriting, spelling, composition, grammar, arithmetic, history, geography, government, science, foreign language, art, and music—acquired at previous levels. Most of the school day is devoted to teaching reading, writing, spelling, language, and arithmetic, using the school district's written guidelines as an instructional base.[2] Standard texts emphasizing basic skills are also used. Teachers do not develop their own materials—this is left to those who specialize in curriculum development.

Homework should be given on a regular basis to encourage independent work and diligent study habits. Teachers must check homework and all classroom assignments daily and return them to the students. In this way students find out where they are succeeding and where they need to work harder.

Teachers keep parents advised of students' progress. In some schools they do this weekly through reports or letters. Report cards with letter grades A, B, C, D, and F are issued four to six times a year. Grade equivalencies on standardized achievement tests measure student progress. Students not reaching grade equivalency at the end of the year are not promoted to the next grade.

The Hoover School in Palo Alto, California, expects its teachers to do the following:

1. Maintain neat, quiet, and orderly classrooms.

2. Stress reading, writing, and language arts in the learning experience.

3. Keep a file of weekly comprehensive tests in basic subject areas.

4. Keep an accurate record of the work completed and test results for each student in all subject areas.

5. Describe their methods of instruction, materials, and units of instruction for the year and file copies with the principal.

6. Assign weekly compositions to students (in grades 4-7) of one to three pages in length.

7. Check completion of *all* homework assignments.

8. Establish homework as a routine by the second week of school.

9. Maintain class routine except for supplemental experiences (speech, learning assistance, music, and so on). Routines will not be broken for student volunteer jobs like library aide, traffic patrol, and so on.

10. Submit a short weekly report to parents concerning each student's progress, work habits, and completion of assignments.

11. Contribute to the formulation of uniform school standards.

12. Teach and encourage students to demonstrate good manners.

---

[2]Wallace Bud Clark, "A More Structured Alternative to Elementary Education in the Palo Alto Unified School District," Palo Alto Unified School District, Palo Alto, Calif., 1975. (Lecture presented at the University of California, Riverside.)

13. Consider all students their responsibility when on the playground whether on duty or off duty.

14. Encourage children's bulletin boards. (Children's work is displayed.)

15. Initiate neither rewards nor a system of points unless the entire school is involved.

In addition, teachers are responsible for providing moral training, developing a sense of respect, and maintaining law and order in the classroom and on the school grounds.

SCHEDULE

The following are typical schedules for classes in the Fundamental School Model.

8:30 Take attendance; collect lunch money; salute flag; song.

8:40 Character-building session.

8:50 Discuss assignments listed on the chalkboard; explain new material in phonics and spelling.

9:15 Call highest reading group to front of room. (Even when children are grouped in classes according to ability, they often differ in reading ability, so that some teachers divide them into three smaller groups.) Other children work on assignments in their seats. Children in group report on individual stories they have read and answer questions the teacher asks about the group assignments. The teacher presents new words and concepts. The children take new assignments to their seats.

9:50 Recess.

10:10 Call the middle reading group. (Follow same procedure as with preceding group.)

10:35 Call lowest reading group. (Follow same procedure as with preceding group.)

11:00 Math—old processes reviewed and tested; new processes explained; assignments are placed on the chalkboard.

11:30 Phonics—work is reviewed and tested; new work explained; assigments placed on the chalkboard.

11:45 Lunch—children sit at tables in orderly fashion; children are excused for play when area is clean.

12:30 Physical education—emphasis on developing strength and skill through competition.

1:00 Time to work on assignments in reading, math, and spelling; teacher helps as needed.

1:50 Recess.

2:10 Music (Monday); science or social studies (Tuesday, Wednesday, and Thursday); Library (Friday).

(Children who have been diagnosed as needing special help in reading or speech work with a specialist at this time.)

3:00 Dismissal.

8:30 Take roll; salute flag; sing national anthem; make announcements; collect lunch money.

8:45 Phonics and spelling—explanation and assignments.

9:15 Reading—explanation and assignments.

10:00 Recess.

10:15 Math—explanation and assignments.

11:00 Handwriting.

11:10 Grammar and composition.

11:45 Lunch.

12:30 Music (Monday and Wednesday); art (Tuesday and Thursday); Library (Friday).

1:15 Science or social studies.

2:00 Recess.

2:15 Physical education.

2:45 Literature appreciation (Story or poem reading by teacher).

3:00 Dismissal.

PHYSICAL ENVIRONMENT

The fundamental school has self-contained classrooms. Desks may or may not be fastened to the floor, but they all face the front of the room and are in straight rows. The teacher's desk and a large chalkboard at the front of the room are the focal points of instruction. A flag is also present in the front of the room. Children's good writing, good arithmetic papers, and other signs of achievement are displayed on bulletin boards. Information about special events and national holidays is also displayed on the bulletin boards.

Book shelves hold supplementary textbooks and some storybooks for extra reading. Games, puzzles, and exploratory materials are *not* present in the room. However, balls, bats, and jump ropes that are used for athletic activities are in evidence.

The room is set up to facilitate the goal of the program: to train children in basic skills.

INTERACTION PATTERNS

The vignette opening this chapter is an example of how a teacher in the Fundamental School Model instructs a class in a new phonics rule. Teachers initiate the discussions, explain new work, point out relationships between ideas and concepts, and monitor the students' understanding of the lessons through question-and-answer sessions.

The following exercise demonstrates the type of interactions that occur in this model. Do the exercise now. The correct answers are given at the end of the chapter.

EXERCISE 8.1 Code the following interactions using the SRI coding system.

Situation: A third-grade teacher examining how well students understand a new list of spelling words is asking the children to make up a sentence for the words. The teacher addresses the whole group.

1. Teacher: "Who can think of a sentence using the word *night*?"

2. Class: (All raise their hands.)

3. Teacher: "Tell us your sentence, Dan."

4. Dan: "The brave knight rode into battle."

5. Teacher: "Is that a correct use for the word *night*?"

6. Class: (Many raise their hands.)

7. Teacher: "Laura?"

8. Laura: "No, because a silent *k* comes before the *night*."

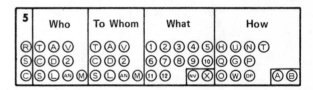

9. Teacher: "Very good, Laura."

9	Who	To Whom	What	How
	ℝ Ⓣ Ⓐ Ⓥ	Ⓣ Ⓐ Ⓥ	① ② ③ ④ ⑤ Ⓗ Ⓤ Ⓝ Ⓣ	
	Ⓢ Ⓒ Ⓓ ②	Ⓒ Ⓓ ②	⑥ ⑦ ⑧ ⑨ ⑩ Ⓠ Ⓖ Ⓟ	
	Ⓒ Ⓢ Ⓛ Ⓐⓝ Ⓜ	Ⓢ Ⓛ Ⓐⓝ Ⓜ	⑪ ⑫ ⓃⓋ Ⓧ Ⓞ Ⓦ Ⓓⓟ	Ⓐ Ⓑ

10. Teacher: "What other word in our list has a silent *k*?"

10	Who	To Whom	What	How
	ℝ Ⓣ Ⓐ Ⓥ	Ⓣ Ⓐ Ⓥ	① ② ③ ④ ⑤ Ⓗ Ⓤ Ⓝ Ⓣ	
	Ⓢ Ⓒ Ⓓ ②	Ⓒ Ⓓ ②	⑥ ⑦ ⑧ ⑨ ⑩ Ⓠ Ⓖ Ⓟ	
	Ⓒ Ⓢ Ⓛ Ⓐⓝ Ⓜ	Ⓢ Ⓛ Ⓐⓝ Ⓜ	⑪ ⑫ ⓃⓋ Ⓧ Ⓞ Ⓦ Ⓓⓟ	Ⓐ Ⓑ

11. Class: (All raise their hands.)

11	Who	To Whom	What	How
	ℝ Ⓣ Ⓐ Ⓥ	Ⓣ Ⓐ Ⓥ	① ② ③ ④ ⑤ Ⓗ Ⓤ Ⓝ Ⓣ	
	Ⓢ Ⓒ Ⓓ ②	Ⓒ Ⓓ ②	⑥ ⑦ ⑧ ⑨ ⑩ Ⓠ Ⓖ Ⓟ	
	Ⓒ Ⓢ Ⓛ Ⓐⓝ Ⓜ	Ⓢ Ⓛ Ⓐⓝ Ⓜ	⑪ ⑫ ⓃⓋ Ⓧ Ⓞ Ⓦ Ⓓⓟ	Ⓐ Ⓑ

12. Teacher: "What word is it, Tim?"

12	Who	To Whom	What	How
	ℝ Ⓣ Ⓐ Ⓥ	Ⓣ Ⓐ Ⓥ	① ② ③ ④ ⑤ Ⓗ Ⓤ Ⓝ Ⓣ	
	Ⓢ Ⓒ Ⓓ ②	Ⓒ Ⓓ ②	⑥ ⑦ ⑧ ⑨ ⑩ Ⓠ Ⓖ Ⓟ	
	Ⓒ Ⓢ Ⓛ Ⓐⓝ Ⓜ	Ⓢ Ⓛ Ⓐⓝ Ⓜ	⑪ ⑫ ⓃⓋ Ⓧ Ⓞ Ⓦ Ⓓⓟ	Ⓐ Ⓑ

13. Tim: "Know."

13	Who	To Whom	What	How
	ℝ Ⓣ Ⓐ Ⓥ	Ⓣ Ⓐ Ⓥ	① ② ③ ④ ⑤ Ⓗ Ⓤ Ⓝ Ⓣ	
	Ⓢ Ⓒ Ⓓ ②	Ⓒ Ⓓ ②	⑥ ⑦ ⑧ ⑨ ⑩ Ⓠ Ⓖ Ⓟ	
	Ⓒ Ⓢ Ⓛ Ⓐⓝ Ⓜ	Ⓢ Ⓛ Ⓐⓝ Ⓜ	⑪ ⑫ ⓃⓋ Ⓧ Ⓞ Ⓦ Ⓓⓟ	Ⓐ Ⓑ

14. Teacher: "That's right."

14	Who	To Whom	What	How
	ℝ Ⓣ Ⓐ Ⓥ	Ⓣ Ⓐ Ⓥ	① ② ③ ④ ⑤ Ⓗ Ⓤ Ⓝ Ⓣ	
	Ⓢ Ⓒ Ⓓ ②	Ⓒ Ⓓ ②	⑥ ⑦ ⑧ ⑨ ⑩ Ⓠ Ⓖ Ⓟ	
	Ⓒ Ⓢ Ⓛ Ⓐⓝ Ⓜ	Ⓢ Ⓛ Ⓐⓝ Ⓜ	⑪ ⑫ ⓃⓋ Ⓧ Ⓞ Ⓦ Ⓓⓟ	Ⓐ Ⓑ

EXERCISE 8.2 Write a vignette based on the Fundamental School Model.

Situation: A third-grade teacher is teaching a new math process.

Teacher: _____

Class: _____

Teacher: _____

Student: _____

Teacher: _____

Class: _____

Teacher: _____

Class: _____

Teacher: _____

Class: _____

Teacher: _____

_____

HANDLING MISBEHAVIOR

Rules for student behavior are made very clear. The following list of rules are typical of most fundamental schools. They were prepared for the students in the Hoover School, Palo Alto, California.

Standards for Students

Students *will*:

1. Remain quiet and orderly in the classroom and be attentive to instruction.

2. Support their teacher, classmates, and school.

3. Behave courteously toward any adult or another student.

4. Use spoken expressions of consideration toward others (e.g., pardon me, please, thank you, etc.).

5. Wear clothing of a neat and modest nature. Clothing should be appropriate for the P.E. program (light leather or tennis shoes and shorts under dresses). Students may change normal wear to P.E. clothing before the P.E. period.

6. Obey Principal's directions for seating, conduct, and dismissal at assemblies.

7. Obey all student monitors.

8. Remove hats after entering the building.

9. Share any athletic equipment brought from home.

10. Move together to assemblies; stragglers will be considered tardy.

11. Keep open games played at recess and at noon.

12. Line up quickly and quietly in the morning and after recesses and the lunch period to enter classes. Students who are late must go to the office for tardy slips.

13. Present a tardy slip to the teacher when late or an absent slip when absent for a day or longer in order to gain admission to the classroom. Teachers are to fill out tardy slips and return them to the secretary daily. Blank tardy slips are to be picked up by late students, and absentees will pick up blank absent slips.

14. (Ball monitors especially) Make sure that all playground equipment is off the playground at the end of a recess, noon period, and P.E. period.

15. Stay out of city park area.

16. Keep balls off the roof. They do not roll back.

17. Stay only on the *red-top* when a *red flag* is displayed.

18. Stay only on the *black-top and red-top* and don't go onto the grassy areas when a *black flag* is displayed.

Students *will not*:

1. Leave the school grounds during school hours at any time without written permission.

2. Use profane language or gestures.

3. Engage in any type of fighting.

4. Intimidate, harass, or threaten other students.

5. Be disrespectful to another's property.

6. Engage in body contact sports on the playground unless authorized by a teacher.

7. Throw objects other than balls while under the school's supervision.

8. Bring toys, magazines, radios, or playground equipment to school without teacher's approval.

9. Eat during class time or chew gum anywhere at school.

10. Run on the red-top.

Lunch standards:

1. Students will be seated at tables assigned by class from 11:45 to 12:00 and will remain seated until they are excused.

2. Before the students are excused, the tables and the area around them must be neat and clean.

3. Talking is permitted, and good table manners are to be practiced.

4. Equipment is *not* to be brought to the lunch table.[3]

Rules are strictly and consistently enforced. If children break a rule once, they are reprimanded, and in the Hoover School in Palo Alto, they have to stay after school to write a letter to their parents, telling them about the bad behavior. If the rule is broken again, the child's parents may be called to school, or the child may be sent home from school. In some fundamental schools corporal punishment is used when all else fails. If misbehavior continues, the teacher, principal, and parents may decide this is not the right school for the child.

The following illustrates several ways in which misbehavior might be handled in this model.

Teacher: Rosa, you know that chewing gum is against school rules. You must stay after school and write a letter to your parents to tell them that you have broken a school rule.

Teacher: George, that is the second time you have used bad language on the playground. The principal will call your parents and have them come here to discuss this problem with us. This cannot continue!

---

[3]From Wallace Bud Clark, "A More Structured Alternative to Elementary Education in the Palo Alto Unified School District," Palo Alto Unified School District, Palo Alto, California, 1975. (Lecture presented at the University of California, Riverside.)

Principal: David, this is the third time you have had a fight on the playground. I have talked this over with your parents and they agreed that if it happened again, you should be spanked. You know the school rules about fighting, and yet you continue to get into fights. Have you anything to say for yourself?

David: No.

Principal: (Spanks David.)

David: (Cries.)

Principal: Don't let this happen again. You can be a good citizen, David.

A CONTEXTUAL VIEW

Classroom aides are not used in most Fundamental School Models. The teacher most often teaches each lesson to the entire group. Advocates feel that if instruction is aimed at all of the children, then none of them have to wait for a turn. Further, children have been placed in classrooms according to their ability, so teaching the entire group at one time is more possible in this model. For example, one second-grade class would be composed of all the children with test scores ranging from the highest down to slightly below the average; another would be composed of children with test scores ranging from slightly above average down to the lowest. Such homogeneous grouping also makes it easier for teachers to prepare only one lesson in reading, math, spelling, and so on. Figure 8.2 shows the teacher working with the entire group in reading. Children who have special learning problems work with a school specialist.

CLASSROOM CHECK LIST (be sure to code **EVERYONE** in the class)

	ONE CHILD	TWO CHILDREN	SMALL GROUPS	LARGE GROUPS
1. Snack, lunch	T ①②③ A ①②③ V ①②③ i ①②③	T ①②③ A ①②③ V ①②③ i ①②③	T ①②③④ A ①②③④ V ①②③④ i ①②③④	T ①② A ①② V ①② i ①②
2. Group time	T ①②③ A ①②③ V ①②③ i ①②③	T ①②③ A ①②③ V ①②③ i ①②③	T ①②③④ A ①②③④ V ①②③④ i ①②③④	T ①② A ①② V ①② i ①②
3. Music — Story / Dancing	T ①②③ A ①②③ V ①②③ i ①②③	T ①②③ A ①②③ V ①②③ i ①②③	T ①②③④ A ①②③④ V ①②③④ i ①②③④	T ①② A ①② V ①② i ①②
4. Arts, Crafts	T ①②③ A ①②③ V ①②③ i ①②③	T ①②③ A ①②③ V ①②③ i ①②③	T ①②③④ A ①②③④ V ①②③④ i ①②③④	T ①② A ①② V ①② i ①②
5. Table Games — Guessing Games / Puzzles	T ①②③ A ①②③ V ①②③ i ①②③	T ①②③ A ①②③ V ①②③ i ①②③	T ①②③④ A ①②③④ V ①②③④ i ①②③④	T ①② A ①② V ①② i ①②
6. Math — Numbers / Arithmetic	T ①②③ A ①②③ V ①②③ i ①②③	T ①②③ A ①②③ V ①②③ i ①②③	T ①②③④ A ①②③④ V ①②③④ i ①②③④	T ①② A ①② V ①② i ①②
7. Reading / Alphabet / Lang. Development	T ①②③ A ①②③ V ①②③ i ①②③	T ①②③ A ①②③ V ①②③ i ①②③	T ①②③④ A ①②③④ V ①②③④ i ①②③④	T ●② A ①② V ①② i ①②
8. Social Studies / Geography	T ①②③ A ①②③ V ①②③ i ①②③	T ①②③ A ①②③ V ①②③ i ①②③	T ①②③④ A ①②③④ V ①②③④ i ①②③④	T ①② A ①② V ①② i ①②
9. Science / Natural World	T ①②③ A ①②③ V ①②③ i ①②③	T ①②③ A ①②③ V ①②③ i ①②③	T ①②③④ A ①②③④ V ①②③④ i ①②③④	T ①② A ①② V ①② i ①②
10. Sewing / Cooking / Pounding / Sawing	T ①②③ A ①②③ V ①②③ i ①②③	T ①②③ A ①②③ V ①②③ i ①②③	T ①②③④ A ①②③④ V ①②③④ i ①②③④	T ①② A ①② V ①② i ①②
11. Blocks / Trucks	T ①②③ A ①②③ V ①②③ i ①②③	T ①②③ A ①②③ V ①②③ i ①②③	T ①②③④ A ①②③④ V ①②③④ i ①②③④	T ①② A ①② V ①② i ①②
12. Dramatic Play / Dress-Up	T ①②③ A ①②③ V ①②③ i ①②③	T ①②③ A ①②③ V ①②③ i ①②③	T ①②③④ A ①②③④ V ①②③④ i ①②③④	T ①② A ①② V ①② i ①②
13. Active Play	T ①②③ A ①②③ V ①②③ i ①②③	T ①②③ A ①②③ V ①②③ i ①②③	T ①②③④ A ①②③④ V ①②③④ i ①②③④	T ①② A ①② V ①② i ①②
14. RELIABILITY SHEET ○				

Side list (next to items 6–9):

○ TV
○ Audio-Visual Materials
○ Exploratory Materials
○ Math and Science Equipment
● Texts, Workbooks
○ Puzzles, Games

Figure 8.2

		ONE CHILD	TWO CHILDREN	SMALL GROUPS	LARGE GROUPS
15. Practical Skills Acquisition		T ①②③	T ①②③	T ①②③④	T ①②
		A ①②③	A ①②③	A ①②③④	A ①②
		v ①②③	v ①②③	v ①②③④	v ①②
		i ①②③	i ①②③	i ①②③④	i ①②
16. Observing		T ①②③	T ①②③	T ①②③④	T ①②
		A ①②③	A ①②③	A ①②③④	A ①②
		v ①②③	v ①②③	v ①②③④	v ①②
		i ①②③	i ①②③	i ①②③④	i ①②
17. Social Interaction Ob [©②⑤]	ⓉⒶⓋ	T ①②③	T ①②③	T ①②③④	T ①②
		A ①②③	A ①②③	A ①②③④	A ①②
		v ①②③	v ①②③	v ①②③④	v ①②
		i ①②③	i ①②③	i ①②③④	i ①②
18. Unoccupied Child		T ①②③	T ①②③	T ①②③④	T ①②
		A ①②③	A ①②③	A ①②③④	A ①②
		v ①②③	v ①②③	v ①②③④	v ①②
		i ①②③	i ①②③	i ①②③④	i ①②
19. Discipline		T ①②③	T ①②③	T ①②③④	T ①②
		A ①②③	A ①②③	A ①②③④	A ①②
		v ①②③	v ①②③	v ①②③④	v ①②
		i ①②③	i ①②③	i ①②③④	i ①②
20. Transitional Activities	ⓉⒶⓋ	T ①②③	T ①②③	T ①②③④	T ①②
		A ①②③	A ①②③	A ①②③④	A ①②
		v ①②③	v ①②③	v ①②③④	v ①②
		i ①②③	i ①②③	i ①②③④	i ①②
21. Classroom Management	ⓉⒶⓋ	T ①②③	T ①②③	T ①②③④	T ①②
		A ①②③	A ①②③	A ①②③④	A ①②
		v ①②③	v ①②③	v ①②③④	v ①②
		i ①②③	i ①②③	i ①②③④	i ①②
22. Out of Room	ⓉⒶⓋ	T ①②③	T ①②③	T ①②③④	T ①②
		A ①②③	A ①②③	A ①②③④	A ①②
		v ①②③	v ①②③	v ①②③④	v ①②
		i ①②③	i ①②③	i ①②③④	i ①②

NUMBER OF ADULTS IN CLASSROOM   ⓪ ● ② ③ ④ ⑤ ⑥ ⑦ ⑧ ⑨ ⑩

In some classrooms (usually in kindergarten, and first and second grades), the teachers divide their reading groups into three smaller groups according to ability so that children are not slowed down or pushed too fast. The schedule provided earlier in the chapter illustrates that plan. In Figure 8.3 the teacher is working with a small group in reading while the rest of the class is working on particular reading assignments.

The following exercise involves a typical fourth-grade classroom in a Fundamental School Model. Do the exercise now and check your answers at the end of the chapter.

CLASSROOM CHECK LIST (be sure to code **EVERYONE** in the class)

	ONE CHILD	TWO CHILDREN	SMALL GROUPS	LARGE GROUPS
1. Snack, lunch	T ①②③ A ①②③ v ①②③ i ①②③	T ①②③ A ①②③ v ①②③ i ①②③	T ①②③④ A ①②③④ v ①②③④ i ①②③④	T ①② A ①② v ①② i ①②
2. Group time	T ①②③ A ①②③ v ①②③ i ①②③	T ①②③ A ①②③ v ①②③ i ①②③	T ①②③④ A ①②③④ v ①②③④ i ①②③④	T ①② A ①② v ①② i ①②
Story **3. Music** Dancing	T ①②③ A ①②③ v ①②③ i ①②③	T ①②③ A ①②③ v ①②③ i ①②③	T ①②③④ A ①②③④ v ①②③④ i ①②③④	T ①② A ①② v ①② i ①②
4. Arts, Crafts	T ①②③ A ①②③ v ①②③ i ①②③	T ①②③ A ①②③ v ①②③ i ①②③	T ①②③④ A ①②③④ v ①②③④ i ①②③④	T ①② A ①② v ①② i ①②
Guessing Games **5. Table Games** Puzzles	T ①②③ A ①②③ v ①②③ i ①②③	T ①②③ A ①②③ v ①②③ i ①②③	T ①②③④ A ①②③④ v ①②③④ i ①②③④	T ①② A ①② v ①② i ①②
Numbers **6. Math** Arithmetic	T ①②③ A ①②③ v ①②③ i ①②③	T ①②③ A ①②③ v ①②③ i ①②③	T ①②③④ A ①②③④ v ①②③④ i ①②③④	T ①② A ①② v ①② i ①②
Reading **7. Alphabet** Lang. Development	T ①②③ A ①②③ v ①②③ i ①②③	T ①②③ A ①②③ v ①②③ i ①②③	T ●②③④ A ①②③④ v ①②③④ i ①②③④	T ①② A ①② v ①② i ●②
Social Studies **8. Geography**	T ①②③ A ①②③ v ①②③ i ①②③	T ①②③ A ①②③ v ①②③ i ①②③	T ①②③④ A ①②③④ v ①②③④ i ①②③④	T ①② A ①② v ①② i ①②
Science **9. Natural World**	T ①②③ A ①②③ v ①②③ i ①②③	T ①②③ A ①②③ v ①②③ i ①②③	T ①②③④ A ①②③④ v ①②③④ i ①②③④	T ①② A ①② v ①② i ①②
Sewing Cooking **10. Pounding** Sawing	T ①②③ A ①②③ v ①②③ i ①②③	T ①②③ A ①②③ v ①②③ i ①②③	T ①②③④ A ①②③④ v ①②③④ i ①②③④	T ①② A ①② v ①② i ①②
Blocks **11. Trucks**	T ①②③ A ①②③ v ①②③ i ①②③	T ①②③ A ①②③ v ①②③ i ①②③	T ①②③④ A ①②③④ v ①②③④ i ①②③④	T ①② A ①② v ①② i ①②
Dramatic Play **12. Dress-Up**	T ①②③ A ①②③ v ①②③ i ①②③	T ①②③ A ①②③ v ①②③ i ①②③	T ①②③④ A ①②③④ v ①②③④ i ①②③④	T ①② A ①② v ①② i ①②
13. Active Play	T ①②③ A ①②③ v ①②③ i ①②③	T ①②③ A ①②③. v ①②③ i ①②③	T ①②③④ A ①②③④ v ①②③④ i ①②③④	T ①② A ①② v ①② i ①②
14. RELIABILITY SHEET ○				

Side legend (next to items 6–9):

○ TV
○ Audio-Visual Materials
○ Exploratory Materials
○ Math and Science Equipment
● Texts, Workbooks
○ Puzzles, Games

Figure 8.3

		ONE CHILD	TWO CHILDREN	SMALL GROUPS	LARGE GROUPS
15. Practical Skills Acquisition		T ①②③	T ①②③	T ①②③④	T ①②
		A ①②③	A ①②③	A ①②③④	A ①②
		v ①②③	v ①②③	v ①②③④	v ①②
		i ①②③	i ①②③	i ①②③④	i ①②
16. Observing		T ①②③	T ①②③	T ①②③④	T ①②
		A ①②③	A ①②③	A ①②③④	A ①②
		v ①②③	v ①②③	v ①②③④	v ①②
		i ①②③	i ①②③	i ①②③④	i ①②
17. Social Interaction Ob [Ⓒ ② Ⓢ]	Ⓣ Ⓐ Ⓥ	T ①②③	T ①②③	T ①②③④	T ①②
		A ①②③	A ①②③	A ①②③④	A ①②
		v ①②③	v ①②③	v ①②③④	v ①②
		i ①②③	i ①②③	i ①②③④	i ①②
18. Unoccupied Child		T ①②③	T ①②③	T ①②③④	T ①②
		A ①②③	A ①②③	A ①②③④	A ①②
		v ①②③	v ①②③	v ①②③④	v ①②
		i ①②③	i ①②③	i ①②③④	i ①②
19. Discipline		T ①②③	T ①②③	T ①②③④	T ①②
		A ①②③	A ①②③	A ①②③④	A ①②
		v ①②③	v ①②③	v ①②③④	v ①②
		i ①②③	i ①②③	i ①②③④	i ①②
20. Transitional Activities	Ⓣ Ⓐ Ⓥ	T ①②③	T ①②③	T ①②③④	T ①②
		A ①②③	A ①②③	A ①②③④	A ①②
		v ①②③	v ①②③	v ①②③④	v ①②
		i ①②③	i ①②③	i ①②③④	i ①②
21. Classroom Management	Ⓣ Ⓐ Ⓥ	T ①②③	T ①②③	T ①②③④	T ①②
		A ①②③	A ①②③	A ①②③④	A ①②
		v ①②③	v ①②③	v ①②③④	v ①②
		i ①②③	i ①②③	i ①②③④	i ①②
22. Out of Room	Ⓣ Ⓐ Ⓥ	T ①②③	T ①②③	T ①②③④	T ①②
		A ①②③	A ①②③	A ①②③④	A ①②
		v ①②③	v ①②③	v ①②③④	v ①②
		i ①②③	i ①②③	i ①②③④	i ①②

NUMBER OF ADULTS IN CLASSROOM   ⓪ ● ② ③ ④ ⑤ ⑥ ⑦ ⑧ ⑨ ⑩

EXERCISE 8.3 Code each person in the situation below on the CCL.

Situation: In a fourth-grade classroom the children are all having a lesson in music. The teacher is leading songs. The songs for the day are listed on the chalkboard. The teacher and the children read through each new song before they try to sing it. Any new words are explained to the children. Then the teacher plays the song on the piano, and the children sing it.

CLASSROOM CHECK LIST (be sure to code EVERYONE in the class)

	ONE CHILD	TWO CHILDREN	SMALL GROUPS	LARGE GROUPS
1. Snack, lunch	T ① ② ③ A ① ② ③ v ① ② ③ i ① ② ③	T ① ② ③ A ① ② ③ v ① ② ③ i ① ② ③	T ① ② ③ ④ A ① ② ③ ④ v ① ② ③ ④ i ① ② ③ ④	T ① ② A ① ② v ① ② i ① ②
2. Group time	T ① ② ③ A ① ② ③ v ① ② ③ i ① ② ③	T ① ② ③ A ① ② ③ v ① ② ③ i ① ② ③	T ① ② ③ ④ A ① ② ③ ④ v ① ② ③ ④ i ① ② ③ ④	T ① ② A ① ② v ① ② i ① ②
Story **3. Music** Dancing	T ① ② ③ A ① ② ③ v ① ② ③ i ① ② ③	T ① ② ③ A ① ② ③ v ① ② ③ i ① ② ③	T ① ② ③ ④ A ① ② ③ ④ v ① ② ③ ④ i ① ② ③ ④	T ① ② A ① ② v ① ② i ① ②
4. Arts, Crafts	T ① ② ③ A ① ② ③ v ① ② ③ i ① ② ③	T ① ② ③ A ① ② ③ v ① ② ③ i ① ② ③	T ① ② ③ ④ A ① ② ③ ④ v ① ② ③ ④ i ① ② ③ ④	T ① ② A ① ② v ① ② i ① ②
Guessing Games **5. Table Games** Puzzles	T ① ② ③ A ① ② ③ v ① ② ③ i ① ② ③	T ① ② ③ A ① ② ③ v ① ② ③ i ① ② ③	T ① ② ③ ④ A ① ② ③ ④ v ① ② ③ ④ i ① ② ③ ④	T ① ② A ① ② v ① ② i ① ②
6. Math — Numbers, Arithmetic	T ① ② ③ A ① ② ③ v ① ② ③ i ① ② ③	T ① ② ③ A ① ② ③ v ① ② ③ i ① ② ③	T ① ② ③ ④ A ① ② ③ ④ v ① ② ③ ④ i ① ② ③ ④	T ① ② A ① ② v ① ② i ① ②
7. Reading, Alphabet, Lang. Development	T ① ② ③ A ① ② ③ v ① ② ③ i ① ② ③	T ① ② ③ A ① ② ③ v ① ② ③ i ① ② ③	T ① ② ③ ④ A ① ② ③ ④ v ① ② ③ ④ i ① ② ③ ④	T ① ② A ① ② v ① ② i ① ②
8. Social Studies, Geography	T ① ② ③ A ① ② ③ v ① ② ③ i ① ② ③	T ① ② ③ A ① ② ③ v ① ② ③ i ① ② ③	T ① ② ③ ④ A ① ② ③ ④ v ① ② ③ ④ i ① ② ③ ④	T ① ② A ① ② v ① ② i ① ②
9. Science, Natural World	T ① ② ③ A ① ② ③ v ① ② ③ i ① ② ③	T ① ② ③ A ① ② ③ v ① ② ③ i ① ② ③	T ① ② ③ ④ A ① ② ③ ④ v ① ② ③ ④ i ① ② ③ ④	T ① ② A ① ② v ① ② i ① ②
Sewing Cooking **10.** Pounding Sawing	T ① ② ③ A ① ② ③ v ① ② ③ i ① ② ③	T ① ② ③ A ① ② ③ v ① ② ③ i ① ② ③	T ① ② ③ ④ A ① ② ③ ④ v ① ② ③ ④ i ① ② ③ ④	T ① ② A ① ② v ① ② i ① ②
11. Blocks Trucks	T ① ② ③ A ① ② ③ v ① ② ③ i ① ② ③	T ① ② ③ A ① ② ③ v ① ② ③ i ① ② ③	T ① ② ③ ④ A ① ② ③ ④ v ① ② ③ ④ i ① ② ③ ④	T ① ② A ① ② v ① ② i ① ②
12. Dramatic Play Dress-Up	T ① ② ③ A ① ② ③ v ① ② ③ i ① ② ③	T ① ② ③ A ① ② ③ v ① ② ③ i ① ② ③	T ① ② ③ ④ A ① ② ③ ④ v ① ② ③ ④ i ① ② ③ ④	T ① ② A ① ② v ① ② i ① ②
13. Active Play	T ① ② ③ A ① ② ③ v ① ② ③ i ① ② ③	T ① ② ③ A ① ② ③ v ① ② ③ i ① ② ③	T ① ② ③ ④ A ① ② ③ ④ v ① ② ③ ④ i ① ② ③ ④	T ① ② A ① ② v ① ② i ① ②
14. RELIABILITY SHEET ○				

Within the box beside items 6–9:

○ TV
○ Audio-Visual Materials
○ Exploratory Materials
○ Math and Science Equipment
○ Texts, Workbooks
○ Puzzles, Games

Exercise 8.3

	ONE CHILD	TWO CHILDREN	SMALL GROUPS	LARGE GROUPS
15. Practical Skills Acquisition	T ①②③ A ①②③ v ①②③ i ①②③	T ①②③ A ①②③ v ①②③ i ①②③	T ①②③④ A ①②③④ v ①②③④ i ①②③④	T ①② A ①② v ①② i ①②
16. Observing	T ①②③ A ①②③ v ①②③ i ①②③	T ①②③ A ①②③ v ①②③ i ①②③	T ①②③④ A ①②③④ v ①②③④ i ①②③④	T ①② A ①② v ①② i ①②
17. Social Interaction Ob [©②⑤] (T)(A)(V)	T ①②③ A ①②③ v ①②③ i ①②③	T ①②③ A ①②③ v ①②③ i ①②③	T ①②③④ A ①②③④ v ①②③④ i ①②③④	T ①② A ①② v ①② i ①②
18. Unoccupied Child	T ①②③ A ①②③ v ①②③ i ①②③	T ①②③ A ①②③ v ①②③ i ①②③	T ①②③④ A ①②③④ v ①②③④ i ①②③④	T ①② A ①② v ①② i ①②
19. Discipline	T ①②③ A ①②③ v ①②③ i ①②③	T ①②③ A ①②③ v ①②③ i ①②③	T ①②③④ A ①②③④ v ①②③④ i ①②③④	T ①② A ①② v ①② i ①②
20. Transitional Activities (T)(A)(V)	T ①②③ A ①②③ v ①②③ i ①②③	T ①②③ A ①②③ v ①②③ i ①②③	T ①②③④ A ①②③④ v ①②③④ i ①②③④	T ①② A ①② v ①② i ①②
21. Classroom Management (T)(A)(V)	T ①②③ A ①②③ v ①②③ i ①②③	T ①②③ A ①②③ v ①②③ i ①②③	T ①②③④ A ①②③④ v ①②③④ i ①②③④	T ①② A ①② v ①② i ①②
22. Out of Room (T)(A)(V)	T ①②③ A ①②③ v ①②③ i ①②③	T ①②③ A ①②③ v ①②③ i ①②③	T ①②③④ A ①②③④ v ①②③④ i ①②③④	T ①② A ①② v ①② i ①②

NUMBER OF ADULTS IN CLASSROOM   ⓪ ① ② ③ ④ ⑤ ⑥ ⑦ ⑧ ⑨ ⑩

CLASSROOM REQUIREMENTS

For this model to succeed, a strong commitment to teaching basic skills is required of parents, teachers, and principal. The support of parents is essential since homework is a part of the program. Also, the strict discipline of the school must be supported by parents if the school's rules of conduct are to be upheld. Teachers must be totally committed to the basic idea of the model.

The principal must also be committed to these ideas and support the teachers in their efforts. Final disciplining steps are taken by the principal.

Required classroom space is minimal since all activities take place with children sitting in their seats. The materials required are paper, pencil, erasers, textbooks, and workbooks for each subject, and some storybooks. Teaching machines, math measuring tools, science equipment, or games are *not* needed. This is a low-cost model to implement.

RESEARCH FINDINGS ON HOW CHILDREN GROW AND DEVELOP

Reports from fundamental schools that were started in the mid-1970s indicate that their children are achieving more in basic skills than children in comparison schools. Dr. Henry Myers, Jr. of Pasadena, California, reports that significant differences have been found in the test scores of black children attending fundamental schools and black children not attending fundamental schools. In the school district as a whole, black children test approximately in the 30th percentile, which is lower than the white children test, but in the Fundamental School Models, the average for black and white children is the same. The average for classes from kindergarten through eighth grade, composed of both black and white children, ranges from the 50th to the 60th percentile on standardized achievement tests. This is impressive since many of the children included in the fundamental schools were low achievers.

A report of the Hoover School, issued by James Hessler of the Palo Alto Research Department,[4] indicates that the children progressed more in reading and math during the school year than the children who had been used to set the norms for the achievement tests. The last column in the following table shows the increase of percentile points in each grade level. In September, the average score in math at every grade level was at or above the nationally established 50th percentile. In May, all grades were at or above the 70th percentile. In reading, all but grade 2 had an average score above the 50th percentile on the September tests. In the May testing, all grades were above the 60th percentile. A positive difference in percentile scores indicates that the group tested has made gains greater than the average of all children tested.

In the report, Hessler writes, however, that the results of the comparison between the Hoover students and the others can only be very tentative because the comparison was limited and Hoover has been in operation only a short time. Also, the other schools knew they were competing with Hoover School, and this probably increased their incentive to achieve.

Principals of fundamental schools report that the start of a fundamental school within a school district is likely to challenge other schools to tend more to basic skill training. In the case of Palo Alto, the Hoover School and the comparison schools are operating well above national norms.

The following is a summary of the findings on the Hoover School that appeared in Hessler's report.

1. Parents are highly satisfied with the Hoover program.

2. Parents share the "More Structured" philosophy.

3. Parents see Hoover's activities as important in most cases.

4. Hoover students score consistently above national norms on standardized tests in reading and math.

5. In its first year of operation, Hoover has not produced achievement significantly greater than a comparison group of single-grade, self-contained classes elsewhere in Palo Alto.

6. Classes at Hoover are quiet.

7. Most instruction at Hoover is group instruction and highly teacher directed.

8. Students at Hoover interact with one another very little during class instruction.

9. Students concentrate on their work most of the time.

---

[4]James Hessler and Ann Porteus, "Hoover School Evaluation," Palo Alto Unified School District, Palo Alto, Calif., February 1976. (Unpublished report.)

Hoover School

No. of Students	Grade	Subject	September		May		Difference in Percentile Ranks
			Grade Equivalent	Percentile Rank	Grade Equivalent	Percentile Rank	
21	1	Reading	1.3	78	2.2	78	0
		Math	1.2	76	2.4	82	+6
23	2	Reading	2.0	42	2.9	62	+20
		Math	2.2	56	3.2	76	+20
24	3	Reading	3.2	52	4.9	82	+30
		Math	3.0	50	4.7	77	+27
24	4	Reading	4.4	58	5.5	68	+10
		Math	4.2	56	5.7	70	+14
26	5	Reading	5.8	66	7.1	76	+10
		Math	5.3	58	8.1	92	+24
24	6	Reading	6.6	60	7.8	72	+12
		Math	6.4	58	8.6	80	+22

Source: James Hessler and Ann Porteus, "Hoover School Evaluation" (Palo Alto, Calif., February 1976).

10. Overall, students and teachers relate to each other in a positive manner.

11. Classroom behaviors are generally consistent with the expressed philosophy of the school.

Like the children in Programmed Models, children in Fundamental School Models achieve well in math and reading. It could also be hypothesized that, like children in the Programmed Models, children in fundamental classrooms would test lower on the Raven's Coloured Progressive Matrices test, be less self-directive, attribute their success to their teachers, cooperate less frequently with classmates, and ask fewer questions since they do not experience the freedom of choice and the use of exploratory materials that are associated with these outcomes. However, there is no data to support these hypotheses.

A longitudinal study of the Fundamental School Model is needed and more student outcomes should be assessed. The Council for Basic Education, while supportive of the traditional alternative being offered in some districts, say, in their January 1975 bulletin: "We should enter some words of caution. The oldest of these schools are only in their second year and their results are yet to be seen. Some of the programs contain some simplistic battle cries of doubtful merit; such as 'bring back the paddle,' teach truth, justice, and patriotism, and what we need is a dress code—no tee shirts and skirts must be of moderate length."[5] How the rules and regulations affect child development is yet to be seen.

OBSERVABLE COMPONENTS

Many important components of the Fundamental School Model, such as materials being used, the activities occurring, and interactions between the teacher and the students, can be recorded on the SRI observation system.

Materials

In the Fundamental School Model, very few materials are used. The Physical Environment Information form would have textbooks, workbooks, and instructional charts marked. The children would be assigned to groups and the desks would be in rows (see Figure 8.4).

Activities and Groupings

Since one teacher is in charge of the classroom, the entire class is usually given instruction at one time. The teacher might then divide the children into three groups and instruct one group while the other two do their assignments. Usually, however, the Classroom Check List would have all children marked in one activity. Several activities might occur during the day, but all the children would be participating in it (see Figure 8.5).

---

[5]George Weber, *Council for Basic Education Bulletin* (Washington, D.C.: Council for Basic Schools, January 1975), p. 2.

Physical Environment Information
(Mark all that apply.)

Seating Patterns:
○ Movable tables and chairs for seating purposes.
● Stationary desks in rows.
○ Assigned seating for at least part of the day.
○ Children select their own seating locations.
● Teacher assigns children to groups.
○ Children select their own work groups.

For each of the items below, mark all that apply:

① Present
② Used today

GAMES, TOYS, PLAY EQUIPMENT
①② small toys (trucks, cars, dolls and accessories
①② puzzles, games
①② wheel toys
①② small play equipment (jumpropes, balls)
①② large play equipment (swings, jungle gym)
①② children's storybooks
①② animals, other nature objects
①② sandbox, water table
①② carpentry materials, large blocks
①② cooking and sewing supplies

INSTRUCTIONAL MATERIALS
①② Montessori, other educational toys
① ● children's texts, workbooks
①② math/science equipment, concrete objects
① ● instructional charts

AUDIO, VISUAL EQUIPMENT
①② television
①② record or tape player
①② audio-visual equipment

GENERAL EQUIPMENT, MATERIALS
● ② children's own products on display
①② displays reflecting children's ethnicity
● ② other displays especially for children
①② magazines
● ② achievement charts
①② child-size sink
①② child-size table and chairs
①② child-size shelves
①② arts and crafts materials
● ② blackboard, feltboard
①② child's own storage space
①② photographs of the children on display

OTHER
①② please specify . . . . . .

MAKE NO

STRAY MARKS

IN BLANK AREAS

Figure 8.4

CLASSROOM CHECK LIST (be sure to code EVERYONE in the class)

		ONE CHILD	TWO CHILDREN	SMALL GROUPS	LARGE GROUPS
1. Snack, lunch		T ①②③ / A ①②③ / v ①②③ / i ①②③	T ①②③ / A ①②③ / v ①②③ / i ①②③	T ①②③④ / A ①②③④ / v ①②③④ / i ①②③④	T ①② / A ①② / v ①② / i ①②
2. Group time		T ①②③ / A ①②③ / v ①②③ / i ①②③	T ①②③ / A ①②③ / v ①②③ / i ①②③	T ①②③④ / A ①②③④ / v ①②③④ / i ①②③④	T ①② / A ①② / v ①② / i ①②
3. Music	Story / Dancing	T ①②③ / A ①②③ / v ①②③ / i ①②③	T ①②③ / A ①②③ / v ①②③ / i ①②③	T ①②③④ / A ①②③④ / v ①②③④ / i ①②③④	T ①② / A ①② / v ①② / i ①②
4. Arts, Crafts		T ①②③ / A ①②③ / v ①②③ / i ①②③	T ①②③ / A ①②③ / v ①②③ / i ①②③	T ①②③④ / A ①②③④ / v ①②③④ / i ①②③④	T ●② / A ①② / v ①② / i ①②
5. Table Games	Guessing Games / Puzzles	T ①②③ / A ①②③ / v ①②③ / i ①②③	T ①②③ / A ①②③ / v ①②③ / i ①②③	T ①②③④ / A ①②③④ / v ①②③④ / i ①②③④	T ①② / A ①② / v ①② / i ①②
6. Math	Numbers / Arithmetic	T ①②③ / A ①②③ / v ①②③ / i ①②③	T ①②③ / A ①②③ / v ①②③ / i ①②③	T ①②③④ / A ①②③④ / v ①②③④ / i ①②③④	T ①② / A ①② / v ①② / i ①②
7. Alphabet	Reading / Lang. Development	T ①②③ / A ①②③ / v ①②③ / i ①②③	T ①②③ / A ①②③ / v ①②③ / i ①②③	T ①②③④ / A ①②③④ / v ①②③④ / i ①②③④	T ①② / A ①② / v ①② / i ①②
8.	Social Studies / Geography	T ①②③ / A ①②③ / v ①②③ / i ①②③	T ①②③ / A ①②③ / v ①②③ / i ①②③	T ①②③④ / A ①②③④ / v ①②③④ / i ①②③④	T ①② / A ①② / v ①② / i ①②
9.	Science / Natural World	T ①②③ / A ①②③ / v ①②③ / i ①②③	T ①②③ / A ①②③ / v ①②③ / i ①②③	T ①②③④ / A ①②③④ / v ①②③④ / i ①②③④	T ①② / A ①② / v ①② / i ①②
10.	Sewing / Cooking / Pounding / Sawing	T ①②③ / A ①②③ / v ①②③ / i ①②③	T ①②③ / A ①②③ / v ①②③ / i ①②③	T ①②③④ / A ①②③④ / v ①②③④ / i ①②③④	T ①② / A ①② / v ①② / i ①②
11.	Blocks / Trucks	T ①②③ / A ①②③ / v ①②③ / i ①②③	T ①②③ / A ①②③ / v ①②③ / i ①②③	T ①②③④ / A ①②③④ / v ①②③④ / i ①②③④	T ①② / A ①② / v ①② / i ①②
12.	Dramatic Play / Dress-Up	T ①②③ / A ①②③ / v ①②③ / i ①②③	T ①②③ / A ①②③ / v ①②③ / i ①②③	T ①②③④ / A ①②③④ / v ①②③④ / i ①②③④	T ①② / A ①② / v ①② / i ①②
13. Active Play		T ①②③ / A ①②③ / v ①②③ / i ①②③	T ①②③ / A ①②③ / v ①②③ / i ①②③	T ①②③④ / A ①②③④ / v ①②③④ / i ①②③④	T ①② / A ①② / v ①② / i ①②
14. RELIABILITY SHEET	○				

Side category list (next to items 6–9):

○ TV
○ Audio-Visual Materials
○ Exploratory Materials
○ Math and Science Equipment
○ Texts, Workbooks
○ Puzzles, Games

Figure 8.5

		ONE CHILD	TWO CHILDREN	SMALL GROUPS	LARGE GROUPS
15. Practical Skills Acquisition		T ①②③	T ①②③	T ①②③④	T ①②
		A ①②③	A ①②③	A ①②③④	A ①②
		v ①②③	v ①②③	v ①②③④	v ①②
		i ①②③	i ①②③	i ①②③④	i ①②
16. Observing		T ①②③	T ①②③	T ①②③④	T ①②
		A ①②③	A ①②③	A ①②③④	A ①②
		v ①②③	v ①②③	v ①②③④	v ①②
		i ①②③	i ①②③	i ①②③④	i ①②
17. Social Interaction Ob [©②⑤] Ⓣ Ⓐ Ⓥ		T ①②③	T ①②③	T ①②③④	T ①②
		A ①②③	A ①②③	A ①②③④	A ①②
		v ①②③	v ①②③	v ①②③④	v ①②
		i ①②③	i ①②③	i ①②③④	i ①②
18. Unoccupied Child		T ①②③	T ①②③	T ①②③④	T ①②
		A ①②③	A ①②③	A ①②③④	A ①②
		v ①②③	v ①②③	v ①②③④	v ①②
		i ①②③	i ①②③	i ①②③④	i ①②
19. Discipline		T ①②③	T ①②③	T ①②③④	T ①②
		A ①②③	A ①②③	A ①②③④	A ①②
		v ①②③	v ①②③	v ①②③④	v ①②
		i ①②③	i ①②③	i ①②③④	i ①②
20. Transitional Activities	Ⓣ Ⓐ Ⓥ	T ①②③	T ①②③	T ①②③④	T ①②
		A ①②③	A ①②③	A ①②③④	A ①②
		v ①②③	v ①②③	v ①②③④	v ①②
		i ①②③	i ①②③	i ①②③④	i ①②
21. Classroom Management	Ⓣ Ⓐ Ⓥ	T ①②③	T ①②③	T ①②③④	T ①②
		A ①②③	A ①②③	A ①②③④	A ①②
		v ①②③	v ①②③	v ①②③④	v ①②
		i ①②③	i ①②③	i ①②③④	i ①②
22. Out of Room	Ⓣ Ⓐ Ⓥ	T ①②③	T ①②③	T ①②③④	T ①②
		A ①②③	A ①②③	A ①②③④	A ①②
		v ①②③	v ①②③	v ①②③④	v ①②
		i ①②③	i ①②③	i ①②③④	i ①②

NUMBER OF ADULTS IN CLASSROOM ⓪ ● ② ③ ④ ⑤ ⑥ ⑦ ⑧ ⑨ ⑩

Interaction Observations

Teachers dominate most of the verbal communication in the classroom. The high rate of teacher talk compared to student talk makes this model different from the others described previously.

Most of the teacher's instruction would be addressed to the large group. There would be a high proportion of teacher instruction (TL4A) and direct requests (TL1A) in academic subjects. The entire class would respond by raising their hands (LT3NVA), or if one child is called upon, that child would respond (CT3A). The following is a typical interaction in the Fundamental School Model. The interaction is coded in Figure 8.6.

Situation: A teacher is giving a spelling lesson to a second-grade class.

1. Teacher: Boys and girls, take out your spelling books and turn to page 32.

2. Children: (Quietly take their books out.)

3. Teacher: Write a sentence using each of these spelling words. Remember to use capitals where needed and use the correct punctuation.

4. Teacher: Where do we use capitals, John?

5. John: At the beginning of sentences, for people's names, for days of the week, and months, cities, and states and countries.

6. Teacher: That is very good, John.

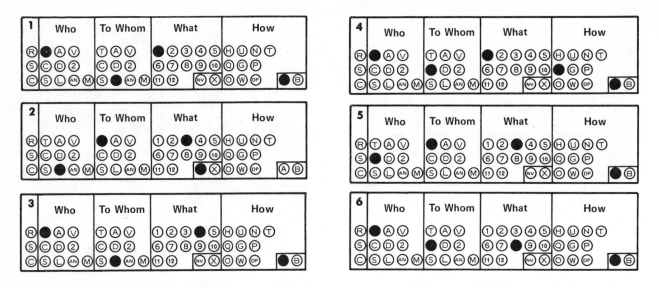

Figure 8.6 Coded Interaction of a Fundamental School Model Classroom

IMPORTANCE OF TEACHER OBSERVATION

Teachers who understand this observation system could learn from the observation records whether or not the Fundamental School Model was being faithfully implemented. If the record showed that the teacher was being interrupted during explanations or that children were not complying with requests, the teacher would attempt to meet the goals of the model by improving classroom control.

SUMMARY OF COMPONENTS

Theorist or theory: Mental discipline

Oriented toward: Factual knowledge

Goals: To develop basic skills

Stress: Good study habits and discipline

Structure: Teacher-centered

Grouping patterns: Large group

Materials: Standard textbooks and workbooks

Where to teach: Front of room

Who initiates: Teacher

Questioning strategy: Narrow focus requiring single answers

Feedback from: Teacher and test scores

Who evaluates: Teacher

Evaluation tools: Achievement tests

BIBLIOGRAPHY

Following are additional readings on the Fundamental School
Model, including articles reporting on the founding of fundamental
schools in several communities. Since this model is so current,
however, not many books are available. The principals and teachers
at the schools themselves are the best resources of information on
this model. The education department in a city that has a fundamental school would be able to direct you to the school and the appropriate spokesperson.

Where Fundamental School Models Can Be Seen

Interested readers should contact the Follow Through offices in
the school districts of the cities listed or contact the Council for
Basic Education, 725 Fifteenth Street N.W., Washington, D.C. 20005.

Cupertino, California	Dade County, Florida
Monterey Peninsula, California	Prince Georges County, Maryland
Palo Alto, California	Cambridge, Massachusetts
Pasadena, California	Great Neck, New York
San Geronimo, California	Long Beach, New York
Santa Ana, California	Charlotte, North Carolina
Aurora, Colorado	Cincinnati, Ohio
Denver, Colorado	Columbus, Ohio
Jefferson County, Colorado	Philadelphia, Pennsylvania
Broward County, Florida	Houston, Texas

Suggested Readings

Why and How the Fundamental Schools Started

"Back to Basics in the Schools." *Newsweek*, October 21, 1974,
    pp. 87-88.

Lloyd, Dick. "Hardy: Fundamental Best for Blacks." *Star News*
    (Pasadena, Calif.), August 12, 1975, p. A-1.

Ryan, Terry. "Back to Basics: Hoover School." *Palo Alto Times*
    (Palo Alto, Calif.), February 27, 1975, Associated Press Re-
    lease, p. 15.

Shaw, Jane S. "The New Conservative Alternative." *Nations Schools
    and Colleges* (February 1975), pp. 31-39.

Weber, George. *Council for Basic Education Bulletin*. Washington,
    D.C.: Council for Basic Schools, December 1976.

Wright, Guy. "Calm Classrooms." *San Francisco Examiner*, December
    15, 1974, Section B, p. 2.

Implementing the Fundamental School Model

Clark, Wallace Bud. "A More Structured Alternative to Elementary
    Education." (Lecture presented at University of California,
    Riverside.) Palo Alto Unified School District, Palo Alto,
    California, 1975.

Hansen, Dr. Carl F. *The Amidon Elementary School: A Successful Demonstration in Basic Education.* Englewood Cliffs, N.J.: Prentice-Hall, 1962.

Myers, Henry, Jr. "A Report of Fundamental Education in the Public Schools." Pasadena School District, Pasadena, California, 1975.

Commercially Available Materials

Standard school textbooks and workbooks are used in this model. New books do not need to be purchased, with the exception of phonics books, which are recommended.

Research Findings

Cities in which Fundamental School Models are being implemented are carefully watching the progress of the children involved. Although comprehensive studies require several years, some findings are now available. Findings, on the progress of children in the Pasadena fundamental schools might be obtained from Dr. Henry Myers at the John Marshall School in Pasadena, California. Also, James Hessler and Ann Porteus have made an evaluation of the Hoover School in Palo Alto, California, and their findings too might be shared upon request. Contact the Palo Alto School District in Palo Alto, California.

ANSWERS: CORRECT CODING FOR EXERCISE 8.1

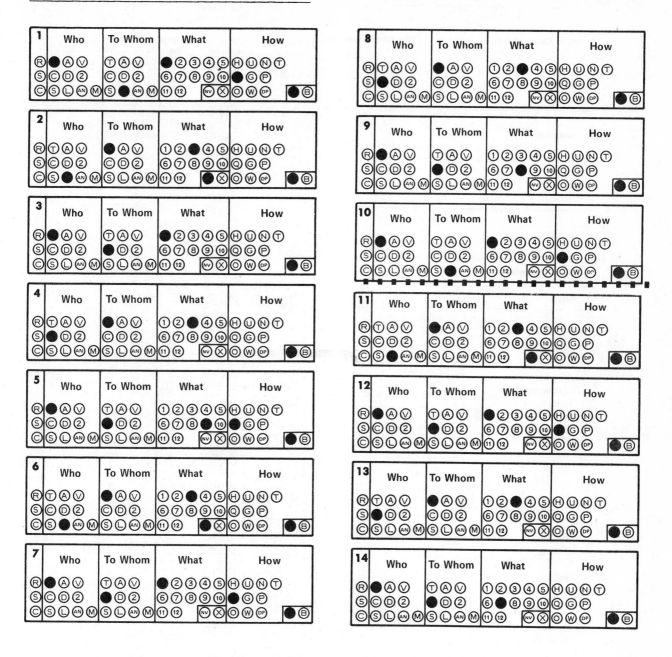

CLASSROOM CHECK LIST (be sure to code **EVERYONE** in the class)

	ONE CHILD	TWO CHILDREN	SMALL GROUPS	LARGE GROUPS
1. Snack, lunch	T ①②③ A ①②③ v ①②③ i ①②③	T ①②③ A ①②③ v ①②③ i ①②③	T ①②③④ A ①②③④ v ①②③④ i ①②③④	T ①② A ①② v ①② i ①②
2. Group time	T ①②③ A ①②③ v ①②③ i ①②③	T ①②③ A ①②③ v ①②③ i ①②③	T ①②③④ A ①②③④ v ①②③④ i ①②③④	T ①② A ①② v ①② i ①②
Story **3. Music** Dancing	T ①②③ A ①②③ v ①②③ i ①②③	T ①②③ A ①②③ v ①②③ i ①②③	T ①②③④ A ①②③④ v ①②③④ i ①②③④	T ●② A ①② v ①② i ①②
4. Arts, Crafts	T ①②③ A ①②③ v ①②③ i ①②③	T ①②③ A ①②③ v ①②③ i ①②③	T ①②③④ A ①②③④ v ①②③④ i ①②③④	T ①② A ①② v ①② i ①②
Guessing Games **5. Table Games** Puzzles	T ①②③ A ①②③ v ①②③ i ①②③	T ①②③ A ①②③ v ①②③ i ①②③	T ①②③④ A ①②③④ v ①②③④ i ①②③④	T ①② A ①② v ①② i ①②
Numbers **6. Math** Arithmetic	T ①②③ A ①②③ v ①②③ i ①②③	T ①②③ A ①②③ v ①②③ i ①②③	T ①②③④ A ①②③④ v ①②③④ i ①②③④	T ①② A ①② v ①② i ①②
Reading **7. Alphabet** Lang. Development	T ①②③ A ①②③ v ①②③ i ①②③	T ①②③ A ①②③ v ①②③ i ①②③	T ①②③④ A ①②③④ v ①②③④ i ①②③④	T ①② A ①② v ①② i ①②
Social Studies **8.** Geography	T ①②③ A ①②③ v ①②③ i ①②③	T ①②③ A ①②③ v ①②③ i ①②③	T ①②③④ A ①②③④ v ①②③④ i ①②③④	T ①② A ①② v ①② i ①②
Science **9.** Natural World	T ①②③ A ①②③ v ①②③ i ①②③	T ①②③ A ①②③ v ①②③ i ①②③	T ①②③④ A ①②③④ v ①②③④ i ①②③④	T ①② A ①② v ①② i ①②
Sewing Cooking **10.** Pounding Sawing	T ①②③ A ①②③ v ①②③ i ①②③	T ①②③ A ①②③ v ①②③ i ①②③	T ①②③④ A ①②③④ v ①②③④ i ①②③④	T ①② A ①② v ①② i ①②
11. Blocks Trucks	T ①②③ A ①②③ v ①②③ i ①②③	T ①②③ A ①②③ v ①②③ i ①②③	T ①②③④ A ①②③④ v ①②③④ i ①②③④	T ①② A ①② v ①② i ①②
12. Dramatic Play Dress-Up	T ①②③ A ①②③ v ①②③ i ①②③	T ①②③ A ①②③ v ①②③ i ①②③	T ①②③④ A ①②③④ v ①②③④ i ①②③④	T ①② A ①② v ①② i ①②
13. Active Play	T ①②③ A ①②③ v ①②③ i ①②③	T ①②③ A ①②③ v ①②③ i ①②③	T ①②③④ A ①②③④ v ①②③④ i ①②③④	T ①② A ①② v ①② i ①②

For items 6–9 (side column):

○ TV
○ Audio-Visual Materials
○ Exploratory Materials
○ Math and Science Equipment
○ Texts, Workbooks
○ Puzzles, Games

14. RELIABILITY SHEET ○

		ONE CHILD	TWO CHILDREN	SMALL GROUPS	LARGE GROUPS
15. Practical Skills Acquisition		T ①②③	T ①②③	T ①②③④	T ①②
		A ①②③	A ①②③	A ①②③④	A ①②
		v ①②③	v ①②③	v ①②③④	v ①②
		i ①②③	i ①②③	i ①②③④	i ①②
16. Observing		T ①②③	T ①②③	T ①②③④	T ①②
		A ①②③	A ①②③	A ①②③④	A ①②
		v ①②③	v ①②③	v ①②③④	v ①②
		i ①②③	i ①②③	i ①②③④	i ①②
17. Social Interaction Ob [Ⓒ ② Ⓢ]	Ⓣ Ⓐ Ⓥ	T ①②③	T ①②③	T ①②③④	T ①②
		A ①②③	A ①②③	A ①②③④	A ①②
		v ①②③	v ①②③	v ①②③④	v ①②
		i ①②③	i ①②③	i ①②③④	i ①②
18. Unoccupied Child		T ①②③	T ①②③	T ①②③④	T ①②
		A ①②③	A ①②③	A ①②③④	A ①②
		v ①②③	v ①②③	v ①②③④	v ①②
		i ①②③	i ①②③	i ①②③④	i ①②
19. Discipline		T ①②③	T ①②③	T ①②③④	T ①②
		A ①②③	A ①②③	A ①②③④	A ①②
		v ①②③	v ①②③	v ①②③④	v ①②
		i ①②③	i ①②③	i ①②③④	i ①②
20. Transitional Activities	Ⓣ Ⓐ Ⓥ	T ①②③	T ①②③	T ①②③④	T ①②
		A ①②③	A ①②③	A ①②③④	A ①②
		v ①②③	v ①②③	v ①②③④	v ①②
		i ①②③	i ①②③	i ①②③④	i ①②
21. Classroom Management	Ⓣ Ⓐ Ⓥ	T ①②③	T ①②③	T ①②③④	T ①②
		A ①②③	A ①②③	A ①②③④	A ①②
		v ①②③	v ①②③	v ①②③④	v ①②
		i ①②③	i ①②③	i ①②③④	i ①②
22. Out of Room	Ⓣ Ⓐ Ⓥ	T ①②③	T ①②③	T ①②③④	T ①②
		A ①②③	A ①②③	A ①②③④	A ①②
		v ①②③	v ①②③	v ①②③④	v ①②
		i ①②③	i ①②③	i ①②③④	i ①②

NUMBER OF ADULTS IN CLASSROOM   ⓪ ① ② ③ ④ ⑤ ⑥ ⑦ ⑧ ⑨ ⑩

Chapter 9

Bibliography

Suggested Readings

Summary

A number of educational models have been developed and are available for use in classrooms: this book describes five. Muska Mosston describes seven models in *Teaching from Demand to Discovery*,[1] and Bruce Joyce and Marsha Weil in *Models of Teaching* describe sixteen.[2] Similar models are quite often given different names by different authors, and the reader is advised to look beyond the name to the theory, goals, structure, and processes of each. The table on page 236 compares the five models presented in this book.

Through systematic observation in these different kinds of classrooms, the reader—now able to use the SRI Classroom Observation System—could tell which model they were based on. For example, if, during most of a school day, you see all the children reading at their seats while the teacher stands at the front of the room, what model of classroom are you in?

If, during the school day, you see the children frequently working in different learning centers and the teacher working with one child in reading, what model of classroom are you in?

If, during most of the day, you see a teacher teaching reading, one aide teaching math, and a second aide teaching writing and spelling—all at the same time—what model are you in?

If you hear a teacher asking children, "What have you done today in reading?" and then asking them to evaluate their work, what model are you in?

If you hear a teacher asking a group of children how they feel when they are trying to read and the noise level gets very high, and then asking them to suggest solutions to the noise problem, what model are you in?[3]

EXERCISE 9.1 To help your understanding of the models, try to develop five questions like those preceding that contrast the five models.

---

[1]Muska Mosston, *Teaching: From Command to Discovery* (Belmont, Calif.: Wadsworth, 1972).
[2]Bruce Joyce and Marsha Weil, *Models of Teaching* (Engelwood Cliffs, N.J.: Prentice-Hall, 1972).
[3]Fundamental, Exploratory, Programmed, Developmental Cognitive, Group Process.

A Comparison of Five Models of Teaching by Theory and Practice

Component	Exploratory	Group Process	Developmental Cognitive	Programmed	Fundamental
Theorist or theory	Gestalt theory Dewey, Taba	Lewin field theory, Glasser	Piaget	Skinner	Mental discipline
Oriented toward	Self-motivation	Social-emotional development	Cognitive growth	Behavior modification	Factual knowledge
Goals	To develop creativity and independence	To develop self-awareness, responsibility, and cooperation	To develop cognitive skills	To develop basic skills	To develop basic skills
Stress	Inquiring skills	Social problem-solving skills	Classification, planning, and evaluation skills	Drill, practice, and memory skills	Good study habits and discipline
Structure	Student-centered	Student-centered	Student-centered	Teacher-centered	Teacher-centered
Grouping patterns	Individual student	Large group and individual student	Small group	Small group	Large group
Materials	Teaching machines and exploratory materials	Textbooks and exploratory objects	Exploratory objects, building and cooking materials	Programmed workbooks	Standard textbooks and workbooks
Where to teach	Learning centers	Large group circle or individual desks	Learning centers or around a table	Small group of chairs in a half circle	Front of room
Who initiates	Child	Child	Teacher and child	Teacher	Teacher
Questioning strategy	Open-ended	Open-ended	Open-ended and direct single answers	Direct single answers	Narrow focus requires single answers
Feedback from	Materials	Other students and teacher	Materials and teacher	Teacher and test scores	Teacher and test scores
Who evaluates	Student and teacher	Students and teacher	Students and teacher	Teacher	Teacher
Evaluation tools	Problem-solving tests, locus of control tests, child observations	Problem-solving tests, achievement tests, child observations, locus of control tests	Problem-solving tests, cognitive tests, child observations, achievement tests	Achievement tests	Achievement tests

Ways in which children can be expected to grow and develop in each model have been discussed at the end of each appropriate chapter. However, although learning theorists have ideas about the effects the various models are likely to have on children, there is very little data to support their hypotheses. (See the bibliography at the end of this chapter for studies that report findings on teaching effects.) The following table summarizes both the findings reported by Stallings and Kaskowitz and, for the Group Process Model and the Fundamental School Model, the reports of involved school districts.[4]

It is clear from the table that no one model is optimal for developing all facets of a child. Models that emphasize development of basic skills and ignore development of social abilities and emotional expression may find they have developed children not well prepared to take part in decision making or to be responsible citizens.

Growth and Development of Children in the Five Models

	Exploratory	Group Process	Developmental Cognitive	Programmed	Fundamental
Reading achievement		N+		C+	N+
Math achievement		N+		C+	N+
Nonverbal problem solving	C+		C+		
Questioning	C+				
Independence	C+		C+		
Cooperation with others	C+		C+		
Accepts responsibility for success	C+		C+		
Accepts responsibility for failure				C+	
Absence rate	C+		C+		

N+ = Better than national norms
C+ = Better than control group in the Follow Through study

Models that fail to provide some structure and ignore cognitive development may find they have developed children deficient in basic skills and unable to make connections between their varied experiences.

In selecting a model of education, both the advantages and disadvantages of children's growth should be considered. No one model is likely to be perfect, and no one model is likely to be the

---

[4]Jane A. Stallings and David Kaskowitz, *Follow Through Classroom Observation Evaluation 1972-1973.* SRI Project URU-7370. (Menlo Park, Calif.: Stanford Research Institute, 1974). ERIC Accession No. ED 104 969.

best for children for each of their school years. Children who show good progress in a fundamental school during the first three grades, for example, may prosper more in an open education model during the upper elementary school years. For this reason, it is important, I think, to have several educational alternatives within any school system, from which parents and students can choose.

In addition, teachers should be allowed to select and use from each model what they consider to be the best components. For instance, they may prefer the Programmed Model for teaching reading and math; the Group Process Model for teaching social values and developing problem-solving skills; and the Exploratory Model for allowing children to explore science materials. To learn the advantages and disadvantages, teachers should study all the literature available on the different models and, at the same time, study local needs. A model of education must be chosen in the context of the students, parents, school, and community.

The pendulum of educational emphasis swings back and forth. The movement of the 1960s and 1970s concentrated on the individual. Open classrooms, schools without walls, and street academies tried to lure school dropouts back to education by tailoring programs to meet individual student needs. This swing toward personalized education brought many structural changes—open classrooms, for example—to education. Too often however, the teachers' goals for educating children and the methods they used were not considered when these changes were planned. In some cases, after open classroom schools were built, it was discovered that teachers were not prepared to work in open space. Those who did not feel comfortable in a "fishbowl" quickly erected walls of book shelves or made other room dividers. School communities caught in the "It's new—it's good—let's do it" syndrome often made decisions without careful consideration of teachers, and then found that their innovations did not necessarily promote the desired growth and development of children.

It is important for teachers, parents, and administrators to consider for now and for the future what kind of citizens the school system should be developing. What kind of people are required to make a democracy work? These topics must be considered when selecting a model of education for children.

More recently, with the resurgence of fundamental schools, emphasis has been placed on discipline, orderliness, and patriotism, an emphasis that reflects society's fears of radical, rebellious youth born in the 1950s and 1960s. Many older people feel that these fundamental schools are needed, that the open schools failed—that they allowed children to become undisciplined, disrespectful of authority, unpatriotic, uneducated, and dangerous to the established order. I disagree. I feel that the open schools trained children to be independent and self-aware, to ask questions and value their own ideas; it trained them to not follow blindly. Where these schools may have failed was in not getting the children to value knowledge, to have patience, and to develop wisdom.

Many skills developed in the open education schools have not yet been tested or evaluated. Indeed, few reliable tests for measuring social, emotional, and higher cognitive development are available. Only Standard Achievement Tests are widely used to evaluate school success. Thus, it is hard to compare open education and its success with the success of other models in other decades. A young person needs to know a lot to contribute toward solving the problems of world hunger, dwindling energy supplies, environmental pollution, and international political crises. Basic skills in reading, composition, and communication are essential if a person is to gain the technological background necessary to be able to solve these problems in an innovative way. The skills developed in the basic schools' programs are as essential to good scholarship as the questioning and evaluating skills developed in the open education programs are essential to creativity and problem solving.

Perhaps this time we can stop the pendulum's swing from the open school program back to basic education. Perhaps we can find a middle position that will allow children to benefit from both these extremes. As classroom teachers we have a special trust. What we do in the classroom does make a difference in how children grow and develop.

BIBLIOGRAPHY

Suggested Readings

Education Theory and Practice

Gage, Nathan L., and Berliner, David C. *Educational Psychology*. Chicago: Rand McNally, 1975.

Joyce, Bruce, and Weil, Marsha. *Models of Teaching*. Englewood, Cliffs, N.J.: Prentice-Hall, 1972.

Mosston, Muska. *Teaching from Command to Discovery*. Belmont, Calif.: Wadsworth, 1972.

Perkins, Hugh V. *Human Development and Learning*, 2d ed. Belmont, Calif.: Wadsworth, 1974.

Shulman, Lee S., and Keislar, Evan R., eds. *Learning by Discovery, A Critical Appraisal*. Chicago, Ill.: Rand McNally, 1966.

Taba, Hilda. *Curriculum Development: Theory and Practice*. New York: Harcourt Brace and World, 1962.

Student Outcomes and Educational Practices

Anderson, Linda M., and Brophy, Jere E. "An Experimental Investigation of First Grade Reading Group Instruction." Austin, Texas: Research and Development Center for Teacher Education, University of Texas, 1976. (Report No. 76-3) ERIC Accession No. 124 921.

Bennett, Neville. *Teaching Styles and Pupil Progress*. Cambridge, Mass.: Harvard University Press, 1976.

Berliner, David C. *Impediments to the Study of Teacher Effectiveness*. San Francisco, Calif.: Far West Laboratory for Educational Research and Development, 1975. ERIC Accession No. ED 128 343.

Brophy, Jere, and Evertson, Carolyn M. *Learning from Teaching: A Developmental Perspective*. Boston: Allyn and Bacon, 1976.

————. *Process-Product Correlations in the Texas Teacher Effectiveness Study: Final Report*. Austin, Texas: University of Texas, 1974. ERIC Accession No. ED 091 394.

Brophy, Jere E., and Good, Thomas L. *Teacher-Student Relationships: Causes and Consequences*. New York: Holt, Rinehart and Winston, 1974.

Calfee, Robert, and Calfee, Kathryn H. "Reading and Mathematics Observation System: Description and Analysis of Time Expenditures." In *Beginning Teacher Evaluation Study: Phase II, 1973-74, Final Report*, Vol. 3, edited by F. McDonald and P. Elias, ch. 2. Princeton, N.J.: Educational Testing Service, 1976. ERIC Accession No. 127 367.

Dunkin, M., and Biddle, J. *The Study of Teaching*. New York: Holt, Rinehart and Winston, 1974.

Flanders, Ned A. *Analyzing Teaching Behavior*. New York: Addison-Wesley, 1970.

Gage, Nathan L. "Evaluating Ways to Help Teachers Behave Desirably." In *Competency Assessment, Research, and Evaluation: A Report of a National Conference, March 12-15, 1974*. Washington, D.C.: American Association of Colleges for Teacher Education, 1974, pp. 173-185.

Gage, N. L., ed. *The Psychology of Teaching Methods: Seventy-Fifth Yearbook Part I*. Chicago: National Society for the Study of Education, University of Chicago Press, 1976.

Good, Thomas L. and Brophy, J. E. "Changing Teacher and Student Behavior: An Empirical Investigation." *Journal of Educational Psychology* 66 (1974): 390-405.

Good, T., et al. *Teacher Behavior and Student Outcomes in the Missouri Teacher Effectiveness Study*. Columbia, Mo.: College of Education, University of Missouri, 1975.

Good, T., et al. *Teachers Make a Difference*. New York: Holt, Rinehart and Winston, 1975.

Hall, G. E. *The Effects of "Change" on Teachers and Professors—Theory, Research, and Implications for Decision Makers*. Austin, Tx.: Research and Development Center for Teacher Education, University of Texas, 1975.

"How Teachers Make a Difference." Washington, D.C.: U.S. Government Printing Office, 1971 (No. 1780-0813).

Lambert, Nadine M., and Hartsough, Carolyn S. "APPLE Observation Variables and Their Relationship to Reading and Mathematics Achievement." In *Beginning Teacher Evaluation Study: Phase II, 1973-74, Final Report*, Vol. 3, edited by F. McDonald and P. Elias, ch. 1. Princeton, N.J.: Educational Testing Service, 1976. ERIC Accession No. ED 127 366.

McDonald, Frederick, and Elias, Patricia. "The Effects of Teaching Performances on Pupil Learning." *Beginning Teacher Evaluation Study: Phase II, 1973-74, Final Report*, Vol. 1. Princeton, N.J.: Educational Testing Service, 1976. ERIC Accession No. 127 364.

McDonald, F. J., et al. *Beginning Teacher Education Study, Phase II: Final Report*. Princeton, N.J.: Educational Testing Service, 1975.

Rist, Ray C. *The Urban School: A Factory for Failure*. Cambridge, Mass.: M.I.T. Press, 1973.

Rosenshine, Barak, and Furst, N. F. "The Use of Direct Observation to Study Teaching." In *Second Handbook of Research on Teaching*, edited by R.M.W. Travers. Chicago: Rand McNally, 1973.

Rosenshine, Barak, and Martin, Marilyn. "Teacher Education and Teaching Behavior Comments on the State-of-the-Research." *Educational Researcher* 3 (July/August 1974): 11-14.

Soar, R. S. *Follow Through Classroom Process Measurement and Pupil Growth (1970-1971): Final Report*. Gainesville, Fla.: College of Education, University of Florida, 1973.

Spaulding, Robert L. *Classroom Behavior Analysis and Treatment*. San Jose, Calif.: San Jose State College, 1970.

Stallings, Jane. "Evaluation of Implementation in Follow Through Classrooms and an Assessment of the Relationship between Classroom Process and Children Outcomes." *Monographs of the Society for Research in Child Development* 40 (1976).

Stallings, Jane A., and Kaskowitz, David H. *Follow Through Classroom Observation Evaluation 1972-1973*. Menlo Park, Calif.: Stanford Research Institute, 1974. ERIC Accession No. ED 104 969.

Tikunoff, William J.; Berliner, David C.; and Rist, Ray C. *An Ethnographic Study of the Forty Classrooms of the Beginning Teacher Evaluation Study Known Sample Technical Report No. 75-10-5*. San Francisco, Calif.: Far West Laboratory for Educational Research and Development, 1975.

Walker, Decker F., and Schaffarzick, Jon. "Comparing Curricula." *Review of Educational Research* 44 (Winter, 1974): 83-111.

Wiley, D. E. "Another Hour, Another Day: Quantity of Schooling, A Potent Path for Policy." *Studies of Educative Processes*, no. 3. (July 1973). University of Chicago.

Wiley, David E., and Harnischfeger, Annegret. "Explosion of a Myth: Quantity of Schooling and Exposure to Instruction, Major Educational Vehicles." *Educational Research* 3 (April 1974): 7-12.

Wright, R. J. "The Affective and Cognitive Consequences of an Open Education Elementary School." *American Educational Research Journal* 12 (1975): 449-468.

Appendix A

THE STANFORD RESEARCH INSTITUTE CLASSROOM OBSERVATION SYSTEM FOR USE
IN KINDERGARTEN THROUGH SIXTH-GRADE CLASSROOMS

CLASSROOM OBSERVATION INSTRUMENT
Classroom Summary Information

DIRECTIONS: Make sure that all of the identifying information has been entered on the Classroom Summary Information form prior to your observation of physical environment. Do not make any stray marks outside the boxes provided in places where written information is required. Make sure you code the classroom summary information form booklet Identification Number in the I. D. grid of all booklets used in the observation.

TEACHER NUMBER

⓪⓪⓪⓪⓪⓪⓪⓪
①①①①①①①①
②②②②②②②②
③③③③③③③③
④④④④④④④④
⑤⑤⑤⑤⑤⑤⑤⑤
⑥⑥⑥⑥⑥⑥⑥⑥
⑦⑦⑦⑦⑦⑦⑦⑦
⑧⑧⑧⑧⑧⑧⑧⑧
⑨⑨⑨⑨⑨⑨⑨⑨

Grade

Ⓚ
①
②
③
Ⓜ

OBSERVER NUMBER

⓪⓪⓪⓪
①①①①
②②②②
③③③③
④④④④
⑤⑤⑤⑤
⑥⑥⑥⑥
⑦⑦⑦⑦
⑧⑧⑧⑧
⑨⑨⑨⑨

TODAY'S DATE

MO.	DAY	YR.

⓪⓪⓪⓪⓪⓪
①①①①①①
②②②②②②
③③③③③③
④④④④④④
⑤⑤⑤⑤⑤⑤
⑥⑥⑥⑥⑥⑥
⑦⑦⑦⑦⑦⑦
⑧⑧⑧⑧⑧⑧
⑨⑨⑨⑨⑨⑨

I. D. NUMBER

⓪⓪⓪⓪
①①①①
②②②②
③③③③
④④④④
⑤⑤⑤⑤
⑥⑥⑥⑥
⑦⑦⑦⑦
⑧⑧⑧⑧
⑨⑨⑨⑨

Teacher _____

School _____

City _____

Observer _____

CLASSROOM SUMMARY INFORMATION

⓪①②③④ Number of teachers that regularly work in the classroom.

⓪①②③④ Number of aides that regularly work in the classroom.

⓪①②③④ Number of volunteers/visitors present today.

Classroom Summary Information (Cont.)

A	B

⓪⓪
①①
②②
③③
④④
⑤⑤
⑥⑥
⑦⑦
⑧⑧
⑨⑨

A. Number of children enrolled

B. Number of children present today

Total Class Duration

○ 2½ hours
○ 3 hours
○ 3½ hours
○ 4 hours
○ 4½ hours
○ 5 hours
○ 5½ hours
○ 6 hours
○ 6½ hours
○ 7 or more hours

NCS Trans-Optic S387A-3

Physical Environment Information
(Mark all that apply.)

For each of the items below, mark all that apply:

① Present
② Used today

Seating Patterns:
○ Movable tables and chairs for seating purposes.
○ Stationary desks in rows.
○ Assigned seating for at least part of the day.
○ Children select their own seating locations.
○ Teacher assigns children to groups.
○ Children select their own work groups.

GAMES, TOYS, PLAY EQUIPMENT
① ② small toys (trucks, cars, dolls and accessories
① ② puzzles, games
① ② wheel toys
① ② small play equipment (jumpropes, balls)
① ② large play equipment (swings, jungle gym)
① ② children's storybooks
① ② animals, other nature objects
① ② sandbox, water table
① ② carpentry materials, large blocks
① ② cooking and sewing supplies

INSTRUCTIONAL MATERIALS
① ② Montessori, other educational toys
① ② children's texts, workbooks
① ② math/science equipment, concrete objects
① ② instructional charts

AUDIO, VISUAL EQUIPMENT
① ② television
① ② record or tape player
① ② audio-visual equipment

GENERAL EQUIPMENT, MATERIALS
① ② children's own products on display
① ② displays reflecting children's ethnicity
① ② other displays especially for children
① ② magazines
① ② achievement charts
① ② child-size sink
① ② child-size table and chairs
① ② child-size shelves
① ② arts and crafts materials
① ② blackboard, feltboard
① ② child's own storage space
① ② photographs of the children on display

OTHER
① ② please specify . . . . . .

MAKE NO

STRAY MARKS

IN BLANK AREAS

CLASSROOM CHECK LIST (be sure to code **EVERYONE** in the class)

Activity	ONE CHILD	TWO CHILDREN	SMALL GROUPS	LARGE GROUPS
1. Snack, lunch	T ①②③ / A ①②③ / V ①②③ / i ①②③	T ①②③ / A ①②③ / V ①②③ / i ①②③	T ①②③④ / A ①②③④ / V ①②③④ / i ①②③④	T ①② / A ①② / V ①② / i ①②
2. Group time	T ①②③ / A ①②③ / V ①②③ / i ①②③	T ①②③ / A ①②③ / V ①②③ / i ①②③	T ①②③④ / A ①②③④ / V ①②③④ / i ①②③④	T ①② / A ①② / V ①② / i ①②
Story / 3. Music / Dancing	T ①②③ / A ①②③ / V ①②③ / i ①②③	T ①②③ / A ①②③ / V ①②③ / i ①②③	T ①②③④ / A ①②③④ / V ①②③④ / i ①②③④	T ①② / A ①② / V ①② / i ①②
4. Arts, Crafts	T ①②③ / A ①②③ / V ①②③ / i ①②③	T ①②③ / A ①②③ / V ①②③ / i ①②③	T ①②③④ / A ①②③④ / V ①②③④ / i ①②③④	T ①② / A ①② / V ①② / i ①②
Guessing Games / 5. Table Games / Puzzles	T ①②③ / A ①②③ / V ①②③ / i ①②③	T ①②③ / A ①②③ / V ①②③ / i ①②③	T ①②③④ / A ①②③④ / V ①②③④ / i ①②③④	T ①② / A ①② / V ①② / i ①②
6. Numbers / Math / Arithmetic	T ①②③ / A ①②③ / V ①②③ / i ①②③	T ①②③ / A ①②③ / V ①②③ / i ①②③	T ①②③④ / A ①②③④ / V ①②③④ / i ①②③④	T ①② / A ①② / V ①② / i ①②
7. Reading / Alphabet / Lang. Development	T ①②③ / A ①②③ / V ①②③ / i ①②③	T ①②③ / A ①②③ / V ①②③ / i ①②③	T ①②③④ / A ①②③④ / V ①②③④ / i ①②③④	T ①② / A ①② / V ①② / i ①②
8. Social Studies / Geography	T ①②③ / A ①②③ / V ①②③ / i ①②③	T ①②③ / A ①②③ / V ①②③ / i ①②③	T ①②③④ / A ①②③④ / V ①②③④ / i ①②③④	T ①② / A ①② / V ①② / i ①②
9. Science / Natural World	T ①②③ / A ①②③ / V ①②③ / i ①②③	T ①②③ / A ①②③ / V ①②③ / i ①②③	T ①②③④ / A ①②③④ / V ①②③④ / i ①②③④	T ①② / A ①② / V ①② / i ①②
10. Sewing / Cooking / Pounding / Sawing	T ①②③ / A ①②③ / V ①②③ / i ①②③	T ①②③ / A ①②③ / V ①②③ / i ①②③	T ①②③④ / A ①②③④ / V ①②③④ / i ①②③④	T ①② / A ①② / V ①② / i ①②
11. Blocks / Trucks	T ①②③ / A ①②③ / V ①②③ / i ①②③	T ①②③ / A ①②③ / V ①②③ / i ①②③	T ①②③④ / A ①②③④ / V ①②③④ / i ①②③④	T ①② / A ①② / V ①② / i ①②
12. Dramatic Play / Dress-Up	T ①②③ / A ①②③ / V ①②③ / i ①②③	T ①②③ / A ①②③ / V ①②③ / i ①②③	T ①②③④ / A ①②③④ / V ①②③④ / i ①②③④	T ①② / A ①② / V ①② / i ①②
13. Active Play	T ①②③ / A ①②③ / V ①②③ / i ①②③	T ①②③ / A ①②③ / V ①②③ / i ①②③	T ①②③④ / A ①②③④ / V ①②③④ / i ①②③④	T ①② / A ①② / V ①② / i ①②

(Left column categories, beside items 6–9)
○ TV
○ Audio-Visual Materials
○ Exploratory Materials
○ Math and Science Equipment
○ Texts, Workbooks
○ Puzzles, Games

14. **RELIABILITY SHEET** ○

			ONE CHILD	TWO CHILDREN	SMALL GROUPS	LARGE GROUPS
15. Practical Skills Acquisition			T ①②③ / A ①②③ / v ①②③ / i ①②③	T ①②③ / A ①②③ / v ①②③ / i ①②③	T ①②③④ / A ①②③④ / v ①②③④ / i ①②③④	T ①② / A ①② / v ①② / i ①②
16. Observing			T ①②③ / A ①②③ / v ①②③ / i ①②③	T ①②③ / A ①②③ / v ①②③ / i ①②③	T ①②③④ / A ①②③④ / v ①②③④ / i ①②③④	T ①② / A ①② / v ①② / i ①②
17. Social Interaction	Ob [© ② Ⓢ]	Ⓣ Ⓐ Ⓥ	T ①②③ / A ①②③ / v ①②③ / i ①②③	T ①②③ / A ①②③ / v ①②③ / i ①②③	T ①②③④ / A ①②③④ / v ①②③④ / i ①②③④	T ①② / A ①② / v ①② / i ①②
18. Unoccupied Child			T ①②③ / A ①②③ / v ①②③ / i ①②③	T ①②③ / A ①②③ / v ①②③ / i ①②③	T ①②③④ / A ①②③④ / v ①②③④ / i ①②③④	T ①② / A ①② / v ①② / i ①②
19. Discipline			T ①②③ / A ①②③ / v ①②③ / i ①②③	T ①②③ / A ①②③ / v ①②③ / i ①②③	T ①②③④ / A ①②③④ / v ①②③④ / i ①②③④	T ①② / A ①② / v ①② / i ①②
20. Transitional Activities		Ⓣ Ⓐ Ⓥ	T ①②③ / A ①②③ / v ①②③ / i ①②③	T ①②③ / A ①②③ / v ①②③ / i ①②③	T ①②③④ / A ①②③④ / v ①②③④ / i ①②③④	T ①② / A ①② / v ①② / i ①②
21. Classroom Management		Ⓣ Ⓐ Ⓥ	T ①②③ / A ①②③ / v ①②③ / i ①②③	T ①②③ / A ①②③ / v ①②③ / i ①②③	T ①②③④ / A ①②③④ / v ①②③④ / i ①②③④	T ①② / A ①② / v ①② / i ①②
22. Out of Room		Ⓣ Ⓐ Ⓥ	T ①②③ / A ①②③ / v ①②③ / i ①②③	T ①②③ / A ①②③ / v ①②③ / i ①②③	T ①②③④ / A ①②③④ / v ①②③④ / i ①②③④	T ①② / A ①② / v ①② / i ①②

NUMBER OF ADULTS IN CLASSROOM ⓪ ① ② ③ ④ ⑤ ⑥ ⑦ ⑧ ⑨ ⑩

PREAMBLE

Focus Person Codes:
00 – The original class teacher
1-76 – Child codes
77 – Volunteer
88 – Teacher other than designated class teacher
99 – Aide to teacher

Activity	Focus Person Code
⓪⓪	⓪⓪
①①	①①
②②	②②
③③	③③
④④	④④
⑤⑤	⑤⑤
⑥⑥	⑥⑥
⑦⑦	⑦⑦
⑧⑧	⑧⑧
⑨⑨	⑨⑨

FOCUS PERSON
○ Child
○ Teacher
○ Aide
○ Volunteer

CONTINUATION OF PREVIOUS FOCUS ACTIVITY
○ Yes
○ No

Focus Person's Name and Number

(Do not write outside this box)

Number of Children ① ② ⑤ Ⓛ

FOR NCS USE ONLY
⓪⓪⓪⓪⓪
①①①①①
②②②②②
③③③③③
④④④④④
⑤⑤⑤⑤⑤
⑥⑥⑥⑥⑥
⑦⑦⑦⑦⑦
⑧⑧⑧⑧⑧
⑨⑨⑨⑨⑨

ADULT	Directing	Participating	Observing	Not Involved
Teacher	○	○	○	○
Aide	○	○	○	○
Volunteer	○	○	○	○

TIME STARTED

Hour		Minute	
⑧ ⑨ ⑩ ⑪ ⑫	⓪ ① ②	⓪ ① ② ③ ④	
① ② ③ ④ ⑤	③ ④ ⑤	⑤ ⑥ ⑦ ⑧ ⑨	

Each numbered observation block (1–20) contains four columns with the following coded options:

Who | **To Whom** | **What** | **How**

- **Who:** R T A V / S C D 2 / C S L AN M
- **To Whom:** T A V / C D 2 / S L AN M
- **What:** 1 2 3 4 5 / 6 7 8 9 10 / 11 12
- **How:** H U N T / Q G P / NV X O W DP / A B

The numbered blocks are:

1, 2, 3, 4, 5, 6, 7, 8, 9, 10 (left column)

11, 12, 13, 14, 15, 16, 17, 18, 19, 20 (right column)

Coding forms numbered 21 through 40, each with columns: **Who | To Whom | What | How**

Each card contains the following printed elements:

- **Who:** R, T, A, V / S, C, D, 2 / C, S, L, AN, M
- **To Whom:** T, A, V / C, D, 2 / S, L, AN, M
- **What:** 1, 2, 3, 4, 5 / 6, 7, 8, 9, 10 / 11, 12 / NV, X
- **How:** H, U, N, T / Q, G, P / O, W, DP / A, B

21	Who	To Whom	What	How
22	Who	To Whom	What	How
23	Who	To Whom	What	How
24	Who	To Whom	What	How
25	Who	To Whom	What	How
26	Who	To Whom	What	How
27	Who	To Whom	What	How
28	Who	To Whom	What	How
29	Who	To Whom	What	How
30	Who	To Whom	What	How
31	Who	To Whom	What	How
32	Who	To Whom	What	How
33	Who	To Whom	What	How
34	Who	To Whom	What	How
35	Who	To Whom	What	How
36	Who	To Whom	What	How
37	Who	To Whom	What	How
38	Who	To Whom	What	How
39	Who	To Whom	What	How
40	Who	To Whom	What	How

41

Who	To Whom	What	How
Ⓡ Ⓣ Ⓐ Ⓥ	Ⓣ Ⓐ Ⓥ	① ② ③ ④ ⑤	Ⓗ Ⓤ Ⓝ Ⓣ
Ⓢ Ⓒ Ⓓ ②	Ⓒ Ⓓ ②	⑥ ⑦ ⑧ ⑨ ⑩	Ⓠ Ⓖ Ⓟ
Ⓒ Ⓢ Ⓛ ⒜ⓝ Ⓜ	Ⓢ Ⓛ ⒜ⓝ Ⓜ	⑪ ⑫	ⓃⓋ Ⓧ Ⓞ Ⓦ ⒹⓅ Ⓐ Ⓑ

42

Who	To Whom	What	How
Ⓡ Ⓣ Ⓐ Ⓥ	Ⓣ Ⓐ Ⓥ	① ② ③ ④ ⑤	Ⓗ Ⓤ Ⓝ Ⓣ
Ⓢ Ⓒ Ⓓ ②	Ⓒ Ⓓ ②	⑥ ⑦ ⑧ ⑨ ⑩	Ⓠ Ⓖ Ⓟ
Ⓒ Ⓢ Ⓛ ⒜ⓝ Ⓜ	Ⓢ Ⓛ ⒜ⓝ Ⓜ	⑪ ⑫	ⓃⓋ Ⓧ Ⓞ Ⓦ ⒹⓅ Ⓐ Ⓑ

43

Who	To Whom	What	How
Ⓡ Ⓣ Ⓐ Ⓥ	Ⓣ Ⓐ Ⓥ	① ② ③ ④ ⑤	Ⓗ Ⓤ Ⓝ Ⓣ
Ⓢ Ⓒ Ⓓ ②	Ⓒ Ⓓ ②	⑥ ⑦ ⑧ ⑨ ⑩	Ⓠ Ⓖ Ⓟ
Ⓒ Ⓢ Ⓛ ⒜ⓝ Ⓜ	Ⓢ Ⓛ ⒜ⓝ Ⓜ	⑪ ⑫	ⓃⓋ Ⓧ Ⓞ Ⓦ ⒹⓅ Ⓐ Ⓑ

44

Who	To Whom	What	How
Ⓡ Ⓣ Ⓐ Ⓥ	Ⓣ Ⓐ Ⓥ	① ② ③ ④ ⑤	Ⓗ Ⓤ Ⓝ Ⓣ
Ⓢ Ⓒ Ⓓ ②	Ⓒ Ⓓ ②	⑥ ⑦ ⑧ ⑨ ⑩	Ⓠ Ⓖ Ⓟ
Ⓒ Ⓢ Ⓛ ⒜ⓝ Ⓜ	Ⓢ Ⓛ ⒜ⓝ Ⓜ	⑪ ⑫	ⓃⓋ Ⓧ Ⓞ Ⓦ ⒹⓅ Ⓐ Ⓑ

45

Who	To Whom	What	How
Ⓡ Ⓣ Ⓐ Ⓥ	Ⓣ Ⓐ Ⓥ	① ② ③ ④ ⑤	Ⓗ Ⓤ Ⓝ Ⓣ
Ⓢ Ⓒ Ⓓ ②	Ⓒ Ⓓ ②	⑥ ⑦ ⑧ ⑨ ⑩	Ⓠ Ⓖ Ⓟ
Ⓒ Ⓢ Ⓛ ⒜ⓝ Ⓜ	Ⓢ Ⓛ ⒜ⓝ Ⓜ	⑪ ⑫	ⓃⓋ Ⓧ Ⓞ Ⓦ ⒹⓅ Ⓐ Ⓑ

46

Who	To Whom	What	How
Ⓡ Ⓣ Ⓐ Ⓥ	Ⓣ Ⓐ Ⓥ	① ② ③ ④ ⑤	Ⓗ Ⓤ Ⓝ Ⓣ
Ⓢ Ⓒ Ⓓ ②	Ⓒ Ⓓ ②	⑥ ⑦ ⑧ ⑨ ⑩	Ⓠ Ⓖ Ⓟ
Ⓒ Ⓢ Ⓛ ⒜ⓝ Ⓜ	Ⓢ Ⓛ ⒜ⓝ Ⓜ	⑪ ⑫	ⓃⓋ Ⓧ Ⓞ Ⓦ ⒹⓅ Ⓐ Ⓑ

47

Who	To Whom	What	How
Ⓡ Ⓣ Ⓐ Ⓥ	Ⓣ Ⓐ Ⓥ	① ② ③ ④ ⑤	Ⓗ Ⓤ Ⓝ Ⓣ
Ⓢ Ⓒ Ⓓ ②	Ⓒ Ⓓ ②	⑥ ⑦ ⑧ ⑨ ⑩	Ⓠ Ⓖ Ⓟ
Ⓒ Ⓢ Ⓛ ⒜ⓝ Ⓜ	Ⓢ Ⓛ ⒜ⓝ Ⓜ	⑪ ⑫	ⓃⓋ Ⓧ Ⓞ Ⓦ ⒹⓅ Ⓐ Ⓑ

48

Who	To Whom	What	How
Ⓡ Ⓣ Ⓐ Ⓥ	Ⓣ Ⓐ Ⓥ	① ② ③ ④ ⑤	Ⓗ Ⓤ Ⓝ Ⓣ
Ⓢ Ⓒ Ⓓ ②	Ⓒ Ⓓ ②	⑥ ⑦ ⑧ ⑨ ⑩	Ⓠ Ⓖ Ⓟ
Ⓒ Ⓢ Ⓛ ⒜ⓝ Ⓜ	Ⓢ Ⓛ ⒜ⓝ Ⓜ	⑪ ⑫	ⓃⓋ Ⓧ Ⓞ Ⓦ ⒹⓅ Ⓐ Ⓑ

49

Who	To Whom	What	How
Ⓡ Ⓣ Ⓐ Ⓥ	Ⓣ Ⓐ Ⓥ	① ② ③ ④ ⑤	Ⓗ Ⓤ Ⓝ Ⓣ
Ⓢ Ⓒ Ⓓ ②	Ⓒ Ⓓ ②	⑥ ⑦ ⑧ ⑨ ⑩	Ⓠ Ⓖ Ⓟ
Ⓒ Ⓢ Ⓛ ⒜ⓝ Ⓜ	Ⓢ Ⓛ ⒜ⓝ Ⓜ	⑪ ⑫	ⓃⓋ Ⓧ Ⓞ Ⓦ ⒹⓅ Ⓐ Ⓑ

50

Who	To Whom	What	How
Ⓡ Ⓣ Ⓐ Ⓥ	Ⓣ Ⓐ Ⓥ	① ② ③ ④ ⑤	Ⓗ Ⓤ Ⓝ Ⓣ
Ⓢ Ⓒ Ⓓ ②	Ⓒ Ⓓ ②	⑥ ⑦ ⑧ ⑨ ⑩	Ⓠ Ⓖ Ⓟ
Ⓒ Ⓢ Ⓛ ⒜ⓝ Ⓜ	Ⓢ Ⓛ ⒜ⓝ Ⓜ	⑪ ⑫	ⓃⓋ Ⓧ Ⓞ Ⓦ ⒹⓅ Ⓐ Ⓑ

51

Who	To Whom	What	How
Ⓡ Ⓣ Ⓐ Ⓥ	Ⓣ Ⓐ Ⓥ	① ② ③ ④ ⑤	Ⓗ Ⓤ Ⓝ Ⓣ
Ⓢ Ⓒ Ⓓ ②	Ⓒ Ⓓ ②	⑥ ⑦ ⑧ ⑨ ⑩	Ⓠ Ⓖ Ⓟ
Ⓒ Ⓢ Ⓛ ⒜ⓝ Ⓜ	Ⓢ Ⓛ ⒜ⓝ Ⓜ	⑪ ⑫	ⓃⓋ Ⓧ Ⓞ Ⓦ ⒹⓅ Ⓐ Ⓑ

52

Who	To Whom	What	How
Ⓡ Ⓣ Ⓐ Ⓥ	Ⓣ Ⓐ Ⓥ	① ② ③ ④ ⑤	Ⓗ Ⓤ Ⓝ Ⓣ
Ⓢ Ⓒ Ⓓ ②	Ⓒ Ⓓ ②	⑥ ⑦ ⑧ ⑨ ⑩	Ⓠ Ⓖ Ⓟ
Ⓒ Ⓢ Ⓛ ⒜ⓝ Ⓜ	Ⓢ Ⓛ ⒜ⓝ Ⓜ	⑪ ⑫	ⓃⓋ Ⓧ Ⓞ Ⓦ ⒹⓅ Ⓐ Ⓑ

53

Who	To Whom	What	How
Ⓡ Ⓣ Ⓐ Ⓥ	Ⓣ Ⓐ Ⓥ	① ② ③ ④ ⑤	Ⓗ Ⓤ Ⓝ Ⓣ
Ⓢ Ⓒ Ⓓ ②	Ⓒ Ⓓ ②	⑥ ⑦ ⑧ ⑨ ⑩	Ⓠ Ⓖ Ⓟ
Ⓒ Ⓢ Ⓛ ⒜ⓝ Ⓜ	Ⓢ Ⓛ ⒜ⓝ Ⓜ	⑪ ⑫	ⓃⓋ Ⓧ Ⓞ Ⓦ ⒹⓅ Ⓐ Ⓑ

54

Who	To Whom	What	How
Ⓡ Ⓣ Ⓐ Ⓥ	Ⓣ Ⓐ Ⓥ	① ② ③ ④ ⑤	Ⓗ Ⓤ Ⓝ Ⓣ
Ⓢ Ⓒ Ⓓ ②	Ⓒ Ⓓ ②	⑥ ⑦ ⑧ ⑨ ⑩	Ⓠ Ⓖ Ⓟ
Ⓒ Ⓢ Ⓛ ⒜ⓝ Ⓜ	Ⓢ Ⓛ ⒜ⓝ Ⓜ	⑪ ⑫	ⓃⓋ Ⓧ Ⓞ Ⓦ ⒹⓅ Ⓐ Ⓑ

55

Who	To Whom	What	How
Ⓡ Ⓣ Ⓐ Ⓥ	Ⓣ Ⓐ Ⓥ	① ② ③ ④ ⑤	Ⓗ Ⓤ Ⓝ Ⓣ
Ⓢ Ⓒ Ⓓ ②	Ⓒ Ⓓ ②	⑥ ⑦ ⑧ ⑨ ⑩	Ⓠ Ⓖ Ⓟ
Ⓒ Ⓢ Ⓛ ⒜ⓝ Ⓜ	Ⓢ Ⓛ ⒜ⓝ Ⓜ	⑪ ⑫	ⓃⓋ Ⓧ Ⓞ Ⓦ ⒹⓅ Ⓐ Ⓑ

56

Who	To Whom	What	How
Ⓡ Ⓣ Ⓐ Ⓥ	Ⓣ Ⓐ Ⓥ	① ② ③ ④ ⑤	Ⓗ Ⓤ Ⓝ Ⓣ
Ⓢ Ⓒ Ⓓ ②	Ⓒ Ⓓ ②	⑥ ⑦ ⑧ ⑨ ⑩	Ⓠ Ⓖ Ⓟ
Ⓒ Ⓢ Ⓛ ⒜ⓝ Ⓜ	Ⓢ Ⓛ ⒜ⓝ Ⓜ	⑪ ⑫	ⓃⓋ Ⓧ Ⓞ Ⓦ ⒹⓅ Ⓐ Ⓑ

57

Who	To Whom	What	How
Ⓡ Ⓣ Ⓐ Ⓥ	Ⓣ Ⓐ Ⓥ	① ② ③ ④ ⑤	Ⓗ Ⓤ Ⓝ Ⓣ
Ⓢ Ⓒ Ⓓ ②	Ⓒ Ⓓ ②	⑥ ⑦ ⑧ ⑨ ⑩	Ⓠ Ⓖ Ⓟ
Ⓒ Ⓢ Ⓛ ⒜ⓝ Ⓜ	Ⓢ Ⓛ ⒜ⓝ Ⓜ	⑪ ⑫	ⓃⓋ Ⓧ Ⓞ Ⓦ ⒹⓅ Ⓐ Ⓑ

58

Who	To Whom	What	How
Ⓡ Ⓣ Ⓐ Ⓥ	Ⓣ Ⓐ Ⓥ	① ② ③ ④ ⑤	Ⓗ Ⓤ Ⓝ Ⓣ
Ⓢ Ⓒ Ⓓ ②	Ⓒ Ⓓ ②	⑥ ⑦ ⑧ ⑨ ⑩	Ⓠ Ⓖ Ⓟ
Ⓒ Ⓢ Ⓛ ⒜ⓝ Ⓜ	Ⓢ Ⓛ ⒜ⓝ Ⓜ	⑪ ⑫	ⓃⓋ Ⓧ Ⓞ Ⓦ ⒹⓅ Ⓐ Ⓑ

59

Who	To Whom	What	How
Ⓡ Ⓣ Ⓐ Ⓥ	Ⓣ Ⓐ Ⓥ	① ② ③ ④ ⑤	Ⓗ Ⓤ Ⓝ Ⓣ
Ⓢ Ⓒ Ⓓ ②	Ⓒ Ⓓ ②	⑥ ⑦ ⑧ ⑨ ⑩	Ⓠ Ⓖ Ⓟ
Ⓒ Ⓢ Ⓛ ⒜ⓝ Ⓜ	Ⓢ Ⓛ ⒜ⓝ Ⓜ	⑪ ⑫	ⓃⓋ Ⓧ Ⓞ Ⓦ ⒹⓅ Ⓐ Ⓑ

60

Who	To Whom	What	How
Ⓡ Ⓣ Ⓐ Ⓥ	Ⓣ Ⓐ Ⓥ	① ② ③ ④ ⑤	Ⓗ Ⓤ Ⓝ Ⓣ
Ⓢ Ⓒ Ⓓ ②	Ⓒ Ⓓ ②	⑥ ⑦ ⑧ ⑨ ⑩	Ⓠ Ⓖ Ⓟ
Ⓒ Ⓢ Ⓛ ⒜ⓝ Ⓜ	Ⓢ Ⓛ ⒜ⓝ Ⓜ	⑪ ⑫	ⓃⓋ Ⓧ Ⓞ Ⓦ ⒹⓅ Ⓐ Ⓑ

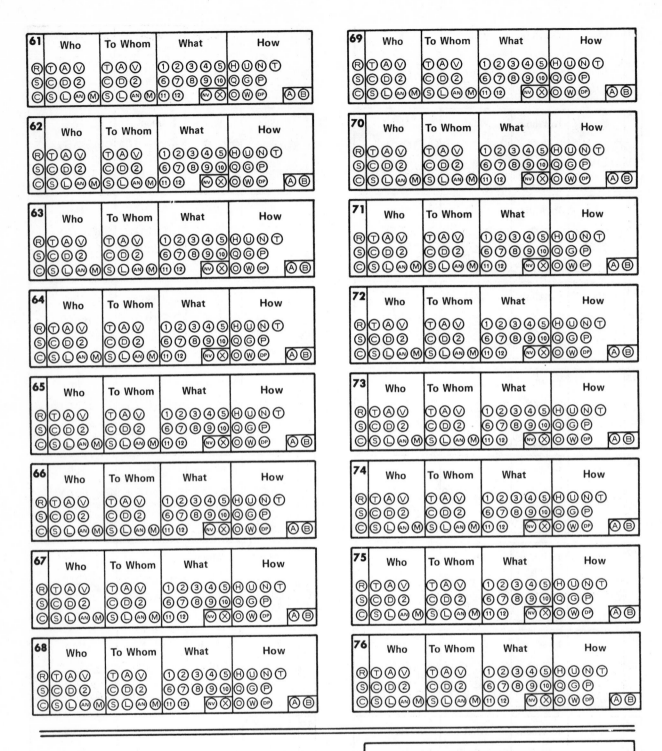

TIME STOPPED

Hour		Minute
⑧ ⑨ ⑩ ⑪ ⑫		⓪ ① ② | ⓪ ① ② ③ ④
① ② ③ ④ ⑤		③ ④ ⑤ | ⑤ ⑥ ⑦ ⑧ ⑨

ACTIVITY CHANGE

1 2 3 4 5 6 7 8 9 10 11
○ ○ ○ ○ ○ ○ ○ ○ ○ ○ ○

12 13 14 15 16 17 18 19 20 21 22
○ ○ ○ ○ ○ ○ ○ ○ ○ ○ ○

Appendix B

THE CLASSROOM CHECK LIST

    Classroom Check List Activities

    Classroom Check List Materials

    Example of Coded Classroom Check List

CLASSROOM OBSERVATION PROCEDURE

CLASSROOM CHECK LIST (be sure to code EVERYONE in the class)

	ONE CHILD	TWO CHILDREN	SMALL GROUPS	LARGE GROUPS
1. Snack, lunch	T ①②③ / A ①②③ / V ①②③ / i ①②③	T ①②③ / A ①②③ / V ①②③ / i ①②③	T ①②③④ / A ①②③④ / V ①②③④ / i ①②③④	T ①② / A ①② / V ①② / i ①②
2. Group time	T ①②③ / A ①②③ / V ①②③ / i ①②③	T ①②③ / A ①②③ / V ①②③ / i ①②③	T ①②③④ / A ①②③④ / V ①②③④ / i ①②③④	T ①② / A ①② / V ①② / i ①②
3. Music Story / Dancing	T ①②③ / A ①②③ / V ①②③ / i ①②③	T ①②③ / A ①②③ / V ①②③ / i ①②③	T ①②③④ / A ①②③④ / V ①②③④ / i ①②③④	T ①② / A ①② / V ①② / i ①②
4. Arts, Crafts	T ①②③ / A ①②③ / V ①②③ / i ①②③	T ①②③ / A ①②③ / V ①②③ / i ①②③	T ①②③④ / A ①②③④ / V ①②③④ / i ①②③④	T ①② / A ①② / V ①② / i ①②
5. Table Games Guessing Games / Puzzles	T ①②③ / A ①②③ / V ①②③ / i ①②③	T ①②③ / A ①②③ / V ①②③ / i ①②③	T ①②③④ / A ①②③④ / V ①②③④ / i ①②③④	T ①② / A ①② / V ①② / i ①②
6. Math Numbers / Arithmetic	T ①②③ / A ①②③ / V ①②③ / i ①②③	T ①②③ / A ①②③ / V ①②③ / i ①②③	T ①②③④ / A ①②③④ / V ①②③④ / i ①②③④	T ①② / A ①② / V ①② / i ①②
7. Alphabet Reading / Lang. Development	T ①②③ / A ①②③ / V ①②③ / i ①②③	T ①②③ / A ①②③ / V ①②③ / i ①②③	T ①②③④ / A ①②③④ / V ①②③④ / i ①②③④	T ①② / A ①② / V ①② / i ①②
8. Social Studies / Geography	T ①②③ / A ①②③ / V ①②③ / i ①②③	T ①②③ / A ①②③ / V ①②③ / i ①②③	T ①②③④ / A ①②③④ / V ①②③④ / i ①②③④	T ①② / A ①② / V ①② / i ①②
9. Science / Natural World	T ①②③ / A ①②③ / V ①②③ / i ①②③	T ①②③ / A ①②③ / V ①②③ / i ①②③	T ①②③④ / A ①②③④ / V ①②③④ / i ①②③④	T ①② / A ①② / V ①② / i ①②
10. Sewing / Cooking / Pounding / Sawing	T ①②③ / A ①②③ / V ①②③ / i ①②③	T ①②③ / A ①②③ / V ①②③ / i ①②③	T ①②③④ / A ①②③④ / V ①②③④ / i ①②③④	T ①② / A ①② / V ①② / i ①②
11. Blocks / Trucks	T ①②③ / A ①②③ / V ①②③ / i ①②③	T ①②③ / A ①②③ / V ①②③ / i ①②③	T ①②③④ / A ①②③④ / V ①②③④ / i ①②③④	T ①② / A ①② / V ①② / i ①②
12. Dramatic Play / Dress-Up	T ①②③ / A ①②③ / V ①②③ / i ①②③	T ①②③ / A ①②③ / V ①②③ / i ①②③	T ①②③④ / A ①②③④ / V ①②③④ / i ①②③④	T ①② / A ①② / V ①② / i ①②
13. Active Play	T ①②③ / A ①②③ / V ①②③ / i ①②③	T ①②③ / A ①②③ / V ①②③ / i ①②③	T ①②③④ / A ①②③④ / V ①②③④ / i ①②③④	T ①② / A ①② / V ①② / i ①②
14. RELIABILITY SHEET ○				

Left-side list (adjacent to rows 6–9):

○ TV
○ Audio-Visual Materials
○ Exploratory Materials
○ Math and Science Equipment
○ Texts, Workbooks
○ Puzzles, Games

			ONE CHILD	TWO CHILDREN	SMALL GROUPS	LARGE GROUPS
15. Practical Skills Acquisition			T ①②③ A ①②③ v ①②③ i ①②③	T ①②③ A ①②③ v ①②③ i ①②③	T ①②③④ A ①②③④ v ①②③④ i ①②③④	T ①② A ①② v ①② i ①②
16. Observing			T ①②③ A ①②③ v ①②③ i ①②③	T ①②③ A ①②③ v ①②③ i ①②③	T ①②③④ A ①②③④ v ①②③④ i ①②③④	T ①② A ①② v ①② i ①②
17. Social Interaction	Ob [ⓒ ② Ⓢ]	Ⓣ Ⓐ Ⓥ	T ①②③ A ①②③ v ①②③ i ①②③	T ①②③ A ①②③ v ①②③ i ①②③	T ①②③④ A ①②③④ v ①②③④ i ①②③④	T ①② A ①② v ①② i ①②
18. Unoccupied Child			T ①②③ A ①②③ v ①②③ i ①②③	T ①②③ A ①②③ v ①②③ i ①②③	T ①②③④ A ①②③④ v ①②③④ i ①②③④	T ①② A ①② v ①② i ①②
19. Discipline			T ①②③ A ①②③ v ①②③ i ①②③	T ①②③ A ①②③ v ①②③ i ①②③	T ①②③④ A ①②③④ v ①②③④ i ①②③④	T ①② A ①② v ①② i ①②
20. Transitional Activities		Ⓣ Ⓐ Ⓥ	T ①②③ A ①②③ v ①②③ i ①②③	T ①②③ A ①②③ v ①②③ i ①②③	T ①②③④ A ①②③④ v ①②③④ i ①②③④	T ①② A ①② v ①② i ①②
21. Classroom Management		Ⓣ Ⓐ Ⓥ	T ①②③ A ①②③ v ①②③ i ①②③	T ①②③ A ①②③ v ①②③ i ①②③	T ①②③④ A ①②③④ v ①②③④ i ①②③④	T ①② A ①② v ①② i ①②
22. Out of Room		Ⓣ Ⓐ Ⓥ	T ①②③ A ①②③ v ①②③ i ①②③	T ①②③ A ①②③ v ①②③ i ①②③	T ①②③④ A ①②③④ v ①②③④ i ①②③④	T ①② A ①② v ①② i ①②

NUMBER OF ADULTS IN CLASSROOM ⓪ ① ② ③ ④ ⑤ ⑥ ⑦ ⑧ ⑨ ⑩

The Classroom Check List (CCL), or classroom "snapshot," is the second of three parts of the Classroom Observation Instrument. It precedes the Preamble and the Five-Minute Interaction and is coded four times an hour, just before each interaction recording.

A reproduction of the two CCL pages appears on pages 259-260.

The CCL records a picture of the distribution of adults and children within activities at a particular time. Essentially, it shows (1) activities occurring, (2) materials used within activities, (3) grouping patterns, (4) teacher and aide responsibilities, and (5) child independence.

The CCL records how teachers (T), aides (A), volunteers (V), and children spend their time during the day, with whom they spend it, and how often children are left to work independently (i). It consists of twenty-two activity categories in which a class might be routinely engaged during an ordinary day.

CLASSROOM CHECK LIST ACTIVITIES

The CCL activities are listed and defined as follows:

1. Snack, lunch—This activity refers to any and all eating.

2. Group time—This refers to nonacademic activities that usually involve the full group: morning activities (such as the pledge of allegiance), planning for the day or for a future event, sharing ideas or items ("Show and Tell"), resting after lunch, or watching television for entertainment rather than for curriculum-related work.

3. Story, Singing, Dancing—Activities in this category include telling a story, music and music-related activities, and dancing of any kind, by one person or by a group.

4. Arts, Crafts—These refer to activities that use arts and crafts materials and teach art concepts (composition) or art techniques (shading, use of brushes).

5. Guessing Games, Table Games, Puzzles—This category includes all games or puzzles in the classroom that are provided for the enjoyment of the children—tiddlywinks, jacks, checkers, and the like. Games and puzzles used for reading or math instruction are not recorded in this category.

Activities 6, 7, 8, and 9 are placed to the right of the column listing various materials and equipment that can be used in teaching the category subjects: TV; Audio-Visual Materials; Exploratory Materials; Math and Science Equipment; Text Books, Workbooks; and Puzzles, Games. See page 257 for definitions of these materials.

6. Arithmetic, Numbers, Math—This category refers to any activity involving numbers, computation, measurements or math concepts; e.g., comparing sizes, learning to change

money, telling time, reading scales, and so on.

7. Reading, Alphabet, Language Development—This category includes any activity directed to the process of teaching or learning language; e.g., letter recognition, reading, writing, speaking, phonics, grammar, and labeling.

8. Social Studies, Geography—This category includes any activities related to teaching or learning about peoples, life styles, cultural patterns, social environments, social roles, current events, countries, bodies of water, and so forth.

9. Science, Natural World—This category refers to activities involved with teaching or learning about the earth and its plants, animals, and minerals (caring for them, collecting them, comparing them) and about the basic concepts of physical science (sunshine and evaporation, rain and condensation, gravity, moonlight, stars and planets, and so on). Health and safety studies are also coded here.

10. Sewing, Cooking, Pounding, Sawing—Activities in this category involve teaching or learning about measurements, numbers, and proportions, or they may be used in exploratory activities. Real materials must be used.

11. Blocks, Trucks—This category involves using building blocks, trucks, and other small toys in free play.

12. Dramatic Play, Dress-up—These are activities in which individuals are playing make-believe or are pretending; they include puppet shows and plays.

13. Active play—This refers to classroom or outdoors play that is organized or permitted by the teacher as part of the classroom routine and is energetic rather than quiet or passive.

14. RELIABILITY SHEET—This circle is to be marked when two people code simultaneously in order to measure inter-observer reliability.

15. Practical Skills Acquisition—This category covers the instruction, practice, or self-learning of classroom-related or other practical skills, like operation of all kinds of equipment (projectors, phonographs, typewriters, brooms), personal grooming, dressing oneself, safety procedures, and the like.

16. Observing—This category is to be used for persons who are watching other people or activities: a teacher who is overseeing children in an activity, a child watching another group playing, and so on.

17. Social Interaction—This category applies to two or more persons who are not involved in activity but are interacting socially with one another, e.g., talking, whispering, laughing, hitting, hugging, or walking and holding hands. When a child or children attempt to interact with the observer during the coding of the CCL, the appropriate circle is also marked. If a teacher, aide, or volunteer are interacting with each other, the appropriate circles for them are marked.

18. Unoccupied Child—This refers to a child sitting or standing alone or wandering about with no evident purpose or goal. (Note, however, that a child observing is coded in Activity 16.)

19. Discipline—This category is coded when an adult is dis-

ciplining a child (scolding, spanking) or when a child is being punished, e.g., standing in a corner alone at the request of an adult.

20. Transitional Activities—This category applies to periods of time when adults and/or children are "between" activities or preparing for activities, e.g., getting coats on to go out, standing in line, and so on. It also includes going to the bathroom and washing hands.

21. Classroom Management—Activities in this category are daily, routine classroom activities or events—distributing materials, setting up equipment and furniture, taking roll, checking materials in cupboard, gathering up materials and equipment, correcting papers, and cleaning up.

22. Out of Room—If a person or group is temporarily out of the room—e.g., on an errand or on a field trip—this fact is coded in Activity 22.

NUMBER OF ADULTS IN CLASSROOM—This entry records the total number of adults (excluding SRI observers) included in the CCL.

CLASSROOM CHECK LIST MATERIALS

The six categories of materials listed on the CCL to the left of Activities 6 through 9—Arithmetic, Numbers, Math; Reading, Alphabet, Language Development; Social Studies, Geography; Science, Natural World—apply only to those four categories.

When the materials are used in one of these activities, the appropriate materials category, as well as the appropriate grouping, is coded. The following coded example shows a teacher with a small group in a science lesson using a microscope.

		ONE CHILD	TWO CHILDREN	SMALL GROUPS	LARGE GROUPS
○ TV	Numbers 6. Math Arithmetic	T ①②③ A ①②③ V ①②③ i ①②③	T ①②③ A ①②③ V ①②③ i ①②③	T ①②③④ A ①②③④ V ①②③④ i ①②③④	T ①② A ①② V ①② i ①②
○ Audio-Visual Materials ○ Exploratory Materials	7. Reading Alphabet Lang. Development	T ①②③ A ①②③ V ①②③ i ①②③	T ①②③ A ①②③ V ①②③ i ①②③	T ①②③④ A ①②③④ V ①②③④ i ①②③④	T ①② A ①② V ①② i ①②
● Math and Science Equipment	8. Social Studies Geography	T ①②③ A ①②③ V ①②③ i ①②③	T ①②③ A ①②③ V ①②③ i ①②③	T ①②③④ A ①②③④ V ①②③④ i ①②③④	T ①② A ①② V ①② i ①②
○ Texts, Workbooks ○ Puzzles, Games	9. Science Natural World	T ①②③ A ①②③ V ①②③ i ①②③	T ①②③ A ①②③ V ①②③ i ①②③	T ●②③④ A ①②③④ V ①②③④ i ①②③④	T ①② A ①② V ①② i ①②

Below are definitions of each of these materials categories and examples of how to code them:

TV—This includes any TV program whose content concerns any of the four subject areas (Activities 6, 7, 8, and 9).

Example: On "Sesame Street," Oscar is playing an alphabet game with Kermit. (Code TV and Activity 7.)

Audio-Visual Materials—This category includes any audiovisual equipment other than TV—record players, tape recorders, film strips, and earphones—that is used within these subject activities.

Example: The children are being shown a film strip on wildlife. (Code Audio-Visual Materials and Activity 9.)

Exploratory Materials—Materials in this category are those that are not included in other categories and that a child uses in self-learning (manipulation, experimentation, observation) or that an adult uses to teach any of the four subject areas. They can be nature objects (rocks, leaves, butterflies), sandpaper letters, charts, graphs, and clay.

Example: Each child has been given a pine cone to look at during a nature lesson. (Code Exploratory Materials and Activity 9.)

Math and Science Equipment—This includes equipment manufactured especially for science or math that is used within Activity 6 or 9. Some examples are: scales, weights and balances, magnifying glass, microscope, abacus.

Example: A teacher illustrates the principles of conservation with test tubes of varying sizes. (Code Math and Science Equipment and Activity 9.)

Texts, Workbooks—This includes printed materials specifically designed to teach any of the four subject areas through sequential or graduated lessons or chapters. Storybooks and magazines are also in the category.

Example: A child is doing an assignment in a math workbook. (Code Texts, Workbooks and Activity 6.)

Puzzles, Games—This category includes games or puzzles that drill or instruct in any of the four subject areas.

Example: Children are playing a game in which one child chooses a number from 1 to 20 and others must guess it by elimination. (Code Puzzles, Games and Activity 6.)

EXAMPLE OF CODED CLASSROOM CHECK LIST

On page 258 is a diagram of a classroom situation placing each child (C), teacher (T), aide (A), volunteer (V), and the observer (Ob), in various activities. This "snapshot" is coded on the CCL that follows and an explanation of the coding is given (Figure B.1).

Remember that all activities are occurring at the same time and that every person in the room is placed on the CCL, but in only one place; for example, a teacher moving from group to group is coded with only one of them. Going clockwise around the room, starting from the door through which the observer entered, the observer records each child and adult on the grid one time. This requires about sixty seconds.

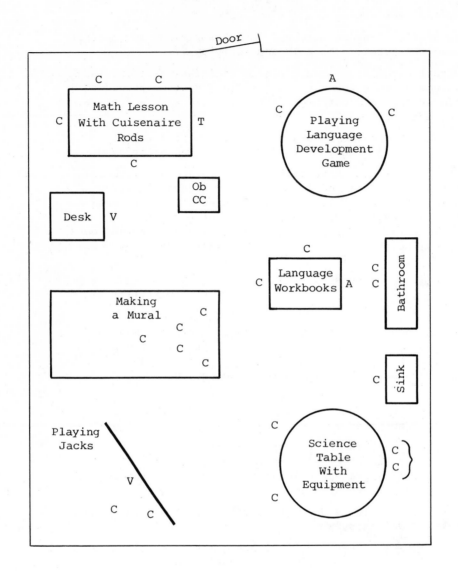

CLASSROOM OBSERVATION PROCEDURE

CLASSROOM CHECK LIST (be sure to code **EVERYONE** in the class)

		ONE CHILD	TWO CHILDREN	SMALL GROUPS	LARGE GROUPS
1. Snack, lunch	T	① ② ③	① ② ③	① ② ③ ④	① ②
	A	① ② ③	① ② ③	① ② ③ ④	① ②
	v	① ② ③	① ② ③	① ② ③ ④	① ②
	i	① ② ③	① ② ③	① ② ③ ④	① ②
2. Group time	T	① ② ③	① ② ③	① ② ③ ④	① ②
	A	① ② ③	① ② ③	① ② ③ ④	① ②
	v	① ② ③	① ② ③	① ② ③ ④	① ②
	i	① ② ③	① ② ③	① ② ③ ④	① ②
3. Story / Music / Dancing	T	① ② ③	① ② ③	① ② ③ ④	① ②
	A	① ② ③	① ② ③	① ② ③ ④	① ②
	v	① ② ③	① ② ③	① ② ③ ④	① ②
	i	① ② ③	① ② ③	① ② ③ ④	① ②
4. Arts, Crafts	T	① ② ③	① ② ③	① ② ③ ④	① ②
	A	① ② ③	① ② ③	① ② ③ ④	① ②
	v	① ② ③	① ② ③	① ② ③ ④	① ②
	i	① ② ③	① ② ③	● ② ③ ④	① ②
5. Guessing Games / Table Games / Puzzles	T	① ② ③	① ② ③	① ② ③ ④	① ②
	A	① ② ③	① ② ③	① ② ③ ④	① ②
	v	① ② ③	● ② ③	① ② ③ ④	① ②
	i	① ② ③	① ② ③	① ② ③ ④	① ②
6. Math: Numbers / Arithmetic	T	① ② ③	① ② ③	● ② ③ ④	① ②
	A	① ② ③	① ② ③	① ② ③ ④	① ②
	v	① ② ③	① ② ③	① ② ③ ④	① ②
	i	① ② ③	① ② ③	① ② ③ ④	① ②
7. Reading / Alphabet / Lang. Development	T	① ② ③	① ② ③	① ② ③ ④	① ②
	A	① ② ③	① ● ③	① ② ③ ④	① ②
	v	① ② ③	① ② ③	① ② ③ ④	① ②
	i	① ② ③	① ② ③	① ② ③ ④	① ②
8. Social Studies / Geography	T	① ② ③	① ② ③	① ② ③ ④	① ②
	A	① ② ③	① ② ③	① ② ③ ④	① ②
	v	① ② ③	① ② ③	① ② ③ ④	① ②
	i	① ② ③	① ② ③	① ② ③ ④	① ②
9. Science / Natural World	T	① ② ③	① ② ③	① ② ③ ④	① ②
	A	① ② ③	① ② ③	① ② ③ ④	① ②
	v	① ② ③	① ② ③	① ② ③ ④	① ②
	i	① ● ③	● ② ③	① ② ③ ④	① ②
10. Sewing / Cooking / Pounding / Sawing	T	① ② ③	① ② ③	① ② ③ ④	① ②
	A	① ② ③	① ② ③	① ② ③ ④	① ②
	v	① ② ③	① ② ③	① ② ③ ④	① ②
	i	① ② ③	① ② ③	① ② ③ ④	① ②
11. Blocks / Trucks	T	① ② ③	① ② ③	① ② ③ ④	① ②
	A	① ② ③	① ② ③	① ② ③ ④	① ②
	v	① ② ③	① ② ③	① ② ③ ④	① ②
	i	① ② ③	① ② ③	① ② ③ ④	① ②
12. Dramatic Play / Dress-Up	T	① ② ③	① ② ③	① ② ③ ④	① ②
	A	① ② ③	① ② ③	① ② ③ ④	① ②
	v	① ② ③	① ② ③	① ② ③ ④	① ②
	i	① ② ③	① ② ③	① ② ③ ④	① ②
13. Active Play	T	① ② ③	① ② ③	① ② ③ ④	① ②
	A	① ② ③	① ② ③	① ② ③ ④	① ②
	v	① ② ③	① ② ③	① ② ③ ④	① ②
	i	① ② ③	① ② ③	① ② ③ ④	① ②

14. RELIABILITY SHEET ○

Left-hand list (associated with items 6–9):

○ TV
○ Audio-Visual Materials
○ Exploratory Materials
● Math and Science Equipment
● Texts, Workbooks
● Puzzles, Games

Figure B.1

		ONE CHILD	TWO CHILDREN	SMALL GROUPS	LARGE GROUPS
15. Practical Skills Acquisition		T ①②③ / A ①②③ / v ①②③ / i ①②③	T ①②③ / A ①②③ / v ①②③ / i ①②③	T ①②③④ / A ①②③④ / v ①②③④ / i ①②③④	T ①② / A ①② / v ①② / i ①②
16. Observing		T ①②③ / A ①②③ / v ①②③ / i ①②③	T ①②③ / A ①②③ / v ①②③ / i ①②③	T ①②③④ / A ①②③④ / v ①②③④ / i ①②③④	T ①② / A ①② / v ①② / i ①②
17. Social Interaction	Ob [©] ● [Ⓢ] Ⓣ Ⓐ Ⓥ	T ①②③ / A ①②③ / v ①②③ / i ①②③	T ①②③ / A ①②③ / v ①②③ / i ①②③	T ①②③④ / A ①②③④ / v ①②③④ / i ①②③④	T ①② / A ①② / v ①② / i ①②
18. Unoccupied Child		T ①②③ / A ①②③ / v ①②③ / i ①②③	T ①②③ / A ①②③ / v ①②③ / i ①②③	T ①②③④ / A ①②③④ / v ①②③④ / i ①②③④	T ①② / A ①② / v ①② / i ①②
19. Discipline		T ①②③ / A ①②③ / v ①②③ / i ①②③	T ①②③ / A ①②③ / v ①②③ / i ①②③	T ①②③④ / A ①②③④ / v ①②③④ / i ①②③④	T ①② / A ①② / v ①② / i ①②
20. Transitional Activities	Ⓣ Ⓐ Ⓥ	T ①②③ / A ①②③ / v ①②③ / i ①②●	T ①②③ / A ①②③ / v ①②③ / i ①②③	T ①②③④ / A ①②③④ / v ①②③④ / i ①②③④	T ①② / A ①② / v ①② / i ①②
21. Classroom Management	Ⓣ Ⓐ ●	T ①②③ / A ①②③ / v ①②③ / i ①②③	T ①②③ / A ①②③ / v ①②③ / i ①②③	T ①②③④ / A ①②③④ / v ①②③④ / i ①②③④	T ①② / A ①② / v ①② / i ①②
22. Out of Room	Ⓣ Ⓐ Ⓥ	T ①②③ / A ①②③ / v ①②③ / i ①②③	T ①②③ / A ①②③ / v ①②③ / i ①②③	T ①②③④ / A ①②③④ / v ①②③④ / i ①②③④	T ①② / A ①② / v ①② / i ①②

NUMBER OF ADULTS IN CLASSROOM ⓪ ① ② ③ ④ ● ⑥ ⑦ ⑧ ⑨ ⑩

In Activity 4, Arts and Crafts, the ① circle is filled in next to i (independent) in the Small Groups column. This refers to the five children who are making a mural in the diagram—one small group without an adult in an arts and crafts activity.

In Activity 5, Guessing Games, Table Games, Puzzles, the ① circle is filled in next to V (volunteer) in the Two Children column. This refers to the group of two children and a volunteer who are playing jacks.

In Activity 6, Arithmetic, Numbers, Math, the ① circle is filled in next to T (teacher) in the column headed Small Groups. This means that one teacher is with one small group. For the same item, the circle next to Math and Science Equipment is filled in to indicate that the group is doing a math lesson with the aid of concrete objects like Cuisenaire rods.

In Activity 7, Reading, Alphabet, Language Development, the ② circle is filled in next to A (aide) in the Two Children column. This means that two aides are each working with a group of two children in a language lesson. The circles next to Texts, Workbooks, and Puzzles, Games are also filled in to indicate that the groups are using books and games.

In Activity 9, Science, Natural World, the ② circle next to i (independent) in the One Child column is marked. This means that two children are working independently in a science activity; that is, two instances of one child working independently. In the Two Children column, the ① circle next to i is filled in, indicating that two children are working together in some kind of science activity, that is, one instance of two children working together without an adult. The circle next to Math and Science Equipment is also filled in because the diagram indicates that the children are using science equipment.

In Activity 17, Social Interaction, the ②circle is filled in next to Ob, indicating that two children are attempting to talk with the observer at the moment she is coding the CCL.

In Activity 20, Transitional Activities, the ③circle is marked next to the i (independent) in the One Child column. This means that three children are engaged independently in transitional activities. (In the diagram, one child is at the sink and two children are waiting in line at the bathroom.)

In Activity 21, Classroom Management, the single V is filled in, meaning that a volunteer without any children is performing some kind of management task. In the diagram, a volunteer is at a desk, perhaps correcting papers.

Finally, the ⑤circle following Number of Adults in Classroom is filled in. This indicates that five adults—one teacher, two aides, and two volunteers—are coded on the CCL. The observer is not included in this number.

EXERCISE B.1 Here is a picture of an open classroom. Record each person in the picture, going clockwise around the room, or on the CCL grid that follows.
Be certain each adult and child is accounted for. When you have finished,
check your codes with the correct ones, given on pages 265-266.

CLASSROOM CHECK LIST (be sure to code **EVERYONE** in the class)

	ONE CHILD	TWO CHILDREN	SMALL GROUPS	LARGE GROUPS
1. Snack, lunch	T ①②③ A ①②③ v ①②③ i ①②③	T ①②③ A ①②③ v ①②③ i ①②③	T ①②③④ A ①②③④ v ①②③④ i ①②③④	T ①② A ①② v ①② i ①②
2. Group time	T ①②③ A ①②③ v ①②③ i ①②③	T ①②③ A ①②③ v ①②③ i ①②③	T ①②③④ A ①②③④ v ①②③④ i ①②③④	T ①② A ①② v ①② i ①②
3. Music — Story / Music / Dancing	T ①②③ A ①②③ v ①②③ i ①②③	T ①②③ A ①②③ v ①②③ i ①②③	T ①②③④ A ①②③④ v ①②③④ i ①②③④	T ①② A ①② v ①② i ①②
4. Arts, Crafts	T ①②③ A ①②③ v ①②③ i ①②③	T ①②③ A ①②③ v ①②③ i ①②③	T ①②③④ A ①②③④ v ①②③④ i ①②③④	T ①② A ①② v ①② i ①②
5. Table Games — Guessing Games / Table Games / Puzzles	T ①②③ A ①②③ v ①②③ i ①②③	T ①②③ A ①②③ v ①②③ i ①②③	T ①②③④ A ①②③④ v ①②③④ i ①②③④	T ①② A ①② v ①② i ①②
6. Math — Numbers / Math / Arithmetic	T ①②③ A ①②③ v ①②③ i ①②③	T ①②③ A ①②③ v ①②③ i ①②③	T ①②③④ A ①②③④ v ①②③④ i ①②③④	T ①② A ①② v ①② i ①②
7. Alphabet — Reading / Alphabet / Lang. Development	T ①②③ A ①②③ v ①②③ i ①②③	T ①②③ A ①②③ v ①②③ i ①②③	T ①②③④ A ①②③④ v ①②③④ i ①②③④	T ①② A ①② v ①② i ①②
8. Social Studies / Geography	T ①②③ A ①②③ v ①②③ i ①②③	T ①②③ A ①②③ v ①②③ i ①②③	T ①②③④ A ①②③④ v ①②③④ i ①②③④	T ①② A ①② v ①② i ①②
9. Science / Natural World	T ①②③ A ①②③ v ①②③ i ①②③	T ①②③ A ①②③ v ①②③ i ①②③	T ①②③④ A ①②③④ v ①②③④ i ①②③④	T ①② A ①② v ①② i ①②
10. Sewing / Cooking / Pounding / Sawing	T ①②③ A ①②③ v ①②③ i ①②③	T ①②③ A ①②③ v ①②③ i ①②③	T ①②③④ A ①②③④ v ①②③④ i ①②③④	T ①② A ①② v ①② i ①②
11. Blocks / Trucks	T ①②③ A ①②③ v ①②③ i ①②③	T ①②③ A ①②③ v ①②③ i ①②③	T ①②③④ A ①②③④ v ①②③④ i ①②③④	T ①② A ①② v ①② i ①②
12. Dramatic Play / Dress-Up	T ①②③ A ①②③ v ①②③ i ①②③	T ①②③ A ①②③ v ①②③ i ①②③	T ①②③④ A ①②③④ v ①②③④ i ①②③④	T ①② A ①② v ①② i ①②
13. Active Play	T ①②③ A ①②③ v ①②③ i ①②③	T ①②③ A ①②③ v ①②③ i ①②③	T ①②③④ A ①②③④ v ①②③④ i ①②③④	T ①② A ①② v ①② i ①②
14. RELIABILITY SHEET ○				

Sub-list (associated with items 6–9):

○ TV
○ Audio-Visual Materials
○ Exploratory Materials
○ Math and Science Equipment
○ Texts, Workbooks
○ Puzzles, Games

Exercise B.1

		ONE CHILD	TWO CHILDREN	SMALL GROUPS	LARGE GROUPS
15. Practical Skills Acquisition		T ①②③	T ①②③	T ①②③④	T ①②
		A ①②③	A ①②③	A ①②③④	A ①②
		v ①②③	v ①②③	v ①②③④	v ①②
		i ①②③	i ①②③	i ①②③④	i ①②
16. Observing		T ①②③	T ①②③	T ①②③④	T ①②
		A ①②③	A ①②③	A ①②③④	A ①②
		v ①②③	v ①②③	v ①②③④	v ①②
		i ①②③	i ①②③	i ①②③④	i ①②
17. Social Interaction Ob [Ⓒ ② Ⓢ]	Ⓣ Ⓐ Ⓥ	T ①②③	T ①②③	T ①②③④	T ①②
		A ①②③	A ①②③	A ①②③④	A ①②
		v ①②③	v ①②③	v ①②③④	v ①②
		i ①②③	i ①②③	i ①②③④	i ①②
18. Unoccupied Child		T ①②③	T ①②③	T ①②③④	T ①②
		A ①②③	A ①②③	A ①②③④	A ①②
		v ①②③	v ①②③	v ①②③④	v ①②
		i ①②③	i ①②③	i ①②③④	i ①②
19. Discipline		T ①②③	T ①②③	T ①②③④	T ①②
		A ①②③	A ①②③	A ①②③④	A ①②
		v ①②③	v ①②③	v ①②③④	v ①②
		i ①②③	i ①②③	i ①②③④	i ①②
20. Transitional Activities	Ⓣ Ⓐ Ⓥ	T ①②③	T ①②③	T ①②③④	T ①②
		A ①②③	A ①②③	A ①②③④	A ①②
		v ①②③	v ①②③	v ①②③④	v ①②
		i ①②③	i ①②③	i ①②③④	i ①②
21. Classroom Management	Ⓣ Ⓐ Ⓥ	T ①②③	T ①②③	T ①②③④	T ①②
		A ①②③	A ①②③	A ①②③④	A ①②
		v ①②③	v ①②③	v ①②③④	v ①②
		i ①②③	i ①②③	i ①②③④	i ①②
22. Out of Room	Ⓣ Ⓐ Ⓥ	T ①②③	T ①②③	T ①②③④	T ①②
		A ①②③	A ①②③	A ①②③④	A ①②
		v ①②③	v ①②③	v ①②③④	v ①②
		i ①②③	i ①②③	i ①②③④	i ①②

NUMBER OF ADULTS IN CLASSROOM   ⓪ ① ② ③ ④ ⑤ ⑥ ⑦ ⑧ ⑨ ⑩

CLASSROOM CHECK LIST (be sure to code **EVERYONE** in the class)

	ONE CHILD	TWO CHILDREN	SMALL GROUPS	LARGE GROUPS
1. Snack, lunch	T ①②③ / A ①②③ / v ①②③ / i ①②③	T ①②③ / A ①②③ / v ①②③ / i ①②③	T ①②③④ / A ①②③④ / v ①②③④ / i ①②③④	T ①② / A ①② / v ①② / i ①②
2. Group time	T ①②③ / A ①②③ / v ①②③ / i ①②③	T ①②③ / A ①②③ / v ①②③ / i ①②③	T ①②③④ / A ①②③④ / v ①②③④ / i ①②③④	T ①② / A ①② / v ①② / i ①②
3. Story, Music, Dancing	T ①②③ / A ①②③ / v ①②③ / i ●②③	T ①②③ / A ①②③ / v ①②③ / i ①②③	T ①②③④ / A ①②③④ / v ①②③④ / i ①②③④	T ①② / A ①② / v ①② / i ①②
4. Arts, Crafts	T ①②③ / A ①②③ / v ①②③ / i ①②③	T ①②③ / A ①②③ / v ①②③ / i ①②③	T ①②③④ / A ①②③④ / v ①②③④ / i ①②③④	T ①② / A ①② / v ①② / i ①②
5. Guessing Games, Table Games, Puzzles	T ①②③ / A ①②③ / v ①②③ / i ①②③	T ①②③ / A ①②③ / v ①②③ / i ①②③	T ①②③④ / A ①②③④ / v ①②③④ / i ①②③④	T ①② / A ①② / v ①② / i ①②
6. Math — Numbers, Arithmetic	T ①②③ / A ①②③ / v ①②③ / i ①②③	T ①②③ / A ①②③ / v ①②③ / i ①②③	T ●②③④ / A ①②③④ / v ①②③④ / i ①②③④	T ①② / A ①② / v ①② / i ①②
7. Reading, Alphabet, Lang. Development	T ①②③ / A ①②③ / v ①②③ / i ①②③	T ①②③ / A ①②③ / v ①②③ / i ①②③	T ①②③④ / A ●②③④ / v ①②③④ / i ①②③④	T ①② / A ①② / v ①② / i ①②
8. Social Studies, Geography	T ①②③ / A ①②③ / v ①②③ / i ①②③	T ①②③ / A ①②③ / v ①②③ / i ①②③	T ①②③④ / A ①②③④ / v ①②③④ / i ①②③④	T ①② / A ①② / v ①② / i ①②
9. Science, Natural World	T ①②③ / A ①②③ / v ①②③ / i ①②③	T ①②③ / A ①②③ / v ①②③ / i ①②③	T ①②③④ / A ●②③④ / v ①②③④ / i ①②③④	T ①② / A ①② / v ①② / i ①②
10. Sewing, Cooking, Pounding, Sawing	T ①②③ / A ①②③ / v ①②③ / i ①②③	T ①②③ / A ①②③ / v ①②③ / i ①②③	T ①②③④ / A ①②③④ / v ①②③④ / i ①②③④	T ①② / A ①② / v ①② / i ①②
11. Blocks, Trucks	T ①②③ / A ①②③ / v ①②③ / i ①②③	T ①②③ / A ①②③ / v ①②③ / i ●②③	T ①②③④ / A ①②③④ / v ①②③④ / i ①②③④	T ①② / A ①② / v ①② / i ①②
12. Dramatic Play, Dress-Up	T ①②③ / A ①②③ / v ①②③ / i ①②③	T ①②③ / A ①②③ / v ①②③ / i ①②③	T ①②③④ / A ①②③④ / v ①②③④ / i ①②③④	T ①② / A ①② / v ①② / i ①②
13. Active Play	T ①②③ / A ①②③ / v ①②③ / i ①②③	T ①②③ / A ①②③ / v ①②③ / i ①②③	T ①②③④ / A ①②③④ / v ①②③④ / i ①②③④	T ①② / A ①② / v ①② / i ①②
14. RELIABILITY SHEET	○			

Left-side checklist (between items 6 and 9):

○ TV
○ Audio-Visual Materials
○ Exploratory Materials
● Math and Science Equipment
● Texts, Workbooks
○ Puzzles, Games

			ONE CHILD	TWO CHILDREN	SMALL GROUPS	LARGE GROUPS
15. Practical Skills Acquisition			T ①②③	T ①②③	T ①②③④	T ①②
			A ①②③	A ①②③	A ①②③④	A ①②
			V ①②③	V ①②③	V ①②③④	V ①②
			i ①②③	i ①②③	i ①②③④	i ①②
16. Observing			T ①②③	T ①②③	T ①②③④	T ①②
			A ①②③	A ①②③	A ①②③④	A ①②
			V ①②③	V ①②③	V ①②③④	V ①②
			i ①②③	i ①②③	i ①②③④	i ①②
17. Social Interaction	Ob ⎡©⎤ ⎢②⎥ ⎣Ⓢ⎦	Ⓣ Ⓐ Ⓥ	T ①②③	T ①②③	T ①②③④	T ①②
			A ①②③	A ①②③	A ①②③④	A ①②
			V ①②③	V ①②③	V ①②③④	V ①②
			i ①②③	i ①②③	i ①②③④	i ①②
18. Unoccupied Child			T ①②③	T ①②③	T ①②③④	T ①②
			A ①②③	A ①②③	A ①②③④	A ①②
			V ①②③	V ①②③	V ①②③④	V ①②
			i ①②③	i ①②③	i ①②③④	i ①②
19. Discipline			T ①②③	T ①②③	T ①②③④	T ①②
			A ①②③	A ①②③	A ①②③④	A ①②
			V ①②③	V ①②③	V ①②③④	V ①②
			i ①②③	i ①②③	i ①②③④	i ①②
20. Transitional Activities		Ⓣ Ⓐ Ⓥ	T ①②③	T ①②③	T ①②③④	T ①②
			A ①②③	A ①②③	A ①②③④	A ①②
			V ①②③	V ①②③	V ①②③④	V ①②
			i ①②③	i ①②③	i ①②③④	i ①②
21. Classroom Management		Ⓣ Ⓐ Ⓥ	T ①②③	T ①②③	T ①②③④	T ①②
			A ①②③	A ①②③	A ①②③④	A ①②
			V ①②③	V ①②③	V ①②③④	V ①②
			i ①②③	i ①②③	i ①②③④	i ①②
22. Out of Room		Ⓣ Ⓐ Ⓥ	T ①②③	T ①②③	T ①②③④	T ①②
			A ①②③	A ①②③	A ①②③④	A ①②
			V ①②③	V ①②③	V ①②③④	V ①②
			i ①②③	i ①②③	i ①②③④	i ①②

NUMBER OF ADULTS IN CLASSROOM ⓪ ① ② ● ④ ⑤ ⑥ ⑦ ⑧ ⑨ ⑩

Appendix C

THE INTERACTION CODES AND STUDENT EXERCISES

The Who Column

The To Whom Column

The What Column

The How Column

The R, S, and C Codes

Training Exercises

The Who and To Whom codes are used to indicate the participants in an interaction. These codes make it possible to designate the person or group of persons initiating or receiving an action.

The twelve What codes refer to the action categories; these are the ones that have survived several years of use and review. They preserve the distinctions that seem to be important in describing varying classroom processes.

The How categories are used in conjunction with the What codes to specify emotional or descriptive aspects of an interaction and to define strategies used to control behavior.

Operational definitions of the codes used in the classroom observation instrument are given in the following subsections.

THE WHO COLUMN

The Who column indicates who is doing the talking or the action:

Code	Code Usage
T - Teacher	The one person who is ultimately responsible for the everyday conduct of the classroom.
A - Aide	Adults who work in the classroom regularly and are paid by the school district.
V - Volunteer	Any other adult who works in the classroom, such as a parent.
C - Child	When the focus of an observation is a specific child, that child is "C" (all other children are "D," Different Child). When the focus is an adult, C refers to any individual child with whom the adult is interacting.
D - Different Child	A second child in an interaction when the focus child, C, is being observed.
2 - Two Children	
S - Small Group	Three to eight children.
L - Large Group	More than eight children.
An - Animal	Any live animal in the classroom (including birds and fish).
M - Machine	Record player, tape recorder, TV, and so on.

THE TO WHOM COLUMN

The To Whom column indicates the person, group, or machine that is being talked to or interacted with: These codes are the same as the codes for the Who Column.

THE WHAT COLUMN

It is assumed that all interactions coded in the What column are verbal unless marked NV (nonverbal). (NOTE: NV and certain codes from the How column are used in the examples below. See the How column definitions on pages 273-275).

Code	Code Usage
1 - Command or Request	Code 1 asks for a response free of argument or speculation. There is one expected, acceptable response that is to be carried out, verbally or nonverbally: Code 1A refers to academic information.

- "Open the door, please." TC1
- "Read this sentence." TC1A
- "Draw a line." TC1
- "Zip me up." CT1
- "Gimme that book." CD1

1Q - Direct Question	Code 1Q questions are those that ask for direct recall of material already learned, or anticipate a specific or automatic response or a yes-or-no answer. Code 1Q questions elicit the following responses: statements of preference, statements of fact, itemizing, classifying, and definitions.

- "In the story, did you like Mr. Brown?" TC1Q
- "What is one-half and one-half?" CD1QA
- "What was on the list of mountain climbing equipment we made yesterday?" TL1Q
- "If you had two pears and three apples, what would you have five of?" TS1Q
- "Is this dog a Great Dane or a St. Bernard?" CD1Q
- "What does this word mean?" TC1QA

2 - Open-Ended Question	Code 2 questions are those that allow a free expression of ideas or feelings and invite opinions. Code 2 questions encourage responses that require: interpreting ideas, cause and effect establishing relationships, making comparisons, reasoning, applying previously learned material to a new situation, and describing a process. Code 2 can be a request for information not a question.

Code 2 may be phrased as a statement as well as a question.

- "What do you think of the Eskimo way of life?" TC2
- "Why did you like Mr. Brown in the story?" CD2
- "State the problem in your own words." TC2
- "Tell me how an electric train works." CD2
- "In what ways are the things in this picture alike?" TC2
- "Use these sticks to see if you can find all the different groupings that add up to ten." TC2A

3 – Response	Code 3 is a response to a command (Code 1) or a question (Code 1Q, 2), or is corrective (Code 9).

When the response is concerned with basic academic skills, Code 3 is used with A in the How column; it is used with B in the How column when it follows acknowledgment, praise, or a corrective for behavior.

- "Read the next sentence, Jimmy."   TC1A
  "The dog chased the ball."   CT3A

- "Will you add two and two?"   TC1QA
  "Two and two makes four."   CT3A

- "Guess what I've brought for you."   CT2
  "Flowers—or an apple."   CT3

- "Please shut the door."   TC1
  The child shuts the door (nonverbal).   CT3NV

- "Did you save my painting?"   CT1Q
  "Yes, it's hanging up."   TC3

- "We can't hear when you do that, Alice."   TC9GB
  Alice is quiet.   CT3NVB

4 – Instruction, Explanation	Code 4 is used when a teacher or child is:

(a) Verbally giving new information to others, reviewing lessons, or explaining rules of behavior.

(b) Nonverbally engaged in demonstrating or in an activity that is productive, organized, or exploratory (including playing with games, blocks, and dolls, and water play).

When the interaction is concerned with the basic skills of reading, writing, spelling, and computation, Code 4 is used with A in the How column. If an object is being used in self-instruction, Code 4 is used with O in the How column.

- "Flowers grow everywhere. There are many different
  kinds of flowers and they grow in many shapes and
  colors."   CL4

- "Here is a game called 'Community People.' You play by
  matching the pictures on your card with those on the
  large card."   TS4

- "This is how I'd like you to do these exercises:
  First, fold your paper in half like this. Then in
  half again like this. Then put the first problem in
  this square and the second here."   TS4

- "I made my puppet out of an old sock and I made the
  eyes from pieces of crayon (holding puppet)."   CS4

- "You have to add three to seven here and carry the
  one over to this column; then add those."   CD4A

- Child learning the shape of a letter by running a
  finger over a sandpaper letter on a card. (NOTE:
  When the action involves only one person, the Who
  and To Whom columns are coded with the same letter.)   CC4NVOA

- Child reading aloud to a small group of children.   CS4A

- A child building a block tower.   CC4NVO

- Child reading to himself.   CC4NVA

5 – General Comments/ General Action	Greetings, personal compliments, social or non-task-related comments and remarks. Irrelevant remarks are also coded 5.	

- "Hello." "Good morning."   TC5
- "That's a pretty dress."   CT5
- "I can't stand you today."   CD5N

Classroom management activities, general movement about the room, mild horseplay, eating, napping, are coded 5NV. (NOTE: 5NV is coded only if there is no talking along with the general action; otherwise, the observer codes the kind of remark that is accompanying the general action.)

- Child setting the table for lunch or snack.   CC5NV
- Two children jostling in a line   225NV
- Teacher walking around the room.   TT5NVX

6 – Task-Related Comment

Code 6 is used for a statement about the activity or problem at hand.

- Two children making clay animals:

  C: "This clay makes my hands sticky."   CD6
  D: "The horn won't stay on my cow."   DC6
  C: "Mine doesn't have a horn."   CD6

- Teacher is conducting a Show-and-Tell period:

  T: "What did you do over the weekend?"   TL1Q
  C: "I went to the zoo with my daddy."   CT3
  D: "The tigers are really big."   DT6
  C: "The elephants are bigger."   CD6

- Three children are working with metal washers and a balance:

  C: "I think three big washers will balance four small ones." C26A
  D: "I'll try it."   DC6A
  D: "I sure like your cowboy boots."   DC5
  C: "It balanced!"   C26A

7 – Acknowledge

An indication that a response, product, or behavior is recognized or agreed with is coded 7. Another form of acknowledgment is to repeat someone else's statement immediately.

Code 7 with A in the How column is used to indicate acknowledgment of a response having to do with academic subject matter; it is used with B in the How column to indicate acknowledgment of a response having to do with behavior.

- Nodding (nonverbal) to indicate that a painting is acceptable.   TC7NV
- "Yes, that's the right way to knead clay."   TC7
- "That math problem is correct."   TC7A
- "Thank you for sitting down when I asked you."   TC7B
- "What do you think is in this bag, Peter?"   TC2
- "I think it's a carrot."   CT3
- "You think it's a carrot."   TC7

8 - Praise

Code 8 is used to praise a response, product, or behavior. Praise in academic areas is coded 8 with A in the How column, praise for behavior is coded 8 with B in the How column.

- "What a pretty picture you've made!"   TC8
- "I like the story you wrote about your trip, Jim."   TC8A
- "You've done a fine job on your math workbook."   TC8A
- "I'm really proud of you, class, for behaving so well while Mr. Mendelsohn was here."   TL8B

9 - Corrective Feedback

Corrective feedback is the attempt to change or modify a response, product, or behavior. Code 9 is used when the subject of the observation tries to change another's behavior or corrects another's answers or work.

Codes G, Q, N, and P from the How column can be coded with 9 to show the method used to effect behavior modification.

Code 9 is used with A in the How column to indicate corrective feedback in academic areas and with B to indicate corrective feedback having to do with classroom behavior.

- "Don't throw your ball against the wall; come and play on the swing."   TC9GB
- "You'll have to stay in at recess if you continue to talk."   TC9NB
- "Are you sure Sacramento is the capital of New Mexico?"   TC9Q
- "The answer to that math problem is wrong."   TC9A
- "No, that word is spelled b-u-i-l-d."   TC9GA
- "You have not mixed that paint correctly."   TC9

10 - No Response

Code 10 is used for no response when a response is called for to complete the interaction but none is forthcoming. (NOTE: NV is not coded with 10, because 10 is by definition nonverbal.)

- "Teacher, may I be next?"   CT1Q

  Teacher does not reply because he is talking to another child.   TC10

- "Jimmy, let me play with you."   CD1

  Jimmy does not look up or answer.   DC10

11 - Waiting

Code 11 is used when the subject of the observation is waiting in line or for materials, attention, use of equipment, or activity change. It is also used when the subject is not attending or is not involved with anyone or anything. (NOTE: NV is not coded with 11 because it is nonverbal by definition.)

- Child waiting at the teacher's desk while the teacher works with another child.   CC11
- Child has finished work and is sitting at the desk staring off into space.   CC11

12 - Observing, Listening

Code 12 is used when the subject of the observation is listening to or watching other people, other activities, TV, slides, films, and the like. (NOTE: NV is not coded with 12.)

- A child sitting on a chair is watching a small group play with blocks on the rug.   CS12
- Child listens to another child give a report.   CD12

	• Teacher stands watching the children and the activities in the room.	TL12
NV - Nonverbal	When the action being coded is not accompanied by words, NV is coded in the What column, along with the other relevant codes.	
	• Child laughing.	CC5NVH
	• Teacher passes out material silently to a small group.	TS5NV
	• Child taps the teacher's arm without speaking, requesting her attention.	CT1NVT
	• Child sits down in response to a request from the teacher.	CT3NV
X - Movement	Code X is used when the subject of the observation or a person with whom the subject is interacting moves. X can be used with any What code. If the movement is nonverbal and no What code is applicable, code X with 5 (general action).	
	• Teacher moves about the room while lecturing to the class.	TL4X
	• Child asks, "Ms. Hughes, will you help me?" while moving to the teacher.	CT1QX
	• Child walks over to close the door in response to a request from the teacher.	CT3NVX
	• Child runs to the door when recess is announced.	CC5NVX

THE HOW COLUMN

Categories in the How column are used in conjunction with the What codes.

Code   Code Usage

H - Happy	Obvious behavioral expressions of happiness or positive affect, such as laughing, smiling, and giggling are coded with H.	
	• A child jumping up and down, clapping hands, and grinning over a new puppet.	CC5NVH
	• A child laughing at a joke.	CC5NVH
	• Teacher smiles as she says, "What are you doing?"	TC1QH
	• Child smiles—in reply to the teacher's praise.	CT3NVH
	• Two girls giggling and talking in the corner.	225H
U - Unhappy	Code U is used for obvious behavioral expressions of sadness or unhappiness, such as crying or welling tears.	
	• Child with tear-filled eyes waiting in a line.	CC11NVU
	• Child crying.	CC5NVU
N - Negative	Expressions of annoyance or anger, negative content (e.g., sarcasm, insults, threats), scolding, rejection, and destructive behavior are coded N.	

Code	Code Usage	
N - Negative (Cont'd.)	• "You're stupid!"	CD5N
	• Teacher, red-faced and tight-lipped with anger, glares at class.	TL12N
	• "Johnny, if you can't leave Sandy alone, I will ask you to sit in the corner."	TC9NB
	• Child hits child ahead of him in line.	CD5NVNT
	• Child throws jar of paint on the floor in anger.	CC5NVN
T - Touch	Whenever one person touches another person, T is coded—with H to denote a positive touch, with N to denote a negative touch (hit, slap, pinch), and with P to denote a punishing touch from an adult to a child.	
	• Girl pinches another girl's arm.	CD5NVNT
	• Teacher puts her arm around a child and smiles as she says, "Jenny, will you help Lily with her puzzle?"	TC1QHT
	• Teacher moves around the class and touches a child on the head momentarily as she passes.	TC5NVXT
	• Teacher holds a child's hand.	TC5NVT
	• Teacher spanks child.	TC9NVPTB
Q - Question	Code Q is used with 1 for a direct question and with 9 when corrective feedback is in question form.	
	• "Are you sure that eight is the correct answer?"	TC9QA
	• "What color should I use?"	CT1Q
	• "Didn't I tell you not to bother Jimmy?"	TC9QB
	• "You weren't paying attention when I explained it, were you?"	TC9QB
G - Guide/Reason	G is coded with 9 when corrective feedback is positive and guides to an alternative activity, approach to a problem, and the like, or when the corrective includes a reason or explanation.	
	• "It might work better if you turned it around."	TC9G
	• "Sit down so the others can see, Gerald."	TC9GB
	• "If you knock that over it will make Jim angry, so please build your own tower."	TC9GB
P - Punish	Code P covers a range of adult disciplinary or behavior-modifying techniques, including withholding of privileges, isolation of a child, and physical punishment (coded with T). P is coded only with 9 in the How column.	
	• "Angela, go over to the corner and sit there alone until we're through!"	TC9PB
	• "Okay, Fred, no recess for you!"	TC9PB
	• Teacher spanks child for disruptive behavior.	TC9NVPT
O - Object	Code O is used with concrete, inanimate objects that are used in nonverbal self-instruction. (NOTE: When an object—token, candy, and the like—is given as a reward for a correct response or good behavior, O is coded with 8.)	
	• Child working on math using Cuisenaire rods.	CC4NVOA
	• Child building a block tower.	CC4NVO
	• Child fitting together pieces of a puzzle.	CC4NVO

Code	Code Usage	
O - Object (Cont'd.)	• Small group using pennies in working out math problems.	SS4NVOA
	• Child examining several kinds of pine cones.	CC4NVO
W - Worth	Code W is used with child statements of self-worth, self-praise, or self-esteem; exclamations of accomplishment; positive remarks about one's self; bragging.	
	• "I did it!"	CT6W
	• "I can do three cartwheels in a row!"	CD6W
	• "Isn't my dress pretty?"	CT1QW
DP - Dramatic Play/ Pretend	Code DP describes playacting, puppet shows, and other dramatic presentations, talking to toys or dolls, pretending or making believe, role playing.	
	• Boy walking on all fours, howling like a wolf.	CC5NVDP
	• Two children giving a puppet show to the rest of the class: "Oh, here comes the prince!"	CL6DP
	• Child talking to her doll: "Now, Mary Pat, you know I've told you not to do that." (NOTE: Because there is no code in the Who and To Whom columns to symbolize a toy, doll, or other object of that kind, the example above must be coded as if the child is talking to herself.)	CC9BDP
A - Academic	Interactions that have to do with the development of basic skills as measured on achievement tests are coded with A: reading (letter and word recognition, vocabulary, pronunciation, grammar), writing, and computation (number recognition, counting, adding, subtracting).	
	• "What is two plus two?"	TC1QA
	• "Two and two is five."	CT3A
	• "No, it's four."	TC9GA
	• "You read beautifully today, Aaron."	TC8A
	• "Will you show me how to do this problem, Robert?"	CD1QA
	• "I figured out that word all by myself!"	CT6WA
B - Behavior	Code B describes interactions concerned with classroom behavior (deportment, conduct). Code B is used only with the feedback codes (7, 8, 9) and with the responses to them.	
	• "Sit down—now!"	TC9B
	Child sits down.	CT3NVB
	• "You were very quiet in group time today, Ralph, and we all appreciated it. Good for you!"	TC8B
	Ralph smiles.	CT3NVHB
	• "Betty, please go over and work on your collage instead of bothering Gina."	TC9GB
	Betty replies, "O.K."	CT3B

(NOTE: If neither A nor B is coded, it is assumed that the frame concerns other task-related content.)

THE R, S, AND C CODES

These codes are located in the left margin of each interaction frame.

Code	Code Usage
R - Repeat	If the interaction being observed continues without change or interruption, code R is used in subsequent frames (approximately every five seconds) until the action is interrupted by another interaction, or stops. Code R repeats the interaction from the frame above.
S - Simultaneous	The simultaneous code is used to record inattention by a child or children while an adult-led activity is going on. It allows the observer to record what the child or children are doing, as well as the activity to which they should be attending.

In child-focused observations, the simultaneous code is used to record the activity that the child is ignoring.

A child is listening to a math lesson:

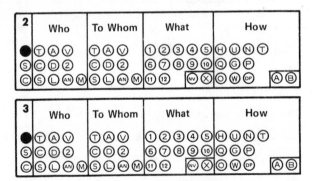

CT12A

She continues to listen for ten seconds:

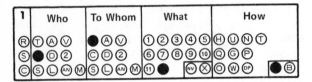

R

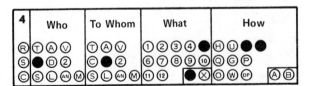

R

The child starts to pull the hair of the girl sitting next to her:

CD5NVNT

If the teacher continues with the math lesson while the child is
pulling her neighbor's hair, the teacher's actions are coded and
the S is recorded with it to show the activity that the child is
ignoring.

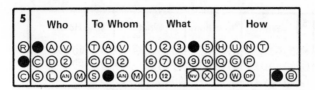

S TL4A

In the case of activity/adult-focused observations, the code is
used to show inattention on the part of a small or large group.
It is not used to show inattention on the part of only one or two
children within the larger group.

The teacher is giving a math lesson to a large group of children:

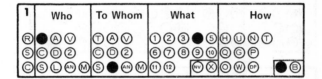

TL4A

He continues with his uninterrupted lecture (R is coded every five
seconds as he continues):

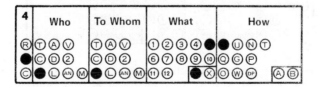

R

R

When a small group starts giggling while the teacher continues
lecturing, code S is used in the left margin of the next interaction block; then the new interaction (small group giggling) is
coded in the same block to show the children's inattention:

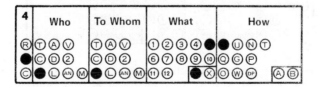

S SS5NVH

If the dual activity of "teacher lecturing-children giggling" continues for more than five seconds, code R is used in the next
interaction block(s) to show this continuation of the dual activities:

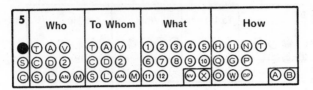

R

If a different interruption occurs (e.g., small group of children
arguing) during the same lecture, the first coding (TL4A) is repeated before the new interruption is coded:

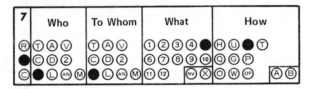

TL4A

S SS5N

C - Cancel

When a mistake is made in coding an interation, code C is used
in the left margin of the miscoded frame and the next frame is
coded correctly.

Teacher is lecturing to a large group. Observer mistakenly codes
TL5. Code C is used in that frame to show the error and Code TL4
is marked in the following frame:

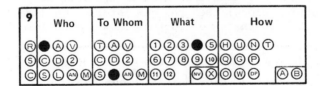

C TL5

TL4

Observer is coding an interaction. She forgets a code, is
momentarily blank. She records code C and begins again. For
example:

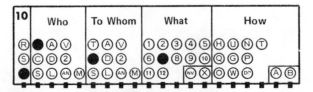

C TC7

C - Cancel
    (Cont'd.)

11	Who	To Whom	What	How
Ⓡ ●ⒶⓋ	ⓉⒶⓋ	①②③④⑤● ⓤⓃⓉ	
Ⓢ ⒸⒹ②	●Ⓓ②	⑥⑦⑧⑨⑩ ⓆⒼⓅ	
Ⓒ ⒮Ⓛ⒜ⓜ	⒮Ⓛ⒜ⓜ	⑪● ⓃⓥⓍⓄⓌ⒟⒫	ⒶⒷ

TC12H

TRAINING EXERCISES

On the following pages are some exercises for you to complete.[1]
They are to be completed in the order in which they are given.

Each exercise consists of a series of interactions you might
find in a classroom. Beneath each interaction is an interaction
frame. Code the frame to the best of your ability. This is a learning device and you are encouraged to refer to the definitions as you
do the exercises. The page following each exercise gives the correct
coding and a brief explanation. If, after reading the explanation,
you still do not understand why the frame was completed that way, go
back to the definitions.

EXERCISE C.1   Situation: A first-grade teacher is asking a child questions in arithmetic.

1. Teacher: "Johnny, what is
   two minus one?"

1	Who	To Whom	What	How
ⓇⓉⒶⓋ	ⓉⒶⓋ	①②③④⑤ⒽⓤⓃⓉ	
ⓈⒸⒹ②	ⒸⒹ②	⑥⑦⑧⑨⑩ⓆⒼⓅ	
Ⓒ⒮Ⓛ⒜ⓜ	⒮Ⓛ⒜ⓜ	⑪⑫ ⓝⓥⓍⓄⓌ⒟⒫	ⒶⒷ

2. Child: "Two minus one is
   one."

2	Who	To Whom	What	How
ⓇⓉⒶⓋ	ⓉⒶⓋ	①②③④⑤ⒽⓤⓃⓉ	
ⓈⒸⒹ②	ⒸⒹ②	⑥⑦⑧⑨⑩ⓆⒼⓅ	
Ⓒ⒮Ⓛ⒜ⓜ	⒮Ⓛ⒜ⓜ	⑪⑫ ⓝⓥⓍⓄⓌ⒟⒫	ⒶⒷ

3. Teacher: "What is three
   minus one?"

3	Who	To Whom	What	How
ⓇⓉⒶⓋ	ⓉⒶⓋ	①②③④⑤ⒽⓤⓃⓉ	
ⓈⒸⒹ②	ⒸⒹ②	⑥⑦⑧⑨⑩ⓆⒼⓅ	
Ⓒ⒮Ⓛ⒜ⓜ	⒮Ⓛ⒜ⓜ	⑪⑫ ⓝⓥⓍⓄⓌ⒟⒫	ⒶⒷ

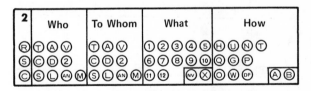

---

[1]Jane Stallings et al., "Training Materials for the SRI Classroom Observation System" (Menlo Park, Ca.: Stanford Research Institute, 1972).

4. Child: "Two."

4	Who	To Whom	What	How
	Ⓡ Ⓣ Ⓐ Ⓥ	Ⓣ Ⓐ Ⓥ	① ② ③ ④ ⑤	Ⓗ Ⓤ Ⓝ Ⓣ
	Ⓢ Ⓒ Ⓓ ②	Ⓒ Ⓓ ②	⑥ ⑦ ⑧ ⑨ ⑩	Ⓠ Ⓖ Ⓟ
	Ⓒ Ⓢ Ⓛ AN Ⓜ	Ⓢ Ⓛ AN Ⓜ	⑪ ⑫ NV Ⓧ	Ⓞ Ⓦ DP Ⓐ Ⓑ

5. Teacher: "And what is four minus one?"

5	Who	To Whom	What	How
	Ⓡ Ⓣ Ⓐ Ⓥ	Ⓣ Ⓐ Ⓥ	① ② ③ ④ ⑤	Ⓗ Ⓤ Ⓝ Ⓣ
	Ⓢ Ⓒ Ⓓ ②	Ⓒ Ⓓ ②	⑥ ⑦ ⑧ ⑨ ⑩	Ⓠ Ⓖ Ⓟ
	Ⓒ Ⓢ Ⓛ AN Ⓜ	Ⓢ Ⓛ AN Ⓜ	⑪ ⑫ NV Ⓧ	Ⓞ Ⓦ DP Ⓐ Ⓑ

6. Child: "Three."

6	Who	To Whom	What	How
	Ⓡ Ⓣ Ⓐ Ⓥ	Ⓣ Ⓐ Ⓥ	① ② ③ ④ ⑤	Ⓗ Ⓤ Ⓝ Ⓣ
	Ⓢ Ⓒ Ⓓ ②	Ⓒ Ⓓ ②	⑥ ⑦ ⑧ ⑨ ⑩	Ⓠ Ⓖ Ⓟ
	Ⓒ Ⓢ Ⓛ AN Ⓜ	Ⓢ Ⓛ AN Ⓜ	⑪ ⑫ NV Ⓧ	Ⓞ Ⓦ DP Ⓐ Ⓑ

7. Teacher: "Tell me what five minus one is."

7	Who	To Whom	What	How
	Ⓡ Ⓣ Ⓐ Ⓥ	Ⓣ Ⓐ Ⓥ	① ② ③ ④ ⑤	Ⓗ Ⓤ Ⓝ Ⓣ
	Ⓢ Ⓒ Ⓓ ②	Ⓒ Ⓓ ②	⑥ ⑦ ⑧ ⑨ ⑩	Ⓠ Ⓖ Ⓟ
	Ⓒ Ⓢ Ⓛ AN Ⓜ	Ⓢ Ⓛ AN Ⓜ	⑪ ⑫ NV Ⓧ	Ⓞ Ⓦ DP Ⓐ Ⓑ

8. Child: "Four."

8	Who	To Whom	What	How
	Ⓡ Ⓣ Ⓐ Ⓥ	Ⓣ Ⓐ Ⓥ	① ② ③ ④ ⑤	Ⓗ Ⓤ Ⓝ Ⓣ
	Ⓢ Ⓒ Ⓓ ②	Ⓒ Ⓓ ②	⑥ ⑦ ⑧ ⑨ ⑩	Ⓠ Ⓖ Ⓟ
	Ⓒ Ⓢ Ⓛ AN Ⓜ	Ⓢ Ⓛ AN Ⓜ	⑪ ⑫ NV Ⓧ	Ⓞ Ⓦ DP Ⓐ Ⓑ

9. Teacher: "Correct."

9	Who	To Whom	What	How
	Ⓡ Ⓣ Ⓐ Ⓥ	Ⓣ Ⓐ Ⓥ	① ② ③ ④ ⑤	Ⓗ Ⓤ Ⓝ Ⓣ
	Ⓢ Ⓒ Ⓓ ②	Ⓒ Ⓓ ②	⑥ ⑦ ⑧ ⑨ ⑩	Ⓠ Ⓖ Ⓟ
	Ⓒ Ⓢ Ⓛ AN Ⓜ	Ⓢ Ⓛ AN Ⓜ	⑪ ⑫ NV Ⓧ	Ⓞ Ⓦ DP Ⓐ Ⓑ

ANSWERS: CORRECT CODING FOR EXERCISE C.1

Exercise C.1 illustrates two basic interaction sequences: question—response and question—response—feedback.

1. <u>TC1QA</u>. The teacher (T) has asked the child (C) an academic (A) direct question (1Q). The question calls specifically for recall of facts related to basic computation skills.

1	Who	To Whom	What	How
	Ⓡ ● Ⓐ Ⓥ	Ⓣ Ⓐ Ⓥ	● ② ③ ④ ⑤	Ⓗ Ⓤ Ⓝ Ⓣ
	Ⓢ Ⓒ Ⓓ ②	● Ⓓ ②	⑥ ⑦ ⑧ ⑨ ⑩	● Ⓖ Ⓟ
	Ⓒ Ⓢ Ⓛ AN Ⓜ	Ⓢ Ⓛ AN Ⓜ	⑪ ⑫ NV Ⓧ	Ⓞ Ⓦ DP ● Ⓑ

2. <u>CT3A</u>. The child's (C) response (3) to the teacher (T) is academic (A). This is a reaction to the question.

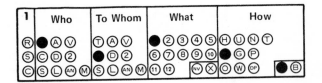

3. TC1QA. (See explanation, frame 1, this exercise.)

4. CT3A. (See explanation, frame 2, this exercise.)

5. TC1QA. (See explanation, frame 1, this exercise.)

6. CT3A. (See explanation, frame 2, this exercise.)

7. TC1A. The teacher (T) requests (1) academic (A) information of the child (C). The request is not in question form.

8. CT3A. (See explanation, frame 2, this exercise.)

9. TC7A. The teacher (T) acknowledges (7) the child's (C) academic (A). Here acknowledgment is simply informing the child that the answer is correct.

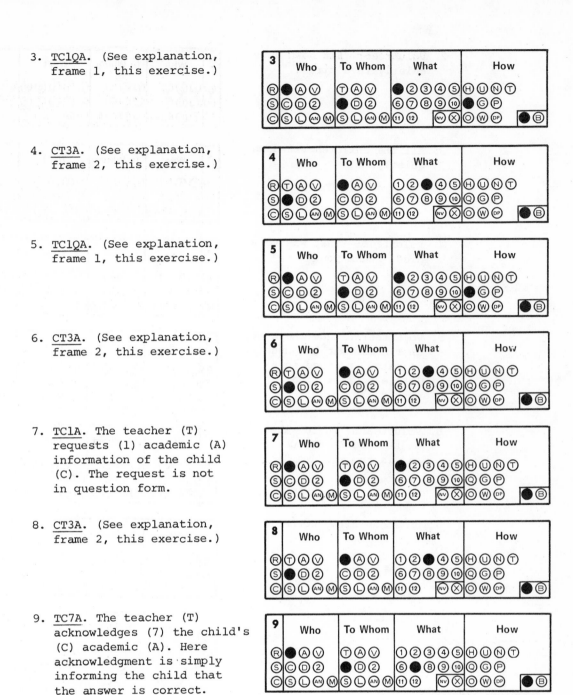

EXERCISE C.2   Situation: A volunteer is reading to a small group of first-grade children.

1. Volunteer: "I'm going to read a story to you now."

2. Volunteer: "Sit down very quietly in a circle."

2	Who	To Whom	What	How
	Ⓡ Ⓣ Ⓐ Ⓥ	Ⓣ Ⓐ Ⓥ	① ② ③ ④ ⑤	Ⓗ Ⓤ Ⓝ Ⓣ
	Ⓢ Ⓒ Ⓓ ②	Ⓒ Ⓓ ②	⑥ ⑦ ⑧ ⑨ ⑩	Ⓠ Ⓖ Ⓟ
	Ⓒ Ⓢ Ⓛ ⒶⓃ Ⓜ	Ⓢ Ⓛ ⒶⓃ Ⓜ	⑪ ⑫ Ⓝⓥ ⓧ	Ⓞ Ⓦ ⒹⓅ Ⓐ Ⓑ

3. All the children sit down quietly.

3	Who	To Whom	What	How
	Ⓡ Ⓣ Ⓐ Ⓥ	Ⓣ Ⓐ Ⓥ	① ② ③ ④ ⑤	Ⓗ Ⓤ Ⓝ Ⓣ
	Ⓢ Ⓒ Ⓓ ②	Ⓒ Ⓓ ②	⑥ ⑦ ⑧ ⑨ ⑩	Ⓠ Ⓖ Ⓟ
	Ⓒ Ⓢ Ⓛ ⒶⓃ Ⓜ	Ⓢ Ⓛ ⒶⓃ Ⓜ	⑪ ⑫ Ⓝⓥ ⓧ	Ⓞ Ⓦ ⒹⓅ Ⓐ Ⓑ

4. Volunteer: "That was very nice, thank you."

4	Who	To Whom	What	How
	Ⓡ Ⓣ Ⓐ Ⓥ	Ⓣ Ⓐ Ⓥ	① ② ③ ④ ⑤	Ⓗ Ⓤ Ⓝ Ⓣ
	Ⓢ Ⓒ Ⓓ ②	Ⓒ Ⓓ ②	⑥ ⑦ ⑧ ⑨ ⑩	Ⓠ Ⓖ Ⓟ
	Ⓒ Ⓢ Ⓛ ⒶⓃ Ⓜ	Ⓢ Ⓛ ⒶⓃ Ⓜ	⑪ ⑫ Ⓝⓥ ⓧ	Ⓞ Ⓦ ⒹⓅ Ⓐ Ⓑ

5. Volunteer: "Once there was an old man who had hundreds of cats. He lived in a little house in the country."

5	Who	To Whom	What	How
	Ⓡ Ⓣ Ⓐ Ⓥ	Ⓣ Ⓐ Ⓥ	① ② ③ ④ ⑤	Ⓗ Ⓤ Ⓝ Ⓣ
	Ⓢ Ⓒ Ⓓ ②	Ⓒ Ⓓ ②	⑥ ⑦ ⑧ ⑨ ⑩	Ⓠ Ⓖ Ⓟ
	Ⓒ Ⓢ Ⓛ ⒶⓃ Ⓜ	Ⓢ Ⓛ ⒶⓃ Ⓜ	⑪ ⑫ Ⓝⓥ ⓧ	Ⓞ Ⓦ ⒹⓅ Ⓐ Ⓑ

6. Volunteer: "There were cats on the chairs and the bed and in the windows."

6	Who	To Whom	What	How
	Ⓡ Ⓣ Ⓐ Ⓥ	Ⓣ Ⓐ Ⓥ	① ② ③ ④ ⑤	Ⓗ Ⓤ Ⓝ Ⓣ
	Ⓢ Ⓒ Ⓓ ②	Ⓒ Ⓓ ②	⑥ ⑦ ⑧ ⑨ ⑩	Ⓠ Ⓖ Ⓟ
	Ⓒ Ⓢ Ⓛ ⒶⓃ Ⓜ	Ⓢ Ⓛ ⒶⓃ Ⓜ	⑪ ⑫ Ⓝⓥ ⓧ	Ⓞ Ⓦ ⒹⓅ Ⓐ Ⓑ

7. Jonathan hits another child, Ann.

7	Who	To Whom	What	How
	Ⓡ Ⓣ Ⓐ Ⓥ	Ⓣ Ⓐ Ⓥ	① ② ③ ④ ⑤	Ⓗ Ⓤ Ⓝ Ⓣ
	Ⓢ Ⓒ Ⓓ ②	Ⓒ Ⓓ ②	⑥ ⑦ ⑧ ⑨ ⑩	Ⓠ Ⓖ Ⓟ
	Ⓒ Ⓢ Ⓛ ⒶⓃ Ⓜ	Ⓢ Ⓛ ⒶⓃ Ⓜ	⑪ ⑫ Ⓝⓥ ⓧ	Ⓞ Ⓦ ⒹⓅ Ⓐ Ⓑ

8. Volunteer: "Leave Ann alone!"

8	Who	To Whom	What	How
	Ⓡ Ⓣ Ⓐ Ⓥ	Ⓣ Ⓐ Ⓥ	① ② ③ ④ ⑤	Ⓗ Ⓤ Ⓝ Ⓣ
	Ⓢ Ⓒ Ⓓ ②	Ⓒ Ⓓ ②	⑥ ⑦ ⑧ ⑨ ⑩	Ⓠ Ⓖ Ⓟ
	Ⓒ Ⓢ Ⓛ ⒶⓃ Ⓜ	Ⓢ Ⓛ ⒶⓃ Ⓜ	⑪ ⑫ Ⓝⓥ ⓧ	Ⓞ Ⓦ ⒹⓅ Ⓐ Ⓑ

9. Jonathan sits down quietly complying with the volunteer's command.

9	Who	To Whom	What	How
	Ⓡ Ⓣ Ⓐ Ⓥ	Ⓣ Ⓐ Ⓥ	① ② ③ ④ ⑤	Ⓗ Ⓤ Ⓝ Ⓣ
	Ⓢ Ⓒ Ⓓ ②	Ⓒ Ⓓ ②	⑥ ⑦ ⑧ ⑨ ⑩	Ⓠ Ⓖ Ⓟ
	Ⓒ Ⓢ Ⓛ ⒶⓃ Ⓜ	Ⓢ Ⓛ ⒶⓃ Ⓜ	⑪ ⑫ Ⓝⓥ ⓧ	Ⓞ Ⓦ ⒹⓅ Ⓐ Ⓑ

10. Volunteer: "There were cats on the roof and cats in the garden. There were cats by the mailbox and cats on the fence."

10	Who	To Whom	What	How
	Ⓡ Ⓣ Ⓐ Ⓥ	Ⓣ Ⓐ Ⓥ	① ② ③ ④ ⑤	Ⓗ Ⓤ Ⓝ Ⓣ
	Ⓢ Ⓒ Ⓓ ②	Ⓒ Ⓓ ②	⑥ ⑦ ⑧ ⑨ ⑩	Ⓠ Ⓖ Ⓟ
	Ⓒ Ⓢ Ⓛ ⒶⓃ Ⓜ	Ⓢ Ⓛ ⒶⓃ Ⓜ	⑪ ⑫ Ⓝⓥ ⓧ	Ⓞ Ⓦ ⒹⓅ Ⓐ Ⓑ

11. Two children begin giggling as volunteer pauses.

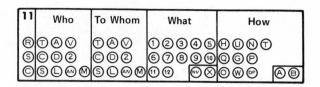

12. Volunteer: "Be quiet so that the other children can listen to the story."

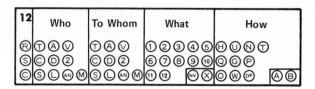

13. The two children stop giggling and start listening.

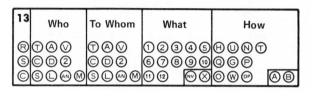

ANSWERS: CORRECT CODING FOR EXERCISE C.2

1. VS4. The volunteer (V) is introducing the activity (4) to the small group (S).

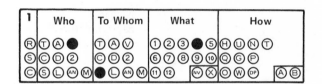

2. VS1. The volunteer (V) has made a request (1) of the small group (S).

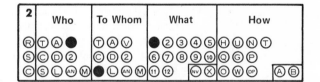

3. SV3NV. The small group (S) responds (3) nonverbally (NV) to the volunteer's (V) request.

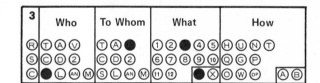

4. VS8. The volunteer (V) praises (8) the small group (S).

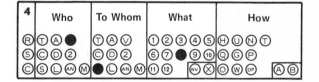

5. VS4A. The volunteer (V) begins reading to the small group (S); that is considered academic (A) instruction (4).

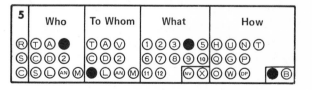

6. R. The Volunteer continues reading, so this frame is coded Repeat (R). No other code is filled in when Repeat is coded.

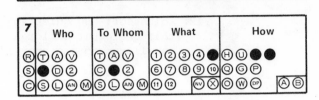

7. CD5NT. A child (C) hits another child (D); this is a negative (N) touch (T). Since a What code must be coded in each frame, code General Action (5) is used for such cases.

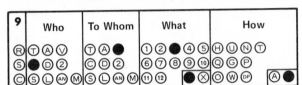

8. VC9B. The volunteer (V) corrects (9) the child's (C) behavior (B).

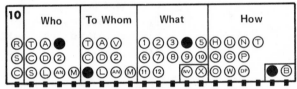

9. CB3NVB. The child (C) responds (3) nonverbally (NV) to the volunteer's (V) behavioral (B) correction.

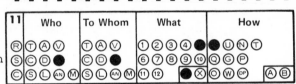

10. VS4A. The volunteer (V) resumes reading (4A; see frame 5 above) to the small group (S).

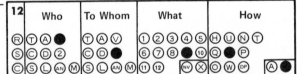

11. 225NVH. Two children (2) interrupt the volunteer with their giggling (5NVH). Giggling is coded General Action (5), Happy (H) and Nonverbal (NV), because only recognizable words are considered verbalization.

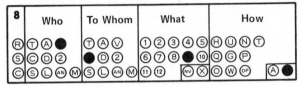

12. V29GB. The volunteer (V) corrects (9) the two children's behavior (B) by giving them a reason (G).

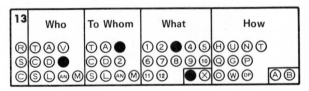

13. 2V3NVB. The two children (2) respond (3) nonverbally (NV) to the volunteer's corrections of their behavior (B).

EXERCISE C.3 Situation: The teacher is discussing tooth care with a small group of second-grade children.

1. Teacher: "Today, we will review yesterday's discussion on the care of teeth."

1	Who	To Whom	What	How
	R T A V	T A V	1 2 3 4 5 H U N T	
	S C D 2	C D 2	6 7 8 9 10 Q G P	
	C S L AN M	S L AN M	11 12 NV X O W DP	A B

2. Child: "I went to the dentist yesterday!"

2	Who	To Whom	What	How
	R T A V	T A V	1 2 3 4 5 H U N T	
	S C D 2	C D 2	6 7 8 9 10 Q G P	
	C S L AN M	S L AN M	11 12 NV X O W DP	A B

3. Teacher: "You went to the dentist yesterday."

3	Who	To Whom	What	How
	R T A V	T A V	1 2 3 4 5 H U N T	
	S C D 2	C D 2	6 7 8 9 10 Q G P	
	C S L AN M	S L AN M	11 12 NV X O W DP	A B

4. Child: "He cleaned my teeth with a machine and I have to brush them a lot now."

4	Who	To Whom	What	How
	R T A V	T A V	1 2 3 4 5 H U N T	
	S C D 2	C D 2	6 7 8 9 10 Q G P	
	C S L AN M	S L AN M	11 12 NV X O W DP	A B

5. Teacher: "Larry, are there other ways to take care of teeth?"

5	Who	To Whom	What	How
	R T A V	T A V	1 2 3 4 5 H U N T	
	S C D 2	C D 2	6 7 8 9 10 Q G P	
	C S L AN M	S L AN M	11 12 NV X O W DP	A B

6. Child: "Eat the right foods."

6	Who	To Whom	What	How
	R T A V	T A V	1 2 3 4 5 H U N T	
	S C D 2	C D 2	6 7 8 9 10 Q G P	
	C S L AN M	S L AN M	11 12 NV X O W DP	A B

7. Different Child: "I have to go get a drink of water!"

7	Who	To Whom	What	How
	R T A V	T A V	1 2 3 4 5 H U N T	
	S C D 2	C D 2	6 7 8 9 10 Q G P	
	C S L AN M	S L AN M	11 12 NV X O W DP	A B

8. Child: "Me, too!"

8	Who	To Whom	What	How
	R T A V	T A V	1 2 3 4 5 H U N T	
	S C D 2	C D 2	6 7 8 9 10 Q G P	
	C S L AN M	S L AN M	11 12 NV X O W DP	A B

9. Teacher: "You can wait
   I think."

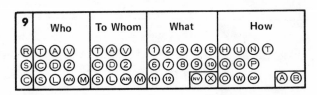

10. Teacher: "To prevent tooth
    decay, you should stay very
    healthy, exercise, drink
    milk, and clean your teeth."

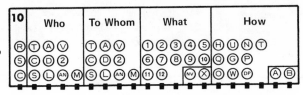

ANSWERS: CORRECT CODING FOR EXERCISE C.3

1. TS4. The teacher (T) is
   introducing the subject of
   today's instruction (4) to
   the small group.

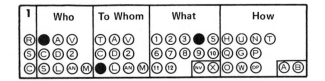

2. CT6. A child (C) addresses
   a task-related statement
   (6) to the teacher.

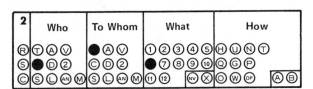

3. TC7. The teacher (T)
   acknowledges (7) the child's
   (C) statement through repe-
   tition.

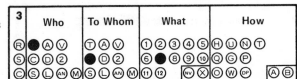

4. CT6. The child (C) directs
   another task-related statement (6) to the teacher (T).

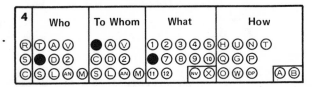

5. TC1Q. The teacher (T) asks
   a child (C) a direct question (1Q) that asks for
   recall of material already
   learned.

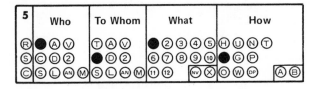

6. CT3. The child (C) responds
   (3) to the teacher (T).

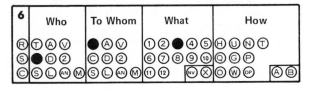

7. <u>DT5</u>. Another child (D) makes an irrelevant comment (5) to the teacher (T).

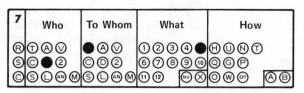

8. <u>CT5</u>. Another child (C) also makes an irrelevant comment (5) to the teacher (T).

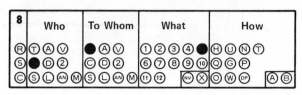

9. <u>T29GB</u>. The teacher (T) gives both children (2) corrective feedback (9) which guides (G) them to an alternative (i.e., waiting). Behavior (B) is coded because the Teacher is not correcting academic or other task-related work, but behavior (B).

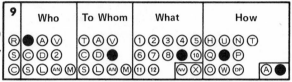

10. <u>TS4</u>. The teacher (T) resumes instructing (4) the small group (S).

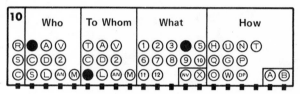

EXERCISE C.4 Situation: A fourth-grade teacher is discussing science with one child.

1. Teacher: "Donald, do you re-member what we talked about yesterday in science?"

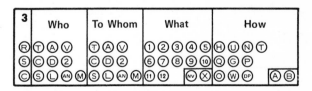

2. Donald: "Yes, evaporation."

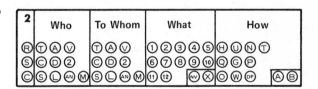

3. Teacher: "Yes, it was evaporation."

4. Teacher: "The water in the glass jar evaporated over the weekend."

5. Teacher: "Think about what happened to that water and tell me some examples of evaporation in the real world."

5	Who	To Whom	What	How
	Ⓡ Ⓣ Ⓐ Ⓥ	Ⓣ Ⓐ Ⓥ	① ② ③ ④ ⑤	Ⓗ Ⓤ Ⓝ Ⓣ
	Ⓢ Ⓒ Ⓓ ②	Ⓒ Ⓓ ②	⑥ ⑦ ⑧ ⑨ ⑩	Ⓠ Ⓖ Ⓟ
	Ⓒ Ⓢ Ⓛ ⒜ⓝ Ⓜ	Ⓢ Ⓛ ⒜ⓝ Ⓜ	⑪ ⑫	ⓝⓥ Ⓧ Ⓞ Ⓦ Ⓓⓟ Ⓐ Ⓑ

6. Donald: "Mud puddles. After it rains they're there, then later they're gone."

6	Who	To Whom	What	How
	Ⓡ Ⓣ Ⓐ Ⓥ	Ⓣ Ⓐ Ⓥ	① ② ③ ④ ⑤	Ⓗ Ⓤ Ⓝ Ⓣ
	Ⓢ Ⓒ Ⓓ ②	Ⓒ Ⓓ ②	⑥ ⑦ ⑧ ⑨ ⑩	Ⓠ Ⓖ Ⓟ
	Ⓒ Ⓢ Ⓛ ⒜ⓝ Ⓜ	Ⓢ Ⓛ ⒜ⓝ Ⓜ	⑪ ⑫	ⓝⓥ Ⓧ Ⓞ Ⓦ Ⓓⓟ Ⓐ Ⓑ

7. Teacher: "A very good example, Donald."

7	Who	To Whom	What	How
	Ⓡ Ⓣ Ⓐ Ⓥ	Ⓣ Ⓐ Ⓥ	① ② ③ ④ ⑤	Ⓗ Ⓤ Ⓝ Ⓣ
	Ⓢ Ⓒ Ⓓ ②	Ⓒ Ⓓ ②	⑥ ⑦ ⑧ ⑨ ⑩	Ⓠ Ⓖ Ⓟ
	Ⓒ Ⓢ Ⓛ ⒜ⓝ Ⓜ	Ⓢ Ⓛ ⒜ⓝ Ⓜ	⑪ ⑫	ⓝⓥ Ⓧ Ⓞ Ⓦ Ⓓⓟ Ⓐ Ⓑ

8. Donald: "Some creeks dry up in the summer when it's hot and dry."

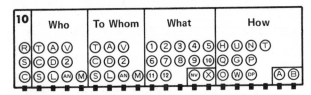

8	Who	To Whom	What	How
	Ⓡ Ⓣ Ⓐ Ⓥ	Ⓣ Ⓐ Ⓥ	① ② ③ ④ ⑤	Ⓗ Ⓤ Ⓝ Ⓣ
	Ⓢ Ⓒ Ⓓ ②	Ⓒ Ⓓ ②	⑥ ⑦ ⑧ ⑨ ⑩	Ⓠ Ⓖ Ⓟ
	Ⓒ Ⓢ Ⓛ ⒜ⓝ Ⓜ	Ⓢ Ⓛ ⒜ⓝ Ⓜ	⑪ ⑫	ⓝⓥ Ⓧ Ⓞ Ⓦ Ⓓⓟ Ⓐ Ⓑ

9. Teacher: "Yes, indeed."

9	Who	To Whom	What	How
	Ⓡ Ⓣ Ⓐ Ⓥ	Ⓣ Ⓐ Ⓥ	① ② ③ ④ ⑤	Ⓗ Ⓤ Ⓝ Ⓣ
	Ⓢ Ⓒ Ⓓ ②	Ⓒ Ⓓ ②	⑥ ⑦ ⑧ ⑨ ⑩	Ⓠ Ⓖ Ⓟ
	Ⓒ Ⓢ Ⓛ ⒜ⓝ Ⓜ	Ⓢ Ⓛ ⒜ⓝ Ⓜ	⑪ ⑫	ⓝⓥ Ⓧ Ⓞ Ⓦ Ⓓⓟ Ⓐ Ⓑ

10. Teacher: "What makes this water 'disappear'?"

10	Who	To Whom	What	How
	Ⓡ Ⓣ Ⓐ Ⓥ	Ⓣ Ⓐ Ⓥ	① ② ③ ④ ⑤	Ⓗ Ⓤ Ⓝ Ⓣ
	Ⓢ Ⓒ Ⓓ ②	Ⓒ Ⓓ ②	⑥ ⑦ ⑧ ⑨ ⑩	Ⓠ Ⓖ Ⓟ
	Ⓒ Ⓢ Ⓛ ⒜ⓝ Ⓜ	Ⓢ Ⓛ ⒜ⓝ Ⓜ	⑪ ⑫	ⓝⓥ Ⓧ Ⓞ Ⓦ Ⓓⓟ Ⓐ Ⓑ

11. Donald: "Evaporation."

11	Who	To Whom	What	How
	Ⓡ Ⓣ Ⓐ Ⓥ	Ⓣ Ⓐ Ⓥ	① ② ③ ④ ⑤	Ⓗ Ⓤ Ⓝ Ⓣ
	Ⓢ Ⓒ Ⓓ ②	Ⓒ Ⓓ ②	⑥ ⑦ ⑧ ⑨ ⑩	Ⓠ Ⓖ Ⓟ
	Ⓒ Ⓢ Ⓛ ⒜ⓝ Ⓜ	Ⓢ Ⓛ ⒜ⓝ Ⓜ	⑪ ⑫	ⓝⓥ Ⓧ Ⓞ Ⓦ Ⓓⓟ Ⓐ Ⓑ

12. Teacher: "Yes, evaporation."

12	Who	To Whom	What	How
	Ⓡ Ⓣ Ⓐ Ⓥ	Ⓣ Ⓐ Ⓥ	① ② ③ ④ ⑤	Ⓗ Ⓤ Ⓝ Ⓣ
	Ⓢ Ⓒ Ⓓ ②	Ⓒ Ⓓ ②	⑥ ⑦ ⑧ ⑨ ⑩	Ⓠ Ⓖ Ⓟ
	Ⓒ Ⓢ Ⓛ ⒜ⓝ Ⓜ	Ⓢ Ⓛ ⒜ⓝ Ⓜ	⑪ ⑫	ⓝⓥ Ⓧ Ⓞ Ⓦ Ⓓⓟ Ⓐ Ⓑ

ANSWERS: CORRECT CODING FOR EXERCISE C.4

1. <u>TC1Q</u>. The teacher (T) asks
   a child (C) a direct question (1Q) which asks for
   recall of material already
   learned.

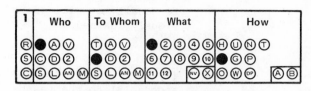

2. <u>CT3</u>. Child (C) responds (3)
   to the teacher (T).

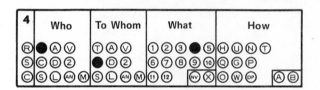

3. <u>TC7</u>. The teacher (T)
   acknowledges (7) the child's
   (C) response by confirming
   the answer as correct.

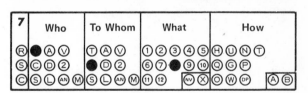

4. <u>TC4</u>. The teacher (T) is
   instructing (4) the
   child (C).

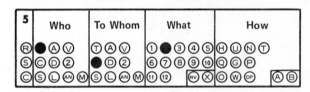

5. <u>TC2</u>. The teacher (T) asks
   the child (C) an open-ended
   question (2) which asks him
   to apply a learned idea to
   new situations.

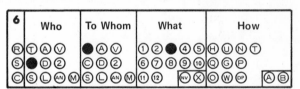

6. <u>CT3</u>. The child (C) responds
   (3) to the teacher (T).

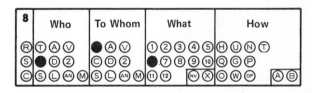

7. <u>TC8</u>. The teacher (T)
   praises (8) the child's
   (C) response.

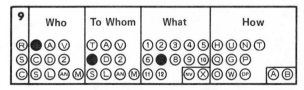

8. <u>CT6</u>. The child (C) volunteers a task-related statement (6) to the teacher
   (T).

9. <u>TC7</u>. The teacher (T)
   acknowledges (7) the
   child's (C) remark.

10. <u>TC1Q</u>. The teacher (T) asks
the child (C) a direct
question (1Q) to get him
to recall material pre-
viously learned.

11. $\dfrac{CT3}{(T)}$. The child (C) responds (3) to the teacher
(T).

12. <u>TC7</u>. The teacher (T)
acknowledges (7) the
child's (C) correct answer.

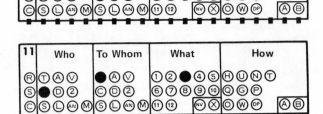

Appendix D

CASE STUDY OF MARCY

The teacher must be aware of home, school, and community values and understand how these values affect a child. Although there are many ways for teachers in an open classroom model to fulfill their responsibility, I want to describe how I studied the children in a group I taught and how I used the Group Process Model. To begin with, I kept copious notes and made frequent observations of each child—each was a case study. Also, I was, fortunately, able to teach the same group of children for two consecutive years, first and second grades. Only five new children entered the second-grade class. One of these new children was Marcy. Her case study in particular is presented here to show how a child is enculturated into the group, how a teacher can understand and aid in this process through systematic observations, and how a model can help in the process (in this case, through group meetings).

MARCY

What do children value? Do they value stars on papers, pats on heads, lollipops, or chewing gum? What do they value in themselves and in each other? What is good or bad in their eyes? What role does parental expectation play in a child's value system? How does a child, new to a group, earn a passport to acceptance by his or her peers without the sacrifice of unique special qualities? One fall semester I recorded and attempted to understand the valuing system of a group of second-grade children and the enculturation of a seven-year-old girl who came to my class from the Summerhill School in England.

My first meeting with Marcy took place two weeks before school was due to open. At the private school, the enrollment included a formal application, an interview with the director, and acceptance by the classroom teacher. For a few months after leaving the Summerhill School, Marcy had attended a public school in San Marin, California. The San Marin school's report of her scholastic achievement was quite negative. They recommended retaining her in the first grade, and described her as having difficulty in adjusting to a structured school system; they also described her as being immature for her age. Further, they said she was strong willed and creative. At first glance this report raised doubts in my mind about how comfortable Marcy would feel in a group of highly skilled and productive second-grade children. Even though our structure and facilities are more similar to Summerhill than the public school she had attended, the children's expectations of themselves and each other were quite high.

With these doubts foremost in my mind, I made an appointment to meet Marcy's family at school. It was moving day. We had to move all of my things from the first-grade room to the second-grade room. I had just filled the trunk of my car with a load of books, dress-up clothes, and games, when a little moppet with long, shiny-brown hair, dressed in jeans and no shoes, appeared beside me and said, "I'm Marcy." Her eyes were deep brown, and they didn't seem to look at me but rather to take in all the surroundings. "Would you like to ride with me to our new room?" I asked. "It is on the other side of the school grounds." She nodded, and climbed into the car. "This is like my first school," she volunteered, "only there we stayed all night. Do you ever stay all night here?" "No, at the end of the day we all go home. Sometimes we have camping trips, and then we all sleep together. Do you like to camp?" "I would like to, but I haven't." By this time we were at the second-grade room. She looked in the trunk and spied the dress-up clothes. "May I use these?" she asked. She carried an armload inside and soon appeared in a chiffon gown with a piece of velvet drape around her shoulders. She strutted and preened before the mirror. She talked in a grown-up voice to her image. I was struck by her natural and unaffected manner. She was not trying to please me. In fact, she was now oblivious to me. She had entered the child's world. She was bright and creative, and it seemed we would be able to communicate. I wanted her for my class. Most likely she would have some problems in feeling comfortable with the group: she lacked the academic sophistication of the others. But she had other essentials for acceptance to this group of children such as a flair for fantasy. I felt that she was enough like them and that she would be happy among us.

Her parents talked with me briefly while she played. They said she had been quite unhappy in the public school. On their application the father had said that he hoped the school would look to her, rather than to any other criteria, for guidance as to how and in what direction she wanted to be led in her development. He felt she needed steady warmth and encouragement. Both parents had become full-time graduate students and were most anxious to get their three children enrolled in school.

I told them I would be happy to have Marcy in our group and explained that we did have structured work times in which all of the children participated. That the lessons were individualized and each child progressed at his own speed. That there was a choice of work, and the children helped in planning the program, but that there was no choice as to whether or not they would join the group at study times. The father said that he understood this was how we operated, and thought our system would best fit his children since there was no Summerhillian school available.

Marcy, it seemed, had been at Summerhill as a boarding student at 4½ years of age. I wondered how the time away from home, when she was so young, had affected Marcy's emotional and social development.

That day I asked our school secretary to write A. S. Neill for a report on the time Marcy had spent with them. The reply spoke glowingly of her older sister, but merely said, "Marcy is another matter. She was ill a great deal with us, but I suppose her parents have already filled you in on that." Marcy's illness had not been mentioned, either on the application form or in our initial interview. Was it an oversight on their part, or did it seem insignificant once it was past? Or did they feel guilty about leaving a child so young? At any rate, it was the only thing Mr. Neill mentioned about Marcy, and it must have affected to a considerable extent the time she spent there, or he would not have mentioned the illness to the exclusion of everything else about her. Her parents were busy and could not be reached for another parent conference.

On the first day of school, Marcy came into the room and looked around for the dress-up clothes. She put on the same things she had worn during her previous visit. At first, I thought she was talking to Wendy who had just arrived, but then I realized she was addressing her cocktail-type conversation to the general atmosphere. I introduced her to Wendy and suggested that she select a desk next to her. Wendy is a friendly, helpful child who can respond to the needs of others. Marcy giggled and said, "Do you want to come to my cocktail party?" I left to greet other arriving children, and Marcy was off to explore more of her new environment. She seemed more interested in the things around her than in the people. Her words continued to be addressed to the air, rather than to anyone in particular.

At reading time Marcy insisted that she could read. We tried book after book, but there were no words she could recognize. We looked at individual letters and sounds; many of these she did not know. We would have to start at the beginning in both reading and writing.

Marcy did not like this. She continued to claim a great reading ability. It was true she was a great picture reader, but the written word escaped her.

In a birthday card and story she wrote, the word *Happy* appeared several times among the scrawls, carefully and clearly written. This card seemed to symbolize her communication system. She communicated with herself, and only once in a while did she reveal herself to the outside world. Then, what she revealed was "happy."

We continued the next week to study letter sounds and small base words: at, cat, rat, an, man, fan, and so on. When I sat down beside her, she bowed her head in such a way that her hair fell over her face and the page. When I pulled the hair back, she gave it a little shake, and with a laugh she was hidden again. She repeated the sounds in a muffled voice but learned very quickly. Another child new to the group said, "I did that baby work in kindergarten." Marcy did not respond but continued to do her seat work hidden under her hair.

The next day she announced, "I did that baby work in kindergarten."

I smiled and said, "Do you want to read, Marcy?"

"Yes," came her small voice.

"Then this is where we begin."

She fussed about the baby books in the presence of other children, but never again to me. She worked with a great deal of concentration every day for nearly thirty minutes. In two weeks she could read a very simple hardbacked book named *Come and Have Fun.* It is the story of a cat and a mouse. She was delighted. It was a real book.

The other children were amazed at Marcy's lack of reading skills. Most of them were reading well above the second-grade level, and many were above the fourth-grade level. Marcy was on the edge of the group. In a sociogram given at the end of the second week, she was not chosen by anyone as the friend he or she would like to sit by. What factors besides reading ability were separating her?

In order to check further into the valuing system of this group, I constructed a questionnaire asking:

I want to sit by _____ because _____.
_____ makes a good chairman because _____.
I like to play with _____ because _____.
I like myself because _____.

From this I found that those qualities which they valued in themselves and each other included gentleness, the ability to comfort, help with seat work, quiet at work times, good ideas for dramatic play, ability at reading or math, and being a good sport. For leadership in a chairman, they wanted someone who would speak loud and clear, be fair in calling on everybody, keep people quiet, not be silly, comfort people, and trust people. With these values in mind, we could better assess Marcy's struggle to become a participating member of the group.

She was lonely. She started bringing a red-haired stuffed rag doll to school. She talked to the doll and said, "I am teaching my dolly her lessons. She is learning to read." She talked to her doll and used the physical environment with a great deal of pleasure. She did not complain or seem unhappy, just unrelated to the other children.

At the end of the second week of school we went on the bus to San Francisco to take a trip on the Red and White Fleet. This was the opening of our study of the San Francisco Bay. That morning Marcy seemed anxious. "I can go on this trip," she said when she arrived.

"Yes, I know. Your daddy sent a note saying that you could."

She stayed close to me as we walked to the bus. She sat down in the first seat and held her dolly close. Her thumb popped into her mouth and she sat concentrating on something inside herself. She did not ask to sit with me as many other children were clamoring to do. She seemed accustomed to comforting herself. She moved through the day with childish delight, but remote from other people. She and her doll had a lovely time.

The next week Marty Marcus, our special math and science consultant, assisted our afternoon math group. We were working out special problems with the Cuisenaire rods. Marcy paid no attention. She ran a little toy car across her desk, making a motor noise. She said to the car in a loud voice, "He is not the math teacher!" She built with the rods. "That's four." She counted incorrectly: "one, two, four, eight." "I said something silly." She continued to give incorrect answers and did not work the problems the math specialist was presenting. She picked up a bright orange rod—the longest—and turned to Wendy, saying, "Orange is the Prince, the hero!" Wendy smiled at this and went on doing her problems. Martha said, "Marcy is silly."

The second-grade group of children with whom Marcy was confronted was fortunate and unusual in its possession of physical, mental, and sociological qualities well above the average.

Twenty of the twenty-five children had been in the first grade with me. They were creative and highly intelligent. There were eleven boys, three of whom had led the others in exciting batman adventures. They had also organized a fine baseball team that was the undisputed champion of the first, second, and third grades.

The enthusiasm of the first-grade class had been equally great for reading, writing, and arithmetic. The class median for the total battery of California Achievement Tests had been in the 97th percentile. The had worked very hard, and each could measure his own success. By Christmas of their first-grade year, two children had finished their first-grade math book and had started into the second-grade book. Six of the first-grade children whose interest was primarily in math, had tested lower in reading than in math, but we had decided in the fall to see whether a child's interest in math and reading would even out if he was allowed to do a minimum in reading, his second love, and a maximum in math, his first love.

After the Christmas holidays, we found that these children were indeed more interested and ready for reading. When a child is self-motivated and enthusiastic, he can accomplish with pleasure and ease in a very short time those tasks which seemed overwhelmingly difficult when imposed from the outside at an inappropriate time. We concluded from this experiment that if children are given choices and encouraged in major fields of interest, they are likely to carry that enthusiasm into a new interest.

The first-grade group had done a great deal of its own planning. This had come about slowly. I think it is important that children think about, and implement their own plans, and develop problem-solving skills. An opportunity for planning and problem solving took place in a group meeting that we held each morning. Here a child could share an adventure, register a complaint, or propose a plan for the future.

When there was a dispute, we encouraged each child involved to say what he felt and thought. A problem was described as a big puzzle to which many people might have a part, and it was stressed that it was important to have all the parts so that we could complete the puzzle. By spring this group had learned to speak rather precisely and listen carefully to each other when matters of importance were being discussed. Together they had made some group rules which all had to follow. When the batman game had become too rough, they decided that there should be no grabbing around the neck and no pushing from behind; no one else could jump on if two guys were wrestling; if Batman or the Riddler touched you, you had to go to his hideout, and if you broke these rules, you had to sit on the couch for ten minutes. The group had also created two plays which they performed for the entire school, and earned five dollars for the scholarship fund. They had constructed a permanent store where they sold cookies and cake to the other school children. In this way, they had learned to use pennies, nickels, dimes, and dollars. They were able, with minimum assistance, to plan an overnight camping trip for the class.

As I examined the demographics of these twenty former first-grade students who were returning for the second grade, I found that ages ranged from 6.3 to 8.0 years. Eight of them were the first children in their families, seven were second children, four were third children, and one was the fourth child. Three of the children had been in the school since they were three years old; three had entered at four years, five more had come to the school for kindergarten; and nine had had their first experience here in the first grade. I would expect the core of these children to feel quite safe and secure in an environment with which they were familiar. Their home life also seemed to reflect a high degree of stability. Only one child was from a divorced family. Five of the parents were professors, three were physicians, five were businessmen, and five were teachers. There were two scientists, two counselors, two professional musicians, and two contractors represented in this group—along with a real estate man, a policeman, a secretary, and six housewives. The educational background of the parents included eight doctoral degrees, nine Masters degrees, thirteen Bachelor of Science degrees, two Junior College Certificates, and three high school diplomas.

What did this kind of parent value for his child? Did it come near to what the child valued for himself? To better understand the parent's wishes, I examined their enrollment forms under the question "Why do you wish to send your child to this school?" Three of the parents had attended the school and wished their children to have the same opportunity. Four of the children had older brothers and sisters in the school and their parents were happy with it. Two of the children were coming because their parents felt they had had a negative public school experience. Ten of the parents wished their children to have individualized work, and wanted them to work at their own speed. Four parents mentioned the physical environment, where children could climb trees and build forts and use their active bodies. Six mentioned intellectual achievement and excellence in the basic skills. A relaxed atmosphere where warmth and love could be received from an adult was valued by eight parents. Seven parents cited many avenues of creativity as a quality they wished for in their child's education. This was a highly skilled and talented group of parents. Their expectations, at least as indicated by their responses to this question, were clear—intellectual achievement, creativity, individual achievement, warmth in their relationships—and their values were implicit within those expectations.

In order to check, among other things, what relation the children's value system bore to those of their parents, I asked these second-grade children to list the things they liked or didn't like about our school. Eighteen of them mentioned liking academic achievement in reading, spelling, writing, math, or French. Outlets for creativity in music, art, crafts, clay, shop, dramatics, and dance were mentioned many times. Physical facilities such as trees, rope-swings, puddles, and the big building (upon which a child can climb) were mentioned ten times. Eighteen children liked the long recesses and the free time to choose their own activities. Four children mentioned that they liked being able to wear pants or long dresses or old clothes or no shoes. Eight children said they valued their relationships with adults and children.

Seemingly the children were receiving what their parents had hoped for them in their educations. What they valued was very similar to their parent's stated expectation for the school. What was Marcy's value system? She did not respond to the questions. I read each question to her, but there was no response. She sat rocking her dolly and shaking her head as I read to her. She shut me and the questions out.

One night after school Frances said, "Most kids don't like Marcy." "Why?" I asked. "Because she is stupid and can't read—and they most like smart kids like John and Martha."

I told her that some schools, like the one Marcy had gone to last year, felt that other things were more important to learn in the first grade, and that they did not teach reading as much as we did. I told her that Marcy was learning to read as fast as any child I had ever taught.

This was true, but she still had difficulty in making relationships with the children. To questions on a sociogram about friends and choice of seats, her answer was "I want to sit by Wendy . . . on a cloud with my friend—because she is my best friend and she plays with me sometimes."

At recess the next day Martha asked Marcy to change seats with her. This was accomplished when I was absent from the room. When I returned Marcy was seated next to Julie who was showing open hostility to her. When I asked Marcy why she had changed seats, she said, "Oh, I don't care who I sit by. Martha just said she wanted to sit by Wendy and I don't care."

Even though I assured her that there was no need for her to give up her seat—that she could say, "No, I would rather not"—she still gave up her seat next to the only child in the room who was truly friendly to her and accepted a seat by a child who was hostile to her, in order to please Martha.

Did she recognize Martha as a group leader? Was this a move toward the group, or was it a statement about herself—that she had no rights or value?

The next day in a math game using play money she gave one of her one hundred dollar bills to each of the other children, saying "I don't get as much because I am not as good."

It seemed both elements were there. She wanted friends, and she also felt inferior.

Each afternoon at closing she would ask several children if she could go home with them. As each mother came in the door she would ask, "Can I go home with you?" Many of the mothers responded kindly, and she visited a number of the children's homes. Her parents picked her up at school thirty minutes to an hour after closing time, so that it was a relief to her to be able to go to someone's home. One parent observed that Marcy gave the impression of great spontaneity and curiosity, but had no patterns or techniques for dealing with children or adults.

One morning Marcy announced in the group meeting, "My name isn't Marcy anymore. It is Veelee." She wrote "Veelee" on all of her books and would respond only to that name. She seemed a little more assertive with the new name, and we went along with her to try to discover what it meant in her terms.

Marcy held conversations with Veelee, sometimes grumbling about the hard school work. One of the boys commented, "I like Marcy, but I don't like Veelee." "Why?" I asked. "Well, you can't talk to Marcy when Veelee is there. They talk to each other."

I felt a need for help in understanding what was going on in Marcy and Veelee. I had had children assume another name before, but not to this extent. Her relationship to things rather than to people concerned me. I made an appointment with our consulting school psychologist, Paul Wanner. He suggested that she might have been deficient in making primary relationships when she was little. If a primary relationship does not occur, it may be difficult to make other relationships. He suggested that we talk soon with her parents concerning the year in England, and learn of the illness to which Mr. Neill referred.

Her father came to a conference on Saturday morning at 9:30. He outlined chronologically the time the family had spent abroad. When Marcy was three, she lived at home and went to morning nursery. It wasn't a very happy experience for her. She wanted to go to Summerhill where her brother and sister were. In the summer before she turned five, she was accepted as a student at Summerhill. The father took her to the train with her brother and sister and waved goodbye. She had had a kidney ailment for which she had been hospitalized in the spring, but the school had agreed to give her the needed daily medication. For her first two weeks at Summerhill she received a great deal of attention and care. Soon the other children grew tired of her and she was left alone. She grew quite ill, and was hospitalized again. The father and mother were in Greece at this time. She was not seriously ill, but she needed the consistent care of a hospital. At this time she started having imaginary friends, and she continued to have them. Her father reported that her older brother also had imaginary friends, but her sister did not. The sister was much lonelier, he thought, because she did not have this way of coping with a situation. I asked if he thought Marcy was happy at school, and he said he felt she was happier at school than at home. Because of a demanding graduate school schedule, neither parent had much time to be with Marcy. Her father was interested in her academic progress, and seemed impressed at how much she had accomplished in such a short time. I told him how important learning to read seemed to be to her, and he said that perhaps they could make a bit more of it at home. I agreed that it would probably make her happy to share it with them.

This father was forty-seven, and the mother was forty. They had lived a semi-nomadic life. The family was not extremely wealthy, but was able to move about and do primarily as they wished. There was no reason to expect that Marcy's life was going to change. She needed whatever tools she could develop to cope with her life as it was. At that time, her thumb, her dolly, a bit of cloth that she carried, and Veelee were ways of coping. To the best of our ability we would support her in developing her good, bright mind, and provide outlets for her creative nature. There was much Marcy could learn from this group of children, and there was much she could give to them.

While the social part of her living remained much the same, she finished a workbook on the short vowel sounds and started a new book that taught her blend sounds and long vowel sounds. Even though it was a little over her head we put her in a textbook in which two other children were reading. We wanted her and the class to see how rapidly she was going. It was very difficult for her at first, and I feared that in my haste to boost her self-esteem, I had exposed her to failure. She was such a plucky creature, however, that after stumbling over nearly every word on a page she would say, "Let's do it again." And surely as she did it again, the words became her own. Soon she was not stumbling over each word, but moving along at a slow, steady pace.

During one afternoon math session, we were working on some new time concepts. Marcy was one of the first to complete her work and have it correct. Lydia turned to her and said, "You are smart, Marcy."

"Yes, you are smart, Marcy. I never said you were stupid," added Martha.

"Yes, you did say that lots and lots of times," countered Julie. "Everybody has heard you say Marcy is stupid."

"Well, so did everybody else," was Martha's retort.

"No," said Marcy timidly, and stretched the truth a bit—"You just said that I was not as fast as you."

Marcy was now beaming but not riding too high on her newfound glory. As these other girls opened themselves to Marcy, would they also learn from her and incorporate some of her values into their own systems? Marcy was an exceedingly kind, willing, and able child. She had courage and the strength to endure. It seemed to me that she was beginning to pick up some of the finer signals of communication, as the exchange with the girls might indicate. There was no way to tell what would happen during the remainder of the year. A sociogram given in the last week of December revealed that Marcy was chosen neither in a positive nor a negative relationship. Her tautological responses had decreased and her social and personal responses on a sentence completion test had increased. This indicated to me that the group's verbalized rejection was decreasing, and that Marcy was becoming more able to reveal herself and connect with people as well as things.

Hopefully this enculturation would be a two-way street. If we were a little bit wise and very lucky, we would be able to incorporate some of her spontaneity, her integrity, her courage, and her forgiveness into ourselves—and leave her with that quiet spot where she seemed to find strength. And we never heard from Veelee again.

Such in-depth studies of children provided me with information from which I could develop the kind of program each child needed. My responsibility was to provide the nutrients each child needed to grow. The group process helped to reveal each child's cognitive, social, and emotional needs.

Appendix E

FLASH CARDS FOR LEARNING CODES

OPEN-ENDED QUESTION	RESPONSE	INSTRUCTION, EXPLANATION, LEARNING	COMMENT, GREETING, GENERAL ACTION
MATERIALS	ANIMAL	SIMPLE QUESTION	COMMAND OR REQUEST
DIFFERENT CHILD	TWO CHILDREN	SMALL GROUP	LARGE GROUP
TEACHER	AIDE	VOLUNTEER	CHILD

5	4	3	2
1	1Q	An	M
1	S	2	D
C	V	A	T

TASK-RELATED COMMENT	"I DON'T KNOW" NO RESPONSE, IGNORING	NONVERBAL	TOUCHING
ACKNOWLEDGMENT ENCOURAGEMENT	REFUSAL, REJECTION	POSITIVE, HAPPY FEELING	QUESTIONING
PRAISE	OBSERVING	UNHAPPY FEELING, SADNESS, CRYING	GUIDE TO ALTERNATIVE
CORRECTIVE FEEDBACK	MOVEMENT	DEMEANING OR NASTY STATEMENT	PUNISHING

P	G	Q	T
N	U	H	AV
X	12	11	10
9	8	7	6

CONCRETE OBJECT	STATEMENTS OF SELF-WORTH	DRAMATIC PLAY	ACADEMIC
BEHAVIOR			

A	DP	W	O
			B

INDEX

146; and Exploratory Model, 72; and Fundamental School Model, 222; and Group Process Model, 109; and Programmed Model, 184
Rayder, Nicholas F., 60, 74
Reality Therapy, 91
Resnick, Lauren, 171
Responsive Classroom Observation Schedule, 74
Responsive Educational model, 79
Rhodes, Anne, 60, 74
Rist, Ray C., 10
Rogers, Carl R., 25, 50, 52
Rosman, Bernice L., 15, 18

Schutz, William, 50
Sears, Pauline S., 10
Sensorimotor stage, 126
Shaftel, Fannie R., 92, 93, 104
Shaftel, George, 92, 93, 104
Sherman, Vivian S., 10
Siegel, Irving, 130
Sign Level, 131
Simon, Anita, 19
Skills, basic: in behavior modification models, 54; in Developmental Cognitive Model, 146-147; in Exploratory Model, 61, 73; in Fundamental School Model, 203-205, 206, 219-220; in fundamental school programs, 53-54, 238-239; in open education, 50, 238-239; in Programmed Model, 170-172, 183-184
Skinner, B. F., 25, 169
Soar, R. M., 53
Soar, Robert S., 15, 17, 53
Social Competence Scale, 15, 18
Stallings, Jane A., 9, 13, 37, 42, 53, 72, 108, 146, 184, 237, 279
Stanford Research Institute (SRI) observation system, 25-34, 242-250; and Developmental Cognitive Model, 147-153; and Exploratory Model, 73-79;

and Fundamental School Model, 222-226; and Group Process Model, 109-114; modifications in, 38; and Programmed Model, 182, 184-189; using, 35-37, 235. *See also* Classroom Check List; Five-Minute Interaction; Physical Environment Information
Suchman, J. Richard, 131
Summerhill School, 49
Symbol Level, 131
Systematic observation: analyzing data from, 41-42; importance of, in Developmental Cognitive Model, 153; importance of, in Exploratory Model, 79; importance of, in Fundamental School Model, 226; importance of, in Group Process Model, 114; importance of, in Programmed Model, 189; planning, 40-41; value of, 4-5. *See also* Observation

Taba, Hilda, 60, 91
Teachers, responsibilities of: in Developmental Cognitive Model, 130-131, 146; in Exploratory Model, 61-62; in Fundamental School Model, 205-207; in Group Process Model, 92-93, 108; in Programmed Model, 170, 172-173
Tikunoff, William J., 10
Time sample, 13
Turner, Marion E., 93

Wang, Margaret, 171
Weber, George, 222
Weikart, David, 130, 147, 154
Weil, Marsha, 50, 91, 92, 169, 235
Wilcox, Mary, 13
Wiley, David E., 52, 53, 54
Wodtke, Kenneth H., 50
Wolfson, Bernice J., 50
Wright, Robert J., 53